Contents

Articles

References

Article Licenses

Recruitment

Recruitment refers to the process of attracting, screening, and selecting qualified people for a job. For some components of the recruitment process, mid- and large-size organizations often retain professional recruiters or outsource some of the process to recruitment agencies.

The recruitment industry has four main types of agencies: employment agencies, recruitment websites and job search engines, "headhunters" for executive and professional recruitment, and niche agencies which specialize in a particular area of staffing. Some organizations use employer branding strategy and in-house recruitment instead of agencies. Recruitment-related functions are generally carried out by an organization's human resources staff.

The stages in recruitment include sourcing candidates by advertising or other methods, screening potential candidates using tests and/or interviews, selecting candidates based on the results of the tests and/or interviews, and on-boarding to ensure the candidate is able to fulfill their new role effectively.

Agency types

The recruitment industry is based on the goal of providing a candidate to a client for a price. On one end of the spectrum there are agencies that are paid only if they deliver a candidate that successfully stays with the client beyond the agreed probationary period. On the other end of the spectrum there are agencies that are paid a retainer to focus on a client's needs and achieve milestones in the search for the right candidate, and then again are paid a percentage of the candidate's salary when a candidate is placed and stays with the organization beyond the probationary period. Today's (march 2011) recruitment industry is fairly competitive, therefore agencies have sought out ways to differentiate themselves and add value by focusing on some area of the recruitment life cycle. Here are five types of typical agencies.

Traditional agency

Also known as employment agencies, recruitment agencies have historically had a physical location. A candidate visits a local branch for a short interview and an assessment before being taken onto the agency's books. Recruitment consultants then work to match their pool of candidates to their clients' open positions. Suitable candidates are short-listed and put forward for an interview with potential employers on a contract or direct basis.

Compensation to agencies take several forms, the most popular are:

- A contingency fee paid by the company when a recommended candidate accepts a job with the client company (typically 20%-30% based and calculated on the candidates first-year base salary (though fees as low as 12.5% can be found online, and which usually has some form of guarantee (30–90 days standard), should the candidate fail to perform and is terminated within a set period of time (refundable fully or prorated).
- An advance payment that serves as a retainer, also paid by the company, non-refundable paid in full depending on outcome and success (e.g. 40% up front, 30% in 90 days and the remainder once a search is completed). This form of compensation is generally reserved for high level executive search/headhunters
- Hourly Compensation for temporary workers and projects. A pre-negotiated hourly fee, in which the agency is paid and pays the applicant as a consultant for services as a third party. Many contracts allow a consultant to transition to a full-time status upon completion of a certain number of hours with or without a conversion fee.

Headhunters

A "headhunter" is an industry term for a third-party recruiter who seeks out candidates often when normal recruitment efforts have failed. Headhunters are generally considered more aggressive than in-house recruiters or may have pre-existing industry experience and contacts. They may use advanced sales techniques such as initially posing as clients to gather employee contacts as well as visiting candidate offices. They may also purchase expensive lists of names and job titles but more often will generate their own lists. They may arrange a meeting or a formal interview between their client and the candidate and will usually prepare the candidate for the interview, help negotiate the salary and conduct closure to the search. They are frequently members in good standing of industry trade groups and associations. Headhunters will often attend trade shows and other meetings nationally or even internationally that may be attended by potential candidates and hiring managers.

Headhunters are typically small operations that make high margins on candidate placements (sometimes more than 30% of the candidate's annual compensation). Due to their higher costs, headhunters are usually employed to fill senior management and executive level roles. Headhunters are also used to recruit very specialized individuals; for example, in some fields, such as emerging scientific research areas, there may only be a handful of top-level professionals who are active in the field. In this case, since there are so few qualified candidates, it makes more sense to directly recruit them one-by-one, rather than advertise internationally for candidates. While in-house recruiters tend to attract candidates for specific jobs, headhunters will attract both candidates and actively seek them out as well. To do so, they may network, cultivate relationships with various companies, maintain large databases, purchase company directories or candidate lists and cold call prospective recruits.

Headhunters are increasingly using social media to find and research candidates. This approach is often called social recruiting.

Niche recruiters

Specialized recruiters exist to seek staff with a very narrow specialty. Because of their focus, these firms can very often produce superior results due to their ability to channel all of their resources into networking for a very specific skill set. This specialization in staffing allows them to offer more jobs for their specific demographic which in turn attracts more specialized candidates from that specific demographic over time building large proprietary databases. These niche firms tend to be more focused on building ongoing relationships with their candidates as is very common the same candidates are placed many times throughout their careers. Niche firms also develop knowledge on specific employment trends within their industry of focus (e.g. The energy industry) and are able to identify demographic shifts such as aging and its impact on the industry.[1]

The alternatives to agencies

Lower recruitment budgets and frustration with sub-standard agency practices are encouraging companies to develop new approaches to the challenge of finding and retaining talented staff.[2] A popular alternative to using recruitment agencies is putting in place an employee referral program. This is a system where existing employees recommend people for vacancies and if the recommendation results in a successful hire, the employee receives a cash bonus.

The growing popularity of social media as a way to communicate with staff has seen a handful of companies use custom, in-house platforms to facilitate employee referrals.[3]

In-house recruitment

Under pressure to reduce costs, both large- and medium-sized employers tend to undertake their own in-house recruitment, using their human resources department, front-line hiring managers and recruitment personnel who handle targeted functions and populations. In addition to coordinating with the agencies mentioned above, in-house recruiters may advertise job vacancies on their own websites, coordinate internal employee referrals, work with external associations, trade groups and/or focus on campus graduate recruitment. Some large employers choose to outsource all or some of their recruitment process (recruitment process outsourcing) however a much more common approach is for employers to introduce referral schemes where employees are encouraged to source new staff from within their own network.

Passive candidate research firms and sourcing firms

These firms are the new hybrid firms in the recruitment world able to combine the research aspects (discovering passive candidates) of recruiting and combine them with the ability to make hires for their clients. These firms provide competitive passive candidate intelligence to support companies' recruiting efforts. Normally they will generate varying degrees of candidate information from those people currently engaged in the position a company is looking to fill. These firms usually charge a per hour fee or by candidate lead. Many times this uncovers names that cannot be found with other methods and will allow internal recruiters the ability to focus their efforts solely on recruiting.

Process

Job analysis

The proper start to a recruitment effort is to perform a job analysis, to document the actual or intended requirement of the job to be performed. This information is captured in a job description and provides the recruitment effort with the boundaries and objectives of the search.[4] Oftentimes a company will have job descriptions that represent a historical collection of tasks performed in the past. These job descriptions need to be reviewed or updated prior to a recruitment effort to reflect present day requirements. Starting a recruitment with an accurate job analysis and job description ensures the recruitment effort starts off on a proper track for success.

Sourcing

Sourcing involves 1) advertising, a common part of the recruiting process, often encompassing multiple media, such as the Internet, general newspapers, job ad newspapers, professional publications, window advertisements, job centers, and campus graduate recruitment programs; and 2) recruiting research, which is the proactive identification of relevant talent who may not respond to job postings and other recruitment advertising methods done in #1. This initial research for so-called passive prospects, also called name-generation, results in a list of prospects who can then be contacted to solicit interest, obtain a resume/CV, and be screened (see below).

Screening and selection

Suitability for a job is typically assessed by looking for skills, e.g. communication, typing, and computer skills. Qualifications may be shown through résumés, job applications, interviews, educational or professional experience, the testimony of references, or in-house testing, such as for software knowledge, typing skills, numeracy, and literacy, through psychological tests or employment testing. Other resume screening criteria may include length of service, job titles and length of time at a job. In some countries, employers are legally mandated to provide equal opportunity in hiring. Business management software is used by many recruitment agencies to automate the testing process. Many recruiters and agencies are using an applicant tracking system to perform many of the filtering tasks, along with software tools for psychometric testing.

Onboarding

"Onboarding" is a term which describes the process of helping new employees become productive members of an organization. A well-planned introduction helps new employees become fully operational quickly and is often integrated with a new company and environment. Onboarding is included in the recruitment process for retention purposes. Many companies have onboarding campaigns in hopes to retain top talent that is new to the company; campaigns may last anywhere from 1 week to 6 months.

Internet recruitment and websites

Such sites have two main features: job boards and a résumé/curriculum vitae (CV) database. Job boards allow member companies to post job vacancies. Alternatively, candidates can upload a résumé to be included in searches by member companies. Fees are charged for job postings and access to search resumes. Since the late 1990s, the recruitment website has evolved to encompass end-to-end recruitment.

A British Army etc. recruitment centre in Oxford.

Websites capture candidate details and then pool them in client accessed candidate management interfaces (also online). Key players in this sector provide e-recruitment software and services to organizations of all sizes and within numerous industry sectors, who want to e-enable entirely or partly their recruitment process in order to improve business performance.

The online software provided by those who specialize in online recruitment helps organizations attract, test, recruit, employ and retain quality staff with a minimal amount of administration. Online recruitment websites can be very helpful to find candidates that are very actively looking for work and post their resumes online, but they will not attract the "passive" candidates who might respond favorably to an opportunity that is presented to them through other means. Also, some candidates who are actively looking to change jobs are hesitant to put their resumes on the job boards, for fear that their companies, co-workers, customers or others might see their resumes.

Job search engines

The emergence of meta-search engines allows job-seekers to search across multiple websites. Some of these new search engines index and list the advertisements of traditional job boards. These sites tend to aim for providing a "one-stop shop" for job-seekers. However, there are many other job search engines which index solely from employers' websites, choosing to bypass traditional job boards entirely. These vertical search engines allow job-seekers to find new positions that may not be advertised on traditional job boards, and online recruitment websites.

Recruiting Companies

- Adecco
- Association of Executive Search Consultants
- AIMS International
- Egon Zehnder International
- Gary Kaplan & Associates
- Kelly Services
- Arithon
- Korn/Ferry
- Michael Page International
- Nels Olson
- Nonprofit Professionals Advisory Group
- R. William Funk & Associates
- Raines International
- Randstad Holding
- Rosenzweig & Company
- Talent Zoo
- The Amrop Hever Group
- Transearch International
- Treeline, Inc.

References

[1] http://www.uc.edu/News/NR.aspx?ID=4226

[2] http://www.recruiter.co.uk/the-rise-of-the-internal-recruiter/1006847.article

[3] http://www.itnews.com.au/News/167381,atlassians-social-hiring-spree-pays-off.aspx

[4] http://www.staffing-and-recruiting-essentials.com/Hiring-Checklist.html

Selection ratio

Selection ratio refers to the ratio of the number job positions to the number of job applicants and is used in the context of selection and recruitment.

It is typically assumed to be a number between 0 and 1 where a number closer to zero implies that there are many applicants for any one position.

The selection ratio provides information about the value of assessment tools, such as interviews, work samples, and psychometric tests. When the selection ratio is close to one, most applicants will need to be hired in order to fill the available positions. As such knowing that one applicant is likely to perform better than another is of limited value. In contrast when the selection ratio is closer to zero, assessment tools have greater value in indicating which subset of job applicants are likely to perform best. Estimates of the selection ratio can form part of estimates of utility for a given selection and recruitment system.

Application for employment

An **application for employment**, **job application**, or **application form** (often simply called an **application**) is a form or collection of forms that an individual seeking employment, called an applicant, must fill out as part of the process of informing an employer of the applicant's availability and desire to be employed, and persuading the employer to offer the applicant employment.

Purpose of the application

From the employer's perspective, the application serves a number of purposes. These vary depending on the nature of the job and the preferences of the person responsible for hiring, as "each organization should have an application form that reflects its own environment".[1] At a minimum, an application usually requires the applicant to provide information sufficient to demonstrate that he or she is legally permitted to be employed. The typical application also requires the applicant to provide information regarding relevant skills, education, and previous employment. The application itself is a minor test of the applicant's literacy, penmanship, and communication skills - a careless job applicant might disqualify themselves with a poorly-filled out application.

The application may also require the applicant to disclose any criminal record, and to provide information sufficient to enable the employer to conduct an appropriate background check. For a business that employs workers on a part-time basis, the application may inquire as to the applicant's specific times and days of availability, and preferences in this regard. It is important to note, however, that an employer may be prohibited from asking applicants about characteristics that are not relevant to the job, such as their political view or sexual orientation.[1] [2]

For white collar jobs, particularly those requiring communication skills, the employer will typically require applicants to accompany the form with a cover letter and a résumé.[3] However, even employers who accept a cover letter and résumé will frequently also require the applicant to complete a form application, as the other documents may neglect to mention details of importance to the employers.[4] [5] In some instances, an application is effectively used to dissuade "walk-in" applicants, serving as a barrier between the applicant and a job interview with the person with the authority to hire.[6]

Application blanks are the second most common hiring instrument next to personal interviews. Companies will occasionally use two types of application blanks, short and long. They both help companies with initial screening and the longer form can be used for other purposes as well. The answers that applicants choose to submit are helpful to the company because they can become an interview question for that applicant at a future date.

Application blanks can either be done by hand or electronically, depending on the company. When submitting an application blank typically companies will ask you attach a one-page cover letter as well as a resume. Applicants tend to make the mistake of sharing too much information with the company and their application will be immediately over looked. Offering too much information gives the company a bigger opportunity to find something they do not like. Companies are not allowed to ask certain questions in person or on an application such as: age, health status, religion, marital status, about children, race, height, weight, whom you live with and etc.

Application Sections

Applications usually ask the applicant at the minimum for your name, phone number, and address. In addition to this applications also ask for previous employment information, educational background, emergency contacts, references, as well as any special skills the applicant might have.

The three categories application blanks are very useful for discovering are; physical characteristics, experience, and socio-environmental factors.

Physical Characteristics

If the company has a bona fide occupational qualification (BFOQ) to ask regarding a physical condition, they may ask questions about it. Such as: The job requires a lot of physical labor. Do you have any physical problems that may interfere with this job?

Experience

Experience requirements can be separated into two groups on an application, work experience and educational background. Educational background is important to companies because by evaluating applicants' performance in school tells them what their personality is like as well as their intelligence. Work experience is important to companies because it will inform the company if the applicant meets their requirements. Companies are usually interested when applicants were unemployed and when/why the applicant left their previous job.

Socio-environmental qualifications

Companies are interested in the applicant's socio-environment because it can inform them of their personality, interest, and qualities. If they are extremely active within an organization, that may demonstrate their ability to communicate well with others. Being in management may demonstrate their leadership ability as well as their determination and so on.

[7]

References

[1] Diane Arthur, *Recruiting, Interviewing, Selecting & Orienting New Employees* (1998), p. 111.

[2] Donald H. Weiss, *Fair, Square & Legal: Safe Hiring, Managing & Firing Practices to Keep You and Your Company Out of Court* (2004), p. 45.

[3] Sandra Bunting, *The Interviewer's Handbook: Successful Interviewing Techniques for the Workplace* (2005), p. 82.

[4] Diane Arthur, *Recruiting, Interviewing, Selecting & Orienting New Employees* (1998), p. 168.

[5] Joe Kennedy, *The Small Business Owner's Manual* (2005), p. 122.

[6] Diane Arthur, *Recruiting, Interviewing, Selecting & Orienting New Employees* (1998), p. 59.

[7] "Sample Application" (http://www.asherm.com/research/application.doc). Asher Martin. . Retrieved 2009-11-22.

Audition

An **audition** is a sample performance by an actor, singer, musician, dancer or other performer. It typically involves the performer displaying their talent through a previously memorized and rehearsed solo piece or by performing a work or piece given to the performer at the audition or shortly before. In some cases, such as with a model or acrobat, the individual may be asked to demonstrate a range of professional skills. Actors may be asked to present a monologue. Singers will perform a song in a popular music context or an aria in a Classical context. A dancer will present a routine in a specific style, such as ballet, tap dance or hip-hop, or show his or her ability to quickly learn a choreographed dance piece.

A singer performing a live audition in front of judges on TV for Fox's *American Idol* reality television series.

The audition is a systematic process in which industry professionals select performers, which is in some ways analogous to a job interview in the regular job market. In an audition, the employer is testing the ability of the applicant to meet the needs of the job and assess how well the individual will take directions and deal with changes. After some auditions, after the performer has demonstrated their abilities in a given performance style, the audition panel may ask a few questions that resemble those used in standard job interviews (e.g., regarding availability).

Auditions are required for many reasons in the performing arts world. Often, employing companies or groups use auditions to select performers for upcoming shows or productions. An audition for a performing opportunity may be for a single performance (e.g., doing a monologue at a comedy club), for a series or season of performances (a season of a Broadway play), or for permanent employment with the performing organization (e.g., an orchestra or dance troupe). Auditions for performing opportunities may be for amateur, school, or community organizations, in which case the performers will typically not be paid. As well, auditions are used to select or screen candidates for entry to training programs (ballet school or circus school); university programs (B.Mus, M.Mus, MFA in Theater); performance-related scholarships and grants; or to be considered for representation by a talent agency or individual agent.

Acting

For actors in theater, film, and TV, the "audition is a systematic process in which industry professionals make final casting decisions. Industry professionals may consist of casting directors, producers, directors or agency representatives" [1] . In film and television, the audition is called a screen test, and it is filmed so that the casting director or director can see how the actor appears on screen. Actors who are looking for auditions can find advertisements for auditions in major cities, or pay for the services of an agent. One of the benefits to hiring an agent is that the agent has connections with casting directors and performing companies. However, the agent will take a cut (often 10%) of the performer's earnings. Although an actor's talents comprise crucial criteria in the casting process, an almost equal amount of attention is given to an actor's "type", (a combination of personality, looks and general casting intuition) as required for a particular production.

For actors, monologues and speeches are the "calling card" that they use to demonstrate their skills to casting directors.

Actors who are selecting an audition piece should select a speech by a character who is close to their own age and wear neutral clothing that allows freedom of movement. Auditionees should be careful not to go over the stated time limit, and they should not direct their speech to the audition panel if they are doing an on-stage audition.[2] The exception to the last "rule" is in cases where the audition panel requests that the auditionee interacts with them (e.g., a director may ask the actor to speak the lines while looking directly at the director). An actor who is doing an audition should warm up before the audition, just the same way an athlete would. Just as with any interview outside of the performing arts world, an auditionee should take care to dress well. Even if the clothing is simple, it should be clean and of good quality. Auditionees should keep in mind that during the audition process, the casting directors are also considering "whether or not the actor will be easy to work with, that they know what they are doing and can take direction well" [3] .

The audition piece is typically not from the show being considered; an actor wishing to be cast in *Hamlet* would not likely do a monologue from that play. However, most performers do have a range of audition pieces and select something appropriate; an actor auditioning for *Hamlet* would have a dramatic Shakespearean monologue ready, and not perform a monologue from an Oscar Wilde comedy, or a contemporary playwright. Some auditions involve cold reading, or performing a script that the actor is not familiar with. Auditions often involve monologues or speeches, but not always. In some cases, an auditionee is asked to read a scene (with a second person reading the other character).

For some auditions, auditionees must bring a professional 8"X10" photo called a "headshot" and a resume that indicates their acting experience and training. It is recommended that actors bring additional copies of the headshot and resume, in case there are additional members of the casting team present at the audition. The casting agent or company may "callback" an auditionee days, weeks, or even months after the initial audition for a second audition. At a major audition for a professional company, the time limits are strictly enforced. A musical theater performer may be given a moment to tell the piano accompanist the tempo, and state their name and audition number to the audition panel. Then, once the auditionee starts acting or singing, the clock starts running. A buzzer sounds when the time limit runs out, which may be a minute and a half, two minutes, or three minutes, depending on the company. At this point, the auditionee is expected to stop and leave to free up the stage for the next auditionee.

Right before the audition, the casting director may give new instructions that were not in the advertisement; for example, due to time constraints, the time limit for the monologues might be cut in half, or the vocal selections might be cut. It is important that auditionees follow these last-minute instructions, and not be "thrown off balance" by these changes. At an audition, a director may ask for changes in the delivery of the lines or in other aspects of the performance. The goal may be to see if the auditionee is versatile or because the director disagrees with the initial approach used by the auditionee. In either case, the behavior of the auditionee is important; if the auditionee is cooperative in making the changes, it shows that he or she will be easy to work with. If a script is provided beforehand, actors should try to memorize as much as possible, because this shows that they have prepared and it allows them to look up from the script and show their facial expressions more.

Music

Popular music

Instrumentalists

In some styles of music, such as jazz-oriented stage bands, instrumentalists may be asked to sight read printed music at various levels of difficulty. In jazz groups, auditionees may be asked to perform standard pieces (e.g., a jazz standard such as "Now's the Time") with an ensemble. Similarly, in a rock or blues band, auditionees may be asked to play a rock or blues standard. An auditionee for a rhythm section role (rhythm guitar, electric bass, drumkit, etc.) will be asked to play a range of standard styles or "feels" which are used in a given style. For example, a drummer applying to play in a jazz band might be asked to play a slow ballad, a medium "standard", and an up-tempo swing style. A  bassist auditioning for a pop band might be asked to play in a Motown style bassline, a syncopated 1970s funk "slapping" style line, and a reggae-style bassline. A person auditioning for a role as a rhythm section member in some styles of music may be expected to be able to demonstrate the ability to perform as a backup singer.

A performer auditioning for a solo or "lead" instrument role will typically perform prepared solos that showcase a range of skills, including the ability to perform a melody with sensitivity and expression; the ability to play virtuosic passages; and, in some styles (e.g., fusion jazz or blues), the ability to improvise a melody over a chord progression. In some popular genres, there is relatively less emphasis on "stage presence" and movement onstage, such as classic jazz or traditional 1950s-style country music. In these styles, there is more of a focus on the sound of the music and the expressiveness of the performer with their voice or instrument. In other genres, such as heavy metal "shred guitar" or hardcore punk, it may be very important that a performer can move about in a dramatic fashion onstage. One of the differences between instrumentalist auditions in rock music styles and Classical styles is that in a rock context, the performers will be expected to have memorized most or all of the music. In a Classical context, most or all of the music is read from sheet music (with the exception of a solo Bach suite movement or a solo concerto movement).

Singers

For rock, country, and other forms of popular music, auditions are used to test the ability of an instrumentalist or singer to perform a specific style of music, or several styles. A singer auditioning for a role in a musical theatre production would not, unless instructed otherwise, need to sing opera or country music, and a musician auditioning for a seat in an orchestra would not perform rock. Occasionally a musical theatre audition may require the performer to sing a song in the genre to which the musical pertains. For instance, a singer auditioning for *Destry Rides Again* may be asked to sing a standard country-western song. A person auditioning for *The Rocky Horror Show* may be asked to sing a standard rock song. As well, in some cases, an audition may require a performer to demonstrate pieces in several styles. A hard rock band

Irving Berlin, Rodgers and Hammerstein, and Helen Tamiris watching music theater auditions

auditioning a new singer may request that the individual perform songs from heavy metal and related styles such as blues rock. A pop or rock band that is selecting a new lead singer that has whittled the number of applicants down to the top two or three singers may test out how the singers perform in live shows by performing a few live concerts with each guest singer. This allows the band to see how the singer performs in a full multi-hour concert, including how well the singer can develop a rapport with the audience, deal with the inevitable problems that occur in live music (e.g., microphones failing or stage lights malfunctioning), and maintain their vocal endurance until the end of the evening.

A contestant in the Eurovision Song Contest tries to impress the judges at her live audition

For smaller roles in a large musical theater production, mass auditions are held at which many inexperienced or aspiring performers, most without agents, show up. These are popularly known as "cattle calls" , since the hopefuls are often kept together in one large room. The musical *A Chorus Line* depicts this type of audition. *American Idol* also auditions its aspiring vocalists using this technique, since there are so many auditions. In musical theater and in pop music styles for which onstage dancing is part of the performance (e.g., hip hop), singers who are doing a vocal audition may also be required to demonstrate that they can dance while singing. In some popular music groups, such as a rock band, a backup singer may be expected to be able to play an instrument

while singing, such as strumming a simple rhythm guitar part or playing a percussion instrument (e.g., tambourine or congas). While an ability to sing in multiple languages with the appropriate diction and pronunciation is more associated with Classical music than popular music, there are some popular styles where multiple languages are expected, including Latin jazz styles such as Bossa Nova (Portuguese songs may be requested); Tango (Spanish songs may be requested); folk music (French songs may be requested); and Celtic music (Irish songs may be requested).

Classical music

In classical music, auditions are used to screen candidates for positions as instrumentalists in chamber groups or orchestras or as soloists, and to screen singers for positions as members of a choir or as solo performers. In classical music, auditions are also used to screen candidates for entry to training programs, university or Conservatory programs or degrees, and training festival activities (e.g., classical summer camps). In comparison with some types of pop music auditions, classical auditions tend to be much more formal. The performer may, by tradition, wear a tuxedo or a formal dress, and the judges may sit behind a desk and write comments on clipboards.

Instrumentalists

In classical music, each instrument or vocal type has a standard repertoire of music which is commonly requested at auditions. Instrumentalists in an orchestral context are typically asked to perform excerpts from the orchestral literature, including both exposed solos and "tutti" parts which are particularly demanding. Orchestral auditions are typically held in front of a panel that includes the conductor, the Concertmaster, and a number of Principal players from the orchestra. Since the post-WW II era, professional orchestra auditions often include a musician's union representative, who ensures that the audition is being run in a fair manner. In many major orchestras, a cloth screen may be used at some stages of the audition process, to protect the audition panel from allegations of favouritism or sexism.

An orchestral audition will normally set out a list of orchestral excerpts which each performer has to prepare. As well, each performer plays a movement from a Sonata or Concerto which may be performed with piano accompaniment. When the performer plays the orchestral excerpts, he or she may be given a tempo, or asked to follow the gestures of the conductor. Orchestral auditions are often run in several stages, in order to screen candidates and reduce those who are less likely to meet the needs of the job. A large number of applicants typically apply for a professional orchestra job. The orchestra personnel manager then selects the most promising candidates based on the experience and training indicated in the applicants' CVs (and, in some cases, based on the performing ability demonstrated in a recording of the applicant).

This first "cut" of auditionees then perform in front of the audition panel. The most promising candidates are invited to return for a second or third round of auditions, which allows the conductor and the panel to compare the best candidates. Performers may be asked to sight read orchestral music. The final stage of the audition process in some orchestras is a "test week", in which the performer plays with the orchestra for a week or two, which allows the conductor and Principal players to see if the individual can function well in an actual performance setting.

Singers

There is a standard repertoire of vocal literature for each voice type (e.g., soprano, alto) that is used at auditions for singers. Each sub-type of vocal activity has a separate standard audition repertoire (e.g., choirs, operas, etc.). A person auditioning for a role in a choir will be expected to be able to sight read choral parts. In auditions for opera, a singer will be expected to demonstrate the ability to act out the movements that are associated with the lyrics of the aria, which may include pretending to be dying from a stab wound, miming an activity (e.g., pouring wine), or doing a simple dance routine. Both choral and opera singers are expected to be able to follow the gestures of a conductor in regards to expression and tempo. Since microphones are not used in most classical music performances[4] , the audition panel will be assessing the auditionees ability to project a strong, room-filling vocal tone. In classical music, in addition to judging singing ability (e.g., tone, intonation, etc.), the audition panel will be judging the applicant's ability to use the appropriate diction and pronunciation of the major languages used in Art music: German, Italian, and French. Other languages that the applicant may be asked to sing in include English, Spanish, Portuguese, and Latin.

Dance

There are many types of dance auditions for different performance venues. Dance companies hire employees for ballet and modern dance shows. Broadway companies hire dancers for traditional musicals (Rogers and Hammerstein) and more modern dance musicals (e.g., *Fame* and *Grease*) Casinos, resorts, amusement parks, and cruise ships hire dancers for revue-style shows that can range from jazz dance to hip-hop. For these shows, some backup singing skills or acting skills may be required. Pop music concert producers and pop music video producers recruit dancers to perform onstage during concerts or during videos. For live pop concerts, onstage dancers may be required to perform simple backup singing. Movie and TV producers also hire dancers for short term shoots; even though a dancer may only get several days of work from a movie or TV show, there may be residual payments. Most auditions specify what type of dance skills are required (e.g., Classical, pointe, contemporary, jazz, hip-hop, etc.). In the case of modern dance, some dance companies ask applicants to demonstrate their ability to improvise dance moves.

Two dancers performing modern dance, a style in which performers may be asked to demonstrate improvised movements at an audition.

These dancers from the Braziers troupe are performing Highland dancing, a style at which auditionees must demonstrate a high degree of technique and the ability to quickly learn new steps.

Many dance auditions test the ability of applicants to learning new choreography in a short time period, rather than showcasing a prepared work. In other cases, a short prepared solo piece may also be required (about 90 seconds long). Applicants will be instructed in a technical routine or pattern in a group session. Some auditions require applicants to have completed training at a recognised dance school or conservatoire, and in some cases, auditionees may be requested to bring a reference letter from a dance teacher or dance company director (especially in the case of young dancers with little professional experience). At some auditions, applicants are asked to make a short verbal statement about their dancing goals or why they wish to join the troupe. Auditionees should ensure that they know the major dance terms, because the judges may request that certain dance moves be demonstrated.

Dancers are often asked to bring one or two photographs, such as a "headshot" and a full-body photo of the applicant in a dancing pose. The clothing that auditionees need to wear at auditions varies. At some auditions, particularly Classical auditions, there is a strict dress code: applicants must wear dance leotards and pointe shoes, and long hair must be tied back. Other dance auditions specify loose clothing. For some contemporary dance auditions, applicants must dance barefoot. In some music theater roles, applicants need to bring tap shoes to demonstrate their tap dancing skills. Some auditions where there is a large number of applicants require the performers to wear a number pinned to their shirt, in a similar way to marathon runners. This way, if the casting director sees an exceptional dancer, he or she can take note of the number. Unless jewellery or make-up is an expected part of a dancer's appearance in a certain dance style, dance auditionees should generally avoid jewellery and makeup.

In music theater and pop music, there is a lot of crossover between dancing and singing roles. Almost all dancers in music theater and many dancers in pop music will be expected to have some singing ability as a backup singer (singing harmony parts to accompany the solo vocalists). In rarer cases, dancers will be asked to demonstrate the ability to play a musical instrument (e.g., guitar), because there are some shows in which some of the dancer-actors have to play instruments onstage, such as the *Threepenny Opera*. In music theater, there is also often crossover between dancing and acting roles. Dancers may be expected to be able to take on an acting role and speak lines (often in a supporting role).

Some major dance companies have "open calls" once a year, in which any or almost any applicant can come to demonstrate their dancing skills. At these open calls, the entire group of applicants are taught a dance routine by a choreographer, and then the group of dancers performs the routine while judges assess their performance. It can be hard for a good dancer to get noticed by the judges in such a large group of dancers. For this reason, some dance coaches encourage their students to make an individual appointment at a dance company, so that the dancer will get personal attention during his or her audition. For any audition interviews, dancers should send their resume and headshot to the company director ahead of time.

Circuses and amusement parks

Performers auditioning for Walt Disney Parks and Resorts are heard by a one or more casting directors in a rehearsal hall or a large facility. All Disney auditions are closed auditions, which means that no one is allowed into the audition room who is not auditioning. Vocalists for Disney auditions are asked to prepare two separate vocal selections of contrasting styles. The singers do not sing the entire songs; instead they just need to sing the best 16 bars of each song. Disney provides a piano accompanist for all vocal auditions, and so singers have to bring sheet music in the correct key. Disney does not allow any pre-recorded accompaniment. The casting directors may also ask auditionees to learn additional music or learn a movement combination. Disney Parks & Resorts casts performers for theme parks, resorts, and cruise ships.[5]

At Cirque du Soleil, depending on a performer's discipline, the audition may last an hour, a day or even two days. Depending on a performer's discipline, he or she might have to perform a solo presentation in front of the group of participants and/or participate in individual and group exercises following the solo presentation. Auditions for Cirque du Soleil are filmed. [6]

Modelling

Modelling agencies and other organizations that are looking for models, such as fashion designers and advertising agencies also use auditions to screen and select potential candidates. Aspiring female models for most fashion industry roles need to be in their teens or early twenties and be tall and slim. Although there are "niche markets" for non-svelte models ("plus size models" and "real life models" who model clothes for middle-market clothing catalogues), most female models need to be slender and between 108-125 lbs. Young men who are aspiring models should be between 18 and 25, tall, and fit. While male models who are selected at modelling auditions may well end up having careers that last till beyond age 25 (even in to their 40s), modelling agencies prefer to recruit new models in the 18-25 age range. Most models work with an agent who arranges auditions, bookings, and negotiates fees.At an audition, casting agents will ask the model to demonstrate different poses, which a photographer may record with a digital camera.

For high fashion auditions, the model may be asked to demonstrate the "catwalk" style of modelling clothes on a raised runway. At most modelling auditions, models should wear fairly simple clothes that will allow the talent agents to imagine the model in different garments. Typically, a model should wear fairly body-hugging clothes, so that the judges can see the body type of the model. Some modelling agencies audition a large number of aspiring models in an "open call", in which agents consider applicants for under a minute or so each. Some agencies hold model searches, which is a type of beauty contest in which applicants audition for the opportunity of winning a model portfolio or a photo shoot.

Further reading

- Kohlhaas, Karen. *The Monologue Audition: A Practical Guide for Actors*. Limelight Series. Limelight Editions
- David, Martin A. *The dancer's audition book*. 1982.
- Kayes, Gillyanne and Jeremy Fisher. *Successful Singing Auditions*. Routledge, 2002. ISBN 0878301631, 9780878301638
- Crane, Adam *Audition Mastery Guide"* [7]

References

[1] http://www.auditionmonologues.com/Audition%20Tips.html
[2] http://www.ubishops.ca/ccc/div/hum/dra/audition.html
[3] http://www.auditionmonologues.com/Audition%20Tips.html
[4] The exception is acoustic enhancement systems which apply a subtle amplification in order to balance the volume in the hall and compensate for acoustic problems.
[5] http://corporate.disney.go.com/auditions/experience/prepare.html
[6] http://www.cirquedusoleil.com/en/jobs/casting/how-to-join/step2.aspx
[7] http://www.craneclassical.com

Background check

A **background check** or **background investigation** is the process of looking up and compiling criminal records, commercial records and financial records (in certain instances such as employment screening) of an individual.

Background checks are often requested by employers on job candidates, especially on candidates seeking a position that requires high security or a position of trust, such as in a school, hospital, financial institution, airport, and government. These checks are traditionally administered by a government agency for a nominal fee, but can also be administered by private companies. Results of a background check typically include past employment verification, credit score, and criminal history.

These checks are often used by employers as a means of objectively evaluating a job candidate's qualifications, character, fitness, and to identify potential hiring risks for safety and security reasons. Background check is also used to thoroughly investigate potential government employees in order to be given a security clearance. However, these checks may sometimes be used for illegal purposes, such as unlawful discrimination (or employment discrimination), identity theft, and violation of privacy.

Pre-employment screening

Pre-employment screening refers to the process of investigating the backgrounds of potential employees and is commonly used to verify the accuracy of an applicant's claims as well as to discover any possible criminal history, workers compensation claims, or employer sanctions.

Screening applications in the UK

A number of annual reports, including BDO Stoy Hayward's Fraudtrack 4[1] and CIFAS's [2] (the UK's fraud prevention service) 'The Enemy Within' have showed a rising level of major discrepancies and embellishments on CVs over previous years. Such business fraud cost United Kingdom businesses $1.4 billion in 2005.[3]

Almost half (48%) of organizations with fewer than 100 staff experienced problems with vetted employees.

Thirty-nine percent of UK organizations have experienced a situation where their vetting procedures have allowed an employee to be hired who was later found to have lied or misrepresented themselves in their application.

Since the onset of the Financial crisis of 2007–2010, the level of fraud has almost doubled and some experts have predicted that it will escalate further.[4] Annual research by Powerchex has also shown that the number of applicants lying on their applications has been increasing steadily since the summer of 2007 when the financial crisis of 2007–2010 began.[5] As of August 2009, nearly one in 5 applicants have major lie or discrepancy on their application.[6]

The market

Larger companies are more likely to outsource than their smaller counterparts – the average staff size of the companies who outsource is 3,313 compared to 2,162 for those who carry out in-house checks.

Financial services firms had the highest proportion of respondents who outsource the service, with over a quarter (26%) doing so, compared to an overall average of 16% who outsource vetting to a third party provider.

The construction and property industry showed the lowest level of outsourcing, with 89% of such firms in the sample carrying out checks in-house, making the overall average 16%. This can increase over the years.

Types of checks

- Employment References
- Character Reference Check
- Gaps in employment history
- Identity and Address Verification - whether the applicant is who he or she claims to be. Generally includes verification of the candidate's present and previous addresses. Can include a money laundering, identity and terrorist check and one to verify the validity of passports.
- Whether an applicant holds a directorship
- Credit History - bankruptcies
- Criminal History Report.

Regulation

The Financial Services Authority states in their Training & Competence guidance that regulated firms should have:

- Adequacy of procedures for taking into account knowledge and skills of potential recruits for the role
- Adequacy of procedures for obtaining sufficient information about previous activities and training
- Adequacy of procedures for ensuring that individuals have passed appropriate exams or have appropriate exemptions
- Adequacy of procedures for assessing competence of individuals for sales roles

The Financial Services Authority's statutory objectives:

1. Protecting consumers
2. Maintaining market confidence
3. Promoting public awareness
4. Reducing financial crime

The FCRA (Fair Credit Reporting Act) is the most important regulation governing background screening.

Pre-employment screening in the U.S.

Laws

Due to the sensitivity of the information contained in consumer reports and certain records, there are a variety of important laws regulating the dissemination and legal use of this information. Most notably, the Fair Credit Reporting Act (FCRA) regulates the use of consumer reports (which it defines as information collected and reported by third party agencies) as it pertains to adverse decisions, notification to the applicant, and destruction and safekeeping of records.

If a consumer report is used as a factor in an adverse hiring decision, the applicant must be presented with a "pre-adverse action disclosure," a copy of the FCRA summary of rights, and a "notification of adverse action letter." Individuals are entitled to know the source of any information used against them including a credit reporting company. Individuals must also consent in order for the employer to obtain a credit report.

Florida Law

Florida House Bill H0775, passed in 1999, provides protection for employers from negligent hiring liabilities, provided they attempt to conduct certain screening procedures. Employers who follow these steps will be presumed not to have been negligent when hiring if a background check fails to reveal any records on an applicant. These steps are[7]:

- Ordering a Florida state criminal record check
- Taking reasonable efforts to contact an applicants past employers
- Asking the applicant on the application if they have been convicted of a crime, date of crime and penalty imposed
- Asking the applicant on the application if they were the defendant in a civil action for intentional tort
- A driving record must be ordered if it is relevant to the performed work
- The employer must interview the applicant

Types of checks

There are a variety of types of investigative searches that can be used by potential employers. Many commercial sites will offer specific searches to employers for a fee. Services like these will actually perform the checks, supply the company with adverse action letters, and ensure compliance throughout the process. It is important to be selective about which pre-employment screening agency you use. A legitimate company will be happy to explain the process to you.

Many employers choose to search the most common records such as criminal records, driving records, and education verification. Other searches such as sex offender registry, credential verification, skills assessment, reference checks, credit reports and Patriot Act searches are becoming increasingly common. Employers should consider the position in question when determining which types of searches to include, and should always use the same searches for every applicant being considered for one

Reasons

They are frequently conducted to confirm information found on an employment application or résumé/curriculum vitae. One study showed that half of all reference checks done on prospective employees differed between what the job applicant provided and what the source reported.[8] They may also be conducted as a way to further differentiate potential employees and pick the one the employer feels is best suited for the position. Employers have an obligation to make sure their work environment is safe for all employees and helps prevent other employment problems in the workplace.[9] [10] [11] [12] [13] [14]

In the United States, the Brady Bill requires criminal checks for those wishing to purchase handguns from licensed firearms dealers. Restricted firearms (like machine guns), suppressors, explosives or large quantities of precursor chemicals, and concealed weapons permits also require criminal checks.

Checks are also required for those working in positions with special security concerns, such as trucking, ports of entry, and airports (including airline transportation). Other laws exist to prevent those who do not pass a criminal check from working in careers involving the elderly, disabled, or children.

Recently, many jobs are using pre-employment credit checks and the trend has appear to have grown since 2000 within the United States (Bird, M., 2010) [15]. According to a survey in 2010, 26% of individuals felt that employers should have the right and duty to check credit reports for all jobs, while another 28 percent felt that it depended on the potential employee's job responsibilities such as banking or accounting jobs.

Possible information included

The amount of information included on a background check depends to a large degree on the sensitivity of the reason for which it is conducted—e.g., somebody seeking employment at a minimum wage job would be subject to far fewer requirements than somebody applying to work for a law enforcement agency such as the FBI or jobs related to national security.

Criminal, arrest, incarceration, and sex offender records

> There are several types of criminal record searches available to employers, some more accurate and up to date than others. These "third party" background checking agencies cannot guarantee the accuracy of their information, thus many of them have incomplete records or inaccurate records. The only way to conduct an accurate background check is to go directly through the state. Most times using the state of choice is much cheaper than using a "third party" agency. Many websites offer the "instant" background check, which will search a compilation of databases containing public information for a fee. These "instant" searches originate from a variety of sources, from statewide court and corrections records to law enforcement records which usually stem from county or metro law enforcement offices. There are also other database-type criminal searches, such as statewide repositories and the national crime file. A commonly used criminal search by

employers who outsource is the county criminal search.

Citizenship, immigration, or legal working status

The hiring of illegal workers has become an issue for American businesses since the forming of the Department of Homeland Security and its Immigrations and Customs Enforcement(ICE) division. Many history making immigration raids[16] over the past two years have forced employers to consider including legal working status as part of their background screening process. All employers are required to keep government Form I-9 documents on all employees and some states mandate the use of the federal E-verify program to research the working status of Social Security numbers. With increased concern for right-to-work issues, many outsourcing companies are sprouting in the marketplace to help automate and store Form I-9 documentation. Some jobs are only available to citizens who are residents of that country due to security concerns.

Litigation records

Employers may want to identify potential employees who routinely file discrimination lawsuits. It has also been alleged that in the U.S., employers that do work for the government do not like to hire whistleblowers who have a history of filing *qui tam* suits.

Driving and vehicle records

Employers that routinely hire drivers or are in the transportation sector seek drivers with clean driving records—i.e., those without a history of accidents or traffic tickets. Department of Motor Vehicles and Department of Transportation records are searched to determine a qualified driver.

Drug tests

Drug tests are used for a variety of reasons—corporate ethics, measuring potential employee performance, and keeping workers' compensation premiums down.

Education records

These are used primarily to see if the potential employee had graduated from high school (or a GED) or received a college degree, graduate degree, or some other accredited university degree. There are reports of SAT scores being requested by employers as well.

Employment records

These usually range from simple verbal confirmations of past employment and timeframe to deeper, such as discussions about performance, activities and accomplishments, and relations with others.

Financial information

Credit scores, liens, civil judgments, bankruptcy, and tax information may be included in the report.

Licensing records

A government authority that has some oversight over professional conduct of its licensees will also maintain records regarding the licensee, such as personal information, education, complaints, investigations, and disciplinary actions.

Medical, Mental, and Physiological evaluation and records

These records are generally not available to consumer reporting agencies, background screening firms, or any other investigators without documented, written consent of the applicant, consumer or employee.

Military records

Although not as common today as it was in the past fifty years, employers frequently requested the specifics of one's military discharge.

Social Security Number

(or equivalent outside the US). A fraudulent SSN may be indicative of identity theft, insufficient citizenship, or concealment of a "past life". Background screening firms usually perform a Social Security trace to determine where the applicant or employee has lived.

Other interpersonal interviews

Employers may investigate past employment to verify position and salary information. More intensive checks can involve interviews with anybody that knew or previously knew the applicant—such as teachers, friends, coworkers, neighbors, and family members; however, extensive hearsay investigations in background checks can expose companies to lawsuits. Past employment and personal reference verifications are moving toward standardization with most companies in order to avoid expensive litigation.

Controversies

Drug tests and credit checks for employment are highly controversial practices. According to the Privacy Rights Clearinghouse, a project of the Utility Consumers' Action Network (UCAN): "While some people are not concerned about background investigations, others are uncomfortable with the idea of investigators poking around in their personal histories. In-depth checks could unearth information that is irrelevant, taken out of context, or just plain wrong. A further concern is that the report might include information that is illegal to use for hiring purposes or which comes from questionable sources."

In May 2002, allegedly improper post-hire checks conducted by Northwest Airlines were the subject of a civil lawsuit between Northwest and 10,000 of their mechanics.

In the case of an arrest that did not lead to a conviction, employment checks can continue including the arrest record for up to seven years, per § 605 of the Fair Credit Reporting Act:

Except as authorized under subsection (b) of this section, no consumer reporting agency may make any consumer report containing . . . Civil suits, civil judgments, and records of arrest that from date of entry, antedate the report by more than seven years or until the governing statute of limitations has expired, whichever is the longer period.

Subsection (b) provides for an exception if the report is in connection with "the employment of any individual at an annual salary which equals, or which may reasonably be expected to equal $75,000, or more".[17]

Some proposals for decreasing potential harm to innocent applicants include:

- Furnishing the applicant with a copy of the report before it is given to the employer, so that any inaccuracies can be addressed beforehand; and
- Allowing only conviction (not arrest) records to be reported.

In New Zealand, criminal checks have been affected by the Clean Slate Act 2004, which allows individuals to legally conceal "less serious" convictions from their records provided they had been conviction-free for at least seven years.

In Michigan, the system of criminal checks has been criticized in a recent case where a shooting suspect was able to pass an FBI check to purchase a shotgun although he had failed the check for a state handgun permit. According to the spokesman of the local police department,

... you could have a clear criminal history but still have contacts with law enforcement that would not rise to the level of an arrest or conviction [that can be used] to deny a permit whether or not those involved arrests that might show up on a criminal history.[18]

The Brady Campaign to Prevent Gun Violence has criticized the federal policy, which denies constitutional rights based on a criminal check only if the subject has been accused of a crime.

Public records pay sites

Taking advantage of public records availability in the United States, a number of Web based companies began purchasing U.S. public records data and selling it online, primarily to assist the general public in locating people. Many of these sites advertise background research and provide employers and/or landlords with fee-based checks.

There has been a growing movement on the web to use advertising-based models to subsidize these checks. These companies display targeted ads next to the reports delivered to landlords or employers. Some of the reports provided by these pay sites are only expanded versions of a basic people search providing a 20 year history of addresses, phone numbers, marriages and divorces, businesses owned and property ownership. Usually, these sites will also provide a nationwide criminal report for an added charge.

As a general rule, employers may NOT take adverse action against an applicant or employee (not hiring or terminating them), solely on the basis of results obtained through a database search. Database searches, as opposed to source records searches (search of actual county courthouse records), are notoriously inaccurate, contain incomplete or outdated information, and should only be used as an added safety net when conducting a background check. Failure by employers to follow FCRA guidelines can result in hefty penalties. [19]

References

[1] BDO Fraudtrack 4 Report (http://www.bdo.co.uk/fraudtrack)
[2] CIFAS - The Enemy Within (http://www.cifas.org.uk/default.asp?edit_id=658-57)
[3] Fraud Track 4 Report (http://www.bdo.co.uk/fraudtrack)
[4] Fraud doubles yet expert says the worst is still to come (http://www.bdo.uk.com/news/2009/fraud-doubles-yet-expert-says-the-worst-is-still-to-come.html)
[5] Under-21s told 29% more lies on job applications this year than last (http://www.guardian.co.uk/education/2009/aug/06/young-unemployed-lies-job-applications)
[6] Annual pre-employment Screening Survey (http://www.powerchex.co.uk/interface/files/surveys/PowerchexAnnualPre-EmploymentScreeningSurvey2009.pdf)
[7] IntegraScan Background Check Guide (http://www.integrascan.com/UltimateGuidetoBackgroundChecks.pdf)
[8] http://pre-employmentservices.adp.com/content/PES_wpid205sass_RetailersGuide
[9] http://www.usdoj.gov/olp/ag_bgchecks_report.pdf
[10] http://www.jjkeller.com/humanresources/Background_Check_White_Paper.pdf
[11] http://pre-employmentservices.adp.com/content/PES_wpid201sass_InsideCriminalBackgroundChecks
[12] http://www.choicepoint.com/documents/Background_Screening_Nonprofits.pdf
[13] http://www.kroll.com/news/releases/index.aspx?id=19532
[14] http://www.hireright.com/PDFs/ExtendedWorkforceResearchBrief.pdf
[15] http://importantnews.org/december2010.html
[16] (http://www.ice.gov/pi/nr/0808/080826laurel.htm?searchstring=howard AND industries)
[17] http://www.ftc.gov/os/statutes/fcra.htm
[18] Kathy Barks Hoffman, Associated Press, 10:33 am EDT Apr 13, "Mich. shooting suspect was denied permit"
[19] http://www.workplaceclassaction.com/settlement-issues/bellwether-settlement-for-59-million-given-preliminary-approval-for-fcra-class-action-involving-crim/index.html

External links

- Advocates Complain of Background Check Errors (http://www.abcnews.go.com/TheLaw/story?id=6017227&page=1), ABC News, 13 Oct 2008.

Campus placement

Campus placement or campus interview is the program conducted within educational institutes or in a common place to provide jobs to students pursuing or in the stage of completing the programme. In this programme, industries visit the colleges to select qualified students.

Types of campus placement

There are two types of campus placement. They are on-campus and off-campus

On-campus placement

This is the placement program organized only for the students within the educational institute. In most cases student in the final year of a program will participate in this placement program

Off campus placement

This job placement program is for students from other institutions. This program will be conducted in a common place (it may be in a college or in some public place) where students from different colleges will take part.

Project Placement

Companies recruit students to do their academic project in the industrial environment.

Student Internship Placement

Companies recruit the students as interns. Internship will be during their student period.

Objective

The major objective of campus placement is to identify the talented and qualified professionals before they complete their education. This process reduces the time for an industry to pick the candidates according to their need.

Procedure

Pre-Placement Talk

A presentation about the company will be made during the pre-placement talk. Basically the presentation includes the information like selection procedure, company's milestones, organizational achievements, candidate scope of improvement within the organization if selected, salary, employment benefits. Usually this presentation will end up with question and answer session, students given chance to ask questions about company.

Educational qualification

Companies who interested in campus visit for recruitment purpose will have specific qualification criteria. Qualification criteria include marks or grade range, specific programme.

Written Test

Qualified students will undergo a test. This is usually a simple aptitude test but depending on company and the position looking for, the difficulty level of the test may be at the higher side.

Group discussion

Most of the companies will have this round as a filtering round. This round may or may not be conducted.

A common topic is placed before the group and a formal discussion or knowledge sharing is expected by the judge. Purpose of this round is to check communication skills, etiquette of person, listening ability, convincing power, group leadership, leader or follower and many more thing are evaluated on the basis of requirement or the particular intention of organisation or company.

Technical Interview

Based on outcome of above said process, students will further undergo a round called technical round. This round evaluates the technical ability of the student. In most of the cases this will be an individual round but it may be grouped with the formal interview.

Formal interview

Final round of the selection process, where the student's stability and his confidence level towards the particular work will be evaluated.

Post-Placement Talk

Once the student is selected, he will be given an offer letter. Company's executive may provide guidelines about joining procedure and other prerequisites if needed.

Candidate submittal

Candidate Submittal is an alternative recruitment process offered by companies whereby the candidate submittal agency provides 'coaching' for the job seeker with respect to his/her job application. With candidate submittal, the job seeker usually sources their own prospective job opportunity (e.g. on Job Boards, Company Websites, Newspapers etc...). The job seeker then applies for the job through the candidate submittal agency, which is usually run by ex-recruitment professionals or other industry veterans.

The candidate submittal service will often vett, edit or enhance the job seekers application before passing it on to the employer. The service will then act on behalf of the job seeker in the negotiations and would also may help prepare the job seeker for an interview process or other pre-interview engagement. They would also provide any relevant feedback to the job seeker with regards to his/her application.

Once the job seeker is accepted by the employer, the candidate submittal agency then may then refund a portion of the sign-on fee back to the job seeker . Usually in recognition of the fact that the candidate has completed some of the recruitment process themselves by sourcing their own jobs.

The Market

With up to 80% of companies generally expecting to encounter difficulties in the recruitment process from year to year, [1] . It's obvious that there exists a market for broad recruitment solutions. Companies will generally employ a number of different methods to fill their recruitment needs including employee referral, company websites, recruitment agencies and job boards. Generally, it's found that around 27.1% of recruitment is done through employee referral - making it the largest source of company recruitment [2] , with standard recruitment making up around 5.2% of overall recruitment.

The future of the recruitment industry is generally considered by industry analysts to be in 'Career Networks' [3] , that can provide employee's with the backup necessary to optimize their job searching process - including having access to a 'career coach', utilizing niche recruitment channels, building a profile and receiving positive feedback.

Candidate Submittal vs Agency Recruitment

Candidate Submittal came about because the standard recruitment model was perceived by some in the recruitment industry as being wasteful and providing poor value to both employers and job seekers [4] .

It was argued by these individuals that the standard recruitment model was never meant to be an extension of a company HR department, nor was it designed to accommodate the market share which it currently holds in the recruitment industry and to become the de facto standard for general mass-recruitment needs. They argued that the recruiter in a standard agency is cast both as a 'career coach' by the job seeker and as an 'industry specialist' by the employer. Whereas in fact the recruiter is ill-suited to fulfill either of these rules.

Candidate Submittal agencies aim to re-cast the role of a recruiter into more of a background setting. Using a candidate submittal service, the client will receive feedback and advice with regards to their application. They will not however be interviewed or matched to a position by the candidate submittal agency.

A candidate submittal service will usually offer a substantial discount over standard agency recruitment. Also, because it aims to compensate job seekers for the time they spend sourcing their own opportunities. It means that job seekers are less inclined to leave this job matching process to a recruiter who may or may not be suitably qualified to determine whether a certain candidate fits a certain position. Also since candidate submittal effectively removes the middle man in the recruitment process (the recruiter). It can serve to speed up the process in general and provide more meaningful feedback to the job seeker.

Criticisms

While candidate submittal can help to cut down on recruitment costs for an employer and help to make the job hunting process more efficient, it does require the candidates to spend time sourcing their own employment opportunities, a job that would typically be left to the recruiter to complete.

However it should also be noted that most job seekers only use recruitment agencies as one source of job finding and will typically use the Internet or company job sites to source their own opportunities anyway. [5]

References

[1] RCI. "Recruitment Confidence Index" (http://www.som.cranfield.ac.uk/som/rci/index.asp). RCI. . Retrieved 2007-11-09.

[2] CareerXRoads. "CareerXRoads" (http://www.careerxroads.com/news/SourcesOfHire05.pdf). CareerXRoads. . Retrieved 2007-11-09.

[3] Forrester Research. "The Career Networks" (http://www.marketresearch.com/map/prod/275079.html). Forrester. . Retrieved 2007-11-09.

[4] Dara Burke. "Origins of Candidate Submittal" (http://www.saverecruit.com/blog.php?blog=origins) (html). SaveRecruit. . Retrieved 2007-11-09.

[5] Noras. "National Online Recruitment Survey" (http://www.noras.co.uk/). Noras.co.uk. . Retrieved 2007-11-09.

Careers In The Outdoors

Careers In The Outdoors is an annual careers job fair and exhibition event, promoting the diversity of careers available within the outdoors sector. As part of The Outdoors Show, it is held alongside the London Boat Show, and London Bike Show. The 2011 Outdoors Show will be held at the ExCeL London exhibition centre, between the 13 - 16 January.

History

Careers in the Outdoors is a creation of niche job board network 247recruit, who working in partnership with VOS Media and the Outdoor Industries Association created the event.[1] The first Careers In The Outdoors event was held in March 2010, alongside The Outdoors Show at the NEC Birmingham.

The Outdoors Show is the largest consumer outdoors show in Europe and incorporates up to 250 participating exhibitors each year [2] . With 30,000 visitors in 2010, the number of vistors is expected to be in excess of 125,000 for 2011 [3] .

Exhibition

As well as a classical exhibition style layout, the show is a merger of both jobs fair and careers informational event. A dedicated Careers Zone allows visitors to meet prospective employers, chat to advisers, and browse jobs on the internet at an informal Careers Cafe.

A wide range of key speakers and employers from the outdoors sector speak about their own career journeys, what their day to day roles involve, and their advice for anyone considering a career in the outdoor education or leisure industries. Speakers include:[4]

- Adventure travel companies: Sunsail, Mark Warner
- Outdoor activity centres: Go Ape, PGL, Go Ape
- Youth development charities: Fairbridge
- Expedition organisers:

- Field study centres:
- Outdoor clothing retailers: Blacks Leisure Group
- Equipment manufacturers: Berghaus

All of the talks are recorded on video, which after the close of the physical event, can be viewed on the exhibition website and the OutdoorStaff YouTube Channel.

References

[1] "247recruit Launch Outdoor Careers Event" (http://www.247recruit.net/247recruit_Launch_Outdoor_Careers_Event.html). 247recruit. 10 March 2010. . Retrieved 2010-12-20.

[2] "Show Overview" (http://www.theoutdoorsshow.co.uk/exhibiting/show-overview/). VosMedia. . Retrieved 2010-12-20.

[3] "The Outdoors Show 2010 featuring TriLive 2010 Post Show Report & 2011 Preview" (http://www.outdoorsshowextra.co.uk/data/2011/post_show_report/post_show_report_-_v4.pdf). VosMedia. . Retrieved 2010-12-20.

[4] "PGL at Careers In The Outdoors Zone" (http://www.3d-education.co.uk/PGLWeb/Recruitment/Why-work-for-pgl/Who-are-PGL/Careers-in-the-Outdoors-Event-at-the-Outdoors-Show.htm). PGL. . Retrieved 2010-12-20.

External links

- Careers In The Outdoors Official Website (http://www.careersintheoutdoors.co.uk/)
- The Outdoors Show Official Website (http://www.theoutdoorsshow.co.uk/)
- The Tullet Prebon London International Boat Show Official Website (http://www.londonboatshow.com)
- The London Bike Show Official Website (http://www.thelondonbikeshow.co.uk)
- ExCeL London Official Website (http://www.excel-london.co.uk/)

Common Recruitment Examination

Common Recruitment Examination (綜合招聘考試) is an examination for the recruitment of civil servants in Hong Kong. It consists of three 45-minute papers, namely Use of English (UE), Use of Chinese (UC) and Aptitude Test (AT). Candidates' results in the UE and UC papers are classified as 'Level 2', 'Level 1' or 'Fail', with 'Level 2' being the highest. Results in the AT paper are classified as pass or fail. 'Level 2' and 'Level 1' results of the two language papers and the pass result of the AT paper are of permanent validity. All three papers are in multiple-choice format.

External links

- Official homepage [1]

References

[1] http://www.csb.gov.hk/english/recruit/cre/949.html

Competency-based job description

Competency-based job descriptions are one way to define participant roles while still allowing for evolution. Like well-written typical job descriptions, competency-based job descriptions list job title, job description, key responsibilities, and requisite and preferred education and experience. What competency-based job descriptions add is a focus on less tangible behavioral competencies. These qualities are numerous and elaborate systems developed by human resource consulting firms are available for assistance in developing competency-based job descriptions and related evaluative methods. A few examples of behavioral competencies are leadership, interpersonal communication, multicultural sensitivity, initiative, teamwork, and flexibility. Linked to each competency are indicators of how effectively employees meet each requirement. Enunciating behavioral competencies facilitates personnel selection, role comprehension, and performance evaluation

Cover letter

A **cover letter**, **covering letter**, **motivation letter**, **motivational letter** or a **letter of motivation** is a letter of introduction attached to, or accompanying another document such as a résumé or curriculum vitae.

For employment

Job seekers frequently send a cover letter along with their CV or employment application as a way of introducing themselves to potential employers and explaining their suitability for the desired position. Employers may look for individualized and thoughtfully written cover letters as one method of screening out applicants who are not sufficiently interested in their position or who lack necessary basic skills. Cover letters are typically divided into three categories:

- The application letter or invited cover letter which responds to a known job opening
- The prospecting letter or uninvited cover letter which inquires about possible positions
- The networking letter which requests information and assistance in the sender's job search

Format

Cover letters are generally one page at most in length, divided into a header, introduction, body, and closing...

- *Header.* Cover letters use standard business letter style, with the sender's address and other information, the recipient's contact information, and the date sent after either the sender's or the recipient's address. Following that is an optional reference section (e.g. "RE: Internship Opportunity at Global Corporation") and an optional transmission note (e.g. "Via Email to jobs@example.net"). The final part of the header is a salutation (e.g., "Dear Hiring Managers").
- *Introduction.* The introduction briefly states the specific position desired, and should be designed to catch the employer's immediate interest.
- *Body.* The body highlights or amplifies on material in the resume or job application, and explains why the job seeker is interested in the job and would be of value to the employer. Also, matters discussed typically include skills, qualifications, and past experience. If there are any special things to note such as availability date, they may be included as well.
- *Closing.* A closing sums up the letter and indicates the next step the applicant expects to take. It may indicate that the applicant intends to contact the employer, although many favor the more indirect approach of simply saying that the applicant will look forward to hearing from or speaking with the employer. After the closing is a valediction ("Sincerely"), and then a signature line. Optionally, the abbreviation "ENCL" may be used to indicate that there are enclosures.

Other uses

Cover letters may also serve as marketing devices for prospective job seekers. Cover letters are used in connection with many business documents such as loan applications (mortgage loan), contract drafts and proposals, and executed documents. Many US MBA Schools, such as MIT and Harvard, request a cover letter as part of their admission application. Cover letters may serve the purpose of trying to catch the reader's interest or persuade the reader of something, or they may simply be an inventory or summary of the documents included along with a discussion of the expected future actions the sender or recipient will take in connection with the documents.

External links

- Cover Letter format guidelines [1]
- Cover Letter writing guidelines [2] | CV and Cover Letter Workbook [3]
- How to write a cover letter [4]

References

[1] http://www.career.vt.edu/JobSearchGuide/CoverLetterSamples.html

[2] http://web.mit.edu/career/www/guide/coverletters.pdf

[3] http://web.mit.edu/career/www/students/workbook.pdf

[4] http://www.trincoll.edu/depts/career/guides/cover_ltr.shtml

Cravath System

The **Cravath System** is a hiring practice developed at Cravath, Swaine & Moore in the 19th Century. It has been partially adapted by most large law firms[1] [2] and consulting agencies.

System

Swaine lays out the fundamentals of the Cravath System in the beginning of Volume 2 of the history of the Cravath Firm.[3]

Recruiting staff

> Paul Drennan Cravath preferred to hire the "best of the best" and looked to the better law schools for candidates. Graduates were expected to be members of Phi Beta Kappa/Beta Gamma Sigma and have served as editors for the school law reviews. A graduate from a university outside the top 5 was expected to be at least the equivalent of a "B" student at Harvard. Only new graduates were to be hired, except in extenuating circumstances. The belief was that someone who had worked anywhere else had learned bad habits already.

Training staff

> Associates would be assigned to a partner for a period of time (usually 18 months or less) where they would learn to break down large tasks into manageable pieces.

Compensation

> Early law firm hiring practices paid the associates nothing, except what they could bring in for themselves. By 1910, the Cravath firm was one of the first to hire incoming lawyers on a salary. Since they preferred to hire the best, this led to wide disparities in starting salaries. Collusion among law firms and law schools led to uniform starting salaries across law firms from the end of World War I to World War II.[4].

Tenure

Generally, only partners may have permanent employment at the firm, and as long as an associate is promotable, they may stay. Those who were not suitable for promotion were dismissed in the "up or out" policy.

Choosing partners

Unless there is some need for expertise unavailable within the firm, partners should only be chosen from within the office.

Interests outside the firm

Partners and associates may not have business interests outside the firm. Charitable, educational and artistic interests are permitted. There are no part time associates and partners, and all business in the office is company business.

Relationships of the partners

Partners are expected to work with each other. Silos and cliques are to be avoided.

Scope of the practice

Cravath handled predominantly civil matters in the early years, and the majority of firms adopting this system are likewise civil law firms[5].

Influence

The firm would avoid lobbying or currying favors with politicians. The firm would stick with skill and diligence in applying the law.

As to the firm's management

Cravath believed that a firm must have strong executive direction.

Up or Out

Part of the system was that employees should either be promoted in 3 years, or leave the company. Incoming associates were expected to achieve partner within 7–8 years, and no later than 10 years after the initial hire.

The U.S. military has a similar version to the "up or out" situation. The Defense Officer Personnel Management Act was passed in 1980 (PL 96-513) mandating that officers who had been twice passed over for promotion were required to be discharged from the military.[6]

References

[1] William Henderson (2008) (PDF). *Are We Selling Results or Résumés?: The Underexplored Linkage Between Human Resource Strategies and Firm-Specific Capital* (http://papers.ssrn.com/sol3/papers.cfm?abstract_id=1121238). . Retrieved 2009-06-21.

[2] Henderson, Bill. "How most law firms misapply the "Cravath system"" (http://lawprofessors.typepad.com/legal_profession/2008/07/part-ii-how-mos.html). . Retrieved 2009-06-21.

[3] Swaine, Robert (1948). *The Cravath Firm*. New York: Ad Press. pp. 1–12. ISBN 1581310730.

[4] page 6 of Swaine

[5] Greenfield, Scott. "There's No Cravath System For Criminal Defense" (http://blog.simplejustice.us/2009/06/13/theres-no-cravath-system-for-criminal-defense.aspx). . Retrieved 2009-06-21.

[6] Bernard Rostker, et. al. (1992) (PDF). *The Defense Officer Personnel Management Act of 1980 - A Retrospective Assessment* (http://www.rand.org/pubs/reports/2006/R4246.pdf). ISBN 0833012878. .

e-recruitment

E-recruitment or ecruitment is the process of personnel recruitment using electronic resources, in particular the internet[1] . Companies and recruitment agents have moved much of their recruitment process online so as to improve the speed by which candidates can be matched with live vacancies. Using database technologies, and online job advertising boards and search engines, employers can now fill posts in a fraction of the time previously possible. Using an online e-Recruitment system will save the employer time as usually they can rate the eCandidate and several persons in HR can independently review eCandidates.

Internet, which reach larger number of people and can get immediate feed back become the major source of potential job candidates and well known as online recruitment or E-recruitment. However, It may generates many unqualified candidates and may not increase the diversity and mix of employees. [2]

In terms of HRM, the internet has radically changed the recruitment function from the organisational and job seekers' perspective. Conventional methods of recruitment processes are readily acknowledged as being time-consuming with high costs and limited geographic reach. However, recruitment through World Wide Web (WWW) provides global coverage and easiness. Likewise, the speedy integration of the internet into recruitment processes is primarily recognised due to the internet's unrivalled communications capabilities, which enable recruiters for written communications through e-mails, blogs and job portals.

Some Facts of E-Recruitment

By 2005, expenditure on Internet-based recruiting will be $ 7 billion - Forrester Research Institute. 96% of all companies will use the Internet for their recruitment needs. In the U.S., some companies claim 30% of new hires are from the Internet and 77% of Internet users who are seeking a change, use the Net to do so. A recent survey conducted by Employment Management Association, U.S.A, the cost-per-hire of print Ads was estimated at $3295 and Online Ads, a mere $ 377. Over 16 million resumes floating online. [3]

References

[1] Human Resource Management by R. J. Stone (edition 2006)

[2] Management by Robbins and Coulter (edition 2009)

[3] http://www.selfgrowth.com/articles/Software1.html

Employability

Employability refers to a person's capability of gaining initial employment, maintaining employment, and obtaining new employment if required (Hillage and Pollard, 1998). In simple terms, employability is about being capable of getting and keeping fulfilling work. More comprehensively, employability is the capability to move self-sufficiently within the labour market to realise potential through sustainable employment. For individuals, employability depends on the knowledge, skills and abilities (KSAs) they possess, the way they use those assets and present them to employers, and the context (e.g. personal circumstances and labour market environment) within which they seek work.

Employability is a two-sided equation and many individuals need various forms of support to overcome the physical and mental barriers to learning and personal development (i.e. updating their assets). Employability is not just about vocational and academic skills. Individuals need relevant and usable labour market information to help them make informed decisions about the labour market options available to them. They may also need support to realise when such information would be useful, and to interpret that information and turn it into intelligence. Finally, people also need the opportunities to do things differently, to access relevant training and, most crucially, employment. Both the supply and demand of labour need to be taken into account when defining employability, which is often dependent on factors outside of an individual's control.

Employability was one of the four 'pillars' of the European Employment Strategy until its reformulation in 2000, along with entrepreneurship, adaptability and equal opportunities. It has thus also been a key theme of the EQUAL Community Initiative.

For individuals, employability depends on:

- their assets in terms of the knowledge, skills and attitudes they possess
- the way they use and deploy those assets
- the way they present them to employers
- crucially, the context (e.g. personal circumstances and labour market environment) within which they seek work.

The balance of importance between and within each element will vary for groups of individuals, depending on their relationship to the labour market.

Government policy is aimed:

- more at the development and accreditation of knowledge and vocational skills than at the soft skills and attitudes
- more on the demonstration of assets than their deployment — particularly for adults (e.g. lack of provision of a careers education and guidance service for adults)
- more at individuals looking to enter the labour market (e.g. from education or unemployment) than within
- more on the individual and the supply side, than on employers and the demand side (i.e. the labour market contextual factors).

Origins of Employability

The concept of employability has been in the literature for many years. Current interest has been driven by:

- the changing nature of public employment policy, with increasing emphasis being given to skills-based solutions to economic competition and work-based solutions to social deprivation.
- the supposed end of 'careers' and lifetime job security, which have, of course, only ever applied to a minority of the workforce, the greater uncertainty among employers as to the levels and types of jobs they may have in the future, and the need to build new relationships with employees.

Employability: towards a definition

While there is no singular definition of employability, a review of the literature suggests that employability is about work and the ability to be employed, such as:

- the ability to gain initial employment; hence the interest in ensuring that 'key skills', careers advice and an understanding about the world of work are embedded in the education system
- the ability to maintain employment and make 'transitions' between jobs and roles within the same organization to meet new job requirements, and
- the ability to obtain new employment if required, i.e. to be independent in the labour market by being willing and able to manage their own employment transitions between and within organisations.

It is also, ideally, about:

- the quality of such work or employment. People may be able to obtain work but it may be below their level of skill, or in low paid, undesirable or unsustainable jobs, and so forth.
- The capacity and capability of gaining and maintaining productive work over the period of one's working life. (Muhammad Nawaz Qaisar, MS HRD, NUML, Islamabad, Pakistan)

Four components of employability

This suggests that we can separate out four main elements in respect of individuals' employability: the first three are analogous to the concepts of production, marketing and sales, and the fourth is the marketplace in which they operate.

Assets

An individual's 'employability assets' comprise their knowledge (i.e. what they know), skills (what they do with what they know) and attitudes (how they do it). There are a number of detailed categorisations in the literature which, for instance, distinguish between:

- 'baseline assets' such as basic skills and essential personal attributes (such as reliability and integrity).
- 'intermediate assets' such as occupational specific skills (at all levels), generic or key skills (such as communication and problem solving) and key personal attributes (such as motivation and initiative), and
- 'high level assets' involving skills which help contribute to organizational performance (such as team working, self management, commercial awareness etc.)

Further key points from the literature include the importance of the transferability of these skills from one occupational or business context to another for employability and the increased attention employers are paying to the softer attitudinal skills in selecting employees.

Merely being in possession of employer-relevant knowledge, skills and attitudes is not enough for an individual to either 'move self-sufficiently' in the modern labour market or 'realise their potential'. People also need the capability to exploit their assets, to market them and sell them.

Deployment

These are a linked set of abilities which include:

- Career management skills and life skills — commonly identified as self-awareness (i.e. diagnosing occupational interests and abilities), opportunity awareness (knowing what work opportunities exist and their entry requirements i.e. labour market knowledge), decision-making skills (to develop a strategy of getting from where you are to where you want to be) and transition skills. The latter generally includes:
- Job search skills — i.e. finding suitable jobs. Access to formal and informal networks is an important component of job search and employability.

- Strategic approach — being adaptable to labour market developments and realistic about labour market opportunities, be occupationally and locationally mobile.

There is obviously an important inter-relationship between assets and deployment. The extent to which an individual is aware of what they possess in terms of knowledge, skills and attitudes and its relevance to the employment opportunities available may affect their willingness to undertake training and other activities designed to upgrade their skills etc.

Presentation

Another key aspect of employability is being able to get a particular job, once identified — sometimes included under career management skills, but is given prominence as a separate element here due to its crucial importance to securing employment. It centres around the ability to demonstrate 'employability' assets and present them to the market in an accessible way. This includes:

- the presentation of CVs etc., (including Records of Achievement)
- the qualifications individuals possess (both academic and vocational), perhaps accredited through prior learning
- references and testimonies
- interview technique, and, of particular importance,
- work experience/track record.

In the context of personal circumstances and the labour market

Finally and crucially, the ability to realise or actualise 'employability' assets depends on the individual's personal and external circumstances and the inter-relationship between the two. This includes:

- personal circumstances — e.g. caring responsibilities, disabilities, and household status can all affect their ability to seek different opportunities and will vary during an individual's life cycle; while

- external factors such as macro-economic demand and the pattern and level of job openings in their labour market, be it local or national; labour market regulation and benefit rules; and employer recruitment and selection behaviour.

Priorities for action

For the state, as well as raising the skill profile of the existing workforce, especially at lower levels to boost flexibility and competitiveness, there are a number of potential priority groups including:

- labour market entrants
- labour market re-entrants
- disadvantaged groups
- insecure or under-utilised employees

where different policies may need to be targeted according to different circumstances.

For employers the priorities might be to help key groups of staff to develop both those assets which have explicit, immediate value to the organization as well as those transferable ones which have a wider, longer term currency, thereby engendering a sense of security, encouraging commitment, risk-taking and flexibility among employees.

For the individual the need is to boost those aspects of their employability which will most enhance their opportunities in the light of their circumstances.

Issues for public policy

The above definition of employability provides a basis for analysing the policies affecting the employability of certain groups (e.g. 16 and 17-year-old school leavers), or conversely how major policy initiatives (e.g. the New Deal) impact on employability. A brief review of government initiatives in this area suggests that policy is aimed:

- more at the development and accreditation of knowledge and vocational skills than at the 'softer' skills and attitudes
- more on the demonstration of assets than their deployment — particularly for adults (e.g. lack of provision of a careers education and guidance service for adults)
- more at individuals looking to enter the labour market (e.g. from education or unemployment) than within
- more on the individual and the supply side, than on employers and the demand side (i.e. the labour market contextual factors).

This policy orientation may reflect a variety of factors such as difficulties in defining, assessing and verifying 'soft skills', and difficulties identifying and accessing specific groups of employees at which to target limited resources.

Thus some key questions for future policy interventions include:

- who are the priority groups
- where the most serious gaps are for such groups be they related to e.g. which assets, dimensions of deployment or presentational skills
- how these gaps might best be remedied and
- which of the arms of public policy are best placed to add such value and how through interventions.

Finally, whatever the interventions, they need to be evaluated so that lessons can be fed back into further improvements and to the decision to continue with, change or stop such interventions. Potential measures include those relating to input measures, e.g. possession of vocational qualifications, or the receipt of careers management training; perception measures, e.g. the views of employers and the workforce of their employability; and outcome measures, e.g. the speed at which people are able to get jobs or 'measurements of failure', e.g. the numbers or proportion of people with difficulty finding or keeping work, or the number of job changes, however defined. Obviously there is room for some combination of all three. Whatever route is chosen, it is important to take account of the overall state of the labour market and how it is changing, to take account of any dead-weight effect and assess true additionality.

Duality of Employability

An alternative account of employability takes a more relative approach. Brown and Hesketh define employability as 'the relative chances of getting and maintaining different kinds of employment' (2004).

While most people view employability in absolute terms, focussing on the need for individuals to obtain credentials, knowledge and social status, the concept of employability can also be seen as subjective and dependent on contextual factors. 'Employability not only depends on whether one is able to fulfil the requirements of specific jobs, but also on how one stands relative to others within a hierarchy of job seekers' (Brown and Hesketh, 2004). Taking the supply and demand of labour into account challenges the idea that credentials, knowledge and social status alone will guarantee a good position in the labour market.

With the move to a more knowledge based economy, it is widely thought that there is an increasing demand for high-calibre managerial talent. However, a focus on obtaining skills in order to gain good employment has led to an over-supply of graduates and a larger number of contenders chasing the same top jobs. Brown and Hesketh argue that there is a clear mismatch between individuals' expectations of employability and the realities posed by the labour market.

Under these conditions, students will use a number of tactics in the labour market to maintain competitive advantage. Brown and Hesketh identify two ideal types of individuals entering the labour market. Those who will do anything to get a top job are classed as 'players'. Players are not afraid to take on a different identity if they feel that is what the employer is looking for. The second type, 'purists', are those who believe that job market outcomes should reflect meritocratic achievement. For purists it is important to maintain an authentic sense of self as this will ensure a good fit between individual capabilities and occupational demands. Purists may be as competitive as Players but feel that Players are cheating in order to get ahead.

This view of employability incorporates the dual aspects of supply and demand of labour to show that advancing one's position in the labour market by gaining credentials is partially dependent on structural factors outside the individual's control. The recent financial crisis demonstrates that global economic factors can and do have a significant impact on the likelihood of an individual securing a job regardless of their skills, credentials and social status.

References

- Brown, P and Hesketh, A (2004) The Mismanagement of Talent: Employability and Jobs in the Knowledge Economy: Oxford University Press, Oxford

- Schneider, K. and Otto, H-U (2009) From Employability Towards Capability: Luxembourg

Employee referral

Employee referral is an internal recruitment method employed by organizations to identify potential candidates from their existing employees' social networks. An employee referral scheme encourages a company's existing employees to select and recruit the suitable candidates from their social networks. As a reward, the employer typically pays the referring employee a referral bonus. Recruiting candidates using employee referral is widely acknowledged as being the most cost effective and efficient recruitment method to recruit candidates and as such, employers of all sizes, across all industries are trying to increases the volumes they recruit through this channel.

Proponents of employee referral schemes claim the benefits to be an improved candidate quality, 'fit', and retention levels, while at the same time delivering a significant reduction in recruitment expenditure.However, there are a number of potential drawbacks. One of the greatest concerns tends to be that relying too heavily on employee referrals could limit diversity in the workplace, with new staff recruited in the likeness of existing employees. But, provided that there is already a diverse workforce in place this ceases to be such an issue.

Improved candidate quality, 'fit', and retention

The one-to-one direct relationship between the candidate and the referring employee and the exchange of knowledge that takes place allows the candidate to develop a strong understanding of the company, its business and the application and recruitment process. With this information the candidate is ideally placed to assess their own suitability and likelihood of success at the company and make an informed decision, with the support of the referring employee as to whether to apply. This is the start of the company's recruitment process where, at no cost to the employer, candidates and employees remove unsuitable and poor quality candidates, from the recruitment process ensuring a consistently high quality of applications

Candidates who are interviewed are thoroughly prepared resulting in superior interview to job offer conversion rates. In addition, successful candidates get up to speed faster compared to other recruitment methods. Candidate 'fit' to the company's culture, departments and teams is improved as the expectations of candidate and employer match. This significantly increases the level of staff retention and builds a loyal and committed workforce - ultimately reducing the company's future recruitment requirements

Reduction in Recruitment Expenditure

Employee referral scheme's allows existing employees to screen, select and refer only the best candidates to the recruitment process. This eliminates the often considerable cost of third parties service providers who would have previously conducted the screening and selection process

The costs of operating an employee referral scheme extends to the cash bonus' paid to employees and internal promotion and administration, the total of which is considerably lower than the expense of recruiting using traditional recruitment consultants, headhunters and online recruitment methods

As candidate quality improves and interview to job offer conversion rates increase the amount of time spent interviewing decreases meaning the company's Human Resources headcount can be streamlined and be used more efficiently. Marketing and advertising spend decreases as existing employees source potential candidates from the existing personal networks of friends, family, acquaintances and associates.

The opportunity to improve candidate quality, 'fit', and retention levels, while at the same time significantly reduce recruitment expenditure has seen the emphasis employers place on increasing the volume of recruits by employer referral increase dramatically. However, there are number of obstacles to achieving the desired increase:

- An employees social network is limited – only a small proportion of the network may be suitable for referral
- Recruiting from an employee's limited social network may compromise the diversity of the workforce
- Actively referring candidates increases an employee's workload and may be detrimental to their main responsibilities
- The best and most relevant candidates may not be acquainted with an existing employee of the company and therefore cannot be recruited via the referral scheme

An employee referral scheme is only as good as the volume and quality of candidates applying through the channel.

References

[1]

[1] CareerXRoads, Annual Source of Hire Report, shows Referrals to be the #1 Source or New Hires for major US companies. [Source of Hire Report] (http://www.careerXRoads.com)

Employee value proposition

Employee Value Proposition (EVP) is a term used to denote the balance of the rewards and benefits that are received by employees in return for their performance at the workplace.[1]

Minchington (2005) defines an Employee Value Proposition (EVP) as a set of associations and offerings provided by an organisation in return for the skills, capabilities and experiences an employee brings to the organisation. The EVP is an employee-centered approach that is aligned to existing, integrated workforce planning strategies because it has been informed by existing employees and the external target audience. An EVP must be unique, relevant and compelling if it is to act as a key driver of talent attraction, engagement and retention.[2] [3]

It has become closely related to the concept of employer branding, in terms of the term EVP being used to define the underlying 'offer' on which an organisation's employer brand marketing and management activities are based. In this context, the EVP is often referred to as the Employer Brand Proposition.[4]

Tandehill (2006) reinforces this link to employer branding, and urges all organisations to develop a statement of why the total work experience at their organisation is superior to that at other organisations. The value proposition should identify the unique people policies, processes and programs that demonstrate the organisation's commitment to i.e., employee growth, management development, ongoing employee recognition, community service, etc. Contained within the value proposition are the central reasons that people will choose to commit themselves to an organisation. The EVP should be actively communicated in all recruitment efforts, and in letters offering employment, the EVP should take the focus off of compensation as the primary "offer."

Personal job satisfaction is driven by far more than financial factors such as salary and benefits. An organisation's EVP has thus been described as "critical to attracting, retaining and engaging quality people".[5] Other key factors influencing how an individual may choose to balance his or her career path in an organisation are relocation services, salary, perquisites, career development, location, and so on.

Benefits to an organisation of a well formed EVP include attraction and retention of key talent, helps prioritise the HR agenda, creates a strong people brand, helps re-engage a disenchanted workforce and reduces hire premiums.[6]

Notes and references

[1] "The Employee Value Proposition: 6 Things You Need to Know" (http://www.recruitersnetwork.com/articles/article.cfm?ID=1456). Recruiters Network. . Retrieved 05-06 2008.

[2] Minchington, B (2010) Employer Brand Leadership – A Global Perspective, Collective Learning Australia.

[3] Minchington, B (2006) Your Employer Brand – attract, engage, retain, Collective Learning Australia.

[4] Barrow, S. and Mosley R. (2005), The Employer Brand: Bringing the best of brand management to people at work, John Wiley & Sons

[5] "Developing an Employee Value Proposition" (http://www.canberra.edu.au/pmp/program/courses/developing-an-employee-value-proposition). University of Canberra. . Retrieved 15-01 2009.

[6] "Employee Value Proposition Infosheet" (http://www.talentsmoothie.com/wp-content/uploads/2010/02/Employee-Value-Proposition-infosheet.pdf). talentsmoothie. . Retrieved 2010-04-26.

"The Employment Value Proposition." Article which introduces the original concept, by Tandehill Human Capital. *Workspan Magazine* 10/06
http://www.tandehill.com/pdfs/Total-Rewards.pdf

Employer of last resort

Employers of last resort are employers in an economy which workers go to for jobs when no other jobs are available; the term is by analogy with "lender of last resort". The phrase is used in two sense:

- undesirable jobs, often private sector, which are only taken as a last resort;
- a formal government job guarantee program, where the government promises to act as employer of last resort, employing all comers.

The sense of a job guarantee program is used and advocated by some schools of Post-Keynesian economists, notably Neo-Chartalists in the Kansas City School of Economics and the Australian Centre of Full Employment and Equity, who advocate it as a solution for unemployment.

Use

Colloquially, this may refer to work which is undesirable to most people or pays poorly - for instance, in the United States economy, many fast-food industry jobs represent last-resort employment for many workers.

In economics, the phrase often refers to employers which can hire workers when no other employers are hiring. Their presence may soften the negative impact on employment of downturns in the business cycle. One example of such a program would be the Civilian Conservation Corps, a government agency intended to provide work to young, unemployed men. Military Keynesianism argues that the military can act as an employer of last resort.

External links

- An Introduction to the Employer of Last Resort Proposal [1] from Dollars & Sense magazine
- Center for Full Employment and Price Stability [2]

References

[1] http://www.dollarsandsense.org/archives/2008/0308dodd.html
[2] http://www.cfeps.org

Employment agency

An **employment agency** is an organization which matches employers to employees. In all developed countries there is a publicly funded employment agency and multiple private businesses which also act as employment agencies.

Public employment agencies

Since the beginning of the twentieth century, every developed country has created a public employment agency as a way to combat unemployment and help people find work.

In the United Kingdom the first agency began in London, through the Labour Bureau (London) Act 1902, and subsequently nationwide by the Liberal government through the Labour Exchanges Act 1909. The present public provider of job search help is called Jobcentre plus.

In the United States, a federal programme of employment services was rolled out in the New Deal. The initial legislation was called the Wagner-Peyser Act of 1933 and more recently job services happen through one-stop centres established by the Workforce Investment Act of 1998.

Private employment agencies

The first private employment agency in the United States was opened by Fred Winslow who opened Engineering Agency in 1893. It later became part of General Employment Enterprises who also owned Businessmen's Clearing House (est. 1902). Another of the oldest agencies was developed by Katharine Felton as a response to the problems brought on by the 1906 San Francisco earthquake and fire.

Many temporary agencies specialize in a particular profession or field of business, such as accounting, health care, technical, or secretarial.

Legal status

For most of the twentieth century, private employment agencies were considered quasi illegal entities under international law. The International Labour Organization instead called for the establishment of public employment agencies. To prevent the abusive practices of private agencies, they were either to be fully abolished, or tightly regulated. In most countries they are legal but regulated.

Probably inspired by the dissenting judgments in a US Supreme Court case called *Adams v. Tanner*, the International Labour Organization's first ever Recommendation was targeted at fee charging agencies. The Unemployment Recommendation, 1919 (No.1), Art. 1 called for each member to,

> "take measures to prohibit the establishment of employment agencies which charge fees or which carry on their business for profit. Where such agencies already exist, it is further recommended that they be permitted to operate only under government licenses, and that all practicable measures be taken to abolish such agencies as soon as possible."

The Unemployment Convention, 1919, Art. 2 instead required the alternative of,

> "a system of free public employment agencies under the control of a central authority. Committees, which shall include representatives of employers and workers, shall be appointed to advise on matters concerning the carrying on of these agencies."

In 1933 the Fee-Charging Employment Agencies Convention (No.34) formally called for abolition. The exception was if the agencies were licensed and a fee scale was agreed in advance. In 1949 a new revised Convention (No.96) was produced. This kept the same scheme, but secured an 'opt out' (Art.2) for members that did not wish to sign up. Agencies were an increasingly entrenched part of the labor market. The United States did not sign up to the Conventions. The latest Convention, the Private Employment Agencies Convention, 1997 (No.181) takes a much softer stance and calls merely for regulation.

In most countries, agencies are regulated, for instance in the UK under the Employment Agencies Act 1973, or in Germany under the *Arbeitnehmerüberlassungsgesetz* (Employee Hiring Law of 1972).

Executive recruitment

An executive-search firm is a type of employment agency that specializes in recruiting executive personnel for companies in various industries. This term may apply to job-search-consulting firms who charge job candidates a fee and who specialize in mid-to-upper-level executives. In the United States, some states require job-search-consulting firms to be licensed as employment agencies.

Some third-party recruiters work on their own, while others operate through an agency, acting as direct contacts between client companies and the job candidates they recruit. They can specialize in client relationships only (sales or business development), in finding candidates (recruiting or sourcing), or in both areas. Most recruiters tend to specialize in either permanent, full-time, direct-hire positions, or in contract positions, but occasionally in both. In an executive-search assignment, the employee-gaining client company − not the person being hired − pays the search firm its fee.

Executive Agent

An executive agent is a type of agency that represents executives seeking senior executive positions which are often unadvertised. In the United Kingdom, almost all positions up to £125,000 ($199,000) a year are advertised and 50% of vacancies paying £125,000 - £150,000 are advertised. However 5% of positions which pay more than £150,000 (with the exception of the public sector) are advertised and are often in the domain of around 4,000 executive recruiters in the United Kingdom.[1] . Often such roles are unadvertised to maintain stakeholder confidence and to overcome internal uncertainties. The executive agent would identify the various head-hunters or recruiters who have been given the brief in seeking a candidate. A senior executive would typically pay the agent a fee in a similar fashion to an actor paying a talent agent. Whilst the Employment Agencies Act 1973 prohibited employment agencies charging, in November 2008, there was a European amendment to (c. 35), in section 9 (inspection), subsection (4), of the act[4][2] .

Notes

[1] IR Magazine. "How do I tap into unadvertised job vacancies for senior positions?" (http://www.insideinvestorrelations.com/articles/ 16257/advice-how-do-i-tap-unadvertised-job-vacancies-senior-positions/), *IR Magazine*, August 6, 2010, accessed April 12, 2010

[2] UK Parliament. "Employment Bill" (http://www.publications.parliament.uk/pa/ld200708/ldhansrd/text/81113-0004.htm) *UK Parliament Daily Hansard*, November 2008, accessed April 12, 2011.

References

- DE Balducchi, RW Eberts, CJ O'Leary (eds), *Labour Exchange Policy in the United States* (http://research. upjohn.org/up_press/143/) (W.E. Upjohn Institute for Employment Research 2004)
- P Craig, M Freedland, C Jacqueson and N Kountouris, *Public Employment Services and European Law* (2007)
- International Labour Office, *The role of private employment agencies in the functioning of labour markets* (Report VI 1994) International Labour Conference 81st Session
- R Kellogg, *The United States Employment Service* (University of Chicago Press 1933)
- T Martinez, *The Human Marketplace: An Examination of Private Employment Agencies* (Transaction 1976)
- JB Seymour, *The British Employment Exchange* (PS King & Son 1928)

Employment contract

A **contract of employment** is a category of contract used in labour law to attribute right and responsibilities between parties to a bargain. On the one end stands an "employee" who is "employed" by an "employer". It has arisen out of the old master-servant law, used before the 20th century. Put generally, the contract of employment denotes a relationship of economic dependence and social subordination. In the words of the influential labour lawyer Sir Otto Kahn-Freund,

> "the relation between an employer and an isolated employee or worker is typically a relation between a bearer of power and one who is not a bearer of power. In its inception it is an act of submission, in its operation it is a condition of subordination, however much the submission and the subordination may be concealed by the indispensable figment of the legal mind known as the 'contract of employment'. The main object of labour law has been, and... will always be a countervailing force to counteract the inequality of bargaining power which is inherent and must be inherent in the employment relationship."[1]

Terminology

A contract of employment not usually defined to mean the same as a "contract of service".[2] A contract of service has historically been distinguished from a "contract for services", the expression altered to imply the dividing line between a person who is "employed" and someone who is "self employed". The purpose of the dividing line is to attribute rights to some kinds of people who work from others. This could be the right to a minimum wage, holiday pay, sick leave, fair dismissal, a written statement of the contract, the right to organize in a union, and so on. The assumption is that genuinely self employed people should be able to look after their own affairs, and therefore work they do for others should not carry with it an obligation to look after these rights.

In Roman law the equivalent dichotomy was that between *locatio conductio operarum* and *locatio conductio operis* (lit. a hiring contract of services and by services).[3] [4]

The terminology is complicated by the use of many other sorts of contracts involving one person doing work for another. Instead of being considered an "employee", the individual could be considered a "worker" (which could mean less employment legislation protection) or as having an "employment relationship" (which could mean protection somewhere in between) or a "professional" or a "dependent entrepreneur", and so on. Different countries will take more or less sophisticated, or complicated approaches to the question.

Notes

[1] *Labour and the Law*, Hamlyn Lectures, 1972, 7
[2] in the UK, s.230 Employment Rights Act 1996
[3] see, Sir John MacDonell, *Classification of Forms and Contracts of Labour* (1904) Journal of the Society of Comparative Legislation, New Series, Vol. 5, No. 2, pp. 253-261, at 255-256
[4] "*locatio conductio operarum* is a contract whereby one party agrees to supply the other with a certain quantum of labour. *locatio conductio operis* is a contract whereby one party agrees, in consideration of money payment, to supply the other not with labour, but with the *result* of labour." Sohm, *Institutes of Roman Law*, 311 (1892)

References

• Mark Freedland, *The Personal Employment Contract* (2003) Oxford University Press, ISBN 0199249261

Employment counsellor

An **employment counsellor**, also known as a **career development professional**, advises, coaches, provides information to, and supports people who are planning, seeking and managing their life/work direction.

Duties

Career development professionals help clients of all ages:

- select education and training programs
- balance work and other life roles
- navigate career transitions and stages
- enhance career satisfaction
- find employment or self-employment opportunities, write résumés, develop portfolios and prepare for interviews.

Working with clients individually or in groups, career development professionals may:

- help people develop a better appreciation of their unique characteristics and how those characteristics relate to career choices
- use various assessment tools to help clients identify their interests, values, beliefs, lifestyle preferences, aptitudes and abilities, and relate them to the world of work
- help clients identify educational requirements and develop training plans
- facilitate career management and career decision-making workshops
- work with clients who have disabilities, language and cultural differences, or other special needs that affect their employment prospects
- help clients deal with barriers to achieving their career plans
- help employed clients plan career laddering within organizations, cope successfully with job dissatisfaction, or make occupational or job changes
- provide current labour market information to help clients make realistic occupational or employment decisions
- market clients to potential employers and help clients find job or work experience placements
- assist clients with implementing effective employment search strategies, writing résumés, and developing career portfolios and interview skills
- plan and implement career and employment-related programs
- refer clients to appropriate services to address their particular needs
- work co-operatively with community groups and agencies, businesses and other organizations involved in providing career planning resources
- use computers to write reports and proposals, and research information on the Internet
- perform related administrative tasks such as keeping records.

Working conditions

Career development professionals may work in a variety of settings but usually work in offices where they can conduct private interviews with clients and in classrooms or boardrooms where they conduct group sessions. Depending on the organization, their hours of work may include some evening and weekend work.

Personal characteristics

Career development professionals need the following characteristics:

- a genuine interest in and respect for people from all walks of life
- patience, understanding and the ability to listen non-judgementally
- excellent oral and written communication skills and presentation skills
- objectivity and tact
- the ability to motivate and inspire clients
- the ability to facilitate communication in groups of eight to 20 people
- good organizational and planning skills
- the ability to work effectively with other professionals and community agencies.

They should enjoy consulting with people, compiling information and working with clients to develop innovative solutions to problems.

Educational requirements

Most career development professionals have post-secondary education in a related discipline such as psychology, education, social work or human resources development. Increasingly, employers are looking for applicants who have a certificate, diploma or degree in career development, or an equivalent combination of education and experience.

External links

- National Employment Counseling Association [1] (U.S.A.)
- National Career Development Association [2] (U.S.A.)

References

[1] http://www.employmentcounseling.org
[2] http://www.ncda.org

Europass

Europass is an EU initiative to increase transparency of qualification and mobility of citizens in Europe. It aims to be a Life Long Learning Portfolio of documents containing the descriptions of all learning achievements, official qualifications, work results, skills and competencies, acquired over time, along with the related documentation. The five Europass documents are the CV, Language Passport, Europass Mobility, Certificate supplement and Diploma supplement, sharing a common brand name and logo and aim to make a person's skills and qualifications clearly understood throughout Europe.

Europass web portal

It is a central resource of information related to the Europass documents. Its purpose is also to help all users create, with a simple wizard, a Curriculum vitae or a Language passport in the Europass format. It is available in 26 languages.

Europass is an initiative of the European Commission Directorate General Education and Culture [1].

Cedefop (European centre for the development of vocational training) is responsible for the development and maintenance of the Europass web portal.

In every country (European Union, European Economic Area and candidate countries), a National Europass Centre promotes and provides information on the Europass documents.

Europass Technical Resources

Europass XML Schema

Europass has produced an XML vocabulary to describe the information contained in the CV and Language Passport. A description of this vocabulary is available from the Europass website [2].

People who create a Europass CV or Language passport can save the document in Europass XML format or PDF format with the XML attached. Both formats can be imported to the Europass online editors or any other system that understands the Europass XML, ensuring that all information is properly parsed.

The XML vocabulary is clear and self-explaining, while remaining sound and extensible, and also as close as possible to other related vocabularies, as those defined by HR-XML.

Web services

Europass Web services provide a standard way (web API) for other systems, software and services to utilize Europass services in an automated way. An example is the web service which enables the remote generation of Europass documents in PDF, OpenOffice, Microsoft Word, starting from a Europass XML file.

More information on how to use the Europass web services, as well as a Java-based client application for testing can be found on the Europass website [3]:

Labels and Help texts

Text labels used for the Europass CV and ELP are available in various formats from the Europass website [4]:

- The OASIS XLIFF (XML Localisation Interchange File Format)
- The W3C Xforms
- The PO file format is used in the GNU Gettext toolset

Eures

The European Commission is hosting a jobboard service for European Citizens - the European Job Mobility Portal (EURES) which supports the Europass CV.

Europass CV plug-in for blogs

The Directorate General Education and Culture [1] has co-financed the European project KITE [5] under the Leonardo Da Vinci programme [6]. KITE offers an implementation of the Europass-CV as a plug-in of the open source software weblogs WordPress and DotClear. The plugins allow users of those blogging services to store create a Europass CV in all European official languages and export it into the following formats: PDF, ODT, HTML, XHTML, HR-XML. The plugin is compliant with HR-XML SEP specifications.

External links

- Official sites:
  - Europass [7]
  - Cedefop [8]
  - Eures (European Employment Services) [9], esp. Instructions for Europass CV [10]
  - UK National Europass Centre [11]
- Europass CV creators:
  - Europass CV [12] (Official site)
  - EuroCv [13] (European project)
  - KITE: open source Europass CV plugin for Wordpress and Dotclear [5] (European project)
  - SmartCV [14] free tool to write your own cv in europass format
- Others :
  - Europass at about.com [15]
  - National Europass Centres [16]
  - LaTeX Europass template [17]
  - Europass Admin: Europass profile admin tools [18]

References

[1] http://ec.europa.eu/education/index_en.html/

[2] http://europass.cedefop.europa.eu/europass/home/hornav/Downloads/TechnicalResources/XML.csp

[3] http://europass.cedefop.europa.eu/europass/home/hornav/Downloads/TechnicalResources/Web_Services.csp

[4] http://europass.cedefop.europa.eu/europass/home/hornav/Downloads/TechnicalResources/EuropassLabels.csp

[5] http://www.kite-eu.org/en/

[6] http://ec.europa.eu/education/programmes/llp/leonardo/index_en.html/

[7] http://europass.cedefop.europa.eu/

[8] http://cedefop.europa.eu/

[9] http://ec.europa.eu/eures/

[10] http://www.eea.europa.eu/organisation/jbs/instructions_for_europass_cv.pdf

[11] http://www.uknec.org.uk

[12] https://europass.cedefop.europa.eu/instruments/cv/step0.do

[13] http://www.eurocv.eu/

[14] http://www.smartcv.org

[15] http://jobsearch.about.com/od/cvadvice/a/europasscv.htm

[16] http://europass.cedefop.europa.eu/europass/home/vernav/Information+and++Support/National+Europass+Centres/navigate.action

[17] http://tug.ctan.org/tex-archive/macros/latex/contrib/europecv/

[18] http://europadm.sourceforge.net

Executive pay

Executive pay is financial compensation received by an officer of a firm, often as a mixture of salary, bonuses, shares of and/or call options on the company stock, etc. Over the past three decades, executive pay has risen dramatically beyond the rising levels of an average worker's wage.[1] Executive pay is an important part of corporate governance, and is often determined by a company's board of directors.

Types of compensation

There are six basic tools of compensation or remuneration.

- salary
- bonuses, which provide short-term incentives
- long-term incentive plans (LTIP)
- employee benefits
- paid expenses (perquisites)
- insurance (Golden parachute)

In a modern US corporation, the CEO and other top executives are paid salary plus short-term incentives or bonuses. This combination is referred to as Total Cash Compensation (TCC). Short-term incentives usually are formula-driven and have some performance criteria attached depending on the role of the executive. For example, the Sales Director's performance related bonus may be based on incremental revenue growth turnover; a CEO's could be based on incremental profitability and revenue growth. Bonuses are after-the-fact (not formula driven) and often discretionary. Executives may also be compensated with a mixture of cash and shares of the company which are almost always subject to vesting restrictions (a long-term incentive). To be considered a long-term incentive the measurement period must be in excess of one year (3–5 years is common). The vesting term refers to the period of time before the recipient has the right to transfer shares and realize value. Vesting can be based on time, performance or both. For example a CEO might get 1 million in cash, and 1 million in company shares (and share buy options used). Vesting can occur in two ways: Cliff vesting and Graded Vesting. In case of Cliff Vesting, everything that is due to vest vests at one go i.e. 100% vesting occurs either now or a later point in time at year X. In case of graded vesting, partial vesting occurs at different times in the future. This is further sub-classified into two types: Uniform graded vesting (eg. Same percentage i.e. 20% of the options vest each year for 5 years) and Non-uniform graded vesting (eg. different proportion i.e. 20%, 30% and 50% of the options vest each year for the next three years). Other components of an executive compensation package may include such perks as generous retirement plans, health insurance, a chauffered limousine, an executive jet[2], interest free loans for the purchase of housing, etc.

Stock options

Supporters of stock options say they align the interests of CEOs to those of shareholders, since options are valuable only if the stock price remains above the option's strike price. Stock options are now counted as a corporate expense (non-cash), which impacts a company's income statement and makes the distribution of options more transparent to shareholders. Critics of stock options charge that they are granted excessively and that they invite management abuses such as the options backdating of such grants. Stock options also pose a conflict of interest in which a CEO can artificially raise the stock price to cash in stock options at the expense of the company's long-term health, although this is a problem for any type of incentive compensation that goes unmonitored by directors. Indeed, "reload" stock options allow executives to exercise options and then replace them in part (and sometimes in whole), essentially selling the company stock short (i.e., profiting from the stock's decline). For various reasons, including the accounting charge, concerns about dilution and negative publicity related to stock options, companies have reduced the size of grants to executives.

Stock options also incentivize executives to engage in risk-seeking behavior. This is because the value of a call option increases with increased volatility. (cf. options pricing). Stock options therefore - even when used legitimately - can incentivize excessive risk seeking behavior that can lead to catastrophic corporate failure.

In the Financial crisis of 2007-2009 in the United States, pressure mounted to use more stock options than cash in executive pay. However, since many then-proportionally larger 2008 bonuses were awarded in February, 2009, near the March, 2009, bottom of the stock market, many of the bonuses in the banking industry turned out to have doubled or more in paper value by late in 2009. The bonuses were under particular scrutiny, including by the United States Treasury's new special master of pay, Kenneth R. Feinberg, because many of the firms had been rescued by government Troubled Asset Relief Program (TARP) and other funds.[3]

Restricted stock

Executives are also compensated with restricted stock, which is stock given to an executive that cannot be sold until certain conditions are met and has the same value as the market price of the stock at the time of grant. As the size of stock option grants have been reduced, the number of companies granting restricted stock either with stock options or instead of, has increased. Restricted stock has its detractors, too, as it has value even when the stock price falls. As an alternative to straight time vested restricted stock, companies have been adding performance type features to their grants. These grants, which could be called performance shares, do not vest or are not granted until these conditions are met. These performance conditions could be earnings per share or internal financial targets.

Tax issues

Cash compensation is taxable to an individual at a high individual rate. If part of that income can be converted to long-term capital gain, for example by granting stock options instead of cash to an executive, a more advantageous tax treatment may be obtained by the executive.

Levels of compensation

The levels of compensation in all countries has been rising dramatically over the past decades. Not only is it rising in absolute terms, but also in relative terms.

Fortune 500 compensation

During 2003, about half of Fortune 500 CEO compensation was in cash pay and bonuses, and the other half in vested restricted stock, and gains from exercised stock options according to Forbes magazine.[4] Forbes magazine counted the 500 CEOs compensation to $3.3 billion during 2003 (which makes $6.6 million a piece), a figure that includes gains from stock call options used (the options may have been rewarded many years before the option to buy is used).

Forbes categories of compensation

The categories that Forbes use are (1) salary (cash), (2) bonus (cash), (3) other (market value of restricted stock received), and (4) stock gains from option exercise (the gains being the difference between the price paid for the stock when the option was exercised and that days market price of the stock). If you see someone "making" $100 million or $200 million during the year, chances are 90% of that is coming from options (earned during many years) being exercised.

Typical compensation

The typical salary in the top of the list is $1 million - $3 million.[5] The typical top cash bonus is $10 million - $15 million.[6] The highest stock bonus is $20 million.[7] The highest option exercise have been in the range of $100 million - $200 million.[8]

Compensation protection

Senior executives may enjoy considerable income protection unavailable to many other employees. Often executives may receive a Golden Parachute that rewards them substantially if the company gets taken over or they lose their jobs for other reasons. This can create perverse incentives.

One example is that overly attractive Golden Parachutes may incentivize executives to facilitate the sale of their company at a price that is not in their shareholders' best interests.

It is fairly easy for a top executive to reduce the price of his/her company's stock - due to information asymmetry. The executive can accelerate accounting of expected expenses, delay accounting of expected revenue, engage in off balance sheet transactions to make the company's profitability appear temporarily poorer, or simply promote and report severely conservative (eg. pessimistic) estimates of future earnings. Such seemingly adverse earnings news will be likely to (at least temporarily) reduce share price. (This is again due to information asymmetries since it is more common for top executives to do everything they can to window dress their company's earnings forecasts).

A reduced share price makes a company an easier takeover target. When the company gets bought out (or taken private) - at a dramatically lower price - the takeover artist gains a windfall from the former top executive's actions to surreptitiously reduce share price. This can represent 10s of billions of dollars (questionably) transferred from previous shareholders to the takeover artist. The former top executive is then rewarded with a golden handshake for presiding over the firesale that can sometimes be in the hundreds of millions of dollars for one or two years of work. (This is nevertheless an excellent bargain for the takeover artist, who will tend to benefit from developing a reputation of being very generous to parting top executives).

Similar issues occur when a publicly held asset or non-profit organization undergoes privatization. Top executives often reap tremendous monetary benefits when a government owned, mutual or non-profit entity is sold to private hands. Just as in the example above, they can facilitate this process by making the entity appear to be in financial crisis - this reduces the sale price (to the profit of the purchaser), and makes non-profits and governments more likely to sell. Ironically, it can also contribute to a public perception that private entities are more efficiently run reinforcing the political will to sell of public assets.

Again, due to asymmetric information, policy makers and the general public see a government owned firm that was a financial 'disaster' - miraculously turned around by the private sector (and typically resold) within a few years.

Regulation

There are a number of strategies that could be employed as a response to the growth of executive compensation.

- In the United States, shareholders must approve all equity compensation plans. Shareholders can simply vote against the issuance of any equity plans. This would eliminate huge windfalls that can be due to a rising stock market or years of retained earnings.

- Independent non-executive director setting of compensation is widely practised. Remuneration is the archetype of self dealing. An independent remuneration committee is an attempt to have pay packages set at arms' length from the directors who are getting paid.

- Disclosure of salaries is the first step, so that company stakeholders can know and decide whether or not they think remuneration is fair. In the UK, the Directors' Remuneration Report Regulations 2002[9] introduced a requirement into the old Companies Act 1985, the requirement to release all details of pay in the annual accounts. This is now codified in the Companies Act 2006. Similar requirements exist in most countries, including the U.S., Germany, and Canada.

- A say on pay - a non-binding vote of the general meeting to approve director pay packages, is practised in a growing number of countries. Some commentators have advocated a mandatory binding vote for large amounts (e.g. over $5 million).[10] The aim is that the vote will be a highly influential signal to a board to not raise salaries beyond reasonable levels. The general meeting means shareholders in most countries. In most European countries though, with two-tier board structures, a supervisory board will represent employees and shareholders alike. It is this supervisory board which votes on executive compensation.

- Progressive taxation is a more general strategy that affects executive compensation, as well as other highly paid people. There has been a recent trend to cutting the highest bracket tax payers, a notable example being the tax cuts in the U.S. For example, the Baltic States have a flat tax system for incomes. Executive compensation could be checked by taxing more heavily the highest earners, for instance by taking a greater percentage of income over $200,000.

- Maximum wage is an idea which has been enacted in early 2009 in the United States, where they capped executive pay at $500,000 per year for companies receiving extraordinary financial assistance from the U.S. taxpayers. The argument is to place a cap on the amount that any person may legally make, in the same way as there is a floor of a minimum wage so that people can not earn too little.[11]

- Debt Like Compensation - It has been widely accepted that the risk taking motivation of executives depends on its position in equity based compensation and risky debt. Adding debt like instrument as part of an executive compensation may reduce the risk taking motivation of executives. [12]. Therefore, as of 2011, there are several proposals to enforce financial institutions to use debt like compensation.[13].

- Indexing Operating Performance is a way to make bonus targets business cycle independent. Indexed bonus targets move with the business cycle and are therefore fairer and valid for a longer period of time.

Criticism

Many newspaper stories[14] show people expressing concern that CEOs are paid too much for the services they provide. In *Searching for a Corporate Savior: The Irrational Quest for Charismatic CEOs*, Harvard Business School professor Rakesh Khurana documents the problem of excessive CEO compensation, showing that the return on investment from these pay packages is very poor compared to other outlays of corporate resources.

Defenders of high executive pay say that the global war for talent and the rise of private equity firms can explain much of the increase in executive pay. For example, while in conservative Japan a senior executive has few alternatives to his current employer, in the United States it is acceptable and even admirable for a senior executive to jump to a competitor, to a private equity firm, or to a private equity portfolio company. Portfolio company executives take a pay cut but are routinely granted stock options for ownership of ten percent of the portfolio company, contingent on a successful tenure. Rather than signaling a conspiracy, defenders argue, the increase in executive pay is a mere byproduct of supply and demand for executive talent. However, U.S. executives make substantially more than their European and Asian counterparts.[14]

Shareholders, often members of the Council of Institutional Investors or the Interfaith Center on Corporate Responsibility have often filed shareholder resolutions in protest. 21 such resolutions were filed in 2003.[15] About a dozen were voted on in 2007, with two coming very close to passing (at Verizon, a recount is currently in progress).[16] The U.S. Congress is currently debating mandating shareholder approval of executive pay packages at publicly traded U.S. companies.[17]

The U.S. stood first in the world in 2005 with a ratio of 39:1 CEO's compensation to pay of manufacturing production workers. Britain second with 31.8:1; Italy third with 25.9:1, New Zealand fourth with 24.9:1.[18]

United States

The U.S. Securities and Exchange Commission (SEC) has asked publicly traded companies to disclose more information explaining how their executives' compensation amounts are determined. The SEC has also posted compensation amounts on its website[19] to make it easier for investors to compare compensation amounts paid by different companies. It is interesting to juxtapose SEC regulations related to executive compensation with Congressional efforts to address such compensation.[20]

In 2005, the issue of executive compensation at American companies has been harshly criticized by columnist and Pulitzer Prize winner Gretchen Morgenson in her *Market Watch* column for the Sunday "Money & Business" section of the New York Times newspaper.

A February 2009 report, published by the Institute for Policy Studies notes the impact excessive executive compensation has on taxpayers:

> U.S. taxpayers subsidize excessive executive compensation — by more than $20 billion per year — via a variety of tax and accounting loopholes. For example, there are no meaningful limits on how much companies can deduct from their taxes for the expense of executive compensation. The more they pay their CEO, the more they can deduct. A proposed reform to cap tax deductibility at no more than 25 times the pay of the lowest-paid worker could generate more than $5 billion in extra federal revenues per year.[21] Although a proposal such as this one would tighten controls on pay to executives, this study does take into consideration (or at least does not address) the tax obligations of the individual (CEO) that receives this compensation. Every dollar that is deducted from the firm's income is subject to the personal tax of the individual receiving such pay.

Unions have been very vocal in their opposition to high executive compensation. The AFL-CIO sponsors a website called Executive Paywatch [22] [23] which allows users to compare their salaries to the CEOs of the companies where they work.

In 2007, CEOs in the S&P 500, averaged $10.5 million annually, 344 times the pay of typical American workers. This was a drop in ratio from 2000, when they averaged 525 times the average pay.[18]

To work around the restrictions and the political outrage concerning executive pay practices, banks in particular turned to using life insurance policies to fund bonuses, deferred pay and pensions owed to its executives.[24] [25] Under this scenario, a bank insures thousands of its employees under the life insurance policy, naming itself as the beneficiary of the policy. Bank undertake this practice often without the knowledge or consent of the employee and sometimes with the employee misunderstanding the scope of the coverage or the ability to maintain employee coverage after leaving the company. In recent times, a number of families became outraged by the practice and complained that banks should not profit from the death of the deceased employees.[24] In one case, a family of a former employee filed a lawsuit against the bank after the family questioned the practices of the bank in its coverage of the employee. The insurance company accidentally sent the widow of the deceased employee a check for a $1.6 million that was payable to the bank after the former employee died in 2008. In that case, bank allegedly told the employee in 2001 that the employee was eligible for a $150,000 supplemental life insurance benefit if the employee signed a consent form to allow the bank to add the employee to the bank's life insurance policy. The bank fired the employee four months after the employee consented to the arrangement.[24] After that employee's death, the family collect no benefits from the employee life insurance policies provided by the bank, since the bank had canceled the employee's benefit after the firing. The family claimed that the former employee was "cognitively disabled" because of brain surgery and medical treatments at the time of signing the consent form to understand fully the scope of insurance coverage under the bank's master insurance benefit plan.[24]

The practice of financing executive compensation using corporate-owned life insurance policies remain controversial. On the one hand, observers in the insurance industry note that "businesses enjoy tax-deferred growth of the inside buildup of the [life insurance] policy's cash value, tax-free withdrawals and loans, and income tax-free death benefits to [corporate] beneficiaries."[26] On the other hand, critics frowned upon the use of "janitor's insurance" to collect tax-free death benefits from insurance policies covering retirees and current and former non-key employees that companies rely on as informal pension funds for company executives.[27] To thwart the abuse and reduce the attractiveness of corporate-owned life insurance policies, changes in tax treatment of corporate-owned insurance life insurance policies are under consideration for non-key personnel. These changes would repeal "the exception from the pro rata interest expense disallowance rule for [life insurance] contracts covering employees, officers or directors, other than 20% owners of a business that is the owner or beneficiary of the contracts."[27]

A study by University of Florida researchers found that highly paid CEOs improve company profitability as opposed to executives making less for similar jobs.[28]

On the other hand, a study by Professors Lynne M. Andersson and Thomas S. Batemann published in the *Journal of Organizational Behavior* found that highly paid executives are more likely to behave cynically and therefore show tendencies of unethical performance.[29]

Australia

In Australia, shareholders can vote against the pay rises of board members, but the vote is non-binding.[30] Instead the shareholders can sack some or all of the board members.[31]

Trends in executive compensation

There are some examples of exceptionally high chief executive officer pay in the early twentieth century. When the United States government took control of the railroad industry during the 1910s, they discovered enormous salaries for the railroad bosses.[32] After the Securities and Exchanges Commission was set up in the 1930s, it was concerned enough about excessive executive compensation that it began requiring yearly reporting of company earnings to help reign in abuse.[33] These examples show that exceptionally high CEO pay is not a new phenomenon, just perhaps not as common as today.

Anecdotal evidence for the General Electric corporation suggest that after examples of excess early last century and the Great Depression, following World War II executive pay remained fairly constant at GE for almost three decades.[34] This may have been in part due to high income taxes on the wealthy. To get around this, companies like General Electric began to offer stock options in the late 1950s.[35] The United States government eventually pared down the income taxes on the wealthy – from 91% in the 1950s, to 28% in the 1980s.[36] Thus the level of pay for GE's top three managers increased at a slow rate of about two percent per year from the 1940s to the 1960s but this period of little growth was followed by a rapid acceleration in top management pay. Mostly encouraged by the increasing use of stock options since the 1980s and of restricted stock since the 1990s. From the 1970s to the present, the compensation of the three highest-paid officers at GE has grew at the significantly higher annual rate of eight percent yearly.

The years 1993 -2003 saw executive pay increase sharply with the aggregate compensation to the top five executives of each of the S&P 1500 firms compensation doubling as a percentage of the aggregate earnings of those firms - from 5 per cent in 1993–5 to about 10 per cent in 2001–3.[37]

The Financial Crisis has had a relatively small net effect on executive pay. According to the independent research firm Equilar, median S&P 500 CEO compensation fell significantly for the first time since 2002. From 2007 to 2008, median total compensation declined by 7.5 percent.[38] A sharp decline in bonus payouts contributed most to declines in total pay, with median annual bonus payouts for S&P 500 CEOs dropping to $1.2 million in 2008, down 24.5 percent from the 2007 median of $1.6 million. Additionally, 20.6 percent of CEOs received no bonus payout at all for 2008.[38]

On the other hand, equity compensation changed little from 2007 to 2008, despite the market turmoil. The median value of option awards and stock awards rose by 3.5 percent and 1.4 percent, respectively. Options maintained its place as the most prevalent equity award vehicle, with 72.2 percent of CEOs receiving option awards. In 2008, nearly two-thirds of total CEO compensation was delivered in the form of stock or options.[38]

Notes

[1] see, for one example, *The Guardian*, August 4, 2005, "US executive pay goes off the scale" (http://www.guardian.co.uk/business/story/0,3604,1542100,00.html)

[2] http://www.phoenixair.com/fleet_photos_executive_charter.php

[3] "Windfall Is Seen as Bank Bonuses Are Paid in Stock" (http://www.nytimes.com/2009/11/08/business/08pay.html?hp) by Louise Story, *The New York Times*, November 7, 2009 (Nov. 8, 2009 on p. A1 NY ed.). Retrieved 2009-11-07.

[4] "CEO Compensation" (http://www.forbes.com/lists/2004/04/21/04ceoland.html). *Forbes*. .

[5] see, Immelt (http://www.forbes.com/static/execpay2004/LIR67G5.html?passListId=12&passYear=2004&passListType=Person&uniqueId=67G5&datatype=Person)

[6] see,(Henry R. Silverman (http://www.forbes.com/static/execpay2004/LIR7VML.html?passListId=12&passYear=2004&passListType=Person&uniqueId=7VML&datatype=Person)

[7] see,(Fuld (http://www.forbes.com/static/execpay2004/LIRA9P0.html?passListId=12&passYear=2004&passListType=Person&uniqueId=A9P0&datatype=Person))

[8] see,(Reuben Mark (http://www.forbes.com/static/execpay2004/LIR27R3.html?passListId=12&passYear=2004&passListType=Person&uniqueId=27R3&datatype=Person))

[9] SI 2002/1986 (http://www.opsi.gov.uk/si/si2002/20021986.htm)

[10] Failing Banks' Executive Pay May Face New Rules (http://www.npr.org/templates/story/story.php?storyId=100174138)

[11] Dietl, H., Duschl, T. and Lang, M. (2010): " Executive Salary Caps: What Politicians, Regulators and Managers Can Learn from Major Sports Leagues (http://www.isu.uzh.ch/static/ISU_WPS/129_ISU_full.pdf)", *University of Zurich, ISU Working Paper Series No. 129*.

[12] Raviv, A., and Sisli Ciamarra, E. (2010): " Executive Compensation and Risk Taking: The Impact of Systemic Economic Crisis (http://papers.ssrn.com/sol3/papers.cfm?abstract_id=1719426)".

[13] Bolton, P., Mehran, H. and Shapiro, J. (2010): " Executive Compensation and Risk Taking (http://ideas.repec.org/p/fip/fednsr/456.html)".

[14] "Letter From Washington: As U.S. rich-poor gap grows, so does public outcry" (http://www.iht.com/articles/2007/02/18/news/letter.php). *Bloomberg News*. International Herald Tribune. . Retrieved 2007-02-18.

[15] USA Today May 19, 2003 (http://www.usatoday.com/money/companies/management/2003-05-19-godflys_x.htm)

[16] New York Times, May 4 2007, Verizon Vote On Pay Levels To Be Decided In a Recount (http://www.nytimes.com/2007/05/04/business/04pay.html)

[17] Shareholders one step closer to say on pay, Socialfunds.com May 3 2007 (http://www.socialfunds.com/news/article.cgi/2284.html)

[18] Landy, Heather, Behind the Big Paydays, *The Washington Post*', November 15, 2008

[19] The Securities and Exchange Commission website (http://www.sec.gov)

[20] Kenneth Rosen, Who Killed Katie Couric? And Other Tales from the World of Executive Compensation Reform, 76 Fordham Law Review 2907 (2007) (http://papers.ssrn.com/sol3/papers.cfm?abstract_id=1125295)

[21] Sarah Anderson and Sam Pizzigati. "The CEO Pay Debate: Myths v Facts (http://www.ips-dc.org/getfile.php?id=330)," The Institute for Policy Studies (http://www.ips-dc.org/), 12 February 2009

[22] http://www.aflcio.org/corporatewatch/paywatch/

[23] Forbes.com Best Of The Web (http://www.forbes.com/bow/b2c/review.jhtml?id=7066)

[24] Schultz, Ellen E. (2009-05-20). "Banks Use Life Insurance to Fund Bonuses" (http://online.wsj.com/article/SB124277653430137033. html). The Wall Street Journal. . Retrieved 2009-05-21.

[25] Newman, Richard (2008-02-08). "Banks make money from employees' life insurance" (http://www.northjersey.com/business/news/ Banks_make_money_from_employees_life_insurance.html). NorthJersey.com. . Retrieved 2009-05-21.

[26] Hersch, Warren S. (2006-06-12). "The Market For COLI—Still Strong And Robust" (http://www.lifeandhealthinsurancenews.com/ Issues/2006/23/Pages/The-Market-For-COLI-Still-Strong-And-Robust.aspx). *National Underwriter*. . Retrieved 2009-05-21.

[27] Postal, Arthur D. (2009-05-18). "Industry Gears Up To Fight Tax Changes" (http://www.lifeandhealthinsurancenews.com/Issues/2009/ May 18 2009/Pages/Industry-Gears-Up-To-Fight-Tax-Changes.aspx?k=COLI). *National Underwriter*. . Retrieved 2009-05-21.

[28] Cathy Keen (2009-12-17). "Paying CEOs more than other CEOs results in stockholder dividends" (http://news.ufl.edu/2009/12/17/ ceo-pay-2/). *University of Florida News*. ufl.edu. .

[29] Batemann, Thomas. *Journal of Organizational Behavior* (http://www3.interscience.wiley.com/user/accessdenied?ID=12359& Act=2138&Code=4719&Page=/cgi-bin/fulltext/12359/PDFSTART). **18**. . Retrieved 2010.

[30] The Age article on dealing with board members (http://business.theage.com.au/business/ shareholders-told-to-oust-directors-20090227-8kee.html)

[31] The Age article on executive pay (http://business.theage.com.au/business/shareholders-told-to-oust-directors-20090227-8kee.html)

[32] Frydman, Carola. "Learning from the Past: Trends in Executive Compensation over the Twentieth Century" (http://www.ifo.de/pls/ guestci/download/CESifo Working Papers 2008/CESifo Working Papers November 2008 /cesifo1_wp2460.pdf). Center for Economic Studies. (2008): 15. Accessed 28 Sept. 2009.

[33] ibid p.16 (http://www.ifo.de/pls/guestci/download/CESifo Working Papers 2008/CESifo Working Papers November 2008 / cesifo1_wp2460.pdf)

[34] ibid p.19 (http://www.ifo.de/pls/guestci/download/CESifo Working Papers 2008/CESifo Working Papers November 2008 / cesifo1_wp2460.pdf)

[35] ibid p.17 (http://www.ifo.de/pls/guestci/download/CESifo Working Papers 2008/CESifo Working Papers November 2008 / cesifo1_wp2460.pdf)

[36] Pizziqati, Sam. "Let's Get Serious About CEO Pay" (http://www.ourfuture.org/blog-entry/2008093816/let-s-get-serious-about-ceo-pay). ourfuture.org. 2008. Accessed 28 Sept. 2009.

[37] Bebchuk & Grinstein "The Growth Of Executive Pay" (http://elsmar.com/pdf_files/Growth of Executive Pay.pdf)

[38] Equilar (2009). "2009 CEO Pay Strategies for S&P 500 Companies" (http://www.equilar.com/Executive_Compensation_Reports.php). . Retrieved 5 August 2009.

References

Books

- Lucian Bebchuk and Jesse Fried, *Pay without performance: The Unfulfilled Promise of Executive Compensation* (2006)

Journal articles

- Frydman, Carola; Saks, Raven E. (2007-01-18). "Historical Trends in Executive Compensation 1936-2005" (http://www.vanderbilt.edu/econ/sempapers/Frydman1.pdf).

- Bebchuk, Lucian; Grinstein, Yaniv (April 2005). "The Growth of Executive Pay" (http://www.law.harvard. edu/programs/olin_center/papers/pdf/Bebchuk_et al_510.pdf). Harvard University: John M. Olin Center for Law, Economics and Business.

- Yoram Landskroner and Alon Raviv, ' The 2007-2009 Financial Crisis and Executive Compensation: An Analysis and a Proposal for a Novel Structure (http://papers.ssrn.com/sol3/papers.cfm?abstract_id=1420991)'

- Paolo Cioppa, ' Executive Compensation: The Fallacy of Disclosure (http://works.bepress.com/paolocioppa/1/)'

- Kenneth Rosen, ' Who Killed Katie Couric? And Other Tales from the World of Executive Compensation Reform (http://papers.ssrn.com/sol3/papers.cfm?abstract_id=1125295)' (2007) 76 Fordham Law Review 2907
- Carola Frydman ' Learning from the Past: Trends in Executive Compensation over the Twentieth Century (http://www.ifo.de/pls/guestci/download/CESifo Working Papers 2008/CESifo Working Papers November 2008 / cesifo1_wp2460.pdf)' (2008) Center for Economic Studies

Newspaper articles

- Sean O'Grady, 'Economist Stiglitz blames crunch on 'flawed' City bonuses system' (http://www.independent.co.uk/news/business/news/economist-stiglitz-blames-crunch--on-flawed-city-bonuses-system-799869.html) (24.3.2008) *The Independent*
- Louise Story, ' Windfall Is Seen as Bank Bonuses Are Paid in Stock (http://www.nytimes.com/2009/11/08/business/08pay.html?hp)' (7.11.2009) New York Times
- ' "Chief executives' pay rises to £2.5m average (http://www.guardian.co.uk/business/story/0,3604,1542254,00.html)' (4.8.2005) The Guardian

External links

- Cost-Cutting Strategies in the Downturn: 2009 Pulse Survey (http://www.towersperrin.com/tp/getwebcachedoc?webc=USA/2009/200906/cost-cutting_strategies_pulse-svy_6-5-09.pdf)
- 2008 Executive Compensation (http://www.theglobeopinion.com/section/business/executive-compensation), *The Globe Opinion*
- Forbes.com - Executive Pay (updated with 2004 pay) (http://www.forbes.com/ceos/)

Executive search

Executive search is the consultative process of recruiting individuals to fill senior executive positions in organizations. Executive search may be performed by an organization's board of directors, or by an outside executive search organization.

Executive search profession

Executive search is an extremely lucrative industry and successful search consultants can earn large sums. For this reason there is fierce competition to work in this sector. Generally the office is broken down into three functions: Business Development, Recruiting and Research. Generally the Business Development person receives the largest commission while the Researcher receives the smallest.

The executive search profession ranges in models from "Retained" search to "Contingency" search. Retained search firms are paid a retainer equal to one-third of the fee up front to launch the search process, a third of the fee thirty days from launch and the final third sixty days from launch. If the fee is fully paid before a candidate is hired, the retained firm continues its work until the search is concluded. Contingency search firms, on the other hand, receive their entire fee at the conclusion of the search process. Over the years, many contingency firms have begun receiving retainers while retained firms have expanded their models to include flat fees, capped fees, etc.

Search consultancies are often entrenched in particular market sectors. Their market sector networks are used along with various methods to seek candidates for a particular job. Normally the individuals are not actively seeking a new job. It is the job of the search consultant to approach these individuals with a view to taking them out of their current company and placing them in another, often a competitor.

The service is paid for by the client company or organization, not by the hired job candidate. Potential job candidates are identified, qualified and presented to the client by the executive search firm based upon fit with a written or verbal Job Specification developed in conjunction with the client. Assessing degree of potential fit of the candidate with the job specification is a key activity for the search firm, since the most common reason a search consultant is engaged by a client company is to save time and effort involved with identifying, qualifying and reviewing potential candidates for specific leadership positions.

It is common for a potential candidate to be identified by the search firm via a telephone call. Often the phone call is the result of a recommendation from someone inside the existing network of the search firm. Quality oriented search firms work hard at cultivating and continually updating their network of contacts so that when a search assignment is awarded they will be ready to start recruiting potential candidates. Another way to identify potential candidates involves search firm "research", which is contacting targeted people in specific companies who appear to fit the job profile in some logical manner. Some of the best candidate referrals come from people who could be candidates for the job themselves but for any number of reasons are not interested at that particular time.[1]

Retained executive search firms

Retained executive search firms are firms paid on a retainer-structure that identify, assess, and recruit Corporate Officers, Board Members, C-level executives, Diversity Candidates, and other senior talent.[2] There are large, global firms who engage in this activity, as well as regional "boutique" firms. Some smaller firms act together as a network, thus gaining global reach and being able to compete with the large integrated ones. Some firms specialize in specific industries (for example pharmaceutical, retail, IT) or functions (i.e. sales executives), while others are generalists.

Job seekers who qualify for senior-executive level searches often mistake executive recruiters for career transition, or "outplacement" specialists. Executive recruiters work for their client companies. They do not actively place out-of-work individuals. This would not only be a conflict of interest, it would also be financially unwise. A job seeker does not pay a recruiter when he lands a job. The client company pays the recruiting firm when it fills a position. This nuance is lost on many. It may be worthwhile to contact executive search firms if you qualify, but do not expect them to take time out of their schedule to talk with you or see you. They are driven by their specific assignments for their clients: they find people for roles, not roles for people. Executive search consultants can be "career makers" for some individuals, but for most, this will not be the way they will find their next role.

When choosing a firm, it is a good idea to consider carefully what you want from the relationship. While contingency firms offer a service with no money up front, they will often only work on those searches that can be executed quickly and do not have the time to focus on high-quality candidates. Another option is to hire one firm and give them an "exclusive contingency" arrangement so that the money is still paid at the end of the search, but there is only one firm working on the search. This gives the firm the benefit of time to truly focus on quality and the hiring manager is not flooded with resumes. A third option is to pay the firm an engagement fee. Generally firms with engagement fees are exclusive as well and then have more resources available to them to purchase additional research. This also moves the search to a "retained" level which brings a level of professionalism sought by many upper level candidates. At the retained level, a client could pay a "performance retainer" which means a payment to start the search, a payment when candidates are submitted and final payment when the candidate starts. These milestones are chosen due to the fact that the firm "performed". The more traditional retainer agreements are time based and are set at specific intervals regardless of retainers.

Types of executive search firms

There are broadly two different types of Retained Executive Search firms in operation.

Global: These tend to cover numerous different sectors including financial services, life sciences, automotive, consumer, energy, pharmaceutical, telecommunications, technology, and media companies, as well as other industries. Such executive search companies will have many offices all over the world and the consultants will typically be split by which sector they are expert in. These firms are often public listed and may have over 100 offices.

Boutique: These tend to be more sector specific. That is to say that they will cover only one sector and within this sector, they may only look at certain aspects. For instance, there are a number of boutique firms that operate within financial services and these companies tend to look at senior positions (MD, Director and Vice President) within Investment Banking (M&A, Corporate Finance), Capital Markets (ECM & DCM), Sales, Trading, Research, Interest Rates, Credit, Equities, Derivatives, hedge funds and long-only asset management. As such, these firms would have one or more offices in the major financial centers across the globe; London, New York, Chicago, Dubai, Shanghai, Beijing, Mumbai, Hong Kong, Tokyo and Singapore. While the global firms may have a presence within these areas, they tend to cover board level positions within retail banking, asset & wealth management and insurance. However the larger global firms do periodically work within the capital markets arena.

List of Executive Search Firms

Below are a list of the "Big 5" Generalist Firms These five firms conduct a large share of corporate retained search assignments and are active in most industries and disciplines.[3]

- Korn/Ferry International
- Heidrick & Struggles International Incorporated
- Spencer Stuart and Associates Limited
- Russell Reynolds
- Egon Zehnder International

References

[1] The Riley Guide: Employment Opportunities and Job Resources on the Internet (http://www.rileyguide.com)

[2] http://www.thealexandergroup.com/about

[3] http://mba.yale.edu/alumni/online_resources/career_resources/big5firms.shtml

ForceSelect

ForceSelect is a recruitment consultancy, mentoring service and registered charitable foundation[1] aimed at supporting military service leavers and small military charities across the UK.[2] [3] It aims to raise funds to support smaller military charities that are struggling for funds.[2]

It was founded in 2009 by former Army captain Hugh Andrée.[3]

All recruitment staff are ex-services and partner organisations include British Gas, Sainsbury's and UPS and it was named one of the brightest new organisations of 2010 by a business survey.[4]

The Ministry of Defence has given its support to ForceSelect, recognising the work it does to support military service leavers who are looking for a new career on civvy street.[2]

Other directors include former chief of the general staff General Sir Mike Jackson,[5] bestselling author Andy McNab,[5] and former Royal Artillery officer Lucy Wood.[6]

ForceSelect founder Hugh Andrée grilled UK Chancellor George Osborne on 6 October 2010 at the Conservative Party Conference about the need to support military service leavers in the UK.[7]

Head of the Trustees is General Sir Mike Jackson,[5] while other Trustees include Dame Kelly Holmes,[8] Rebekah Brooks, Sir John Rose, and Stephen Morris.[9]

The ForceSelect Foundation gets its income from a percentage of the profits from the ForceSelect recruitment business as well as a wide range of fundraising activities, such as a collaboration with Lionsgate films for the UK premiere of *The Expendables* in August 2010.[10]

Military charities across the UK are invited to apply for grants which are awarded by the Board of trustees twice a year.[11]

References

[1] FORCESELECT FOUNDATION, Registered Charity no. 1136769 (http://www.charitycommission.gov.uk/ShowCharity/ RegisterOfCharities/searchresulthandler.aspx?chyno=1136769) at the Charity Commission

[2] "Welcome" (http://www.forceselect.com). ForceSelect.com. . Retrieved 18 October 2010.

[3] Larcombe, Duncan; Willetts, David; Hamilton, Jane; Newton Dunn, Tom (22 March 2010). "These heroes risked their lives for us... give them a job, not the dole" (http://www.thesun.co.uk/sol/homepage/news/campaigns/our_boys/2901445/ Sun-launches-Jobs-for-Heroes-campaign.html). The Sun. . Retrieved 18 October 2010.

[4] "Latest News - Forceselect Identified As One Of Uk's Brightest New Businesses In New Survey" (http://www.recruitment-international.co. uk/news/forceselect-identified-as-one-of-ukâ s--brightest-new-businesses-in-new-survey--3915.htm). Recruitment International. 14 October 2010. . Retrieved 18 October 2010.

[5] "The right skills for civvy street" (http://www.forceselect.com/aboutus/senior_management.html). defencemanagement.com. 13 July 2010. . Retrieved 18 October 2010.

[6] "Senior Management" (http://www.forceselect.com/aboutus/senior_management.html). ForceSelect.com. . Retrieved 18 October 2010.

[7] "Osborne grilled by readers: Chancellor praises readers as he listens to ideas for getting Britain back to work" (http://thesun.mobi/sol/ homepage/news/3167043/Chancellor-George-Osborne-grilled-at-Sunemployment-meeting.html?mob=1). The Sun. 6 October 2010. . Retrieved 18 October 2010.

[8] "Forceselect Foundation Appoints Dame Kelly Holmes As Trustee Ahead Of Launch" (http://www.doublegold.co.uk/latestnews/ forceselect-foundation-appoints-dame-kelly-holmes-as-trustee-ahead-of-launch). doublegold.co.uk. 9 June 2010. . Retrieved 18 October 2010.

[9] "Foundation Trustees" (http://www.forceselect.org/aboutus/foundation_trustees.php). ForceSelect Foundation. . Retrieved 18 October 2010.

[10] "Forceselect Foundation Forms Alliance With Lionsgate Films Ahead Of Stallone Premier" (http://www.greymansland.com/andy-mcnab/ forceselect-foundation-forms-alliance-with-lionsgate-films-ahead-of-stallone-premier/). greymansland.com. 11 August 2010. . Retrieved 18 October 2010.

[11] "Welcome" (http://www.forceselect.org/main/index.php). ForceSelect Foundation. . Retrieved 18 October 2010.

External links

- ForceSelect website (http://www.forceselect.com)

Free agent (business)

In business, a **free agent** refers to someone who works independently for oneself, rather than for a single employer.[1] These include self-employed workers, independent contractors and temporary workers, who altogether represent about 22 percent of the U.S. labor force. The term free agent is believed to have been coined by Daniel H. Pink, author of a 1997 cover story in Fast Company titled "Free Agent Nation."[2] In 2001 Pink published a book with the same name. The combination of several workplace trends – including shortened job cycles, the increase of project work, the acceptance of a new lifestyle and the emergence of the Internet and other technology – points to free agent workers becoming more of an employment norm in the coming years. In a 2002 survey sponsored by Kelly Services, a global staffing company, 93 percent of free agents believe demand for their skills is moderate or high.[3]

Effects on Employers

According to Pink and his peers, the free agent trend has measurably benefited numerous U.S. companies. Kinko's, now FedEx Kinko's, restructured itself in 1992 in response to the free agent trend, resulting in a $214 million investment less than four years later by Clayton, Dubilier & Rice.[4] Kelly Services devotes a section of its U.S. web site to free agents and in 2006 hired actor Efren Ramirez to star in a series of podcasts describing free agency.

References

[1] Business & Legal Reports: Study: Free-Agent Workforce Grows (http://hr.blr.com/display.cfm/id/8153)

[2] Fast Company: Free Agent Nation (http://www.fastcompany.com/online/12/freeagent.html)

[3] Ibid. (http://hr.blr.com/display.cfm/id/8153)

[4] Fast Company: Free Agent, Free Spirit (http://www.fastcompany.com/magazine/12/freespirit.html)

Global Career Development Facilitator

The **Global Career Development Facilitator (GCDF)** certification is an evolution of the Career Development Facilitator (CDF) certification developed by the National Career Development Association (NCDA), National Occupational Information Coordinating Committee (NOICC), and the Center for Credentialing in Education (CCE), an affiliate of the National Board for Certified Counselors (Center for Credentialing in Education, 1997). The credential recognizes the education and experience of those working in CDF occupations like careers advisory services, employment services, etc. GCDF have successfully completed an approved CDF training program (over 120+ hours and maintain continuing education credits or lose certification) and have meet and verified specific educational and experience requirements.

Outline

GCDF training is built around 12 core competencies identified by career counseling experts. A period of supervised career facilitation practice also is required prior to certification. The 12 competency areas addressed in GCDF training are Helping Skills, Labor Market Information and Resources, Assessment, Diverse Populations, Ethical and Legal Issues, Career Development Models, Employability Skills, Training Clients and Peers, Program Management and Implementation, Promotion and Public Relations, Technology, and Supervision (Brawley, 2002; National Career Development Association, 2007; Splete & Hoppin, 2000). In light of cultural concerns with the development of the GCDF outside the United States, the tasks within each of the competency areas are adapted to meet the needs of a particular country's context.

In the United States, GCDFs are sometimes still recognized as CDFs and work in government agencies and employment offices, in private practice as "coaches," and in colleges and universities (Splete & Hoppin, 2000). One of the more auspicious places GCDFs are found in the United States is Career One Stop Centers, which are sponsored by the U.S. Department of Labor. The GCDFs at centers like these work with people who are making career transitions. Also, in 2006, the state of South Carolina passed legislation requiring all middle and secondary schools to have a career facilitation and guidance services available to students.

The GCDF certification program for career guidance providers has been implemented in Bulgaria, Canada, China, Germany, Japan, New Zealand, Romania, and Turkey. Worldwide, about 17,600 GCDF have been certified until 2011.

References

Brawley, K. (2002). "Working ahead": The National One-Stop Workforce System and Career Development Facilitator curriculum training for instructors. In *Careers Across America 2002: Best Practices and Ideas in Career Development Conference Proceedings* (pp. 27–32). (ERIC Document Reproduction Service No. ED465911)

Center for Credentialing in Education. (2007). *Global Career Development Facilitator*. Retrieved January 18, 2007 from http://www.cce-global.org/credentials-offered/gcdfmain

National Career Development Association. (2007). *What is a career development facilitator?* Retrieved January 17, 2007 from http://www.ncda.org/

Splete, H. H., & Hoppin, J. (2000). The emergence of career development facilitators. *Career Development Quarterly, 48*, 340-347.

External links

- Center for Credentialing in Education [1]
- National Career Development Association [2]
- United States Department of Labor [2]
- DOL One Stop Career Centers [3]
- GCDF on German wikipedia [4]

References

[1] http://www.cce-global.org
[2] http://www.dol.gov
[3] http://www.careeronestop.org
[4] http://de.wikipedia.org/wiki/Global_Career_Development_Facilitator

Golden hello

A **Golden hello** is a bonus offered by hiring firms if the hired joins the company from a rival firm. It is very similar to the traditional joining bonus offered by firms but will be offered usually for rival firm employees luring them into a firm.

Typically, "Golden hellos" are offered only to high-ranking executives by major corporations and may entail a value measured in millions of dollars.

In the UK a 'golden hello' is a financial incentive to teachers training in shortage subjects for secondary education. The value varies according to the subject with Science and Maths attracting £5000 where as music is offered £2500. The incentive is paid by the TDA teacher development agency.

External links

- Golden Hello [1] Investopedia

References

[1] http://www.investopedia.com/terms/g/goldenhello.asp

Graduate recruitment

Graduate recruitment or campus recruitment refers to the process whereby employers undertake an organised program of attracting and hiring students who are about to graduate from schools, colleges and universities.

Graduate recruitment programs are widespread in most of the developed world. Employers commonly attend campuses to promote employment vacancies and careers opportunities to students who are considering their options following graduation. In the United Kingdom, the process of employers visiting a series of universities to promote themselves is called the milk round.

Selection methods used by employers include interviews, aptitude tests, role plays, written assessments, group discussions and presentations.

Many schools, colleges and universities provide their students with independent advice via a careers advisory service which is staffed by professional careers advisors. The careers advisory service often organises a careers fair or job fair where a large number of employers visit the campus at once giving students the opportunity to meet a range of potential employers.

Employers involved in graduate recruitment programs often form themselves into professional bodies or associations to share best practice or to collaborate in setting a recruitment code of practice.

Careers advisors also form themselves into professional bodies or associations to ensure that current best practice is shared across members and passes onto students.

Examples of professional associations in the graduate recruitment sector include the National Association of Colleges and Employers (NACE) in the United States, the Canadian Association of Careers Educators and Employers (CACEE) in Canada, the Association of Graduate Recruiters (AGR) and the Association of Graduate Careers Advisory Services (AGCAS) in the United Kingdom and the Australian Association of Graduate Employers (AAGE) in Australia, Graduate Daily [1] (GDAILY) in the Russia.

Many of the national professional associations are members of the International Network of Graduate Recruitment and Development Associations (INGRADA).

References

[1] http://gdaily.ru

Greater Chicago HERC

The Greater Chicago Midwest Education Recruitment Consortium is a job-placement and recruitment organization focusing on colleges and universities, research, healthcare, and arts and culture in the Greater Chicago area. It is a part of the National HERC network.

About Greater Chicago Midwest HERC

The Greater Chicago Midwest HERC was established in 2006 and currently serves 25 institutions in northern and central Illinois, SE Wisconsin and NW/Central Indiana. It is one of eleven regional HERCs in the US, consisting of over 450 campuses in 19 states. The Greater Chicago Midwest HERC maintains a web based search engine [1] with listing for faculty and staff job openings at all member institutions along with dual career search option.

Member Institutions

The Greater Chicago Midwest HERC has 25 institutions of higher educations as members:

```
Ancilla College;
```

Argonne National Laboratory; Aurora University; Benedictine University; Chicago State University; Columbia College Chicago; DePaul University; Elmhurst College; Fermi National Accelerator Laboratory; The Field Museum; Harper College; Illinois Institute of Technology; Kendall College; Loyola University Chicago; Midwestern University; National-Louis University; North Central College; Northwestern University; Oakton Community College; Roosevelt University; University of Chicago; University of Illinois at Chicago; University of Illinois at Urbana-Champaign;

```
University of Notre Dame
```

External links

- *National HERC Website* [2]
- *Greater Chicago Midwest HERC website* [3]
- *Greater Chicago Midwest HERC Twitter Page* [4]
- *Greater Chicago Midwest HERC LinkedIn group* [5]

References

[1] http://gcmherc.org/c/search.cfm?site_id=1684
[2] http://www.nationalherc.org
[3] http://gcmherc.org/home/index.cfm?site_id=1684
[4] http://twitter.com/GCMHERC
[5] http://www.linkedin.com/groups?home=&gid=1252827

Haigui

Haigui (Hanzi: 海龟, lit. "sea turtle") is a Chinese language slang term for Chinese people who have returned to mainland China after having studied abroad for several years, but the actual term is 海归.[1] These graduates from foreign universities are highly sought after in Chinese business, and thus can gain employment ahead of those who have graduated from Chinese universities.[1] However, the salary demands of haigui are considered unrealistically high by some employers.[2]

"Sea turtle" in Chinese (海龟) is slang for a student returned from overseas

Motivations

Some haigui have returned to China due to the Late-2000s recession in the US and Europe.[3] According to Chinese government statistics, only a quarter of the 1.2 million Chinese people who have gone abroad to study in the past 30 years have returned.[3] As MIT Sloan School of Management professor Yasheng Huang states:

> The Chinese educational system is terrible at producing workers with innovative skills for Chinese economy. It produces people who memorize existing facts rather than discovering new facts; who fish for existing solutions rather than coming up with new ones; who execute orders rather than inventing new ways of doing things. In other words they do not solve problems for their employers.[4]

The Westernized way of thinking of haigui may be a threat to the politics of the People's Republic of China, which curtail personal freedoms.[5]

Etymology

The word is a pun, as *hai* 海 means "ocean" and *gui* 龟 is a homophone of *gui* 归 meaning "to return." The name was first used by Ren Hong, a young man returning to China as a graduate of Yale University seven years after leaving aboard a tea freighter from Guangzhou to the United States.[6]

Notable haigui

- Sun Yat-Sen
- Zhou Enlai
- Deng Xiaoping
- Lee Kai-fu founding president of Google China
- Qian Xuesen father of the Chinese rocket program

References

[1] Fan, Cindy (March 7, 2010). "Materialism and Social Unrest" (http://roomfordebate.blogs.nytimes.com/2010/03/07/educated-and-fearing-the-future-in-china/?ref=global-home#cindy). New York Times. .

[2] "Overseas Chinese Try to Build a Community in Homeland" (http://www.china.org.cn/living_in_china/news/2006-12/11/content_1191913.htm). China Daily. .

[3] Zhou, Wanfeng (December 17, 2008). "China goes on the road to lure "sea turtles" home" (http://www.reuters.com/article/idUSTRE4BH02220081218). Reuters. .

[4] Huang, Yasheng (March 7, 2010). "A Terrible Education System" (http://roomfordebate.blogs.nytimes.com/2010/03/07/educated-and-fearing-the-future-in-china/?ref=global-home#huang). New York Times. .

[5] "China's long march to the modern world" (http://www.thenational.ae/article/20081219/OPINION/653157655/-1/ART). Abu Dhabi Media Company. December 19. 2008. .

[6] "Hai Gui: The Sea Turtles Come Marching Home" (http://www.apmforum.com/columns/china19.htm). Asia Pacific Management Forum.

External links

- Schott's Vocabulary: Haigui (http://schott.blogs.nytimes.com/2009/01/12/hai-gui/) New York Times January 12, 2009

Higher Education Recruitment Consortium

The Higher Education Recruitment Consortium (HERC) is a job-placement and recruitment organization for institutions of higher education in the United States.

About HERC

The first HERC was established in Northern California in 2000 with Stanford, the University of California at Berkeley, and the University of California at Santa Cruz as lead members, with the goal of allowing colleges and universities to collaborate on the recruitment of faculty, staff, and executives. There are currently eleven regional HERCs in the United States, consisting of over 500 campuses in 19 states.

The National HERC was established in 2007 to support the independent but affiliated regional HERCs. It is a program of the Tides Center, a 501(c)(3) nonprofit organization. The National HERC is governed by an Advisory Board composed of the National HERC Director, *ex officio,* regional HERC directors, a member representative, and a member representative alternate from each regional HERC.

HERC maintains a regional, web-based search engine with listings for faculty and staff job openings at all member institutions, including a dual-career couple search option.

List of Regional HERC Organizations and Member Institutions

- Greater Chicago Midwest HERC [1]

        Ancilla College;

    Argonne National Laboratory; Aurora University; Benedictine University; Chicago State University; DePaul University; Elmhurst College; Fermi National Accelerator Laboratory; The Field Museum; Harper College; Illinois Institute of Technology; Loyola University Chicago;

        McHenry County College;

    Midwestern University; National-Louis University; North Central College; Northwestern University;

        Purdue University Calumet;

Roosevelt University;

```
School of the Art Institute of Chicago;
TCS Education System;
Rush University Medical Center;
```

University of Chicago; University of Illinois at Chicago; University of Notre Dame

- Metro New York and Southern Connecticut HERC

Adelphi University; Barnard College; Brookhaven National Laboratory; Brooklyn Law School; The City University of New York; Cold Spring Harbor Laboratory; Columbia University; Fashion Institute of Technology; Fordham University; The Juilliard School; Laboratory Institute of Merchandising; Manhattanville College Marist College; Memorial Sloan-Kettering Cancer Center; Molloy College; The New School; New York University; Norwalk Community College; Polytechnic University; Pratt Institute; The Rockefeller University; Sarah Lawrence College; Southern Connecticut State University; St. John's University; St. Joseph's College; SUNY Downstate Medical Center; Stony Brook University; Teachers College, Columbia University; Union Theological Seminary; United States Coast Guard Academy; University of Connecticut, Stamford; Vassar College; Wagner College; Weill Medical College of Cornell University; Westchester Community College; Western Connecticut State University; Yale University; Yeshiva University

- Michigan HERC

Alma College; Central Michigan University; College for Creative Studies; Cornerstone University; Davenport University; Delta College; Eastern Michigan University; Ferris State University; Grand Rapids Community College; Grand Valley State University; Henry Ford Community College;

```
Kalamazoo College;
```

Michigan State University; Mott Community College; Oakland Community College; Oakland University; Saginaw Valley State University;

```
Siena Heights University;
```

University of Detroit Mercy; University of Michigan Ann Arbor; University of Michigan Dearborn; University of Michigan Flint; Washtenaw Community College; Wayne County Community College District; Wayne State University; West Shore Community College; Western Michigan University

- Mid-Atlantic HERC

American University; Anne Arundel Community College; College of Notre Dame of Maryland; Community College of Baltimore County; DHHS/FDA/Center for Biologics Evaluation and Research; George Mason University; George Washington University; Georgetown University; Goucher College; Hood College; Johns Hopkins University; Loyola University Maryland; Maryland Institute College of Art; Morgan State University; National Institutes of Health; National Science Foundation; St. Mary's College of Maryland; Stevenson University; Towson University; University of Baltimore; University of Maryland, Baltimore; University of Maryland, Baltimore County; University of Richmond; University of Virginia; Virginia Military Institute; Washington and Lee University

- New England HERC

American Academy of Arts and Sciences; Babson College; Bentley University; Berklee College of Music; Beth Israel Deaconess; Boston College; Boston Conservatory; Boston University; Brandeis University; Bridgewater State College; Brigham and Women's Hospital; Brown University; Bunker Hill Community College; Cape Cod Community College; Champlain College; Children's Hospital Boston; Clark University; College of the Holy Cross; Colleges of the Fenway; Dana-Farber Cancer Institute;

Dartmouth College; Eastern Connecticut State University; Emerson College; Fitchburg State College; Framingham State College; Franklin Pierce University; Harvard University; Institute for Aging Research; Massachusetts College of Liberal Arts; Massachusetts Eye and Ear Infirmary; Massachusetts Institute of Technology; MGH Institute of Health Professions; Middlebury College; Middlesex Community College; Mount Wachusett Community College; New England Institute of Art; North Shore Community College; Northeastern University; Northern Essex Community College; Salem State College; Stonehill College; Suffolk University; Trinity College, Hartford; Tufts University; University of Hartford; University of Massachusetts Boston; University of Massachusetts Dartmouth; University of Massachusetts Lowell; University of Vermont; Wellesley College; Wheaton College; Woods Hole Oceanographic Institution; Worcester Polytechnic Institute; Worcester State College

* New Jersey/Eastern Pennsylvania/Delaware HERC

Albright College; Brookdale Community College; Bryn Mawr College; Bucknell University; Burlington County College; Caldwell College; The College of New Jersey; College of Saint Elizabeth; County College of Morris; Drew University; Drexel University; Fairleigh Dickinson University; Georgian Court University; Gettysburg College; Gloucester County College; Hudson County Community College; Lehigh University; Mercer County Community College; Middlesex County College; Monmouth University; Montclair State University; New Jersey City University; Passaic County Community College; Princeton University; Ramapo College of New Jersey; Richard Stockton College of New Jersey; Rider University; Rowan University; Rutgers University; Saint Peter's College; Seton Hall University; Susquehanna University; Temple University; Thomas Edison State College; Thomas Jefferson University; University of Delaware; University of Medicine and Dentistry of New Jersey; University of Pennsylvania; University of the Sciences in Philadelphia; Ursinus College; Widener University

- Northern California HERC

Butte College; Cabrillo College; California College of the Arts; California Institute of Integral Studies; California State University Chico; California State University East Bay; California State University Monterey Bay; California State University Stanislaus; Carnegie Mellon West; Chabot-Las Positas Community College; College of Marin; Contra Costa Community College District; Gavilan College; Hastings College of Law; Holy Names University; Kern Community College District; Lawrence Berkeley National Lab; Lawrence Livermore National Laboratory; Menlo College; Mills College; Notre Dame de Namur University; Ohlone College; Presidio Graduate School; Sacramento State College; Saint Mary's College of California; Samuel Merritt University; San Francisco Art Institute; San Francisco State University; San Jose State University; San Mateo County Community College District; Santa Clara University; Santa Rosa Junior College; Sonoma State University; Stanford University; State Center Community College District; University of California Berkeley; University of California Davis; University of California Merced; University of California, Office of the President; University of California San Francisco; University of California Santa Cruz; University of Nevada, Reno; University of San Francisco; University of the Pacific; West Valley/Mission Community College District

- Southern California HERC

Antioch University; Azusa Pacific University; California Institute of Technology; Cedars-Sinai Medical Center; Chapman University; Charles R. Drew University of Medicine and Science; The Claremont Colleges; Grossmont-Cuyamaca Community College District; Loyola Marymount University; Mount St. Mary's College; Occidental College; Palomar Community College; Salk Institute for Biological Studies; Santa Monica College; University of California, Irvine; University of California, Los Angeles; University of California, Riverside; University of California, San Diego; University of La Verne; University of Redlands; University of San Diego; Westmont College

- St. Louis Regional HERC

    Barnes-Jewish Hospital; Donald Danforth Plant Science Center;

    Central Methodist University Adult Programs;

    East Central College; Fontbonne University; Harris-Stowe State University; Lewis and Clark Community College; Lindenwood University; Maryville University; Saint Louis University; Southern Illinois University Edwardsville; St. Charles Community College; St. Louis College of Pharmacy; St. Louis Community College; University of Illinois at Springfield; University of Missouri–St. Louis; Washington University in St. Louis

- Upper Midwest HERC

    Alexandria Technical College; Anoka Technical College; Anoka-Ramsey Community College; Augsburg College; Bemidji State University; Carleton College; Central Lakes College; Century College; College of St. Scholastica; Dakota County Technical College; Fond du Lac Tribal and Community College; Hamline University;

    Hazelden Graduate School of Addiction Studies;

    Hennepin Technical College; Hibbing Community College; Inver Hills Community College; Itasca Community College; Lake Superior College; Macalester College; Mesabi Range Community and Technical College; Metropolitan State University; Minneapolis Community and Technical College; Minnesota State College – Southeast Technical; Minnesota State Community and Technical College; Minnesota State University Moorhead; Minnesota State University, Mankato; Minnesota West Community and Technical College; Normandale Community College; North Hennepin Community College; Northland Community and Technical College; Northwest Technical College; Office of the Chancellor for the Minnesota State Colleges and Universities; Pine Technical College; Rainy River Community College; Ridgewater College; Riverland Community College; Rochester Community and Technical College; Saint Paul College; South Central College; Southwest Minnesota State University; St. Catherine University; St. Cloud State University; St. Cloud Technical College; St. Olaf College; University of Minnesota Crookston; University of Minnesota Duluth; University of Minnesota Morris; University of Minnesota Rochester; University of Minnesota Twin Cities; University of St. Thomas;

    University of Wisconsin-Eau Claire;

    University of Wisconsin La Crosse; University of Wisconsin-River Falls; Vermilion Community College; William Mitchell College of Law; Winona State University

- Upstate New York HERC

    Alfred State College; Colgate University; Cornell University; Hamilton College; Hobart and William Smith Colleges; Ithaca College; Le Moyne College; Monroe Community College; Nazareth College of Rochester; Onondaga Community College; Paul Smith's College; Rochester Institute of Technology; SUNY Cortland; SUNY Geneseo; SUNY Oswego; SUNY Potsdam; SUNY College of Environmental Science and Forestry; SUNY Upstate Medical University; Syracuse University; Tompkins Cortland Community College; University of Rochester; Utica College; Wells College

Partners

The National HERC is partnered with both corporate and non-profit partners; both are accorded benefits from their association and provide resources for HERC members.

- Corporate Partners

    Diverse: Issues In Higher Education; Inside Higher Ed; JobElephant; JobTarget OneClick; Monster; Bayard Advertising; Graystone Advertising; GreenJobInterview.com; INSIGHT Into Diversity; Latinos in Higher Ed; LinkedIn; Saad & Shaw; Hispanic Outlook in Higher Education; Indeed.com; Renaissance Strategic Solutions; Women for Hire

- Non-Profit Partners

    American Council on Education; WGBH Education Foundation; Clayman Institute for Gender Research at Stanford University; Collaborative on Academic Careers in Higher Education; College and University Professional Association for Human Resources; Higher Education Dual Career Network; The PhD Project;

References

Harms, William. Higher Education Recruitment Consortium will assist job hunters seeking faculty, research, executive positions. [2] University of Chicago Chronicle. November 1, 2007.

Lewis, Diane. 3 dozen colleges team up to recruit. [3] Boston Globe, October 2, 2006.

Ryssdal, Kai. Studying ways to help 2-career couples. [4] American Public Media. June 18, 2007.

Schiebinger, Londa, Andrea Davis Henderson and Shannon K. Gilmartin. Dual Career Couples: What Universities Need to Know. [5] Michelle R. Clayman Institute for Gender Research, Stanford University. 2008.

Wilson, Robin. Paid Leave at Public Colleges vs. Private Ones; Family-Friendly Benefits That Go Unclaimed; Helping Dual-Career Couples Find Jobs; a Journal's Special Issue on 'Mothering in the Academy.' [6] The Chronicle of Higher Education, April 9, 2004.

American Academy of University Professors. Recommendations on Partner Accommodation and Dual Career Appointments. [7] 2010

External links

- *National HERC Homepage* [2]
- *Regional HERCs and Member Institutions* [8]

References

[1] http://www.gcmherc.org
[2] http://chronicle.uchicago.edu/071101/herc.shtml
[3] http://www.boston.com/business/articles/2006/10/02/3_dozen_colleges_team_up_to_recruit
[4] http://marketplace.publicradio.org/display/web/2007/06/18/studying_ways_to_help_2career_couples
[5] http://www.stanford.edu/group/gender/ResearchPrograms/DualCareer/DualCareerFinalExecSum.pdf
[6] http://chronicle.com/article/Paid-Leave-at-Public-Colleges/19209
[7] http://www.aaup.org/AAUP/comm/rep/dual.htm
[8] http://www.hercjobs.org/site/793/regional_hercs.cfm

Hipsty

HiPSTY is an acronym that stands for Hire People Smarter Than You. It is an informal policy for firms and companies in general. It is a declaration of intent where the employer shows interest in people skills and merits without fearing internal competitiveness. By referring to his company as HiPSTY, the employer intends to suggest an environment where people are dedicated to the company's interest more than to their self-interest, to quality rather than personal pride.

The term HiPSTY is comparable to other terms such as EOE and MFDV.

Homeworker

Homeworkers or **home workers** are defined by the International Labour Organization as people working from their homes or from other premises of their choosing other than the workplace, for remuneration, which results of a product or service specified by the employer. There are an estimated 300 million homeworkers in the world, though because these workers generally function in the informal economy, and are seldom registered and often not contracted, exact numbers are difficult to come by. Recently, the phenomenon of homework has grown with increased communication technology, as well as changes in supply chains, particularly the development of Just In Time inventory systems.

Homeworkers differ from entrepreneurs, or self-employed, or family business, in that they are hired by companies for specific activities or services to be done from their homes. Homeworkers do not own or operate the business they work for. Though there is a significant body of highly skilled homeworkers, particularly in information technology, most homeworkers are considered low skilled labour. Recently, working conditions have worsened for homeworkers, and they are becoming a point of concern for international development organizations and non-governmental organizations.

References

- *Global trade and home work: closing the divide* by Annie Delaney, Gender and Development, Vol 12, No 2, pp 22–28, July 2004
- *Home Work Convention C177, 1996* by ILO, available at

http://www.itcilo.org/actrav/actrav-english/telearn/global/ilo/law/iloc177.htm

- *Organising home-based workers in the global economy: An action-research approach* by Ruth Pearson, Development in Practice, Vol 14, Nos 1&2, pp136–148, February 2004

External links

- Homeworkers Worldwide (HWW) [1] Homepage
- Spezialists Translators Legal Advisors (Homeworker24) [2] Homepage
- Homework defining concept and discussion page [3] at *Demotech.*

References

[1] http://www.homeworkersww.org.uk/
[2] http://www.homeworker.ch/
[3] http://www.demotech.org/d-publications/designA.php?d=77

hResume

hResume is a microformat for publishing résumé or Curriculum Vitae (CV) information [1] using (X)HTML on web pages. Like many other microformats, hResume uses HTML classes and *rel* attributes to make an otherwise non-semantic document more meaningful. A document containing resume information could be modified to use hResume without altering the appearance to the browser.

Structure

hResume provides for ten main areas of information, each denoted with an appropriately named class, and all of them optional except for contact info.

- summary
- contact (uses the hCard microformat)
- experience
- achievements related to this work
- education
- skills/qualifications
- affiliations
- publications
- performance/skills for performance
- individualization/specialization/career objectives

An example of hResume being implemented is the social networking site LinkedIn, where it is used on public profile pages. [2]

References

[1] Microformats: Empowering Your Markup for Web 2.0 (2007) by John Allsopp p. 212
[2] http://microformats.org/wiki/hresume#Examples_in_the_wild

External links

- hResume at the Microformats Wiki (http://microformats.org/wiki/hresume)
- hResume WordPress Plugin at the hResume Project site (http://hresume.org)
- hResume: on-line cv/résumé builder (supports hResume) (http://cv.antix.co.uk)

Independent contractor

An **independent contractor** is a person, business, or corporation that provides goods or services to another entity under terms specified in a contract or within a verbal and physical agreement. Unlike an employee, an independent contractor does not work regularly for an employer but works as and when required, during which time he or she may be subject to the Law of Agency. Independent contractors are usually paid on a freelance basis. Contractors often work through a franchise, which they themselves own, or may work through an umbrella company.

In the United States, any company or organization engaged in a trade or business that pays more than $600 to an independent contractor in one year is required to report this to the Internal Revenue Service (IRS) as well as to the contractor, using Form 1099-MISC.[1] [2] This form is merely a report of monies paid; independent contractors do not have income taxes withheld from their pay as regular employees do.

Independent contractor versus employee

Sometimes, it is not a straightforward matter to determine who is an independent contractor and who should be classified as an employee. To make a determination, the IRS advises taxpayers to look at three aspects of the employment arrangement: financial control, behavioral control, and relationship between the parties.[3] While some independent contractors may work for a number of different organizations throughout the year, there are also many who retain independent contractor status even though they work for the same organization for the entire year.

Generally speaking, independent contractors retain control over their schedule and number of hours worked, jobs accepted, and performance of their job. This contrasts with the situation for regular employees, who usually work at the schedule required by the employer and whose performance is directly supervised by the employer. However many companies (particularly in the freight transport industry) specify the contractor's schedule, require purchase of vehicles from the company and prohibit work for other companies.

Examples of occupations where independent contractor arrangements are typical:

- Accountant
- Author
- Barber or hair stylist
- Boxer
- Courier
- Court Reporter
- Doctor
- Dry cleaner
- Engineering Consultant
- Entertainer
- General contractor
- General Practitioner
- Interpreter or Translator
- Lawn care worker
- Lawyer
- Market stall
- Mason
- Massage therapist
- Nurse
- Newspaper Carrier
- Personal trainer

- Private investigator
- Private military company
- Radio presenter (in radio jargon, referred to as a "swing jock")
- Private security
- Professional wrestler
- Professional athlete
- Real estate agent
- Sales representative
- Stock broker
- Talent agent
- Tattoo artist
- Taxi Driver or limosine driver
- Telephone and live chat psychic
- Tradesman
- Tutor

Pros and Cons

Life as an independent contractor has both benefits and hindrances.

Pros

- Since they are rarely tied to an employer, they are free to set their own rules of business, limited only by bargaining power.
- Since they usually develop a large network of clients, the loss of one or two often has a negligible effect.
- Many people simply like the idea of "being your own boss." Aside from materialistic benefits, many people simply enjoy not having to answer to a supervisor.
- As an artist/author of any tangible artwork, such as paintings, sculptures, photographs, or written works, you are entitled to exclusive copyright ownership if you created the work as an independent contractor. If you created such works while in the employ of another person or corporation, the rights belong to the employer (under most standard employment contracts).

Cons

- In the United States misclassification of employees as "independent contractors" in order to avoid taxation and regulation is widespread.[4]
- Most independent contractors are usually also owners of a sole proprietorship, and as such, bear all the expenses of their product, which can be made up only by charging customers accordingly.
- Income taxes for independent contractors are drastically more complicated than of employees.
- There are several monetary incentives that are guaranteed to employees in the United States, but not independent contractors. Examples include worker's compensation and unemployment insurance.

An independent contractor in tort

The employer of an independent contractor is generally not held vicariously liable for the tortious acts and omissions of the contractor, because the control and supervision found in an employer-employee or Principal-Agent relationship is lacking. However, vicarious liability will be imposed in three circumstances:

1. where the contractor injures an invitee to the real property of the employer,
2. the contractor is involved in an ultra-hazardous activity (one likely to cause substantial injury, such as blasting with explosives), or
3. the employer is estopped from denying liability because he has held out the independent contractor as if he were simply an employee or agent.

References

[1] See generally 26 U.S.C. § 6041 (http://www.law.cornell.edu/uscode/26/6041.html) and 26 C.F.R. sec. 1.6041-1.
[2] Sample form 1099-MISC (http://www.irs.gov/pub/irs-pdf/f1099msc.pdf)
[3] IRS Frequently Asked Questions about form 1099-MISC (http://www.irs.gov/faqs/faq-kw5.html)
[4] "U.S. Cracks Down on 'Contractors' as a Tax Dodge" (http://www.nytimes.com/2010/02/18/business/18workers.html) article by Steven Greenhouse in *The New York Times* February 17, 2010

External links

- Independent Contractor Rights (http://jobsearchtech.about.com/library/weekly/aa121800.htm)
- http://www.irs.gov/taxtopics/tc762.html

Induction (teachers)

Induction is used to refer to a period during which a Newly Qualified Teacher in England or Wales is both supported and assessed to ensure that regulatory standards are met.

Background

Although probation periods for new teachers had only been dropped in 1992, the Teaching and Higher Education Act 1998 introduced arrangements by which the Secretary of State for Education could bring about regulations requiring new teachers to serve a period of induction.[1]

The following year, the then secretary of state, David Blunkett introduced an induction period under The Education (Induction Arrangements for School Teachers) (England) Regulations 1999.[2] These regulations made it a requirement that all teachers complete an induction period equivalent to one year upon qualification as a teacher.

Requirements

Under current regulations, teachers wishing to work in maintained state schools must satisfactorily complete a period of induction. During this period, a newly-qualified teacher is entitled to additional support and subject to regular observation and assessment to ensure that he or she is meeting the required induction standards.

Standards

Having achieved Qualified Teacher Status (QTS), teachers are expected to continue to meet the standards required for that qualification. In addition, they must meet the 6 criteria set out in the induction standards:

1. Seek and use opportunities to work collaboratively with colleagues to raise standards by sharing effective practice in the school.

2. Show a commitment to their professional development by

   1. identifying areas in which they need to improve their professional knowledge, understanding and practice in order to teach more effectively in their current post, and
   2. with support, taking steps to address these needs.

3. Plan effectively to meet the needs of pupils in their classes with special educational needs, with or without statements, and in consultation with the SENCO contribute to the preparation, implementation, monitoring and review of Individual Education Plans or the equivalent.

4. Liaise effectively with parents or carers on pupils' progress and achievements.

5. Work effectively as part of a team and, as appropriate to the post in which they are completing induction, liaise with, deploy, and guide the work of other adults who support pupils' learning.

6. Secure a standard of behaviour that enables pupils to learn, and act to pre empt and deal with inappropriate behaviour in the context of the behaviour policy of the school.

Support

In order to support newly-qualified teachers in meeting the standards, a number of entitlements are guaranteed by regulations:

- a reduced timetable (of no more than 90% of other equivalent teachers)
- support from an induction tutor
- a named induction contact at a Local Education Authority or other body

Assessment

In addition, all teachers undergoing a programme of induction are subject to assessment processes, including:

- regular observations every 6-8 weeks
- a termly review meeting
- a decision at the end of the induction period to ascertain whether the required standards have been met.

Restrictions

Induction can only be completed in a restricted range of school types. Similarly, teachers who have not completed, and are not completing, induction can only be employed in such school types under special circumstances

Completing induction

Induction can only be completed in eligible schools in the United Kingdom, Guernsey, Jersey, Isle of Man, Gibraltar or at Service Children's Education (SCE) schools in Cyprus and Germany. Eligible schools are maintained schools, non-maintained special schools, independent schools (with support from either a Local Education Authority or The Independent Schools' Council Teacher Induction Panel, or a sixth form college under certain circumstances.

Teachers not completing induction

Teachers who have not completed a period of induction are limited in the work they can carry out in eligible schools. Where a teacher is employed in an eligible school for at least one term, he or she must be offered, and must undertake, a programme of induction lasting throughout that period. Teachers who have not completed a period of induction can only work in eligible schools for periods of less than one term during a restricted time-frame. This time-frame begins on the first day that such employment begins, and expires no later than four terms from that date (approximately 16 months). Teachers who have reached this point may seek an extension to this period from the relevant Local Education Authority.

Teachers who have not completed a period of induction are eligible to work in independent schools

Time limits

As stated in the statutory guidance on induction for newly qualified teachers in England, there is no set time limit for starting or completing an induction period. The previous ruling that an NQT needed to complete the induction period within 5 years was abolished in September 2008.

References

[1] HM Government (1998). "Teaching and Higher Education Act 1998" (http://www.opsi.gov.uk/acts/acts1998/80030--d.htm). HMSO. . Retrieved 2007-01-22.

[2] HM Government (1999). "The Education (Induction Arrangements for School Teachers) (England) Regulations 1999 (SI 1999/1065)" (http://www.opsi.gov.uk/si/si1999/19991065.htm). HMSO. . Retrieved 2007-01-21.

Induction programme

An **induction programme** is the process used within many businesses to welcome new employees to the company and prepare them for their new role.

Induction training should, according to TPI-theory, include development of theoretical and practical skills, but also meet interaction needs that exist among the new employees[1].

Benefits of an induction programme

An induction programme is an important process for bringing staff into an organisation. It provides an introduction to the working environment and the set-up of the employee within the organisation. The process will cover the employer and employee rights and the terms and conditions of employment. As a priority the induction programme must cover any legal and compliance requirements for working at the company and pay attention to the health and safety of the new employee.

An induction programme is part of an organisations knowledge management process and is intended to enable the new starter to become a useful, integrated member of the team, rather than being "thrown in at the deep end" without understanding how to do their job, or how their role fits in with the rest of the company.

Good induction programmes can increase productivity and reduce short-term turnover of staff. These programs can also play a critical role under the socialization to the organization in terms of performance, attitudes and organizational commitment[2].

A typical induction programme

A typical induction programme will include at least some of the following:

- any legal requirements (for example in the UK, some Health and Safety training is obligatory)
- any regulatory requirements (for example in the UK banking sector certain forms need to be completed)
- introduction to terms and conditions (for example, holiday entitlement, how to make expense claims, etc)
- a basic introduction to the company, and how the particular department fits in
- a guided tour of the building
- completion of government requirements (for example in UK submission of a P45 or P60)
- set-up of payroll details
- introductions to key members of staff
- specific job-role training

Best practise

In order to fully benefit the company and employee, the induction programme should be planned in advance. A timetable should be prepared, detailing the induction activities for a set period of time (ideally at least a week) for the new employee, including a named member of staff who will be responsible for each activity. This plan should be circulated to everyone involved in the induction process, including the new starter. If possible it should be sent to the new starter in advance, if not co-created with the new starter[3]

It is also considered best practise to assign a buddy to every new starter. If possible this should be a person who the new starter will not be working with directly, but who can undertake some of the tasks on the induction programme, as well as generally make the new employee feel welcome. (For example, by ensuring they are included in any lunchtime social activities.)

References

[1] *Alvenfors, Adam (2010) *Introduction - Integration? On the introduction programs' importance for the integration of new employees* http:// urn.kb.se/resolve?urn=urn:nbn:se:his:diva-4281.

[2] *Alvenfors, Adam (2010) *Introduction - Integration? On the introduction programs' importance for the integration of new employees.* http:// urn.kb.se/resolve?urn=urn:nbn:se:his:diva-4281

[3] "Onboarding - How to Get Your New Employees Up to Speed in Half the Time", George Bradt and Mary Vonnegut (John Wiley & Sons, 2009) - ISBN 0470485817

- ACAS article "Recruitment, selection and induction (http://www.acas.gov.uk/index.aspx?articleid=892)

- Alvenfors, Adam (2010) *Introduction - Integration? On the introduction programs' importance for the integration of new employees.*

- Browning, Guy (15 July 2004) *New kid on the block* People Management Magazine

INGRADA

The **International Network of Graduate Recruitment And Development Associations** (**INGRADA**) consists of a number of associations from around the globe which represent professionals involved in the recruitment and development of university and college graduates.

INGRADA is a non-political, non-profit organisation which provides its members with the capacity to network and share information about graduate recruitment and development across international boundaries.

Existing members of INGRADA include the National Association of Colleges and Employers (NACE), the Association of Graduate Recruiters (AGR), the Canadian Association of Career Educators and Employers (CACEE), the South African Graduate Recruitment Association (SAGRA) and the Australian Association of Graduate Employers (AAGE).

External links

- http://www.ingrada.org

Integrity Inventory

The ***Integrity Inventory - I^2***, is a nationally normed entry-level selection tool initially developed for the public safety sector and now available for use in the private sector. The Integrity Inventory predicts individuals' likelihood of engaging in counterproductive workplace behaviors including, but not limited to, theft, violence and drug abuse.[1] Qualified individuals with a reduced risk of such counterproductive workplace behaviors are selected for employment, leading to a more productive workforce. Counterproductive workplace behaviors lead to real financial losses for business; in the public safety and private sector, such behaviors are hazardous and place the civilian population and coworkers at heightened risk.[2] [3] [4] As such, the prediction of counterproductive workplace behaviors constitutes a "business necessity" as outlined in the U.S. Equal Employment Opportunity Commission's Uniform Guidelines on Employee Selection Procedures.[5]

References

[1] Integrity Inventory Technical Report, 2011, I/O Solutions, Inc., Westchester, Illinois 60154

[2] Barry, C. M., Sackett, P. S., & Wiemann, S. (2007). A review of recent developments in integrity test research. Personnel Psychology, 60, 271-301.

[3] Hough, L. M., & Schneider, R. J. (1996). Personality traits, taxonomies, and applications in organizations. In Murphy KR (ed.), Individual difference and behavior in organizations (pp. 31-88). San Francisco: Jossey-Bass.

[4] National Institute on Drug Abuse. NIDA InfoFacts: Nationwide Trends, accessed May 25, 2011, http://www.drugabuse.gov/Infofacts/nationtrends.html

[5] EEOC's Uniform Guidelines on Employee Selection Procedures document, accessed May 25, 2011, http://www.eeoc.gov/policy/docs/factemployment_procedures.html

External links

- Official Website (http://www.iosolutions.org/)
- Public Safety Recruitment Website (http://www.publicsafetyrecruitment.com/)
- Public Safety Training Website (http://www.publicsafetytesting.com/)

Internal labor market

Internal labor markets are an administrative unit within a firm in which pricing and allocation of labor is governed by a set of administrative rules and procedures. The remainder of jobs within the ILM is filled by the promotion or transfer of workers who have already gained entry. Internal labor markets are shielded from the competition of external labor markets (ELM).[1] However, competition of ILM exists within the firm in the form of job promotions and pay.[2]

The main reasons why internal labor markets were developed are as follows[1] :

Skill specificity

Skill specificity has two effects important to the generation of the ILM: it increases the proportion of training costs borne by the employer, as opposed to by the trainee and it increases the absolute level of such costs.[1] [3] Companies are ever more seeking individuals with specific talents that can be an asset to their organization. Firms that require specifically trained individuals look for a stable labor force.[4]

On the job training

Many firms are willing to train internal employees for other positions.[5] Since they find no use in workers with experience from other places, they prefer to promote young workers and train them on-the-job. Firms want to maintain the investment afterwards; therefore they offer the employees job security and structured promotions. Due to the importance of on the job training, the promotion is often given by seniority. Also, this way of promotion encourages on the job training, since the eldest worker is not afraid that the young one replaces him. Employers benefit from this more stable relationship because they reduce the cost of training.[4]

Analysis

Analysis of Internal Labor Markets concerns the causes of an organization's (or geography's) workforce dynamics − attraction, development, and retention as well as the rewards that motivate them. Statistical models are often used to explain and predict outcomes because internal labor markets are a complex system of interactions between workers, company management practices and labor market dynamics.[6]

Customary Law

Custom at the workplace is an unwritten set of rules based largely upon past practices or precedent. These rules can govern any aspect of the work relationship from discipline to compensation. Work customs appear to be the outgrowth of employment stability within the internal labor markets. Customary law is of special interest in the analysis of internal labor markets both because of the stabilizing influence which it imparts to the rules of the workplace and because the rules governing the pricing and allocation of labor within the market are particularly subject to the influence of custom.[1]

The internal labor market is composed of many facets. The first is ILMs which consist of clusters of jobs related by the skills and capacities required for their successful performance. Second, the sets of skills required within one job cluster are similar, but different from those required in other job clusters. Third, within any one job cluster, there exists a hierarchy of skills and capacities such that the demands for application of skills on certain jobs facilitate the development of further skills required for other jobs. In this hierarchy those with lower-level jobs requiring skills are usually available in the ELM and higher level jobs require capacities developed from the performance of lower-level jobs usually within the ILM. Fourth, different job levels receive different compensation; high level jobs are associated with higher levels of compensation. Finally, selection and assignment of persons to higher level jobs occurs according to the rules that describe the criteria to be used in these decisions.[2]

References

[1] Doeringer, Peter B. & Piore Michael J. (1971). Internal Labor Markets and Manpower Analysis. Massachusetts. D.C. Heath and Company

[2] Pinfield, Lawrence, (1995). The Operation of Internal Labor Markets. New York. Plenum Press.

[3] Chase, Ivan D. Vacancy Chains. Annul. Review Sociology, 1991.

[4] Labor Markets: Institutional Factors (http://www.econ.ubc.ca/ferrer/ec317/lecture 7.pdf#search='internal labor markets , skill specificity), University of British Columbia - Economics, Retrieved on October 10, 2005

[5] Owen, Laura. "History of Labor Turnover in the U.S.". EH.Net Encyclopedia, edited by Robert Whaples. April 30, 2004. Turnover (http://eh.net/encyclopedia/?article=owen.turnover)

[6] Nalbantian, Guzzo, Kieffer and Doherty, Play to Your Strengths, Managing Internal Labor Markets, McGrawHill, 2004

Internet recruiting

Internet recruiting is the act of scouring the Internet to locate both actively-searching job seekers and also individuals who are content in their current position (these are called "passive candidates"). It is a field of dramatic growth and constant change that has given birth to a dynamic multi billion dollar industry.

Traditionally, recruiters use large job boards, niche job boards, as well as social and business networking to locate these individuals. The immediate goal of Internet recruiting is to find individuals that a recruiter or company can present to hiring managers for the purpose of employment. Quite often, Internet recruiters have very short-term goals when it comes to recruiting online. The general catalyst that sparks this process is when a new job requisite comes in (called a REQ). The recruiter scans his or her database to see if anyone's resumes match the requirements. If not, they proceed to search on the Internet.

The challenge arises when recruiters contact passive candidates willy-nilly. If a person is not currently seeking for a job, they generally have no interest in learning about new positions. Excessive contacts of this nature could lead to complaints of spam. A far more logical way to approach Internet recruiting is for recruiters to view themselves as an authority site and answer the WIIFM question that all individuals have: "What's in it for me to act upon your email"?

If a recruiter also offers resources such as career help, salary information, how to manage job stress, and the like, they break out of the stereotypical headhunter mode and enter into the "valued resource" mode to the individuals they contact.

Popular places for Internet recruiting

Internet recruiting can be successfully practiced on:

- Major search engines: Using boolean operators (AND, OR, NOT, etc.), related search syntax (parentheses for clauses, quotation marks around multiple-keyword phrases, etc.) and appropriate special commands (intitle:, inurl:, site:, filetype:, etc.), one can generate very targeted search strings to find just the kinds of candidate resumes and/or prospect biographies desired. These are typically most effective on major engines such as Google, Yahoo, Live, Exalead, etc., that each have billions of pages indexed as well as support for many special commands.

- Niche search engines and job boards: In some cases, it can be more effective to use a more narrow search tool. Blog-specific search engines such as Gigablast can deliver targeted results within that subset of the Internet.

- Discussion lists: Similarly, using Google Groups [1] (formerly Deja) to search Usenet postings can find unique results within newsgroup discussion lists. Yahoo Groups, Topica, etc., are other online communities that each host millions of discussion lists which can be searched. Many portals and individual association sites (see below) offer their own forums where posts (and their posters) can be searched.

- Other virtual communities: LinkedIn, Spoke and [Xing.com] (formerly OpenBC) are currently the largest of the professionally-skewed social networks with differing levels of depth on candidates, though some search capabilities are reserved for paid tier members only. Other larger virtual communities, such as [Facebook] and [MySpace], contain a higher percentage of non-professional content. As a result, these may be less efficient for recruiting purposes even when advanced search techniques are employed.

Association sites: Many local and regional association sites will have targeted niche job boards as a value-added benefit for their members, as well as member directories, local chapter contacts and other data useful for contact name generation/biographical details of passive candidates.

- Local business forums: Towns and cities will often have local business forums in which new jobs can be posted.
- Industry niche sites: Industry niche sites will not only generally have member resumes available but also include vendor lists, discussion forums, and the opportunity to write articles as a career advisor.
- Back to School Nights: The Parents-Teachers Association will often let local businesses advertise during back to school nights. It makes a good fund-raiser, and recruiters have instant access to local professionals.

References

[1] http://groups.google.com

Interview suit

Western dress codes
• Formal wear
• Formal
• Semi-formal
• Informal
• Smart casual
• Business casual
• Casual
• Active attire

For other garments (protective, etc) sometimes called suits, see suit (disambiguation).

In clothing, a **suit** is a set of garments made from the same cloth, consisting of at least a jacket and trousers. **Lounge suits** are the most common style of Western suit, originating in the United Kingdom as country wear.[1] Other types of suit still worn today are the *dinner suit*, part of black tie, which arose as a lounging alternative to dress coats in much the same way as the day lounge suit came to replace frock coats and morning coats; and, rarely worn today, the morning suit. This article discusses the lounge suit (including business suits), elements of informal dress code.

The variations in design, cut, and cloth, such as two- and three- piece, or single- and double- breasted, determine the social and work suitability of the garment. Often, suits are worn, as is traditional, with a collared shirt and necktie.[2] Until around the 1960s, as with all men's clothes, a hat would have been also worn when the wearer was outdoors. Suits also come with different numbers of pieces: a two-piece suit has a jacket and the trousers; a three piece adds a waistcoat; further pieces might include a matching flat cap.

A. G. Murray is pictured in a two-piece suit and a contrasting double-breasted waistcoat with a pocket watch

Originally, as with most clothes, a tailor made the suit from his client's selected cloth; these are now often known as *bespoke* suits. The suit was custom made to the measurements, taste, and style of the man. Since the Industrial Revolution, most suits are mass-produced, and, as such, are sold as ready-to-wear garments (though alteration by a tailor prior to wearing is common). Currently, suits are sold in roughly three ways:

- *bespoke*, in which the garment is custom-made from a pattern created entirely from the customer's measurements, giving the best fit and free choice of fabric;
- *made to measure*, in which a pre-made pattern is modified to fit the customer, and a limited selection of options and fabrics is available;
- and finally *ready-to-wear*, which is least expensive and hence most common.[3]

History

The current styles were founded in the revolution during the early seventeenth century that sharply changed the elaborately embroidered and jewelled formal clothing into the simpler clothing of the British Regency period, which gradually evolved to the stark formality of the Victorian era. It was in the search for more comfort that the loosening of rules gave rise in the late nineteenth century to the modern lounge suit.

Etymology

The word *suit* derives from the French *suite*,[4] meaning "following", from some Late Latin derivative form of the Latin verb *sequor* = "I follow", because the component garments (jacket and trousers and waistcoat) follow each other and have the same cloth and colour and are worn together.

As a suit (in this sense) covers all or most of the wearer's body, the term "suit" was extended to a single garment that covers all or most of the body, such as boilersuits and diving suits and spacesuits (see *Suit*).

Parts of a suit

There are many possible variations in the choice of the style, the garments and the details of a suit.

The cut

The silhouette of a suit is its outline. No suit is skin-tight; the amount of extra fabric and the way it hangs is known as the drape. The shape of the front of the suit is particularly affected by the way the suit buttons. The two main cuts consist firstly of *double-breasted* suits, a conservative design with two vertical rows of buttons, spanned by a large overlap of the left and right sides; and secondly, *single-breasted* suits, on which the sides just meet at the front down a single row of buttons.

British suits are characterised by strongly tapered sides, minimal shoulder padding, and two vents. Italian suits are characterised by strongly padded shoulders, minimally tapered sides, and no vent. American suits are considered more casual than the preceding styles, and are characterised by moderate shoulder padding, moderately tapered sides, and a single vent. The sack suit is a loose American style. *Contemporary* is a term that includes a variety of recently designed garments that do not fit into the preceding categories.[5]

The suit is cut out from a length of fabric from a roll by a cutter using a cutting pattern, a paper outline of the parts. The pattern can be draughted in various ways. With a ready-to-wear suit, the same pattern is used many times to make identical suits. Made-to-measure and bespoke cutters can work by pattern manipulation, altering a stock pattern, or by using a drafting formula to calculate adjusted lengths. Some bespoke tailors work by "Rock Of Eye", drawing and cutting by eye.[6]

A man dressed in a three-piece suit and bowler hat.

Fabric

Suits are made in a variety of fabrics, but most commonly from wool. The two main yarns produce worsteds (where the fibres are combed before spinning) and woollens (where they are not). These can be woven in a number of ways producing flannel, tweed, gabardine, and fresco among others. These fabrics all have different weights and feel, and some fabrics have an S (or Super S) number describing the fineness of the fibres. Although wool has traditionally been associated with warm, bulky clothing meant for warding off cold weather, advances in making finer and finer fiber have made wool suits acceptable for warmer weather, as fabrics have accordingly become lighter and more supple. For hot weather, linen is also used, and in North America cotton seersucker is worn. Other materials are used sometimes, such as cashmere.[7] Silk and silk blended with wool are sometimes used. Synthetic materials, while cheap, are very rarely recommended by experts.

The main four colours for suits worn in business are black, light grey, dark grey, and navy, either with or without patterns. In particular, grey flannel suiting has been worn very widely since the 1930s. In non-business settings or less-formal business contexts, brown is another important colour; olive also occurs. In summer, lighter shades, such as tan or cream, are popular.[8] [9]

A man wearing a pinstriped pattern suit

For non-business use tweed has been popular since Victorian times, and still is commonly worn. A wide range of colour is available, including muted shades of green, brown, red, and grey.[10] Tweeds are usually checked, or plain with a herringbone weave, and are most associated with the country. While full tweed suits are not worn by many now, the jackets are often worn as sports jackets with odd trousers (trousers of different cloth).

The most conventional, universally occurring suit is a 3-button navy blue suit, which can be worn either with matching trousers, or with different, lighter-colored trousers for a more casual look. Other conservative colors are greys, black, and olive. White and light blues are acceptable at some events, especially in the warm season. Red is usually considered "unconventional" and "garish". Tradition calls for a gentleman's suit to be of decidedly plain color, with splashes of bright color reserved for neckties, kerchiefs and, sometimes, hose.

In the US and UK, suits were never traditionally made in plain black, this colour instead being reserved for formal wear[11] (including dinner jackets or strollers), and for undertakers. However, the decline of formal wear in recent years has meant that black, as well as being popular in fashionable scenes,[11] such as clubbing, is now also being worn in formal contexts (such as to a funeral or religious function) in place of the traditional more formal wear.

Traditional business suits are generally in solid colours or with pin stripes;[12] windowpane checks are also acceptable. Outside business, the range of acceptable patterns widens, with plaids such as the traditional glen plaid and herringbone, though apart from some very traditional environments such as London banking, these are worn for business now too. The colour of the patterned element (stripes, plaids, and checks) varies by gender and location. For example, bold checks, particularly with tweeds, have fallen out of use in America, while they continue to be worn as traditionally in Britain. Some unusual old patterns such as diamonds are now rare everywhere.

Inside the jacket of a suit, between the outer fabric and the inner lining, there is a layer of sturdy interfacing fabric to prevent the wool from stretching out of shape; this layer of cloth is called the canvas after the fabric from which it was traditionally made. Expensive jackets have a *floating canvas*, while cheaply manufactured models have a *fused* (glued) canvas.[13] A fused canvas is less soft and, if poorly done, damages the suppleness and durability of the jacket,[14] so many tailors are quick to deride fused canvas as being less durable.[15] However, some selling this type of jacket claim that the difference in quality is very small.[16] A few London tailors state that all bespoke suits should use a floating canvas.[17] In June 2008, the Advertising Standards Authority (ASA), a British advertising regulator, ruled otherwise, citing the Oxford English Dictionary definition of *bespoke* as "made to order".[18]

Jacket

Front buttons

Most single-breasted suits have two or three buttons, and one or four buttons are unusual. It is rare to find a suit with more than four buttons, although zoot suits can have as many as six or more due to their longer length. There is also variation in the placement and style of buttons,[19] since the button placement is critical to the overall impression of height conveyed by the jacket. The centre or top button will typically line up quite closely with the natural waistline.[20]

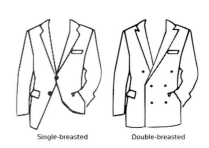

Single-breasted   Double-breasted

Single- vs. double-breasted jacket

Double-breasted jackets have only half their outer buttons functional, as the second row is for display only, forcing them to come in pairs. Some rare jackets can have as few as two buttons, and during various periods, for instance the 1960s and 70s, as many as eight were seen. Six buttons are typical, with two to button; the last pair floats above the overlap. The three buttons down each side may in this case be in a straight line (the 'keystone' layout) or more commonly, the top pair is half as far apart again as each pair in the bottom square. A four-button double-breasted jacket usually buttons in a square.[21] The layout of the buttons and the shape of the lapel are co-ordinated in order to direct the eyes of an observer. For example, if the buttons are too low, or the lapel roll too pronounced, the eyes are drawn down from the face, and the waist appears larger.[22]

The custom that a man's coat should button "left side over right", anecdotally originates in the use of the sword, where such cut avoided catching the top of the weapon in the opening of the cloth (since the sword was usually drawn right-handed).[23] Women's suits are buttoned "right side over left". A similar anecdotal story to explain this is that women were dressed by maids, and so the buttons were arranged for the convenience of their, typically, right-handed servants; men on the other hand dressed themselves and so the buttons were positioned to simplify that task.

Lapels

A notched lapel

The jacket's lapels can be notched (also called "stepped"), peaked ("pointed"), shawl, or "trick" (Mandarin and other unconventional styles). Each lapel style carries different connotations, and is worn with different cuts of suit. Notched lapels are only found on single-breasted jackets and are the most informal style. Double-breasted jackets usually have peaked lapels. Shawl lapels are a style derived from the Victorian informal evening wear, and as such are not normally seen on suit jackets except for dinner suits.[24]

In the 1980s, double-breasted suits with notched lapels were popular with power suits and the New Wave style.

In the late 1920s and 1930s, a design considered very stylish was the single-breasted peaked lapel jacket. This has gone in and out of vogue periodically, being popular once again during the 1970s, and is still a recognised alternative. The ability to properly cut peak lapels on a single-breasted suit is one of the most challenging tailoring tasks, even for very experienced tailors.[25]

A peaked lapel

The width of the lapel is a varying aspect of suits, and has changed over the years. The 1930s and 1970s featured exceptionally wide lapels, whereas during the late 1950s and most of the 1960s suits with very narrow lapels—often only about an inch wide—were in fashion. The 1980s saw mid-size lapels with a low gorge (the point on the jacket that forms the "notch" or "peak" between the collar and front lapel). Current (mid-2000s) trends are towards a narrower lapel and higher gorge.

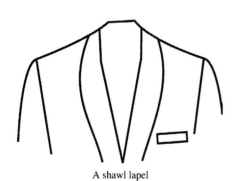

A shawl lapel

Lapels also have a buttonhole, intended to hold a boutonnière, a decorative flower. These are now only commonly seen at more formal events. Usually double-breasted suits have one hole on each lapel (with a flower just on the left), while single-breasted suits have just one on the left.[26]

Pockets

Most jackets have a variety of inner pockets, and two main outer pockets, which are generally either patch pockets, flap pockets, or jetted pockets.[27] The patch pocket is, with its single extra piece of cloth sewn directly onto the front of the jacket, a sporting option, sometimes seen on summer linen suits, or other informal styles. The flap pocket is standard for side pockets, and has an extra lined flap of matching fabric covering the top of the pocket. A jetted pocket is most formal, with a small strip of fabric taping the top and bottom of the slit for the pocket. This style is most often on seen on formalwear, such as a dinner jacket.

A breast pocket is usually found at the left side, where a pocket square or handkerchief can be displayed.

In addition to the standard two outer pockets and breast pocket, some suits have a fourth, the ticket pocket, usually located just above the right pocket and roughly half as wide. While this was originally exclusively a feature of country suits, used for conveniently storing a train ticket, it is now seen on some town suits. Another country feature also worn sometimes in cities is a pair of hacking pockets, which are similar to normal ones, but slanted; this was originally designed to make the pockets easier to open on horseback while hacking.[5] [28]

Sleeves

Suit jackets in all styles typically have three or four buttons on each cuff, which are often purely decorative (the sleeve is sewn closed and cannot be unbuttoned to open). Five buttons are unusual and are a modern fashion innovation. The number of buttons is primarily a function of the formality of the suit; a very casual summer sports jacket might traditionally (1930s) have had only one button, while tweed suits typically have three and city suits four. In the 1970s, two buttons were seen on some city suits. Today, four buttons are common on most business suits and even casual suits.

Although the sleeve buttons usually cannot be undone, the stitching is such that it appears they could. Functional cuff buttons may be found on high-end or bespoke suits; this feature is called a *surgeon's cuff*.[29] Some wearers leave these buttons undone to reveal that they can afford a bespoke suit, although it is proper to leave these buttons done up.[30] Modern bespoke styles and high end off-the-rack suits equipped with surgeon's cuffs have the last two buttons stitched off-centre, so that the sleeve hangs more cleanly should the buttons ever be undone.

A cuffed sleeve has an extra length of fabric folded back over the arm, or just some piping or stitching above the buttons to allude to the edge of a cuff. This was popular in the Edwardian era, as a feature of formalwear such as frock coats carried over to informalwear, but is now rare.

Vents

A vent is a slit in the bottom rear (the "tail") of the jacket.[28] Originally, vents were a sporting option, designed to make riding easier, so are traditional on hacking jackets, formal coats such as a morning coat, and, for practicality, overcoats. Today there are three styles of venting: the single-vented style (with one vent at the centre); the ventless style; and the double-vented style (one vent on each side). Vents are convenient, particularly when using a pocket or sitting down, to improve the hang of the jacket,[31] so are now used on most jackets. Ventless jackets are associated with Italian tailoring, while the double-vented style is typically British.[5] (This is not the case with all types of jackets. For instance, dinner jackets traditionally take no vents.)

Waistcoats

Waistcoats (called *vests* in the USA) were almost always worn with suits prior to the 1940s. After that time their use slowly declined.

Trousers

Suit trousers are always made of the same material as the jacket. Even from the 1910s to 1920s, before the invention of sports jackets specifically to be worn with odd trousers, wearing a suit jacket with odd trousers was seen as an alternative to a full suit.[32] However, with the modern advent of sports jackets, suit jackets are always worn with matching trousers, and the trousers have always been worn with the appropriate jacket.

Trouser width has varied considerably throughout the decades. In the 1920s, trousers were straight-legged and wide-legged, with a standard width at the cuff of 23 inches. After 1935, trousers began to be tapered in at the bottom half of the leg. Trousers remained wide at the top of the leg throughout the 1940s. By the 1950s and 1960s, a more slim look had become popular. In the 1970s, suit makers offered a variety of styles of trousers, including flared, bell bottomed, wide-legged, and more traditional tapered trousers. In the 1980s these styles disappeared in favor of tapered, slim-legged trousers.

One variation in the design of trousers is the use or not of pleats. The most classic style of trouser is to have two pleats, usually forward, since this gives more comfort sitting and better hang standing.[33] This is still a common style, and for these reasons of utility has been worn throughout the twentieth century. The style originally descended from the exaggeratedly widened Oxford bags worn in the 1930s in Oxford, which, though themselves short-lived, began a trend for fuller fronts.[34] The style is still seen as the smartest, featuring on dress trousers with black and white tie. However, at various periods throughout the last century, flat fronted trousers with no pleats have been worn, and the swing in fashions has been marked enough that the more fashion-oriented ready-to-wear brands have not produced both types continuously.

Turn-ups on the bottom of trousers, or cuffs, were initially popularised in the 1890s by Edward VII,[35] and were popular with suits throughout the 1920s and 1930s. After falling out of style in World War II, they were not generally popular again, despite serving the useful purpose of adding weight to straighten the hang of the trousers. They have always been an informal option, being inappropriate on all formalwear.

Other variations in trouser style include the rise of the trouser. This was very high in the early half of the 20th century, particularly with formalwear, with rises above the natural waist,[36] to allow the waistcoat covering the waistband to come down just below the narrowest point of the chest. Though serving less purpose, this high height was duplicated in the daywear of the period. Since then, fashions have changed, and have rarely been that high again with styles returning more to low-rise trousers, even dropping down have waistbands resting on the hips. Other changing aspects of the cut include the length, which determines the break, the bunching of fabric just above the shoe when the front seam is marginally longer than height to the shoe's top. Some parts of the world, such as Europe, traditionally opt for shorter trousers with little or no break, while Americans often choose to wear a slight break.[37]

A final major distinction is made in whether the trousers take a belt or braces (suspenders). While a belt was originally never worn with a suit, the forced wearing of belts during wartime years (caused by restrictions on use of elastic caused by wartime shortages) contributed to their rise in popularity, with braces now much less popular than belts. When braces were common, the buttons for attaching them were placed on the outside of the waistband, because they would be covered by a waistcoat or cardigan, but now it is more frequent to button on the inside of the trouser. Trousers taking braces are rather different in cut at the waist, employing inches of extra girth and also height at the back. The split in the waistband at the back is in the *fishtail* shape.

Breeches

As an alternative to trousers, breeches (or *knickers* in variations of English where this does not refer to underwear) may be worn with informal suits, such as tweed. These are shorter, descending to just below the knees, fastened closely at the top of the calf by a tab or button cuff. While once common, they are now typically only worn when engaged in traditional outdoor sports, such as shooting. The length and design is closely related to the plus-fours (and plus-sixes etc.) worn for sport, but differ in having no bagginess. They are usually designed to be worn with long socks meeting just below the knee, but riding breeches, worn with long boots such as top boots, are long enough to meet the boot and display no sock.[38]

Situations for wearing and perceptions of suits

Former US Secretary of State Condoleezza Rice and Turkish President Abdullah Gül wearing Western-style business suits.

Rock musician Nick Cave wears a pinstripe suit while performing onstage.

Because wearing a suit conveys a respectable image, many people wear suits during the job interview process.[39] An interview suit is usually a conservative style, and often made of blue or grey fabric. Interview suits are frequently composed of wool or wool-blend fabric, with a solid or pin stripe pattern.[40] The style of an interview suit, however, will depend on the organizational culture of the industry in which a person seeks employment.

In modern society, men's suits have become less common as an outfit of daily wear. During the 1990s, the prevailing management philosophy of the time favored more casual attire for employees; the aim was to encourage a sense of openness and egalitarianism. "Business casual" dress still tends to be the norm for most workers up to and sometimes including mid-level management. Traditional business dress as an everyday style is generally limited to middle- and upper-level corporate management (now sometimes collectively referred to as "suits"),[41] and to the professions (particularly law). Casual dress has also become common in Western academic institutions.

For many men, particularly in Western society, wearing a suit is reserved for special occasions, such as weddings, funerals, and other more formal social events. Hence, because they are not a daily outfit for most men, they are often viewed as being "stuffy" and uncomfortable. The combination of a tie, belt and vest can be tight and restrictive compared to contemporary casual wear. The Christian Science Monitor reported that a suit combined with a necktie and slacks was "a design that guarantees that its wearer will be uncomfortable." [42] During the late 1960s and early 1970s, men's suits became less commonly worn, in much the same way that skirts and dresses were dropped by many women in favour of trousers. This was seen as a liberation from the conformity of earlier periods and occurred concurrently with the women's liberation movement.

Suit etiquette for men

Buttoning the suit jacket

The buttoning of the jacket is primarily determined by the *button stance*, a measure of how high the buttons are in relation to the natural waist. In some (now unusual) styles where the buttons are placed high, the tailor would have intended the suit to be buttoned differently from the more common lower stance. Nevertheless, some general guidelines are given here.

Double-breasted suit coats are almost always kept buttoned. When there is more than one to fasten (as in a traditional six-on-two arrangement), only the top one need be fastened; in some configurations, the wearer may elect to fasten only the bottom button, in order to present a longer line (a style popularised by the Prince George, Duke of Kent).

Single-breasted suit coats may be either fastened or unfastened. In two-button suits the bottom button is traditionally left unfastened except with certain unusual cuts of jacket. Legend has it that King Edward VII started the trend of leaving the bottom button of a suit undone.[43]

When fastening a three-button suit, the middle button is fastened, and the top one sometimes, but the bottom is traditionally not designed to be (although in the past some jackets were cut so that it could be fastened without distorting the drape, this is not the case with current clothing). A four-button suit is untraditional and so has no traditional guidelines on buttoning, but the middle ones at least should be fastened. Additionally, the one button suit has regained some popularity (it is also a classic style for some Savile Row tailors). The button should always be fastened while standing.

With a single-breasted suit, it is proper to have the buttons unfastened while sitting down to avoid an ugly drape. A good double-breasted suit is usually able to be left buttoned, to avoid the difficulty of constantly redoing inner buttons when standing up.

Ties with suits

Working with neckties is very much a matter of personal taste, but in conservative terms there are some basic guidelines.

Colour: Ties should always be darker than the wearer's shirt. The background colour of the tie should not be the same as that of the shirt, while the foreground of the tie should contain the colour of the shirt and thereby "pick up" on the colour of the shirt. Ideally, the tie should also integrate the colour of the suit in the same way. Generally, simple or subdued patterns are preferred for conservative dress, though these are terms with a wide range of interpretation. During the late 1990s and early 2000s, it became popular to match the necktie colour with the shirt (a "monochromatic" look popularized by TV personality Regis Philbin) or even wearing a lighter coloured tie with a darker shirt, usually during formal occasions. A light blue shirt with a blue tie that is darker in its colour is also common.

Knot: Some of the most common knots are the Four-in-hand, the Half-Windsor, the Windsor (or Full-Windsor), and the Shelby or Pratt. A Four-in-hand, Half-Windsor, or Windsor is generally the most appropriate with a suit, particularly by contemporary guidelines. Once properly knotted and arranged, the bottom of the tie can extend anywhere from the wearer's navel level, to slightly below the waistband. The thin end should not extend below the wide end, though this can occasionally be seen to be acceptable with thin ties.

Alternatives: In the 1960s, it was fashionable for men as well as women to wear scarves with a suit in a tied knot either inside a shirt as an Ascot or under the collar as would be worn like a tie. This style began to fade by the mid 1970s and came back in the 1990s mainly for women. It did however make a small comeback by 2005 and some famous stars wear them. Although some wore scarves back in the 1960s, ties were still preferred among business workers.

Socks with suits

In the United States it is common for socks to match the trouser leg.[44] This makes the leg appear longer and minimises the attention drawn by a trouser leg tailored to be too short. A more general rule is for socks to be darker than the shade of the trousers, but potentially a different colour. With patterned socks, ideally the background colour of the sock should match the primary colour of the suit. If it is not possible to match the trouser leg, socks may match one's shoes. In particular, pale or even white socks might be worn with, for example, a cream linen suit with white shoes. Although white socks may be worn with very light coloured suits, it is less common and considered a faux pas with darker suits. In practice therefore socks are usually navy, black, or brown, particularly for more conservative occasions.

Socks are preferably at least mid-calf height (*over-the-calf*), if not knee-height, and are usually made predominantly of cotton or wool, though luxury or dress socks may use more exotic blends such as silk and cashmere. Before World War II, patterned socks were common, and a variety of designs like Argyle or contrasting socks was commonly seen. After WWII, socks became more subdued in colour.

Shoes with suits

The correct footwear varies from country to country. Shoes should always be smarter shoes, such as Oxfords (Balmorals in American English), Derbies (Blüchers), or smart slip-ons; never very casual shoes such as trainers (sneakers) or deck shoes. A slip-on is normally only worn with a modern and very informal suit: brown or sometimes navy. Shoes also have differing degrees of decoration, with less ornamentation being more formal, leaving half- and full- brogues as less formal options. Shoes are broadly divided into the two categories of black and not black. Black shoes are worn with all business suits by the English, who traditionally keep brown shoes with suits for tweed or linen only. The rest of the world wears black with grey or black suits, and brown with navy and non-business suits. The shades of brown also vary considerably, as only Americans generally wear colours like cordovan or oxblood; lighter browns are less formal and more appropriate for summer, for example with linen.

Suit etiquette for women

A women's trouser suit

A women's skirt suit

Suit-wearing etiquette for women generally follows the same guidelines used by men, with a few differences and slightly more flexibility.

For women, a dress or skirts are acceptable suits; a blouse (usually white) takes the place of a shirt. Blue and pink blouses are also seen. Women have more leeway in selecting their tops than men have in selecting their shirts. Sometimes a high-quality knitted top replaces the blouse; this is not universally accepted but is common, particularly if the top is made of a luxurious material.

Women's suits come in a larger variety of colors such as darks, pastels, and gem colors. Skirt suits are as popular as pant suits (trouser suits).

Women generally do not wear neckties with their suits. Fancy silk scarves that resemble a floppy ascot tie were popular in North America in the 1970s, worn with pant suits. At that time women entered the white-collar workforce in large numbers and their dress fashions imitated men's business wear.

Notes

[1] Antongiavanni (2006). p. 74

[2] Flusser (2002). p. 146

[3] Antongiavanni (2006). p. 35

[4] Oxford English Dictionary Online (2008). *suit*, n. 19b.

[5] Flusser (1985). ch. 2 (http://www.throughtherye.com/flusser/ch2.htm)

[6] Mahon, Thomas (2005-09-23). "How to draft a pattern" (http://www.englishcut.com/archives/2005_02.html). *English Cut*. . Retrieved 2008-09-20.

[7] Antongiavanni (2006). p. 76

[8] Flusser (2002). pp. 93–99

[9] Antongiavanni (2006). pp. 80–86

[10] Flusser (2002). p. 95

[11] Antongiavanni (2006). p. 81

[12] Flusser (2002). p. 94

[13] Flusser (2002). p. 288

[14] Antongiavanni (2006). p. 66

[15] Mahon, Thomas (2005-02-08). "Fused vs. floating" (http://www.englishcut.com/archives/000020.html). *English Cut*. . Retrieved 2008-09-20.

[16] Merrion, Desmond (2008-11-08). "Recent made to measure tailoring" (http://www.desmerrionbespoketailor.com/folders/weblog/20081108/). . Retrieved 2008-11-19.

[17] Mahon, Thomas (2005-01-06). "How to pick a "bespoke" tailor" (http://www.englishcut.com/archives/000005.html). *English Cut*. . Retrieved 2008-09-20.

[18] Advertising Standards Authority (2008-06-18). "Sartoriani London" (http://www.asa.org.uk/asa/adjudications/Public/TF_ADJ_44555.htm). *ASA Adjudications*. . Retrieved 2008-10-09.

[19] Druesdow (1990). p. vi. "...for often the difference in style from season to season was in the distance between buttons..."

[20] Flusser (2002). p. 83

[21] Antongiavanni (2006). p. 14

[22] Antongiavanni (2006). p. 16

[23] "About Suits and Jackets" (http://www.bensilver.com/style04/about_SuitsJackets.htm). *BenSilver.com*. . Retrieved 2008-09-20.

[24] Flusser (2002). pp. 82–85

[25] Mahon, Thomas (2005-03-29). "Single-breasted, peaked lapel" (http://www.englishcut.com/archives/000052.html). *English Cut*. . Retrieved 2008-09-20.

[26] Boehlke, Will (2007-01-07). "What's in your lapel?" (http://asuitablewardrobe.dynend.com/2007/01/whats-in-your-lapel.html). *A Suitable Wardrobe*. . Retrieved 2008-09-24.

[27] The Nu-Way Course in Fashionable Clothes Making (1926). Lesson 33 (http://vintagesewing.info/1920s/26-fcm/fcm-33.html)

[28] Bookster, a manufacturer of tweed jackets, has illustrations of various features of jackets: "Jacket options" (http://www.tweed-jacket.com/GALLERY PAGE/Bespoke Options/index.htm). . Retrieved 2008-09-20.

[29] Mahon, Thomas (2007-01-18). "Real cuff holes..." (http://www.englishcut.com/archives/000215.html). *English Cut*. . Retrieved 2008-10-26.

[30] Rosenbloom, Stephanie (February 13, 2009). "For Fine Recession Wear, $7,000 Suits From Saks (Off the Rack)" (http://www.nytimes.com/2009/02/14/business/14saks.html). New York Times. . Retrieved 2009-02-14.

[31] Antongiavanni (2006). p. 172

[32] Flusser (2002). p. 100

[33] Flusser (2002). p. 92
[34] Flusser (2002). p. 112
[35] Flusser (2002). p. 284
[36] Croonborg (1907). p. 100 lists tables of trousers heights
[37] Flusser (2002). p. 61
[38] Croonborg (1907). p. 118
[39] Wilson, Eric (2008–11–13). "The Return of the Interview Suit" (http://www.nytimes.com/2008/11/13/fashion/13INTERVIEW.html). *The New York Times*. pp. E1, E10. . Retrieved 2008–11–22.
[40] Canisius College MBA Program (2008-04-24). "Confused about Buying an Interview Suit...This is all you will ever need to know!" (http://www.buffalo-mba.com/confused-about-buying-an-interview-suitthis-is-all-you-will-ever-need-to-know/). . Retrieved 2008–11–22.
[41] *Concise Oxford English Dictionary 10th ed.* Oxford University Press. 2002. p. 1433 "*informal* a high-ranking business executive".
[42] To save power, Bangladesh bans suits and ties (http://features.csmonitor.com/environment/2009/09/05/to-save-power-bangladesh-bans-suits-and-ties/), Christian Science Monitor, September 5, 2009
[43] Matthew, H. C. G. (September 2004; online edition May 2006) "Edward VII (1841–1910)" (http://www.oxforddnb.com/view/article/32975), *Oxford Dictionary of National Biography*, Oxford University Press, doi:10.1093/ref:odnb/32975, retrieved 24 June 2009 (Subscription required)
[44] Flusser (2002). p. 173

References

- Antongiavanni, Nicholas (2006). *The Suit: A Machiavellian Approach to Men's Style*. HarperCollins. ISBN 978-0-06-089186-2.
- Boyer, Bruce (1990). *Eminently Suitable: The Elements of Style In Business Attire*. The Haddon Craftsmen. ISBN 0-393-02877-1.
- Boyer, G. Bruce (September 1990). *Eminently Suitable: The Elements of Style in Business Attire*. W. W. Norton & Company. ISBN 978-0393028775.
- Calasibetta, Charlotte Mankey (2003). *The Fairchild Dictionary of Fashion*. Fairchild Publications. ISBN 1-56367-235-9.
- Croonborg, Frederick (1907). *The Blue Book of Men's Tailoring*. New York and Chicago: Croonborg Sartorial Co.
- Druesedow, Jean L.; Jno. J. Mitchell Co (1990). *Men's Fashion Illustrations from the Turn of the Century: by Jno. J. Mitchell Co*. Courier Dover Publications. ISBN 9780486263533.
- Flusser, Alan (1985). *Clothes and the Man: The Principles of Fine Men's Dress* (http://www.throughtherye.com/flusser/index_current.html). Villard. ISBN 0-394-54623-7. Retrieved 2008-09-20.
- Flusser, Alan (2002). *Dressing the Man: Mastering the Art of Permanent Fashion*. HarperCollins. ISBN 0-06-019144-9.
- Flusser, Alan (1996). *Style and the Man*. HarperCollins. ISBN 0-06-270155-X.
- Keers, Paul (October 1987). *A Gentleman's Wardrobe: Classic Clothes and the Modern Man*. Weidenfeld & Nicolson. ISBN 978-0297791911.
- Kidwill, Claudia, B. (1974). *Suiting Everyone: The Democratization of Clothing in America*. Smithsonian Institution Press.
- *The New-Way Course in Fashionable Clothes-Making* (http://web.archive.org/web/20080705215810/http://www.vintagesewing.info/1920s/26-fcm/fcm-toc-short.html). Fashion Institute. 1926. OCLC 55530806. Archived from the original (http://vintagesewing.info/1920s/26-fcm/fcm-toc-short.html) on 2008-07-05. Retrieved 2008-08-20.

External links

- Emily Post's *Etiquette*: The Clothes of a Gentleman, 1922 (http://www.bartleby.com/95/34.html)
- "Introduction to 18th-century fashion" (http://www.vam.ac.uk/content/articles/i/introduction-to-18th-century-fashion/). *Fashion, Jewellery & Accessories*. Victoria and Albert Museum. Retrieved 2008-08-06.

Jeopardy! audition process

Throughout the run of the quiz show *Jeopardy!*, the production staff has regularly offered **auditions** for potential contestants. Tryouts take place in the Los Angeles area, and occasionally in other locations throughout the United States, in Canada, and at U.S. military installations abroad. Anyone who is at least 18 years old may audition, unless auditioning for one of the special programs, such as the Teen Tournament (ages 13–17), Kids Week (ages 10–12), or the College Championship (full-time undergraduate students). The *Jeopardy!* audition process differs from that of many other game shows in that it involves passing a difficult test of knowledge on a diversity of subjects, approximating the breadth of material encountered by contestants on the show. Since 2006, an online screener test is conducted about once a year.

Historical practices

In the original version, prospective contestants could call the *Jeopardy!* office in New York to make a preliminary determination of eligibility and arrange an appointment to audition. Approximately 10 to 30 individuals would audition at the *Jeopardy!* office at once, the process lasting about an hour and a half, and usually involving a written test, a briefing, and a mock game. Contestants invited to play on the show were generally invited within six weeks of auditioning.[1]

When the current version of *Jeopardy!* premiered in 1984, prospective contestants were given a 50-question written test, with 35 being a passing score. The original contestant tests were written by head writer Jules Minton, and were later written by the show's writers. Initially, 2 new contestant tests were compiled each year, and were given alternately; later, the tests were refreshed every six months to accommodate frequent repeat test takers. The makeup of the test was 15 academic questions, 10 lifestyle, 15 pop culture and 10 wordplay. Beginning in 1987, the number of pop culture questions was reduced to 5 and wordplay to 2. Those who passed the test at an audition were invited to play a mock game to evaluate their stage presence and colorfulness. Initially, all auditions took place in Southern California, and anyone could call to make an appointment to take the test; travelling contestant searches did not begin until after the second season of the show. Local affiliates airing the show sponsored regional contestant searches, paying for the travel expenses and accommodations of the contestant coordinators. Invitations to audition were awarded by postcard drawings and other types of contests.[2]

A 10-question pre-test was first devised when contestant coordinators conducted a two-week East Coast search at Merv Griffin's Resorts Atlantic City hotel and casino.[3] In order to test as many people as possible, hopefuls were invited to take the screener pre-test as often as once per day, and those with a passing score of 7 were invited to return to take the 50-question full test. The 2-week Atlantic City auditions were held annually in February while the show was owned by Griffin,[4] and the 10-question screener is still in use at traveling open auditions.

Internet screenings

Once each year, a series of screenings for potential contestants are conducted on the Internet through the official *Jeopardy!* web site.

Online tests are typically conducted over three days, which each day being targeted at a different time zone (Eastern, Mountain and Pacific). Online test dates for previous years include:

- 2006: March 28-30
- 2007: January 23–25
- 2009: January 27-29
- 2010: January 26-28
- 2011: February 8-10; March 15 (college); March 1 (teen)
- 2012: Early January (Kids)

An online version of the 50-question qualifying exam is administered to pre-registered applicants.[5] [6]

The online test allows 15 seconds to answer each question.[6] Whatever has been typed into the answer bar at the end of 15 seconds is entered as your answer. You are not required to answer in the form of a question, as you would be on the show. Upon completion of the online test, you are not given your actual score.

A random selection of passers (generally understood to be those who get 35 or more questions correct) of this screener are invited to participate in regional in-person auditions.

In-person audition process (regular play games)

Tryouts for regular play games are administered to groups of 18 to 21 people at scheduled dates and times. Upon arriving, contestant applicants are asked to fill out information sheets with their contact information, eligibility information, and availability, and are asked to provide five anecdotes that may be used during the contestant interview portion of the show (a form is emailed in advance).

The first phase of the group audition process is divided into three parts.

1. A contestant coordinator gives an introductory talk reviewing the rules and particularities of the game and providing some guidelines regarding energy, volume, and timing for the applicants. Some sample clues are read aloud (and displayed on a monitor or projection screen) and applicants are called upon to raise their hands and give out the responses.
2. Fifty *Jeopardy!*-style clues in fifty different categories are displayed on the screen at the front of the room and read aloud in a recording by a Clue Crew member (previously, Johnny Gilbert, the show's announcer, did the voice-over on this). A potential contestant has eight seconds to write down his or her response (no need to phrase in the form of a question here) before the next clue is read.
3. The contestant coordinators take the completed response sheets and grade them. Though some sources state that a score of 35 (70%) is passing, the contestant coordinators refuse to confirm or deny any passing score number. Exact scores are not disclosed.

This is followed by a mock *Jeopardy!* competition. A game board is presented, and potential contestants are placed in groups of three to play the game. The emphasis is not on scoring points, or even having correct answers; the contestant coordinators know that they possess the knowledge to compete on the show, as they have already passed the test, and are looking for on-the-air-compatible qualities. Auditionees are encouraged to display energy and use a loud, confident voice.[1] [4] After playing a few clues, the contestant coordinators give each potential contestant a few minutes to talk about themselves. The coordinators request that they finish by telling what they would do with any money they won on *Jeopardy!*[4]

After the end of the tryout, all auditionees who have taken the online test and the in-person test are placed into the "contestant pool" and are eligible to be called to compete for the next eighteen months. The show uses 400 contestants per season, and it is emphasized at the audition that test scores are the most important factor in determining who out of the thousands of applicants will be selected.[5]

The *Jeopardy!* Brain Bus

The *Jeopardy!* promotional vehicle, a 32-foot Winnebago dubbed the "Brain Bus", travels to 12 cities annually[7] conducting traveling contestant searches divided into two activities: a *Pre-Test* section and a *Fun Play* section.

In the Pre-Test, attendees who are at least 18 years old are given a 10-question version of the above qualifying test. (At least three different versions of the test are used, so attendees cannot copy answers from neighbors.) If the attendee passes the test (as above, scores are not given, only pass/fail results), they are given a form that allows them to attend and attempt the full 50-question qualifier (as described above) the next day.

Jeopardy! Brain Bus

The Fun Play area allows attendees, regardless of age, to play a modified "quick game" of *Jeopardy!* for prizes. Attendees queue up in three lines, and are given a static board of six categories. The host—usually a member or members of the Clue Crew--choose one of the attendees at the head of their line to pick a category and "dollar amount" (ranging from $200 to $1000, as in the current *Jeopardy!* Round. A clue is shown, and the line leaders—each using a similar buzzer device to those used on the show—attempt to signal in and answer. After five clues are played, the line leaders hand off the buzzers to the next person in line, and are allowed to choose one of the give-away prizes at the front of the game stage (these usually include *Jeopardy!*-logoed t-shirts, keychains, hats, drink bottles and the like). If, during play, a player finds a *Daily Double* (usually in a specifically identified category), that player plays the clue alone for the chance to win a larger prize (recently, this has been a copy of the reference work *The New York Times Guide To Essential Knowledge*, and the category is ALL THE NEWS THAT'S FIT TO PRINT.) In addition, some attendees are invited to create and sing their own lyrics for the *Jeopardy!* Theme. Those willing to sing the lyrics on stage get a special prize (at recent events, this has been the *Jeopardy!* DVD Home Game System).

Beginning in Season 26, the Brain Bus link was removed from the official *Jeopardy!* website. However, there is a page that indicates test dates for adults, college students, teens, and kids to take the online test.[8]

Kids Week, Holiday Kids Week, and Back to School Week

Tryouts for the Kids Weeks are slightly different. One does bring one's anecdotes and information sheet, but one *first* plays the mock Jeopardy! game, then takes a thirty question test. During the mock game, coordinators sometimes open up triple stumper questions to the other potential contestants. One is called or notified by the station on which one views *Jeopardy!* if one is to appear on the show.[9] Fifteen children who are between ten to twelve years old are chosen for each filming, along with one alternate.

Waiting period

The mandatory waiting period after taking the online contestant exam is one year. Prospective contestants who have completed an in-person test and interview remain in the contestant pool for 18 months, only after the expiration of which may they attend another in-person audition.[8]

Auditions in the Art Fleming era

Tryouts for the original version were conducted somewhat differently.[10] In a classroom-type arrangement, potential contestants wrote their questions to the answers held up by the contestant coordinator, who used cards which had previously actually been used on the show. While the exams were being scored, the staff explained that on any given day, the contestants who actually appear all scored the same number (or very nearly the same number) on this tryout. For the next day, the staff would select two new contestants who had scored a point or two higher than the winner that day, and so on day after day. This typically resulted in a pattern in which almost no contestant was able to win 5 days in a row (because she or he was subsequently competing with contestants who were probably better) -- until the scores escalated to the point at which all three contestants had scored at or near the maximum possible score. When these high scorers, competing against each other day after day, eventually produced an undefeated champion, the contestant pool was "reset" back to scorers who barely passed with the minimum score.

Potential contestants were told that if their score was not in the range that they were seeking that particular day, their names and information would be put into a contestant pool, and that — if they lived near New York — they might be called to come to the studio at any time in the next several months when their "number" came up (although this was, they made it clear, unlikely, due to the large number of contestants who had tried out). Since potential contestants had no idea what the target score was for that day, they had no idea whether it would be a good thing to deliberately score lower than they were capable of scoring.

External links

- Official *Jeopardy!* Web site [11] - Contestant FAQ [12]
- Official *Jeopardy!* message board [13]

References

[1] Fleming, Art (1979), *Art Fleming's TV Game Show Fact Book*, Salt Lake City, Utah: Osmond Publishing Company, pp. 14–15, ISBN 0-89888-005-X

[2] Eisenberg, Harry (1993). *Inside "Jeopardy!": What Really Goes on at TV's Top Quiz Show*. Salt Lake City, Utah: Northwest Publishing Inc.. pp. 32–35. ISBN 1-56901-177-X.

[3] Eisenberg, first edition, page 278.

[4] Dupée, Michael (1998). *How to Get on Jeopardy! and Win!: Valuable Information from a Champion*. Seacaucus, New Jersey: Citadel Press. pp. 3–10. ISBN 0-8065-1991-6.

[5] "Post to the "NYC auditions" thread on the official *Jeopardy!* Message Board" (http://boards.sonypictures.com/boards/showthread. php?p=645614#post645490). 2007-05-04. . Retrieved 2007-05-05.

[6] Geisinger biomedical engineer wins on 'Jeopardy!' (http://dailyitem.com/0100_news/x546128185/ Geisinger-biomedical-engineer-wins-on-Jeopardy) Rick Dandes, December 10, 2009]

[7] Richmond, Ray (2004). *This is Jeopardy!: Celebrating America's Favorite Quiz Show*. New York: Barnes & Noble Books. p. 170. ISBN 0-7607-5374-1.

[8] "This is JEOPARDY! - Contestant FAQ" (http://www.jeopardy.com/beacontestant/contestantfaqs/). . "Online tests may be offered more than once in any 12-month period, but Adults may only take the online test once a year. If you passed the online test and were invited to an "in person" interview, you will be in our active files for 18 months. If at the end of 18 months from the date of your in-person tryout, you have not been booked to appear on the show, you are eligible to take the online test again. If you attended an authorized Jeopardy! contestant event (i.e. Jeopardy! Challenge), passed a qualifying test, and participated in an "in person" interview, you must wait 18 months from the date of that in-person tryout before you are eligible to take the online test. If you did not pass the qualifying test, the regular online test rules apply."

[9] JEOPARDY! Teen FAQ (http://www.jeopardy.com/onlinetests/teen/faq/)-Will I receive my teen's test results?

[10] Jeopardy!:a revealing look inside TV's top quiz show, contestants and question selection process unveiled (http://books.google.com/books?id=zPQiNAAACAAJ) Harry Eisenberg, Lifetime Books, 1997

[11] http://www.jeopardy.com

[12] http://www.jeopardy.com/beacontestant/contestantfaqs/

[13] http://boards.sonypictures.com/boards/forumdisplay.php?f=11

Job description

A **job description** is a list that a person might use for general tasks, or functions, and responsibilities of a position. It may often include to whom the position reports, specifications such as the qualifications or skills needed by the person in the job, or a salary range. Job descriptions are usually narrative,[1] but some may instead comprise a simple list of competencies; for instance, strategic human resource planning methodologies may be used to develop a competency architecture for an organization, from which job descriptions are built as a shortlist of competencies.

Creating a job description

A job description is usually developed by conducting a job analysis, which includes examining the tasks and sequences of tasks necessary to perform the job. The analysis considers the areas of knowledge and skills needed for the job. A job usually includes several roles. The job description might be broadened to form a person specification or may be known as Terms Of Reference

Roles and responsibilities

A job description may include relationships with other people in the organization: Supervisory level, managerial requirements, and relationships with other colleagues.

Goals

A job description need not be limited to explaining the current situation, or work that is currently expected; it may also set out goals for what might be achieved in future.

Limitations

Prescriptive job descriptions may be seen as a hindrance in certain circumstances:[2]

- Job descriptions may not be suitable for some senior managers as they should have the freedom to take the initiative and find fruitful new directions;
- Job descriptions may be too inflexible in a rapidly-changing organisation, for instance in an area subject to rapid technological change;
- Other changes in job content may lead to the job description being out of date;
- The process that an organisation uses to create job descriptions may not be optimal.

References

[1] Torrington & Hall. *Personnel Management: A New Approach*. Prentice Hall International. pp. 205. ISBN 0-13-658501-9.

[2] Ungerson, 1983

Job fair

A **job fair** is also referred commonly as a **career fair** or **career expo**. It is a fair or exposition for employers, recruiters and schools to meet with prospective job seekers. Expos usually include company or organization tables or booths where resumes can be collected and business cards can be exchanged. In the college setting, job fairs are commonly used for entry level job recruiting. Often sponsored by career centers, job fairs provide a convenient location for students to meet employers and perform first interviews. Online job fairs offer the same convenience online.

Job fairs are good places to meet many company representatives from corporations of all industries and sizes during a short period of time. Every job fair has a set of similar, basic elements or processes that require your attention. Job fair networking can be generally described as the process of interacting with, obtaining contact details of, and getting to know corporate recruiters.

A career/job fair

Job fraud

Job fraud refers to fraudulent or deceptive activity or representation on the part of an employee or prospective employee toward an employer. It is not to be confused with *employment fraud*, where an employer scams job seekers or fails to pay wages for work performed. There are several types of job frauds that employees or potential employees commit against employers. While some may be illegal under jurisdictional laws, others do not violate law but may be held by the employer against the employee or applicant.

Résumé fraud

Résumé fraud or *application fraud* refers to any act that involves providing fictitious, exaggerated, or otherwise misleading information on a job application or résumé in hopes of persuading a potential employer to hire an applicant for a job they may be unqualified for or less qualified than other applicants.[1] Depending on the nature of the offense, the type of job, and the jurisdiction where it occurs, such an act may or may not be a violation of criminal law. In any case, knowingly providing inaccurate information to an employer or potential employer, if discovered by the employer, is almost always grounds for immediate dismissal from the job or else denial of that job.

Trends

A number of annual reports, including BDO Hayward's Fraudtrack 4[2] and CIFAS,[3] the UK's fraud prevention service, has shown a rising level of major discrepancies and embellishments on curriculum vitae (CV) over previous years.

Business fraud cost UK businesses £1.4 billion in 2005.[4]

Recent research released by Powerchex has confirmed this trend. Having measured 3,876 applicants to the UK financial sector over the past year, they found that 17% of potential candidates embellished their CV, and found a trend between a graduates choice of university and their likelihood to lie on their CV.[5] [6]

Effects

Almost half (48%) of organizations with fewer than 100 staff experienced problems with vetted employees.

39% of UK organizations have experienced a situation where their vetting procedures have allowed an employee to be hired who was later found to have lied or misrepresented themselves in their application.[7]

Demographics

Younger, more junior people are more likely to have a discrepancy on their CV. Someone in a junior administrative position is 23% more likely to have a discrepancy on their CV than in a managerial role. An applicant aged under 20 is 26% more likely to have a discrepancy than a 51-60 year old.[8]

Women are marginally more likely to have a discrepancy on their CV: 13% of applications submitted by women have a discrepancy compared to only 10% of those for men.[9]

Graduates have marginally fewer discrepancies: 13% of their CVs contain a discrepancy compared to 17% of non-graduates.

Types

- **Fake credentials:** Some applicants provide false documents that are required or strongly recommended to obtain a job. These may include a degree, license, certificate, or other evidence of necessary training or experience that is expected of applicants.
- **Fictitious former employer(s):** The applicant provides a list of previous employers that they never worked for, and that may have never existed. They may include fake reference letters that vouch for the applicant. Absence of contact information may seem plausible if the applicant claims they are no longer in business, living far away, or otherwise out of touch.
- **Fake "live" employer(s):** The applicant arranges with a relative or friend to pose as a former boss. The applicant provides a phone number or other contact information, and when the prospective employer contacts this person, they receive a glowing report about the applicant. Since the widespread use of email, this form of communication may also be used by the applicants themselves to pose as former employers.
- **Exaggerated claims:** The applicant lists a genuine former employer, but leaves out information with the intent to mislead. The employer may have a prestigious reputation, but the applicant's position may have been menial.

Examples of résumé fraud

- The applicant gets past the "20 second resume cull" by making bold statements such as "1st place Academic Standing: Session 1, 2005 and Session 2, 2004", and only later qualifying it as being "First place academic standing amongst Information Systems and Management (ISM) scholars"
- The applicant makes exaggerated or untrue claims, such as having won prizes or other recognition. Similarly, an applicant may claim a scholarship was "for the most outstanding student entering the University" when in fact multiple scholarships were awarded.
- The applicant refers to unknown, unverifiable awards, such as a "Silver Medallion for Academic Excellence.", or an "Emeritus Professor Prize".
- The applicant selectively reports, and uses unofficial terms: rather than reporting an overall grade of credit, reports a "Distinction Average in Finance; High Credit Average in Law."; similarly, a "Distinction average on all core information systems subjects" helps circumvent unflattering grades in information systems electives and other courses. Both "High Credit" and "core information systems subjects" are not defined by the university, and thus are used with impunity.

Fraud by active employees

There are other forms of fraudulent methods that employees of jobs use to obtain payroll money from an employer without actually performing any work. These involve blatant cheating, and do not include those who perform at a sub par level.

These include:

- **Swiping in absence:** The employee arrives at the job site at the beginning of the shift and swipes in to report to work. The employee promptly departs, and the absence goes unnoticed in a large workplace. At the end of the shift, the employee returns to swipe out.
- **False signature:** The employee who is supposed to obtain a supervisor's signature to verify having worked signs the form themselves after skipping work. Such acts are usually possible with temp agencies, where contractors are sent to a variety of job sites, and are not known personally by those they would work with.
- **Training pay:** An applicant obtains a job that will include a fixed amount of paid training. Once the training is finished, the applicant promptly quits. The applicant's original purpose was to obtain pay for training, but not do any further work. Many employers who function this way combat this problem by withholding payment for training until a certain amount of work has been performed.

Depending on the nature of the offense, these violations may be grounds for criminal prosecution for civil damages.

References

[1] "Combat Resume Fraud" (http://web.archive.org/web/20070302165400/http://www.inquestscreening.com/ preemployment_background_Screeening_Combat_Resume_Fraud.asp). Inquest Pre Employment Screening. Archived from the original (http://www.inquestscreening.com/preemployment_background_Screeening_Combat_Resume_Fraud.asp) on 2007-03-02. . Retrieved 2007-07-26.
[2] *Fraudtrack 4* (http://www.bdo.co.uk/fraudtrack)
[3] CIFAS - The Enemy Within (http://www.cifas.org.uk/default.asp?edit_id=658-57)
[4] BDO Fraudtrack 4 (http://www.bdo.co.uk/fraudtrack)
[5] Powerchex Annual Survey 2008 (http://www.powerchex.co.uk/documents/The Powerchex Annual Survey 2008.pdf)
[6] A Degree of Creativity on CVs (http://www.ft.com/cms/s/0/f5112740-56bb-11dd-8686-000077b07658.html)
[7] Powerchex Annual Pre-employment Survey (http://www.powerchex.co.uk/documents/Business Europe - newsfeed.htm)
[8] dofonline (http://dofonline.co.uk/personnel/personnel-2007/drop-in-financial-job-applicant-frauds01807.html)
[9] OnRec (http://www.onrec.com/content2/newsimages/SurveyPowerchex.pdf)

Further reading

- McConnell, Charles R. (2004-09-28). "Watching Out for Resume Fraud" (http://www.nfib.com/object/IO_18008.html). National Federation of Independent Business. Retrieved 2007-07-26.

Job interview

A **job interview** is a process in which a potential employee is evaluated by an employer for prospective employment in their company, organization, or firm. During this process, the employer hopes to determine whether or not the applicant is suitable for the job.

Role

A job interview typically precedes the hiring decision, and is used to evaluate the candidate. The interview is usually preceded by the evaluation of submitted résumés from interested candidates, then selecting a small number of candidates for interviews. Potential job interview opportunities also include networking events and career fairs. The job interview is considered one of the most useful tools for evaluating potential employees.[1] It also demands significant resources from the employer, yet has been demonstrated to be notoriously unreliable in identifying the optimal person for the job.[1] An interview also allows the candidate to assess the corporate culture and demands of the job.

Multiple rounds of job interviews may be used where there are many candidates or the job is particularly challenging or desirable. Earlier rounds may involve fewer staff from the employers and will typically be much shorter and less in-depth. A common initial interview form is the phone interview, a job interview conducted over the telephone. This is especially common when the candidates do not live near the employer and has the advantage of keeping costs low for both sides.

Once all candidates have been interviewed, the employer typically selects the most desirable candidate and begins the negotiation of a job offer.

Interview Constructs

In light of its popularity, a stream of research has attempted to identify the constructs (ideas or concepts) that are measured during the interview to understand why interviews might help us pick the right people for the job. Several reviews of the research on interview constructs revealed that the interview captures a wide variety of applicant attributes.[2] [3] [4] These constructs can be classified into three categories: job-relevant interview content (constructs interview questions are designed to assess), interviewee performance (applicant behaviors unrelated to the applicant characteristics the interview questions are designed to assess but nevertheless influence interviewer evaluations of interviewee responses), and potentially job-irrelevant interviewer biases (personal and demographic characteristics of applicants that may influence interviewer evaluations of interviewee responses in an illegal, discriminatory way).

Job-relevant interview content

Interview questions are generally designed to tap applicant attributes that are specifically relevant to the job for which the person is applying. The job-relevant applicant attributes the questions purportedly assess are thought to be necessary for one to successfully perform on the job. The job-relevant constructs that have been assessed in the interview can be classified into three categories: general traits, experiential factors, and core job elements. The first category refers to relatively stable applicant traits. The second category refers to job knowledge that the applicant has acquired over time. The third category refers to the knowledge, skills, and abilities associated with the job.

General Traits:

- Mental ability: Applicants' capacity to learn and process information[3]

- Personality: Conscientiousness, agreeableness, emotional stability, extroversion, openness to new experiences[2] [3] [4]

- Interest, goals, and values: Applicant motives, goals, and person-organization fit[3]

Experiential Factors:

- Experience: Job-relevant knowledge derived from prior experience[3] [4]
- Education: Job-relevant knowledge derived from prior education
- Training: Job-relevant knowledge derived from prior training

Core Job Elements:

- Declarative knowledge: Applicants' learned knowledge[4]
- Procedural skills and abilities: Applicants' ability to complete the tasks required to do the job[5]
- Motivation: Applicants' willingness to exert the effort required to do the job[6]

Interviewee Performance

Interviewer evaluations of applicant responses also tend to be colored by how an applicant behaves in the interview. These behaviors may not be directly related to the constructs the interview questions were designed to assess, but can be related to aspects of the job for which they are applying. Applicants without realizing it may engage in a number of behaviors that influence ratings of their performance. The applicant may have acquired these behaviors during training or from previous interview experience. These interviewee performance constructs can also be classified into three categories: social effectiveness skills, interpersonal presentation, and personal/contextual factors.

Social Effectiveness Skills:

- Impression management: Applicants' attempt to make sure the interviewer forms a positive impression of them[7] [8]

- Social skills: Applicants' ability to adapt his/her behavior according to the demands of the situation to positively influence the interviewer[9]
- Self-monitoring: Applicants' regulation of behaviors to control the image presented to the interviewer[10]
- Relational control: Applicants' attempt to control the flow of the conversation[11]

Interpersonal Presentation:

- Verbal expression: Pitch, rate, pauses[12]
- Nonverbal behavior: Gaze, smile, hand movement, body orientation[13]

Personal/Contextual Factors:

- Interview training: Coaching, mock interviews with feedback[14]
- Interview experience: Number of prior interviews[15]
- Interview self-efficacy: Applicants' perceived ability to do well in the interview[16]
- Interview motivation: Applicants' motivation to succeed in an interview[17]

Job-irrelevant interviewer biases

The following are personal and demographic characteristics that can potentially influence interviewer evaluations of interviewee responses. These factors are typically not relevant to whether the individual can do the job (that is, not related to job performance), thus, their influence on interview ratings should be minimized or excluded. In fact, there are laws in many countries that prohibit consideration of many of these protected classes of people when making selection decisions. Using structured interviews with multiple interviewers coupled with training may help reduce the effect of the following characteristics on interview ratings.[18] The list of job-irrelevant interviewer biases is presented below.

- Attractiveness: Applicant physical attractiveness can influence interviewer's evaluation of one's interview performance[13]

- Race: Whites tend to score higher than Blacks and Hispanics;[19] racial similarity between interviewer and applicant, on the other hand, has not been found to influence interview ratings[18] [20]
- Gender: Females tend to receive slightly higher interview scores than their male counterparts;[2] gender similarity does not seem to influence interview ratings[18]
- Similarities in background and attitudes: Interviewers perceived interpersonal attraction was found to influence interview ratings[21]
- Culture: Applicants with an ethnic name and a foreign accent were viewed less favorably than applicants with just an ethnic name and no accent or an applicant with a traditional name with or without an accent[22]

The extent to which ratings of interviewee performance reflect certain constructs varies widely depending on the level of structure of the interview, the kind of questions asked, interviewer or applicant biases, applicant professional dress or nonverbal behavior, and a host of other factors. For example, some research suggests that applicant's cognitive ability, education, training, and work experiences may be better captured in unstructured interviews, whereas applicant's job knowledge, organizational fit, interpersonal skills, and applied knowledge may be better captured in a structured interview.[3]

Further, interviews are typically designed to assess a number of constructs. Given the social nature of the interview, applicant responses to interview questions and interviewer evaluations of those responses are sometimes influenced by constructs beyond those the questions were intended to assess, making it extremely difficult to tease out the specific constructs measured during the interview.[23] Reducing the number of constructs the interview is intended to assess may help mitigate this issue. Moreover, of practical importance is whether the interview is a better measure of some constructs in comparison to paper and pencil tests of the same constructs. Indeed, certain constructs (mental ability and skills, experience) may be better measured with paper and pencil tests than during the interview, whereas personality-related constructs seem to be better measured during the interview in comparison to paper and pencil tests of the same personality constructs.[24] In sum, the following is recommended: Interviews should be developed to assess the job relevant constructs identified in the job analysis.[25] [26]

Process

A typical job interview has a single candidate meeting with between one and three persons representing the employer; the potential supervisor of the employee is usually involved in the interview process. A larger *interview panel* will often have a specialized human resources worker. While the meeting can be over in as little as 15 minutes, job interviews usually last less than two hours.

The bulk of the job interview will entail the interviewers asking the candidate questions about his or her job history, personality, work style and other factors relevant to the job. For instance, a common interview question is "What are your strengths and weaknesses?" The candidate will usually be given a chance to ask any questions at the end of the interview. These questions are strongly encouraged since they allow the interviewee to acquire more information about the job and the company, but they can also demonstrate the candidate's strong interest in them.

Candidates for lower paid and lower skilled positions tend to have much simpler job interviews than do candidates for more senior positions. For instance, a lawyer's job interview will be much more demanding than that of a retail cashier. Most job interviews are formal; the larger the firm, the more formal and structured the interview will tend to be. Candidates generally dress slightly better than they would for work, with a suit (called an interview suit) being appropriate for a white-collar job interview.

Additionally, some professions have specific types of job interviews; for performing artists, this is an audition in which the emphasis is placed on the performance ability of the candidate.

In many companies, *assessment days* are increasingly being used, particularly for graduate positions, which may include analysis tasks, group activities, presentation exercises, and psychometric testing.

In recent years it has become increasingly common for employers to request job applicants who are successfully shortlisted to deliver one or more presentations at their interview. The purpose of the presentation in this setting may be to *either* demonstrate candidates' skills and abilities in presenting, or to highlight their knowledge of a given subject likely to relate closely to the job role for which they have applied. It is common for the applicant to be notified of the request for them to deliver a presentation along with their invitation to attend the interview. Usually applicants are only provided with a title for the presentation and a time limit which the presentation should not exceed.

A bad hiring decision nowadays can be immensely expensive for an organization—cost of the hire, training costs, severance pay, loss of productivity, impact on morale, cost of re-hiring, etc. (Gallup international places the cost of a bad hire as being 3.2 times the individual's salary). Studies indicate that 40% of new executives fail in their first 18 months in a new job.[27] This has led to organizations investing in onboarding for their new employees to reduce these failure rates.

Process Model

One way to think about the interview process is as three separate, albeit related, phases: (1) the preinterview phase which occurs before the interviewer and candidate meet, (2) the interview phase where the interview is conducted, and (3) the postinterview phase where the interviewer forms judgments of candidate qualifications and makes final decisions.[28] Although separate, these three phases are related. That is, impressions interviewers form early on may affect how they view the person in a later phase. For instance, consider the first time you met someone you had heard about (maybe from a mutual friend). If the mutual friend had mentioned where this new person is from, what they are like, or what they do in their spare time, this may influence how you act towards them compared to a stranger you had never heard about. If you heard the person was not friendly or nice, perhaps you may choose not to even talk to them. Such a similar situation can occur during the process of an interview. Following is a model depicting these phases, as well as a brief discussion of each stage.

Preinterview Phase: The preinterview phase encompasses the information available to the interviewer beforehand (e.g., resumes, test scores, social networking site information) and the perceptions interviewers form about applicants from this information prior to the actual face-to-face interaction between the two individuals. In this phase, interviewers are likely to already have ideas about the characteristics that would make a person ideal or qualified for the position.[29] Interviewers also have information about the applicant usually in the form of a resume, test scores, or prior contacts with the applicant.[28] Interviewers then often integrate information that they have on an applicant with their ideas about the ideal employee to form a preinterview evaluation of the candidate. In this way, interviewers typically have an impression of you even before the actual face-to-face interview interaction. Nowadays with recent technological advancements, we must be aware that interviewers have an even larger amount of information available on some candidates. For example, interviewers can obtain information from search engines (e.g. Google, Bing, Yahoo), blogs, and even social networks (e.g. Linkedin, Facebook, Twitter). While some of this information may be job-related, some of it may not be. Despite the relevance of the information, any information interviewers obtain about the applicant before the interview is likely to influence their preinterview impression of the candidate. And, why is all this important? It is important because what interviewers think about you before they meet you, can have an effect on how they might treat you in the interview and what they remember about you.[28] [30] Furthermore, researchers have found that what interviewers think about the applicant before the interview (preinterview phase) is related to how they evaluate the candidate after the interview, despite how the candidate may have performed during the interview.[31]

Interview Phase: The interview phase entails the actual conduct of the interview, the interaction between the interviewer and the applicant. Initial interviewer impressions about the applicant before the interview may influence the amount of time an interviewer spends in the interview with the applicant, the interviewer's behavior and questioning of the applicant,[32] and the interviewer's postinterview evaluations.[31] Preinterview impressions also can affect what the interviewer notices about the interviewee, recalls from the interview, and how an interviewer interprets what the applicant says and does in the interview.[30] As interviews are typically conducted face-to-face, over the phone, or through video conferencing[33] (e.g. Skype), they are a social interaction between at least two individuals. Thus, the behavior of the interviewer during the interview likely "leaks" information to the interviewee. That is, you can sometimes tell during the interview whether the interviewer thinks positively or negatively about you.[28] Knowing this information can actually affect how the applicant behaves, resulting in a self-fulfilling prophecy effect.[32] [34] For example, interviewees who feel the interviewer does not think they are qualified may be more anxious and feel they need to prove they are qualified. Such anxiety may hamper how well they actually perform and present themselves during the interview, fulfilling the original thoughts of the interviewer. Alternatively, interviewees who perceive an interviewer believes they are qualified for the job may feel more at ease and comfortable during the exchange, and consequently actually perform better in the interview. It should be noted again, that because of the dynamic nature of the interview, the interaction between the behaviors and thoughts of both parties is a continuous process whereby information is processed and informs subsequent behavior, thoughts, and evaluations.

Postinterview Phase: After the interview is conducted, the interviewer must form an evaluation of the interviewee's qualifications for the position. The interviewer most likely takes into consideration all the information, even from the preinterview phase, and integrates it to form a postinterview evaluation of the applicant. In the final stage of the interview process, the interviewer uses his/her evaluation of the candidate (i.e., in the form of interview ratings or judgment) to make a final decision. Sometimes other selection tools (e.g., work samples, cognitive ability tests, personality tests) are used in combination with the interview to make final hiring decisions; however, interviews remain the most commonly used selection device in North America.[35]

For interviewees: Although the description of the interview process above focuses on the perspective of the interviewer, job applicants also gather information on the job and/or organization and form impressions prior to the interview.[29] The interview is a two-way exchange and applicants are also making decisions about whether the company is a good fit for them. Essentially, the process model illustrates that the interview is not an isolated interaction, but rather a complex process that begins with two parties forming judgments and gathering information, and ends with a final interviewer decision.

Types of Questions

History of Interview Questions

In interviews that are considered "structured interviews," there are typically two types of questions interviewers ask applicants: situational questions [36] and behavioral questions (also known as patterned behavioral description interviews).[37] Both types of questions are based on "critical incidents" that are required to perform the job [38] but they differ in their focus (see below for descriptions). Critical incidents are relevant tasks that are required for the job and can be collected through interviews or surveys with current employees, managers, or subject matter experts [39] [40] One of the first critical incidents techniques ever used in the United States Army asked combat veterans to report specific incidents of effective or ineffective behavior of a leader. The question posed to veterans was "Describe the officer's actions. What did he do?" Their responses were compiled to create a factual definition or "critical requirements" of what an effective combat leader is.[38]

Previous meta-analyses have found mixed results for which type of question will best predict future job performance of an applicant. For example, some studies have shown that situational type questions have better predictability for job performance in interviews,[41] [42] [43] while, other researchers have found that behavioral type questions are better at predicting future job performance of applicants.[44] In actual interview settings it is not likely that the sole use of just one type of interview question (situational or behavioral) is asked. A range of questions can add variety for both the interviewer and applicant.[40] In addition, the use of high-quality questions, whether behavioral or situational based, is essential to make sure that candidates provide meaningful responses that lead to insight into their capability to perform on the job.[45]

Behavioral Questions

Behavioral (experience-based or patterned behavioral) interviews are past-oriented in that they ask respondents to relate what they did in past jobs or life situations that are relevant to the particular job relevant knowledge, skills, and abilities required for success[46] [47] The idea is that past behavior is the best predictor of future performance in similar situations. By asking questions about how job applicants have handled situations in the past that are similar to those they will face on the job, employers can gauge how they might perform in future situations.[48]

Behavioral Interview Question Examples:.

- Describe a situation in which you were able to use persuasion to successfully convince someone to see things your way.
- Give me an example of a time when you set a goal and were able to meet or achieve it.
- Tell me about a time when you had to use your presentation skills to influence someone's opinion.
- Give me an example of a time when you had to conform to a policy with which you did not agree.

One way individuals can prepare for behavioral type questions is to practice the STAR method. The STAR method is a structured manner of responding to a behavioral-based interview question by discussing the specific situation, task, action, and result of the situation you are describing.

Situation: Describe the situation that you were in or the task that you needed to accomplish. This should describe specifics rather than general descriptions of past behavior.

Task: What goal were you working toward?

Action: Describe the actions you took to address the situation with detail and focus on yourself. What specific steps did you take and what was your contribution?

Result: Describe the outcome of your actions. What happened? How did the event end? What did you accomplish? What did you learn? Make sure your answer contains multiple positive results.

Situational Interview Questions

Situational interview questions[36] ask job applicants to imagine a set of circumstances and then indicate how they would respond in that situation; hence, the questions are future oriented. One advantage of situational questions is that all interviewees respond to the same hypothetical situation rather than describe experiences unique to them from their past. Another advantage is that situational questions allow respondents who have had no direct job experience relevant to a particular question to provide a hypothetical response.[48] Two core aspects of the SI are the development of situational dilemmas that employees encounter on the job, and a scoring guide to evaluate responses to each dilemma.[49]

Situational Examples

- You are managing a work group and notice that one of your employees has become angry and hostile in recent weeks, to the point of disrupting the entire group. What would you do? [45]
- You are in a meeting. Your manager blames you for not doing well on a task, in front of all your peers and managers from other divisions. You believe that your manager is wrong in his critique, and that he might have come to this conclusion hastily without knowing all the information. You feel you are being treated unfairly in front of your peers. You feel that your reputation may be affected by this critique. What would you do in this situation?.[50]
- A general request has been issued by the Dean for someone to serve on a new joint government/industry/university committee on business education. The objective of the committee is to design the budgeting allocation for the Faculty for the next fiscal year. It is well known that you have the necessary skill and

expertise to improve the chances that the Faculty will receive budget increases for future operations. You have been told that it will require 2–3 days per month of your time for the next 9 months. Your tenure review is one year away. Although you think you have a good publication record, you have no guarantee of tenure at this point. You are concerned because you have already fallen behind on an important research project that you are pursuing with a colleague at another university. What, if anything, would you do?[49]

- You are in charge of truck drivers in Toronto. Your colleague is in charge of truck drivers in Montreal. Both of you report to the same person. Your salary and bonus are affected 100% by your costs. Your colleague is in desperate need of one of your trucks. If you say no, your costs will remain low and your group will probably win the Golden Flyer award for the quarter. If you say yes, the Montreal group will probably win this prestigious award because they will make a significant profit for the company. Your boss is preaching costs, costs, costs, as well as co-operation with one's peers. Your boss has no control over accounting who are the score keepers. Your boss is highly competitive; he or she rewards winners. You are just as competitive; you are a real winner! What would you do in this situation?[49]

Other types of questions

Other possible types of questions that may be asked in an interview include: background questions, job experience questions, and puzzle type questions. A brief explanation of each follows.

- Background questions include a focus on work experience, education, and other qualifications.[51] For instance, an interviewer may ask "What experience have you had with direct sales phone calls?"
- Job experience questions may ask candidates to describe or demonstrate job knowledge. These are typically highly specific questions.[52] For example, one question may be "What steps would you take to conduct a manager training session on safety?"
- The puzzle interview was popularized by Microsoft in the 1990s, and is now used in other organizations. The most common types of questions either ask the applicant to solve puzzles or brainteasers (e.g., "Why are manhole covers round?") or to solve unusual problems (e.g., "How would you weigh an airplane without a scale?").[53]

Illegal Questions

Current EEOC guidelines state "the information obtained and requested through the pre-employment process should be limited to those essential for determining if a person is qualified for the job; whereas, information regarding race, sex, national origin, age, and religion are irrelevant in such determinations" (EEOC website, 2011). In general, any questions, which may indicate the applicant's race, sex, national origin, disability status, age, religion, color or ancestry, should be avoided. Despite the legal implications, interviewers have been found to request information from job applicants regarding their membership in a protected group. For example, a business magazine sampling of small business respondents indicated most of those employers would ask at least one of following five illegal interview questions: Have you ever filed a workers' compensation claim? Do you have any physical problems or injuries? How many days were you sick last year? Are you currently taking any medications? Have you ever been treated for drug abuse?[54] Other interviewees report being asked questions concerning their age, marital status, and language abilities,[55] [56] and organizations report that they frequently ask questions about arrest record and convictions, age, and handicaps.[57] All of these questions could put the company and interviewer at legal risk. For more information about illegal questions please visit the EEOC.gov website.

Case

Further information: Case interview

A case interview is an interview form used mostly by management consulting firms and investment banks in which the job applicant is given a question, situation, problem or challenge and asked to resolve the situation. The case problem is often a business situation or a business case that the interviewer has worked on in real life.

Panel

Another type of job interview found throughout the professional and academic ranks is the *panel interview*. In this type of interview the candidate is interviewed by a group of panelists representing the various stakeholders in the hiring process. Within this format there are several approaches to conducting the interview. Example formats include;

- Presentation format - The candidate is given a generic topic and asked to make a presentation to the panel. Often used in academic or sales-related interviews.
- Role format - Each panelist is tasked with asking questions related to a specific role of the position. For example one panelist may ask technical questions, another may ask management questions, another may ask customer service related questions etc.
- Skeet shoot format - The candidate is given questions from a series of panelists in rapid succession to test his or her ability to handle stress filled situations.

The benefits of the panel approach to interviewing include: time savings over serial interviewing, more focused interviews as there is often less time spend building rapport with small talk, and "apples to apples" comparison because each stake holder/interviewer/panelist gets to hear the answers to the same questions.[58]

Stress

Stress interviews are still in common use. One type of stress interview is where the employer uses a succession of interviewers (one at a time or *en masse*) whose mission is to intimidate the candidate and keep him/her off-balance. The ostensible purpose of this interview: to find out how the candidate handles stress. Stress interviews might involve testing an applicant's behavior in a busy environment. Questions about handling work overload, dealing with multiple projects, and handling conflict are typical.[59]

Another type of stress interview may involve only a single interviewer who behaves in an uninterested or hostile manner. For example, the interviewer may not make eye contact, may roll his eyes or sigh at the candidate's answers, interrupt, turn his back, take phone calls during the interview, or ask questions in a demeaning or challenging style. The goal is to assess how the interviewee handles pressure or to purposely evoke emotional responses. This technique was also used in research protocols studying stress and type A (coronary-prone) behavior because it would evoke hostility and even changes in blood pressure and heart rate in study subjects. The key to success for the candidate is to de-personalize the process. The interviewer is acting a role, deliberately and calculatedly trying to "rattle the cage". Once the candidate realizes that there is nothing personal behind the interviewer's approach, it is easier to handle the questions with aplomb.

Example stress interview questions:

- Sticky situation: "If you caught a colleague cheating on his expenses, what would you do?"
- Putting you on the spot: "How do you feel this interview is going?"
- Popping the balloon: (deep sigh) "Well, if that's the best answer you can give ... " (shakes head) "Okay, what about this one ...?"
- Oddball question: "What would you change about the design of the hockey stick?"
- Doubting your veracity: "I don't feel like we're getting to the heart of the matter here. Start again - tell me what *really* makes you tick."

Candidates may also be asked to deliver a presentation as part of the selection process. The "Platform Test" method involves having the candidate make a presentation to both the selection panel and other candidates for the same job. This is obviously highly stressful and is therefore useful as a predictor of how the candidate will perform under similar circumstances on the job. Selection processes in academic, training, airline, legal and teaching circles frequently involve presentations of this sort.

Technical

Further information: Microsoft Interview

This kind of interview focuses on problem solving and creativity. The questions aim at your problem-solving skills and likely show your ability and creativity. Sometimes these interviews will be on a computer module with multiple-choice questions.

Telephone

Telephone interviews take place if a recruiter wishes to reduce the number of prospective candidates before deciding on a shortlist for face-to-face interviews. They also take place if a job applicant is a significant distance away from the premises of the hiring company, such as abroad or in another state or province.

Interviewee Strategies and Behaviors

Nonverbal Behaviors

It may not only be what you say in an interview that matters, but also how you say it (e.g., how fast you speak) and how you behave during the interview (e.g., hand gestures, eye contact). In other words, although applicants' responses to interview questions influence interview ratings,[60] their nonverbal behaviors may also affect interviewer judgments.[61] Nonverbal behaviors can be divided into two main categories: vocal cues (e.g., articulation, pitch, fluency, frequency of pauses, speed, etc.) and visual cues (e.g., smiling, eye contact, body orientation and lean, hand movement, posture, etc.).[62] Oftentimes physical attractiveness is included as part of nonverbal behavior as well.[62] There is some debate about how large a role nonverbal behaviors may play in the interview. Some researchers maintain that nonverbal behaviors affect interview ratings a great deal,[60] while others have found that they have a relatively small impact on interview outcomes, especially when considered with applicant qualifications presented in résumés.[63] The relationship between nonverbal behavior and interview outcomes is also stronger in structured interviews than unstructured,[64] and stronger when interviewees' answers are of high quality.[63]

Applicants' nonverbal behaviors may influence interview ratings through the inferences interviewers make about the applicant based on their behavior. For instance, applicants who engage in positive nonverbal behaviors such as smiling and leaning forward are perceived as more likable, trustworthy, credible,[62] warmer, successful, qualified, motivated, competent,[65] and socially skilled.[66] These applicants are also predicted to be better accepted and more satisfied with the organization if hired.[65]

Applicants' verbal responses and their nonverbal behavior may convey some of the same information about the applicant.[61] However, despite any shared information between content and nonverbal behavior, it is clear that nonverbal behaviors do predict interview ratings to an extent beyond the content of what was said, and thus it is essential that applicants and interviewers alike are aware of their impact. You may want to be careful of what you may be communicating through the nonverbal behaviors you display.

Physical Attractiveness

To hire the best applicants for the job, interviewers form judgments, sometimes using applicants' physical attractiveness. That is, physical attractiveness is usually not necessarily related to how well one can do the job, yet has been found to influence interviewer evaluations and judgments about how suitable an applicant is for the job. Once individuals are categorized as attractive or unattractive, interviewers may have expectations about physically attractive and physically unattractive individuals and then judge applicants based on how well they fit those expectations.[67] As a result, it typically turns out that interviewers will judge attractive individuals more favorably on job-related factors than they judge unattractive individuals. People generally agree on who is and who is not attractive and attractive individuals are judged and treated more positively than unattractive individuals.[68] For example, people who think another is physically attractive tend to have positive initial impressions of that person (even before formally meeting them), perceive the person to be smart, socially competent, and have good social skills and general mental health.[67]

Within the business domain, physically attractive individuals have been shown to have an advantage over unattractive individuals in numerous ways, that include, but are not limited to, perceived job qualifications, hiring recommendations, predicted job success, and compensation levels.[67] As noted by several researchers, attractiveness may not be the most influential determinant of personnel decisions, but may be a deciding factor when applicants possess similar levels of qualifications.[67] In addition, attractiveness does not provide an advantage if the applicants in the pool are of high quality, but it does provide an advantage in increased hiring rates and more positive job-related outcomes for attractive individuals when applicant quality is low and average.[69]

Just as physical attractiveness is a visual cue, vocal attractiveness is an auditory cue and can lead to differing interviewer evaluations in the interview as well. Vocal attractiveness, defined as an appealing mix of speech rate, loudness, pitch, and variability, has been found to be favorably related to interview ratings and job performance.[70] [71] In addition, the personality traits of agreeableness and conscientiousness predict performance more strongly for people with more attractive voices compared to those with less attractive voices.[70]

As important as it is to understand how physical attractiveness can influence the judgments, behaviors, and final decisions of interviewers, it is equally important to find ways to decrease potential bias in the job interview. Conducting an interview with elements of structure is a one possible way to decrease bias.[72]

Coaching

An abundance of information is available to instruct interviewees on strategies for improving their performance in a job interview. Information used by interviewees comes from a variety of sources ranging from popular how-to books to formal coaching programs, sometimes even provided by the hiring organization. Within the more formal coaching programs, there are two general types of coaching. One type of coaching is designed to teach interviewees how to perform better in the interview by focusing on how to behave and present oneself. This type of coaching is focused on improving aspects of the interview that are not necessarily related to the specific elements of performing the job tasks. This type of coaching could include how to dress, how to display nonverbal behaviors (head nods, smiling, eye contact), verbal cues (how fast to speak, speech volume, articulation, pitch), and impression management tactics. Another type of coaching is designed to focus interviewees on the content specifically relevant to describing one's qualifications for the job, in order to help improve their answers to interview questions. This coaching, therefore, focuses on improving the interviewee's understanding of the skills, abilities, and traits the interviewer is attempting to assess, and responding with relevant experience that demonstrates these skills.[73] For example, this type of coaching might teach an interviewee to use the STAR approach for answering behavioral interview questions. An example coaching program might include several sections focusing on various aspects of the interview. It could include a section designed to introduce interviewees to the interview process, and explain how this process works (e.g., administration of interview, interview day logistics, different types of interviews, advantages of structured interviews). It could also include a section designed to provide feedback to help the interviewee to improve their performance in the interview, as well as a section involving practice answering example interview questions. An additional section providing general interview tips about how to behave and present oneself could also be included.[74]

It is useful to consider coaching in the context of the competing goals of the interviewer and interviewee. The interviewee's goal is typically to perform well (i.e. obtain high interview ratings), in order to get hired. On the other hand, the interviewer's goal is to obtain job-relevant information, in order to determine whether the applicant has the skills, abilities, and traits believed by the organization to be indicators of successful job performance.[73] Research has shown that how well an applicant does in the interview can be enhanced with coaching.[73] [75] [76] [77] The effectiveness of coaching is due, in part, to increasing the interviewee's knowledge, which in turn results in better interview performance. Interviewee knowledge refers to knowledge about the interview, such as the types of questions that will be asked, and the content that the interviewer is attempting to assess.[78] Research has also shown that coaching can increase the likelihood that interviewers using a structured interview will accurately choose those individuals who will ultimately be most successful on the job (i.e., increase reliability and validity of the structured interview).[73] Additionally, research has shown that interviewees tend to have positive reactions to coaching, which is often an underlying goal of an interview.[74] Based on research thus far, the effects of coaching tend to be positive for both interviewees and interviewers.

Faking

Interviewers should be aware that applicants can intentionally distort their responses or fake during the interview and such applicant faking has the potential to influence interview outcomes if present. Two concepts that relate to faking include social desirability (the tendency for people to present themselves in a favorable light [79]), and impression management (conscious or unconscious attempts to influence one's image during interactions [80]). Faking in the employment interview, then, can be defined as "deceptive impression management or the conscious distortion of answers to the interview questions in order to obtain a better score on the interview and/or otherwise create favorable perceptions".[81] Thus, faking in the employment interview is intentional, deceptive, and aimed at improving perceptions of performance.

Faking in the employment interview can be broken down into four elements.[81] The first involves the interviewee portraying him or herself as an ideal job candidate by exaggerating true skills, tailoring answers to better fit the job, and/or creating the impression that personal beliefs, values, and attitudes are similar to those of the organization.

The second aspect of faking is inventing or completely fabricating one's image by piecing distinct work experiences together to create better answers, inventing untrue experiences or skills, and portraying others' experiences or accomplishments as ones' own.

Thirdly, faking might also be aimed at protecting the applicant's image. This can be accomplished through omitting certain negative experiences, concealing negatively perceived aspects of the applicant's background, and by separating oneself from negative experiences.

The fourth and final component of faking involves ingratiating oneself to the interviewer by conforming personal opinions to align with those of the organization, as well as insincerely praising or complimenting the interviewer or organization.

Of all of the various faking behaviors listed, ingratiation tactics were found to be the most prevalent in the employment interview, while flat out making up answers or claiming others' experiences as one's own is the least common.[81] However, fabricating true skills appears to be at least somewhat prevalent in employment interviews. One study found that over 80% of participants lied about job-related skills in the interview,[82] presumably to compensate for a lack of job-required skills/traits and further their chances for employment.

Most importantly, faking behaviors have been shown to affect outcomes of employment interviews. For example, the probability of getting another interview or job offer increases when interviewees make up answers.[81]

Different interview characteristics also seem to impact the likelihood of faking. Faking behavior is less prevalent, for instance, in past behavioral interviews than in situational interviews, although follow-up questions increased faking behaviors in both types of interviews. Therefore, if practitioners are interested in decreasing faking behaviors among job candidates in employment interview settings, they should utilize structured, past behavioral interviews and avoid the use of probes or follow-up questions.[81]

Validity and predictive power

There is extant data[83] which puts into question the value of job interviews as a tool for selecting employees. Where the aim of a job interview is ostensibly to choose a candidate who will perform well in the job role, other methods of selection provide greater predictive power and often lower costs. Furthermore, given the unstructured approach of most interviews they often have almost no useful predictive power of employee success.

While unstructured interviews are commonly used, structured interviews have yielded much better results and are considered a best practice.[84] Interview structure is defined as "the reduction in procedural variance across applicants, which can translate into the degree of discretion that an interviewer is allowed in conducting the interview".[85] Structure in an interview can be compared to a typical paper and pencil test: we would not think it was fair if every test taker was given different questions and a different number of questions on an exam, or if their answers were each graded differently. Yet this is exactly what occurs in an unstructured interview; thus, a structured interview attempts to standardize this popular selection tool. While there is debate surrounding what is meant specifically by a structured interview,[86] there are typically two broad categories of standardization: 1) content structure, and 2) evaluation structure.[87] Content structure includes elements that refer to the actual content of the interview:

- Base questions on attributes that are representative of the job, as indicated by a job analysis
- Ask the same questions of all interviewees
- Limit prompting, or follow up questions, that interviewers may ask
- Ask better questions, such as behavioral description questions
- Have a longer interview
- Control ancillary information available to the interviewees, such as resumes
- Don't allow questions from applicants during interview

Evaluation structure includes aspects that refer to the actual rating of the interviewee:

- Rate each answer rather than making an overall evaluation at the end of the interview
- Use anchored rating scales (for an example, see BARS)
- Have the interviewer take detailed notes
- Have more than one interviewer view each applicant (i.e. have panel interviews)
- Have the same interviewers rate each applicant
- Don't allow any discussion about the applicants between interviewers
- Train the interviewers
- Use statistical procedures to create an overall interview score

It is important to note that structure should be thought of as a continuum; that is, the degree of structure present in an interview can vary along these various elements listed above.[86]

In terms of reliability, meta-analytic results provided evidence that interviews can have acceptable levels of interrater reliability, or consistent ratings across interviewers interrater reliability (i.e. .75 or above), when a structured panel interview is used.[88] In terms of criterion-related validity, or how well the interview predicts later job performance criterion validity, meta-analytic results have shown that when compared to unstructured interviews, structured interviews have higher validities, with values ranging from .20-.57 (on a scale from 0 to 1), with validity coefficients increasing with higher degrees of structure.[85] [89] [90] That is, as the degree of structure in an interview increases, the more likely interviewers can successfully predict how well the person will do on the job, especially when compared to unstructured interviews. In fact, one structured interview that included a) a predetermined set of questions that interviewers were able to choose from, and b) interviewer scoring of applicant answers after each individual question using previously created benchmark answers, showed validity levels comparable to cognitive ability tests (traditionally one of the best predictors of job performance) for entry level jobs.[85]

Honesty and integrity are attributes that can be very hard to determine using a formal job interview process: the competitive environment of the job interview may in fact promote dishonesty. Some experts on job interviews express a degree of cynicism towards the process.

Legal Issues

In many countries laws are put into place to prevent organizations from engaging in discriminatory practices against protected classes when selecting individuals for jobs.[91] In the United States, it is unlawful for private employers with 15 or more employees along with state and local government employers to discriminate against applicants based on the following: race, color, sex (including pregnancy), national origin, age (40 or over), disability, or genetic information (note: additional classes may be protected depending on state or local law). More specifically, an employer cannot legally "fail or refuse to hire or to discharge any individual, or otherwise discriminate against any individual with respect to his compensation, terms, conditions, or privilege of employment" or "to limit, segregate, or classify his employees or applicants for employment in any way which would deprive or tend to deprive any individual of employment opportunities or otherwise adversely affect his status as an employee."[92] [93]

The Civil Rights Acts of 1964 and 1991 (Title VII) were passed into law to prevent the discrimination of individuals due to race, color, religion, sex, or national origin. The Pregnancy Discrimination Act was added as an amendment and protects women if they are pregnant or have a pregnancy-related condition.[94]

The Age Discrimination in Employment Act of 1967 prohibits discriminatory practice directed against individuals who are 40 years of age and older. Although some states (e.g. New York) do have laws preventing the discrimination of individuals younger than 40, no federal law exists.[95]

The Americans with Disabilities Act of 1990 protects qualified individuals who currently have or in the past have had a physical or mental disability (current users of illegal drugs are not covered under this Act). A person may be disabled if he or she has a disability that substantially limits a major life activity, has a history of a disability, is regarded by others as being disabled, or has a physical or mental impairment that is not transitory (lasting or expected to last six months or less) and minor. In order to be covered under this Act, the individual must be qualified for the job. A qualified individual is "an individual with a disability who, with or without reasonable accommodation, can perform the essential functions of the employment position that such individual holds or desires."[96] Unless the disability poses an "undue hardship," reasonable accommodations must be made by the organization. "In general, an accommodation is any change in the work environment or in the way things are customarily done that enables an individual with a disability to enjoy equal employment opportunities."[97] Examples of reasonable accommodations are changing the workspace of an individual in a wheelchair to make it more wheelchair accessible, modifying work schedules, and/or modifying equipment.[98] Employees are responsible for asking for accommodations to be made by their employer.[94]

The most recent law to be passed is Title II of the Genetic Information Nondiscrimination Act of 2008. In essence, this law prohibits the discrimination of employees or applicants due to an individual's genetic information and family medical history information.

In rare circumstances, it is lawful for employers to base hiring decisions on protected class information if it is considered a Bona Fide Occupational Qualification, that is, if it is a "qualification reasonably necessary to the normal operation of the particular business." For example, a movie studio may base a hiring decision on age if the actor they are hiring will play a youthful character in a film.[99]

Given these laws, organizations are limited in the types of questions they legally are allowed to ask applicants in a job interview. Asking these questions may cause discrimination against protected classes, unless the information is considered a Bona Fide Occupational Qualification. For example, in the majority of situations it is illegal to ask the following questions in an interview as a condition of employment:

- What is your date of birth?[100]
- Have you ever been arrested for a crime?[101]
- Do you have any future plans for marriage and children?[102]
- What are your spiritual beliefs?[103]
- How many days were you sick last year? Have you ever been treated for mental health problems?[104]
- What prescription drugs are you currently taking?[105]

Applicants with Disabilities

Applicants with disabilities may be concerned with the effect that their disability has on both interview and employment outcomes. Research has concentrated on four key issues: how interviewers rate applicants with disabilities, the reactions of applicants with disabilities to the interview, the effects of disclosing a disability during the interview, and the perceptions different kinds of applicant disabilities may have on interviewer ratings.

The job interview is a tool used to measure constructs or overall characteristics that are relevant for the job. Oftentimes, applicants will receive a score based on their performance during the interview. Research has found different findings based on interviewers' perceptions of the disability. For example, some research has found a leniency effect (i.e., applicants with disabilities receive higher ratings than equally qualified non-disabled applicants) in ratings of applicants with disabilities [106] [107] Other research, however, has found there is a disconnect between the interview score and the hiring recommendation for applicants with disabilities. That is, even though applicants with disabilities may have received a high interview score, they are still not recommended for employment.[108] [109] The difference between ratings and hiring could be detrimental to a company because they may be missing an opportunity to hire a qualified applicant.

A second issue in interview research deals with the applicants' with disabilities reactions to the interview and applicant perceptions of the interviewers. Applicants with disabilities and able-bodied applicants report similar feelings of anxiety towards an interview.[110] Applicants with disabilities often report that interviewers react nervously and insecurely, which leads such applicants to experience anxiety and tension themselves. The interview is felt to be the part of the selection process where covert discrimination against applicants with disabilities can occur.[110] Many applicants with disabilities feel they cannot disclose (i.e., inform potential employer of disability) or discuss their disability because they want to demonstrate their abilities. If the disability is visible, then disclosure will inevitably occur when the applicant meets the interviewer, so the applicant can decide if they want to discuss their disability. If an applicant has a non-visible disability, however, then that applicant has more of a choice in disclosing and discussing. In addition, applicants who were aware that the recruiting employer already had employed people with disabilities felt they had a more positive interview experience.[110] Applicants should consider if they are comfortable with talking about and answering questions about their disability before deciding how to approach the interview.

Research has also demonstrated that different types of disabilities have different effects on interview outcomes. Disabilities with a negative stigma and that are perceived as resulting from the actions of the person (e.g., HIV-Positive, substance abuse) result in lower interview scores than disabilities for which the causes are perceived to be out of the individual's control (e.g., physical birth defect).[109] A physical disability often results in higher interviewer ratings than psychological (e.g., mental illness) or sensory conditions (e.g., Tourette Syndrome).[107] [111] In addition, there are differences between the effects of disclosing disabilities that are visible (e.g., wheelchair bound) and non-visible (e.g., Epilepsy) during the interview. When applicants had a non-visible disability and disclosed their disability early in the interview they were not rated more negatively than applicants who did not disclose. In fact, they were liked more than the applicants who did not disclose their disability and were presumed not disabled.[112] Interviewers tend to be impressed by the honesty of the disclosure.[111] Strong caution needs to be taken with applying results from studies about specific disabilities, as these results may not apply to other types of disabilities. Not all disabilities are the same and more research is needed to find whether these results are relevant for other types of disabilities.

Some practical implications for job interviews for applicants with disabilities include research findings that show there are no differences in interviewer responses to a brief, shorter discussion or a detailed, longer discussion about the disability during the interview.[111] Applicants, however, should note that when a non-visible disability is disclosed near the end of the interview, applicants were rated more negatively than early disclosing and non-disclosing applicants. Therefore it is possible that interviewers feel individuals who delay disclosure may do so out of shame or embarrassment. In addition, if the disability is disclosed after being hired, employers may feel deceived by the new hire and reactions could be less positive than would have been in the interview.[113] If applicants want to disclose their disability during the interview, research shows that a disclosure and/or discussion earlier in the interview approach may afford them some positive interview effects.[114] The positive effects, however, are preceded by the interviewers perception of the applicants' psychological well-being. That is, when the interviewer perceives the applicant is psychologically well and/or comfortable with his or her disability, there can be positive interviewer effects. In contrast, if the interviewer perceives the applicant as uncomfortable or anxious discussing the disability, this may either fail to garner positive effect or result in more negative interview ratings for the candidate. Caution must again be taken when applying these research findings to other types of disabilities not investigated in the studies discussed above. There are many factors that can influence the interview of an applicant with a disability, such as whether the disability is physical or psychological, visible or non-visible, or whether the applicant is perceived as responsible for the disability or not. Therefore applicants should make their own conclusions about how to proceed in the interview after comparing their situations with those examined in the research discussed here.

Other Applicant Discrimination: Weight and Pregnancy

Employers are using social networking sites like Facebook and LinkedIn to obtain additional information about job applicants.[115] [116] [117] While these sites may be useful to verify resume information, profiles with pictures also may reveal much more information about the applicant, including issues pertaining to applicant weight and pregnancy.[118]

Job applicants who are underweight (to the point of emaciation), overweight or obese may face discrimination in the interview.[119] [120] The negative treatment of overweight and obese individuals may stem from the beliefs that weight is controllable and those who fail to control their weight are lazy, unmotivated, and lack self-discipline.[121] Alternatively, underweight individuals may be negatively treated partly due to their lack of physical attractiveness.[120] These characteristics, lazy, unmotivated, lacks self-discipline, physically unattractive are not ideal for a future employee.[122] Underweight, overweight and obese applicants are not protected from discrimination by any current United States laws.[119] However, some individuals who are morbidly obese and whose obesity is due to a physiological disorder may be protected against discrimination under the Americans with Disabilities Act.[123] In short, men and women should be aware that their weight, whether underweight, overweight or obese, could hinder their chances of getting hired.

Pregnant job applicants are a group that may face discrimination because of their "disability". Discrimination against pregnant applicants is illegal under the Pregnancy Discrimination Act of 1978, which views pregnancy as a temporary disability and requires employers to treat pregnant applicants the same as all other applicants.[124] Yet, discrimination against pregnant applicants continues both in the United States and internationally.[124] [125] Research shows that pregnant applicants compared to non-pregnant applicants are less likely to be recommended for hire.[126] [127] Interviewers appear concerned that pregnant applicants are more likely than non-pregnant applicants to miss work and even quit.[127] Organizations who wish to reduce potential discrimination against pregnant applicants should consider implementing structured interviews, although some theoretical work suggests interviewers may still show biases even in these types of interviews.[126] [128]

References

[1] State.ne.us (http://www.hhs.state.ne.us/hur/Job/ImpInterview.htm)

[2] Huffcutt, A. I. (2011). An empirical review of the employment interview construct literature. International Journal of Selection and Assessment, 19(1), 62-81.

[3] Huffcutt, A. I., Conway, J. M., Roth, P. L., & Stone, N. J. (2001). Identification and meta-analytic assessment of psychological constructs measured in employment interviews. Journal of Applied Psychcology, 86, 897-913.

[4] Salgado, J. F., & Moscoso, S. (2002). Comprehensive meta-analysis of the construct validity of the employment interview. European Journal of Work and Organizational Psychology, 11, 299-324.

[5] Morgeson, R. P., Reider, M. H., & Campion, M. A. (2005). Selecting individual in team settings: The importance of social skills, personality characteristics, and teamwork knowledge. Personnel Psychology, 58, 583-611.

[6] Campbell, J. P., McCloy, R. A., Oppler, S. H., & Sager, C. E. (1993). A theory of performance. In N. Schmitt & W. C. Borman (Eds.), Personnel selection in organizations (pp. 35-70). San Francisco: Jossey-Bass.

[7] Schlenker, B. R. 1980. Impression management: The self-concept, social identity, and interpersonal relations. Monterey, CA: Brooks/Cole.

[8] Kacmar, K. M., Delery, J. E., & Ferris, G. R. 1992. Differential effectiveness of applicant impression management tactics on employment interview decisions. Journal of Applied Social Psychology, 22, 1250-1272.

[9] Ferris, G. R., Witt, L. A., & Hochwarter, W. A. (2001). Interaction of social skill and general mental ability on job performance and salary. Journal of Applied Psychology, 86, 1075-1082.

[10] Snyder, M. (1974). Self-monitoring of expressive behavior. Journal of Personality and Social Psychology, 30, 526-537.

[11] Tuller, W. L. (1989). Relational control in the employment interview. Journal of Applied Psychology, 74, 971-977.

[12] DeGroot, T., & Motowidlo, S. J. (1999). Why visual and vocal interview cues can affect interviewers' judgments and predict job performance. Journal of Applied Psychology, 84, 986-993.

[13] Burnett, J. R., & Motowidlo, S. J. (1998). Relations between different sources of information in the structured interview. Personnel Psychology, 51, 963-983.

[14] Maurer, T. J., Solamon, J. M., & Lippstreu, M. (2008). How does coaching interviewees affect the validity of a structured interview? Journal of Organizational Behavior, 29, 355-371.

[15] Levashina, J., & Campion, M. A. (2007). Measuring faking in the employment interview: Development and validation of an interview faking behavior scale. Journal of Applied Psychology, 92, 1638-1656.

[16] Tay, C., Ang, S., & Van Dyne, L. (2006). Personality, biographical characteristics, and job interview success: A longitudinal study of the mediating effects of interviewing self-efficacy and the moderating effects of internal locus of causality. Journal of Applied Psychology, 91, 446-454.

[17] Becton, J. B., Field, H. S., Giles, W. F., & Jones-Farmer, A. (2008). Racial differences in promotion candidate performance and reactions to selection procedures: a field study in a diverse top-management context. Journal of Organizational Behavior, 29, 265–285.

[18] McCarthy, J. M., Van Iddekinge, C. H., & Campion, M. A. (2010). Are highly structured job interviews resistant to demographic similarity effects? Personnel Psychology, 63, 325-359.

[19] Huffcutt, A. I., & Roth, P. L. (1998). Racial group differences in employment interview evaluations. Journal of Applied Psychology, 83, 179-189.

[20] McFarland, L. A., Ryan, A. M., Sacco, J. M., & Kriska, S. D. (2004). Examination of structured interview ratings across time: The effects of applicant race, rater race, and panel composition. Journal of Management, 30, 435-452.

[21] Wade, K. J., & Kinicki, A. J. (1997). Subjective applicant qualifications and interpersonal attraction as mediators within a process model of interview selection decisions. Journal of Vocational Behavior, 50, 23-40.

[22] Purkiss, S. L. S., Perrewé, P. L., Gillespie, T. L., Mayes, B. T., & Ferris, G. R. (2006). Implicit sources of bias in employment interview judgments and decisions. Organizational Behavior and Human Decision Processes, 101, 152-167.

[23] Roth, P. L., Van Iddekinge, C. H., Huffcutt, A. I., Eidson, C E. Jr., & Schmit, M. J. (2005). Personality saturation in structured interviews. International Journal of Selection and Assessment, 13, 261-273.

[24] Dipboye, R. L., Macan, T., & Shahani-Denning, C. (in press). The selection interview from the interviewer and applicant perspectives: Can't have one without the other. The Oxford Handbook of Personnel Assessment and Selection.

[25] Van Iddekinge, C. H., Raymark, P. H., & Roth, P. L. (2005). Assessing personality with a structured employment interview: Construct-related validity and susceptibility to response inflation. Journal of Applied Psychology, 90(3), 536-552.

[26] Klehe, U. C., & Latham, G. P. (2005). The predictive and incremental validity of the situational and patterned behavior description interviews for teamplaying behavior. International journal of selection and assessment, 13(2), 108-115.

[27] Internal study by executive search firm, Heidrick & Struggles as cited by their CEO, Kevin Kelly in the Financial Times, March 30, 2009

[28] Dipboye, R. L., & Macan, T. (1988). A process view of the selection-recruitment interview. In R.Schuler, V.Huber, & S.Youngblood (Eds.), Readings in personnel and human resource management (pp. 217–232). New York: West.

[29] Dipboye, R. L., Macan, T., & Shahani-Denning, C. (in press). The selection interview from the interviewer and applicant perspectives: Can't have one without the other. Oxford Handbook of I/O Psychology.

[30] Macan, T., & Dipboye, R. L. (1988). The effect of interviewer's initial impressions on information gathering. Organizational Behavior and Human Decision Processes, 42(3), 364-387.

[31] Macan, T., & Dipboye, R. L. (1990). The relationship of interviewers' preinterview impressions to selection and recruitment outcomes. Personnel Psychology, 43(4), 745-768. Retrieved from EBSCOhost.

[32] Dipboye, R. L. (1982). Self-Fulfilling Prophecies in the Selection-Recruitment Interview. Academy of Management Review, 7(4), 579-586. Retrieved from EBSCOhost.

[33] Straus, S. G., Milesb, J. A., & Levesquec, L. L. (2001). The effects of videoconference, telephone, and face-to-face media on interviewer and applicant judgments in employment interviews. Journal of Management, 27(3), 363-381.

[34] Word, C. O., Zanna, M. P., & Cooper, J. (1974). The nonverbal mediation of self-fulfilling prophecies in interracial interaction. Journal of Experimental Social Psychology, 10, 109–120.

[35] Ryan, A., McFarland, L., Baron, H., & Page, R. (1999). An international look at selection practices: Nation and culture as explanations for variability in practice. Personnel Psychology, 52(2), 359-391.

[36] Latham, G. P., Saari, L. M., Pursell, E. D., & Campion, M. A. (1980). The situational interview. Journal of Applied Psychology, 65, 422-427.

[37] Janz, T. (1982). Initial comparison of patterned behavior description interviews versus unstructured interviews. Journal of Applied Psychology, 67, 577-580.

[38] Flanagan, J. C. (1954). The critical incident technique. Psychological Bulletin, 51, 327-359.

[39] Weekley J. A., & Gier, J. A. (1987). Reliability and validity of the situational interview for a sales position. Journal of Applied Psychology, 72. 484-487.

[40] Campion, M. A., Palmer, D. K., & Campion J. E. (1997). A review of structure in the selection interview. Personnel Psychology, 50, 655–702.

[41] Conway, J. M., & Huffcutt, A. I. (1997). Effects of reliability, constructs, and job on structured interview validity. Paper presented at the 12th Annual Conference of the Society for Industrial and Organizational Psychology, St Louis, MO.

[42] McDaniel, M. A., Whetzel, D. L., Schmidt, F. L., & Maurer, S. (1994). The validity of employment interviews: A comprehensive review and meta-analysis. Journal of Applied Psychology, 79, 599–616.

[43] Searcy, C. A., Woods, P. N., Gatewood, R., & Lance, C. (1993). The validity of structured interviews: A meta-analytical search for moderators. Paper presented at the Annual Conference of the Society for Industrial and Organizational Psychology , San Francisco, CA.

[44] Taylor, P. J. & Small, B. (2002). Asking applicants what they would do versus what they did do: A meta-analytic comparison of situational and past behavior employment interview questions. Journal of Occupational and Organizational Psychology, 75, 277-294.

[45] Huffcutt, A. I. (2010). From science to practice: Seven principles for conducting employment interviews. Applied H.R.M., 12, 121-136.

[46] Janz, T. (1982). "Initial comparison of patterned behavior description interviews versus unstructured interviews.". *Journal of Applied Psychology* **67**: 577–580.

[47] Motowidlo, S.J.; Carter, G.W., Dunnette, M.D., Tippins, N., Werner, S., Burnett, J.R., & Vaughn, M.J.. "Studies of the structured behavioral interview.". *Journal of Applied Psychology* **77**: 571–587.

[48] Pulakos, E. D., & Schmitt, N. (1995). Experienced-based and situational interview questions: Studies of validity. Personnel Psychology, 48, 289–308.

[49] Latham, G. P. & Sue-Chan, C. (1999). A meta-analysis of the situational interview: An enumerative review of reasons for its validity. Canadian Psychology, 40, 56-67.

[50] Banki, S. and Latham, G. P. (2010), The Criterion-Related Validities and Perceived Fairness of the Situational Interview and the Situational Judgment Test in an Iranian Organisation. Applied Psychology, 59: 124–142. doi: 10.1111/j.1464-0597.2009.00418.

[51] Roth P. L., Campion J. E. (1992). An analysis of the predictive power of the panel interview and pre-employment tests. Journal of Occupational and Organizational Psychology, 65, 51–60.

[52] Arvey, R. D., Howard, E. M., Gould, R. & Burch, P. (1987). Interview validity for selecting sales clerks. Personnel Psychology, 40, 1-12.

[53] Honer, J., Wright, C. W., & Sablynski, C. J. (2007). Puzzle interviews: What are they and what do the measure? Applied H.R.M. Research, 11, 79-96. Retrieved from http://www.xavier.edu/appliedhrmresearch/

[54] McShulskis, E. (1997). Small businesses: Be aware of illegal interview questions. HR Magazine, 42, 22–23.

[55] Bennington, L. (2001). Age discrimination: Converging evidence from four Australian studies. Employee Responsibilities and Rights Journal, 13, 125–134.

[56] Saunders, D. M., Leck, J. D., & Vitins, G. (1990). Pre-employment enquiries in Canada: The law and society are dancing to different music. Paper presented at the Annual Meeting of the Law and Society Association, Berkeley, California.

[57] Keyton, J., & Springston, J. K. (1992). Response alternatives to discriminatory inquiries. In D. M. Saunders (Eds.), New approaches to employee management: Fairness in employee selection (pp. 159–184). Greenwich, CT: JAI.

[58] Panel Interviews staffing-and-recruiting-essentials.com (http://www.staffing-and-recruiting-essentials.com/Panel-Interview.html)

[59] Money-zine.com (http://www.money-zine.com/Definitions/Career-Dictionary/Stress-Interview/)

[60] Hollandsworth, Jr., J. G. (1979). Relative contributions of verbal, articulate, and nonverbal communication to employment decisions in the job interview setting. Personnel Psychology, 32, 359-367.

[61] Burnett, J. R., Motowildo, S. J. (1998). Relations between different sources of information in the structured selection interview. Personnel Psychology, 51, 963-983.

[62] DeGroot, T., & Motowildo, S. J. (1999). Why visual and vocal cues can affect interviewers' judgments and predict job performance. Journal of Applied Psychology, 84(6), 986-993.

[63] Rasmussen, Jr., K. G. (1984) Nonverbal behavior, verbal behavior, résumé credentials, and selection interview outcomes. Journal of Applied Psychology, 69(4), 551-556.

[64] Barrick, M. R., Shaffer, J. A., & DeGrassi, S. W. (2009). What you see may not be what you get: Relationship among self-presentation tactics and ratings of interview and job performance. Journal of Applied Psychology, 94(6), 1394-1411.

[65] Imada, A. S., & Hakel, M. D. (1977). Influence of nonverbal communication and rater proximity on impressions and decisions in simulated employment interviews. Journal of Applied Psychology, 62(3), 295-300.

[66] Gilfford, R., Ng, C. F., & Wilkinson, M. (1985). Nonverbal cues in the employment interview: Links between applicant qualities and interview judgments. Journal of Applied Psychology, 70(4), 729-736.

[67] Hosoda, M., Stone-Romero, E. F., & Coats, G. (2003). The effects of physical attractiveness on job-related outcomes: A meta-analysis of experimental studies. Personnel Psychology, 56(2), 431-462.

[68] Langlois, J. H., Kalakanis, L., Rubenstein, A. J., Larson, A., Hallam, M., & Smoot, M. (2000). Maxims or myths of beauty? A meta-analytic and theoretical review. Psychological Bulletin, 126(3), 390-423.

[69] Watkins, L. M., & Johnston, L. (2000). Screening job applicants: The impact of physical attractiveness and application quality. International Journal of Selection and Assessment, 8(2), 76-84.

[70] DeGroot, T., & Kluemper, D. (2007). Evidence of Predictive and Incremental Validity of Personality Factors, Vocal Attractiveness and the Situational Interview. International Journal of Selection and Assessment, 15(1), 30-39.

[71] DeGroot, T., & Motowidlo, S. J. (1999). Why visual and vocal interview cues can affect interviewers' judgments and predict job performance. Journal of Applied Psychology, 84(6), 986-993.

[72] Kutcher, E. J., & Bragger, J. (2004). Selection Interviews of Overweight Job Applicants: Can Structure Reduce the Bias?. Journal of Applied Social Psychology, 34(10), 1993-2022.

[73] Maurer, T., Solamon, J., & Lippstreu, M. (2008). How does coaching interviewees affect the validity of a structured interview? Journal of Occupational Behavior, 29, 355-371.

[74] Maurer, T. & Solamon, J. (2006). The science and practice of a structured employment interview coaching program. Personnel Psychology, 59, 431-454.

[75] Campion, M. & Campion, J. (1987). Evaluation of an interviewee skills training program in a natural field experiment. Personnel Psychology, 40, 675-691.

[76] Maurer, T., Solamon, J., Andrews, K., & Troxtel, D. (2001). Interviewee coaching, preparation strategies and response strategies in relation to performance in situational employment interviews: An extension of Maurer, Solamon & Troxtel (1998). Journal of Applied Psychology, 86, 709–717.

[77] Maurer, T., Solamon, J., & Troxtel, D. (1998). Relationship of coaching with performance in situational employment interviews. Journal of Applied Psychology, 83, 128–136.

[78] Tross, S. & Maurer, T. (2008). The effect of coaching interviewees on subsequent interview performance in structure esperience-based interviews. Journal of Occupational and Organizational Psychology, 81, 589-605.

[79] Edwards, A.L. (1957). The social desirability variable in personality assessment and research. Ft. Worth, TX: Dryden Press.

[80] Ellis, A.P.J., West, B.J., Ryan, A.M., & DeShon, R.P (2002). The use of impression management tactics in structured interviews: A function of question type? Journal of Applied Psychology, 87, 1200-1208.

[81] Levashina, J. & Campion, M.A. (2007). Measuring faking in the employment interview: Development and validation of an Interview Faking Behavior Scale. Journal of Applied Psychology, 92, 1638-1656.

[82] Weiss, B. & Feldman, R.S. (2006). Looking good and lying to do it: Deception as an impression management strategy in job interviews. Journal of Applied Social Psychology, 36, 1070–1086.

[83] Vcu.edu (http://www.people.vcu.edu/~mamcdani/Publications/McDaniel_Whetzel_Schmidt_Maurer (1994).pdf)

[84] Huffcutt, A. I. (2010). From science to practice: Seven principles for conducting employment interviews. Applied H.R.M. Research, 12, 121-136

[85] Huffcutt, A. I., & Arthur, W. Jr. (1994). Hunter & Hunter revisited: Interview validity for entry-level jobs. Journal of Applied Psychology, 79, 184-190

[86] Macan, T. (2009). The employment interview: A review of current studies and directions for future research. Human Resource Management Review, 19, 203-218

[87] Campion, M. A., Palmer, D. A., Campion, J. E. (1997). A review of structure in the selection interview. Personnel Psychology, 50, 655-702

[88] Conway, J. M., Jako, R. A., & Goodman, D. F. (1995). A meta-analysis of interrater and internal consistency reliability of selection interviews. Journal of Applied Psychology, 80, 565-579

[89] Wiesner, W. H., & Cronshaw, S. F. (1988). The moderating impact of interview format & degree of structure on interview validity. Journal of Occupational Psychology, 61, 275-290

[90] McDaniel, M. A., Whetzel, D. L., Schmidt, F. L., & Maurer, S. (1994). The validity of employment interviews: A comprehensive review and meta-analysis. Journal of Applied Psychology, 79, 599-617

[91] This is not meant to be a complete explanation of employment law or should it be construed as legal advice. This merely attempts to explain certain laws that are applicable to the employment interview. Please seek legal counsel before taking action based on the content of this information.

[92] Myors, B., Lievens, F., Schollaert, E., Van Hoye, G., Cronshaw, S.F., Mladinic, A., Rodriguez, V., Aguinis, H., Steiner, D.D., Rolland, F., Schuler, H., Frintrup, A., Nikolaou, I., Tomprou, M., Subramony, S., Ray, S.B., Tzafrir, S., Bamberger, P., Bertolino, M., Mariani, M., Fraccaroli, F., Sekiguchi, T., Onyura, B., Yand, H., Anderson, N., Evers, A., Chernyshenko, O., Englert, P., Kriek, H.J., Joubert, T., Salgado, J.F., Konig, C.J., Thommen, L.A., Chaung, A., Sinangil, H.K., Bayazit, M., Cook, M., Shen, W., & Sackett, P. (2008). International perspectives on the legal environment for selection. Industrial and Organizational Psychology: Perspectives on Science and Practice, 1, 206-246.

[93] Title VII of the Civil Rights Act of 1964; Equal employment Opportunity Commission (www.eeoc.gov)

[94] Equal Employment Opportunity Commission (www.eeoc.gov)

[95] New York State Human Rights Law (Executive Law, Article 15); (http://www.dhr.state.ny.us/doc/hrl.pdf)

[96] Americans with Disability Act; Equal Employment Opportunity Commission (www.eeoc.gov)

[97] Ibid.

[98] DeLeire, T. (2000). The wage and employment effects of the Americans with Disabilities Act. The Journal of Human Resources, 35(4), 693-715.

[99] Arvey, R. D., & Faley, R. H. (1988). Fairness in Selecting Employees. Reading, Massachusetts: Addison-Wesley Publishing Company.

[100] Saks, A. M., & McCarthy, J. M. (2006). Effects of discriminatory interview questions and gender on applicant reactions. Journal of Business and Psychology, 21(2). doi: 10.1007/s10869-006-9024-7

[101] Ibid.

[102] Ibid.

[103] US Equal Employment Opportunity Commission (www.eeoc.gov)

[104] Ibid.

[105] Ibid.

[106] Breecher, E., Bragger, J., & Kutcher, E. (2006). The structured interview: Reducing biases toward job applicants with physical disabilities. Employee Responsibilities and Rights Journal, 18, 155-170.

[107] Nordstrom, C. R., Huffaker, B. J., & Williams, K. B. (1998). When physical disabilities are not liabilities: The role of applicant and interviewer characteristics on employment interview outcomes. Journal of Applied Social Psychology, 28, 283-306

[108] Macan, T. H., & Hayes, T. L. (1995). Both sides of the employment interview interaction: Perceptions of interviewers and applicants with disabilities. Rehabilitation Psychology, 40, 261-278

[109] Miceli, N. S., Harvey, M., & Buckley, M. R. (2002). Potential discrimination in structured employment interviews. Employee Responsibilities and Rights Journal, 13, 15-38.

[110] Duckett, P. S. (2000). Disabling employment interviews: Warfare to work. Disability & Society, 15, 1019-1039.

[111] Dalgin, S. R., & Bellini, J. (2008). Invisible disability disclosure in an employment interview: Impact on employers' hiring decision and views of employability. Rehabilitation Counseling Bulletin, 52, 6-15.

[112] Roberts, L. L., & Macan, T. H. (2006). Disability disclosure effects on employment interview ratings of applicants with nonvisible disabilities. Rehabilitation Psychology, 51, 239-246. doi: 10.1037/0090-5550.51.3.239

[113] Stone, D. L., & Colella, A. (1996). A model of factors affecting the treatment of disabled individuals in organizations. Academy of Management Review, 21, 352–401.

[114] Hebl, M. R., & Skorinko, J. L. (2005). Acknowledging one's physical disability in the interview: Does "when" make a difference? Journal of Applied Social Psychology, 35, 2477-2492. doi: 10.1111/j.1559-1816.2005.tb02111.x

[115] Cross-Tab. (2010). Online reputation in a connected world. Retrieved from http://www.microsoft.com/privacy/dpd/research.aspx

[116] Jobvite, Inc., (2010). Jobvite: 2010 social recruiting survey results. Retrieved from http://recruiting.jobvite.com/resources/social-recruiting-survey.php

[117] Society for Human Resource Management. (2007). 2007 advances in e-recruiting: Leveraging the .jobs domain. Retrieved from http://www.goto.jobs/advances_erecruiting_07.pdf

[118] Grasz, J. (2009). Forty-five percent of employers use social networking sites to research job candidates, CareerBuilder survey finds: Career expert provides dos and don'ts for job seekers on social networking. Retrieved from http://oregonbusinessreport.com/2009/08/45-employers-use-facebook-twitter-to-screen-job-candidates/

[119] Roehling, M. V. (1999). Weight-based discrimination in employment: Psychological and legal aspects. Personnel Psychology, 52, 969-1016.

[120] Swami, V., Chan, F., Wong, V. Furnham, A., & Tovee, M. J. (2008). Weight-based discrimination in occupational hiring and helping behavior. Journal of Applied Social Psychology, 38(4), 968-981.

[121] Greenleaf, C., Starks, M., Gomez, L., Chambliss, H., & Martin, S. (2004). Weight-related words associated with figure silhouettes. Body Image, 1(4), 373-384.

[122] Bellizzi, J. A., & Hasty, R. W. (1998). Territory assignment decisions and supervising unethical selling behavior: The effects of obesity and gender as moderated by job-related factors. Journal of Personal Selling & Sales Management, 18(2), 35-49.

[123] King, E. B., Shapiro, J. R., Hebl, M. R., Singletary, S. L., & Turner, S. (2006). The stigma of obesity in customer service: A mechanism for remediation and the bottom-line consequences of interpersonal discrimination. Journal of Applied Psychology, 91(3), 579-593.

[124] U.S. Equal Employment Opportunity Commission. (2011). Pregnancy discrimination. Retrieved from http://www.eeoc.gov/laws/types/pregnancy.cfm

[125] Gatrell, C. (2011). Managing the maternal body: A comprehensive review and transdisciplinary analysis. International Journal of Management Reviews, 13(1), 97-112. doi: 10.1111/j.1468-2370.2010.00286.x

[126] Bragger, J. D., Kutcher, E., Morgan, J., & Firth, P. (2002). The effects of the structured interview on reducing bias against pregnant job applicants. Sex Roles, 46(7-8), 215-226. doi: 1023/A:1019967231059

[127] Cunningham, J., & Macan, T. (2007). Effects of applicant pregnancy on hiring decisions and interview ratings. Sex Roles, 57, 487-508.

[128] Macan, T., & Merritt, S. (in press). Actions speak too: Uncovering possible implicit and explicit discrimination in the employment interview process. In G.P. Hodgkinson & J.K. Ford (Eds.), International Review of Industrial and Organizational Psychology. New York, NY US: John Wiley & Sons Ltd.

External links

- The Interview Process (http://www1.ctdol.state.ct.us/jcc/viewarticle.asp?intArticle=9) by the Connecticut Department of Labor

Job wrapping

Job wrapping is a term used commonly to describe a process by which jobs can be captured from employer website and posted to the job boards that the employer wants to advertise them.

Corporate recruiters and HR professionals who send job listings to multiple Internet employment sites can sometimes delegate those chores to the employment sites themselves under an arrangement called "job wrapping". Job wrap ensures that employer job openings and updates get wrapped up regularly and posted on the job boards that they have designated.

The term "job wrapping" is synonymous with "spidering", "scraping", or "mirroring". Job wrapping is generally done by a third party vendor.

Labour hire

Labour hire is the term applied (especially in Australia) to provision of outsourced skilled and unskilled blue-collar workers hired for short- or long-term positions.

The workers, known as contractors, field employees, temps, on-hired employees or even just employees, are employed by the labour hire organisation. They are not employed by the company to whom they provide labour. This is an important distinction for the purposes of Occupational Healthy and Safety (OH&S) purposes, in particular who has legislative responsibility for ensuring a safe working environment. This has been tested in court (see below).

Development of labour hire

In Australia, SKILLED Group is credited as creating labour hire as a viable business service. Initially, such services provided short-term additional staff for a client's peak periods or other special needs. Since the early '90's however more and more companies have discarded their base employment workforce, or a substantial portion thereof, and utilised labour hire companies to provide their workforce.[1]

Pay and charge rates

An essential component of any labour hire organisation are the two fundamental concepts of pay and charge rates. The pay rate is the per-hour wage paid to the employees. The charge rate is the fee levied on the client to whom labour is provided. Although this sounds very basic, many factors must be considered when calculating these two items.

The following items have a bearing on the determination of pay rates:

- Industrial agreements
- Statuatory on-costs (at state and national levels)
- Worker's compensation levies
- Comparable pay rates for employees of the client

The following items have a bearing on the determination of charge rates:

- Personal protective equipment (PPE) supplied
- Payment terms
- Superannuation
- Payroll tax
- Casual loading
- Gross margin
- Preferred supplier agreements
- Competition

The gross margin is generally calculated as a percentage value of the pay rate. In certain circumstances, it may be calculated as a specific dollar markup.

A schedule of rates is typically quoted to the client which includes

- Charge rate for each hour of ordinary time
- Charge rate for each hour of overtime (typically time and a half, double time, double time and a half)
- Charge rate for applicable allowances which will be paid to the employee in various circumstances (most commonly meal allowance, but also crib allowance, travel allowance, laundry allowance, plus various industry-specific allowances - for example, an additional amount per hour for working with wet/dirty hanging birds in the poultry sector.)

The charge rates for physical hours of time (ordinary plus overtime) are typically quoted for the position at discrete classification increments, for example, level 1, level 2, etc.

Notable court cases

Most legal proceedings against labour hire companies fall into one of two broad categories. The first is unfair dismissal. There are few successful such cases because of the nature of the industry and because organisations are generally careful to emphasise that the work is casual and periodic and cannot be guaranteed. Many labour hire companies are careful to avoid terminology on their staffing systems that may imply an employee has been "terminated" because that can corrupt a defence against unfair dismissal, namely that the employee has not been terminated, there simply has just been no recent placement opportunities.

There is an argument that labour hire firms ought really to be calling their employees "contractors" which makes more explicit that such workers are providing subcontracted services.[2]

The second broad category is a major issue for labour hire companies, namely workplace safety.

It may have been considered in times past that the client of the labour hire company, i.e. the workplace where the labour is performed, were responsible for the safety of their site. However, Drake Personnel Ltd trading as Drake Industrial v WorkCover Authority (Insp. Ch'ng) (1999) 90 IR432 was a significant court case which established that because the worker is an employee of the labour hire company itself, a joint burden of safety is imposed upon the labour hire company.[3] [4]

In this case, the NSW Industrial Commissions full session judged

> A labour hire agency does not employ people to work for itself but to work for a client, it does not directly on a day to day basis supervise the tasks carried out by the employee and it is usually not in control of the workplace where the work is done. However, these circumstances do not obviate, or diminish, the obligation of the employer under the [employer's general duty]. Indeed ... an employer who sends its employees into another workplace over which they exercise limited control is, for that reason, under a particular positive obligation to ensure that those premises, or the work done, do not present a threat to the health, safety or welfare of those employees. Certainly, there is no basis to consider that such an employer has a lesser liability or obligation under [the employer's general duty].... A labour hire company cannot escape liability merely because the client to whom an employee is hired out is also under a duty to ensure that persons working at their workplace are not exposed to risks to their health and safety or because of some alleged implied obligation to inform the labour hire company of the work to be performed. In our view, a labour hire company is required by the OH&S Act to take positive steps to ensure that the premises to which its employees are sent to work do not present risks to health and safety This obligation would, in appropriate circumstances, require it to ensure that its employees are not instructed to, and do not, carry out work in a manner that is unsafe.

In Labour Co-operative Limited v WorkCover Authority of New South Wales (Inspector Robins) (2003) 121 IR 78 at 84-85 the Full Bench of the New South Wales Industrial Relations Commission upheld the trial judge's finding that it was reasonably practicable for the labour hire agency to have ensured against the risks to the worker's safety by "adopting a positive and pro-active approach with [the client] to require steps to be put in place to avoid the risks as a condition of it making available" the services of the worker. The labour hire agency had sufficient control to ensure the adequacy of instruction, training and supervision, and could refuse to supply its employees to the client "until 14 appropriate and sufficient measures to ensure safety were implemented."[5]

Since 1998 prosecutions of labour hire agencies and host firms have been taken regularly in most Australian jurisdictions, particularly in NSW and Victoria. In NSW, for example, the first prosecution of an agency and a host firm took place in 1997, and there have been half a dozen or so prosecutions of agencies and of host firms each year since 2002. In Victoria the first successful prosecution of an agency and of a host firm took place in 1999 (Extra staff and NCI Speciality Metals respectively), and since 2002 there appear to have been half a dozen prosecutions of agencies and of host firms annually. There have also been successful prosecutions against directors of labour hire companies for failing to prevent the agency from contravening its general duty to the worker.[6] [7]

References

[1] Don Moss. "Labour hire and the advent of Joint Employers" (http://www.apesma.asn.au/newsviews/professional_update/2003/jan_feb/joint_employers.htm). APESMA. . Retrieved 2007-04-13.

[2] Dwyer Durack Barristers and Solicitors. "Unfair dismissal" (http://aussielegal.aol.com.au/informationoutline.asp?nocache=1&SubTopicDetailsID=871). AussieLegal. . Retrieved 2007-04-13.

[3] Janet Chan. "OHS duties, training and job safety" (http://web.archive.org/web/20061024114016/http://www.ee-oz.com.au/resources/misc/2790.pdf). Workcover NSW. Archived from the original (http://www.ee-oz.com.au/resources/misc/2790.pdf) on 2006-10-24. . Retrieved 2007-04-13.

[4] Peter Rozen. "Safeguarding the student: School-to-work transition programs and Occupational Health and Safety Law" (http://www.ascc.gov.au/NR/rdonlyres/A6D66173-2996-4CBE-93D7-82922FFA0400/0/SAFEGUARDINGTHESTUDENTRozenReport2002.pdf). . Retrieved 2007-04-13.

[5] See also WorkCover Authority of New South Wales (Inspector Legge) v Coffey Engineering Pty Ltd (No 2) (2001) 110 IR 447.

[6] See for example Inspector Sharpin v Concrete Civil Pty Ltd and Inspector Sharpin v Daryl Smith [2004] NSWIRComm 173 and Workover Authority of New South Wales (Inspector Mansell) v Daly Smith Corporation (Aust) Pty Limited and Thomas Edwin Curtis Smith [2005] NSWIRComm 101.

[7] Richard Johnstone & Michael Quinlan. "The OHS regulatory challenges posed by agency workers: Evidence from Australia" (http://www.ohs.anu.edu.au/publications/pdf/RJ.labour hire paper.pdf). Australian National University. . Retrieved 2007-04-13.

Military recruitment

Military recruitment is the act of requesting people, usually male adults, to join a military voluntarily. Involuntary military recruitment is known as conscription. Many countries that have abolished conscription use military recruiters to persuade people to join, often at an early age. To facilitate this process, militaries have established recruiting commands. These units are solely responsible for increasing military enlistment.

Military recruitment can be considered part of military science if analysed as part of military history. Acquiring large amounts of forces in a relatively short period of time, especially voluntarily, as opposed to stable development, is a frequent phenomenon in history. One particular example is the regeneration of the military strength of the Communist Party of China from a depleted force of 8,000 following the Long March in 1934 into 2.8 million near the end of the Chinese Civil War 14 years later.

Recent cross-cultural studies suggest that, throughout the world, the same broad categories may be used to define recruitment appeals. They include war, economic motivation, education, family and friends, politics, and identity and psychosocial factors.[1]

French marines recruitement poster

Wartime recruitment strategies in the US

Further information: Recruitment in the United States Military and Conscription in the United States

Prior to the outbreak of World War I, military recruitment in the US was conducted primarily by individual states.[2] Upon entering the war, however, the federal government took on an increased role.

The increased emphasis on a national effort was reflected in World War I recruitment methods. Peter A. Padilla and Mary Riege Laner define six basic appeals to these recruitment campaigns: patriotism, job/career/education, adventure/challenge, social status, travel, and miscellaneous. Between 1915 and 1918, 42% of all army recruitment posters were themed primarily by patriotism.[2] And though other themes - such as adventure and greater social status - would play an increased role during World War II recruitment, appeals to serve one's country remained the dominant selling point.

Recruitment without conscription

After World War II, military recruitment shifted significantly. With no war calling men and women to duty, the United States refocused its recruitment efforts to present the military as a career option, and as a means of achieving a higher education. A majority -

United States Navy recruitment poster from 1918. Note the appeal to patriotism. (Digitally restored).

55% - of all recruitment posters would serve this end. And though peacetime would not last, factors such as the move to an all-volunteer military would ultimately keep career-oriented recruitment efforts in place.[3] The Defense Department turned to television syndication as a recruiting aid from 1957-1960 with a filmed show, *Country Style, USA*.

On February 20, 1970, the President's Commission on an All-Volunteer Armed Force unanimously agreed that the United States would be best served by an all-volunteer military. In supporting this recommendation, the committee noted that recruitment efforts would have to be intensified, as new enlistees would need to be *convinced* rather than *conscripted*. Much like the post-World War II era, these new campaigns put a stronger emphasis on job opportunity. As such, the committee recommended "improved basic compensation and conditions of service, proficiency pay, and accelerated promotions for the highly skilled to make military career opportunities more attractive." These new directives were to be combined with "an intensive recruiting effort." [4] Finalized in mid-1973, the recruitment of a "professional" military was met with success. In 1975 and 1976, military enlistments exceeded expectations, with over 365,000 men and women entering the military. Though this may, in part, have been the result of a lack of civilian jobs during the recession, it nevertheless stands to underline the ways in which recruiting efforts responded to the circumstances of the time.[5]

Indeed, recommendations made by the President's Commission continue to work in present-day recruitment efforts. Understanding the need for greater individual incentive, the US military has re-packaged the benefits of the GI Bill. Though originally intended as compensation for service, the bill is now seen as a recruiting tool. Today, the GI Bill is "no longer a reward for service rendered, but an inducement to serve and has become a significant part of recruiter's pitches." [6]

Controversy

For a description of controversies surrounding current US Military recruitment, refer to this page. It describes controversy over recruiters' honesty, potential exploitation of high-school students, military paying for education and providing job skills, and whether reformation is a better option than disassociation.

Military recruitment in the United Kingdom

Further information: Conscription in the United Kingdom and Recruitment in the British Army

During both world wars and a period after the second, military service was mandatory for at least some of the British population. At other times, techniques similar to those outlined above have been used. The most prominent concern over the years has been the minimum age for recruitment, which has been 16 for many years.[7] This has now been raised to 18 in relation to combat operations. In recent years, there have been various concerns over the techniques used in (especially) army recruitment in relation to the portrayal of such a career as an enjoyable adventure.[8] [9]

Military recruitment in India

From the times of the British Raj, recruitment in India has been voluntary. Using Martial Race theory, the British recruited heavily from selected communities for service in the colonial army.[10] The largest of the colonial military forces the British Indian Army of the British Raj until Indian independence, was a volunteer army, raised from the native population with British officers. The Indian Army served both as a security force in India itself and, particularly during the World Wars, in other theaters. About 1.3 million men served in the First World War. During World War II, the British Indian Army would become the largest volunteer army in history, rising to over 2.5 million men in August 1945.[11] It currently has around 1,414,000 troops.

Recruitment centres

A **recruitment centre** in the UK or **recruiting station** in the U.S. is a building used to recruit people into an organization, and is the most popularized method of military recruitment.

A British Military recruitment centre in Oxford

A United States Military recruiting station on Times Square, NYC

Recruitment posters

A **recruitment poster** is a poster used in advertisement to recruit people into an organization, and was a popularized method of military recruitment.

A Canadian WWI recruitment poster

A World War I recruitment poster featuring Lord Kitchener (British Minister of War)

J. M. Flagg's Uncle Sam recruited soldiers for World War I. Based on the Kitchener poster.

An Australian WWI recruitment poster

A 1944 Waffen SS recruitment poster. "You Too! Your comrades await in the French Division of the Waffen-SS"

"Why aren't you in the army?" Volunteer Army recruitment poster during the Russian Civil War featuring Anton Denikin.

"To Arms! To Arms!" Recuitment poster for Confederate States of America. Floyd County, Virginia, 1862.

References

[1] Brett, Rachel, and Irma Specht. Young Soldiers: Why They Choose to Fight. Boulder: Lynne Rienner Publishers, 2004. ISBN 1-58826-261-8

[2] Padilla, Peter A. and Mary Riege Laner. "Trends in Military Influences on Army Recruitment: 1915-1953." Sociological Inquiry, Vol. 71, No. 4. Fall 2001421-36. Austin: University of Texas Press. Page 423

[3] Padilla, Peter A. and Mary Riege Laner. "Trends in Military Influences on Army Recruitment: 1915-1953." Sociological Inquiry, Vol. 71, No. 4. Fall 2001421-36. Austin: University of Texas Press. Page 433

[4] The Report of the President's Commission on an All-Volunteer Armed Force. New York: The Macmillan Company, 1970. Page 18.

[5] Bliven, Bruce Jr. Volunteers, One and All. New York: Readers Digest Press, 1976. ISBN 0-88349-058-7

[6] White, John B. Lieutenant Commander, US Naval Reserve, Ph. D. "The GI Bill: Recruiting Bonus, Retention Onus." Military Review, July–August 2004.

[7] "Marching orders for teenage soldiers?" (http://news.bbc.co.uk/1/hi/uk/117504.stm). *BBC News*. June 22, 1998. . Retrieved May 12, 2010.

[8] "MoD denies 'war glamour' claim" (http://news.bbc.co.uk/1/hi/uk/7174431.stm). *BBC News*. January 7, 2008. . Retrieved May 12, 2010.

[9] "Teachers reject 'Army propaganda'" (http://news.bbc.co.uk/1/hi/education/7311917.stm). *BBC News*. March 25, 2008. . Retrieved May 12, 2010.

[10] http://www.expressindia.com/latest-news/compulsory-military-service-could-be-an-option-in-future/416902/

[11] "Commonwealth War Graves Commission Report on India 2007–2008" (http://www.cwgc.org/admin/files/cwgc_india.pdf). Commonwealth War Graves Commission. . Retrieved 2009-09-07.

External links

- United States Navy Recruiting Information (http://www.navy.com)
- United States Army Recruiting Information (http://www.goarmy.com)
- United States Marine Corps Recruiting Information (http://www.marines.com)
- United States Air Force Recruiting Information (http://www.airforce.com)
- United States Coast Guard Recruiting Information (http://www.gocoastguard.com)
- Indian Navy Recruiting Information (http://www.nausena-bharti.nic.in/New/Careers.htm)
- Indian Army Recruiting Information (http://joinindianarmy.nic.in/)
- Indian Air Force Recruiting Information (http://careerairforce.nic.in/)
- Indian Coast Guard Recruiting Information (http://indiancoastguard.nic.in/IndianCoastGuard/jobs/jobs.html)
- Pashto Linguists Recruiting / Arabic Native Speaking (http://www.allied-media.com/Services/native_linguist_recruiting_arabic_pashto.html)

For Further Reading

Manigart, Philippe. "Risks and Recruitment in Postmodern Armed Forces: The Case of Belgium." *Armed Forces & Society*, Jul 2005; vol. 31: pp. 559–582.

- http://afs.sagepub.com/cgi/content/abstract/31/4/559

Dandeker, Christopher and Alan Strachan. "Soldier Recruitment to the British Army: a Spatial and Social Methodology for Analysis and Monitoring." *Armed Forces & Society*, Jan 1993; vol. 19: pp. 279–290.

- http://afs.sagepub.com/cgi/content/abstract/19/2/279

Snyder, William P. "Officer Recruitment for the All-Volunteer Force: Trends and Prospects." *Armed Forces & Society*, Apr 1984; vol. 10: pp. 401–425.

- http://afs.sagepub.com/cgi/content/abstract/10/3/401

Griffith, James. "Institutional Motives for Serving in the U.S. Army National Guard: Implications for Recruitment, Retention, and Readiness." *Armed Forces & Society*, Jan 2008; vol. 34: pp. 230–258.

- http://afs.sagepub.com/cgi/content/abstract/34/2/230

Fitzgerald, John A. "Changing Patters of Officer Recruitment at the U.S. Naval Academy." *Armed Forces & Society*, Oct 1981; vol. 8: pp. 111–128.

- http://afs.sagepub.com/cgi/reprint/8/1/111

Eighmey, John. "Why Do Youth Enlist?: Identification of Underlying Themes." *Armed Forces & Society*, Jan 2006; vol. 32: pp. 307–328.

- http://afs.sagepub.com/cgi/content/abstract/32/2/307

Multiple mini interview

The **multiple mini interview** (MMI)[1] is an interview format that uses many short independent assessments, typically in a timed circuit, to obtain an aggregate score of each candidate's soft skills. In 2001, the Michael DeGroote School of Medicine at McMaster University began developing the MMI system, to address two widely recognized problems. First, it has been shown that traditional interview formats or simulations of educational situations do not accurately predict performance in medical school. Secondly, when a licensing or regulatory body reviews the performance of a physician subsequent to patient complaints, the most frequent issues of concern are those of the non-cognitive skills, such as interpersonal skills, professionalism and ethical/moral judgment.

Introduction

Interviews have been used widely for different purposes, including assessment and recruitment. Candidate assessment is normally deemed successful when the scores generated by the measuring tool predict for future outcomes of interest, such as job performance or job retention. Meta-analysis of the human resource literature has demonstrated low to moderate ability of interviews to predict for future job performance.[2] How well a candidate scores on one interview is only somewhat correlated with how well that candidate scores on the next interview. Marked shifts in scores are buffered when collecting many scores on the same candidate, with a greater buffering effect provided by multiple interviews than by multiple interviewers acting as a panel for one interview.[3] The score assigned by an interviewer in the first few minutes of an interview is rarely changed significantly over the course of the rest of the interview, an effect known as the halo effect.

Therefore, even very short interviews within an MMI format provide similar ability to differentiate reproducibly between candidates.[4] Ability to reproducibly differentiate between candidates, also known as overall test reliability, is markedly higher for the MMI than for other interview formats.[1] This has translated into higher predictive validity, correlating for future performance much more highly than standard interviews.[5] [6] [7] [8]

History

Aiming to enhance predictive correlations with future performance in medical school, post-graduate medical training, and future performance in practice, McMaster University began research and development of the MMI in 2001. The initial pilot was conducted on 18 graduate students volunteering as "medical school candidates". High overall test reliability (0.81) led to a larger study conducted in 2002 on real medical school candidates, many of whom volunteered after their standard interview to stay for the MMI. Overall test reliability remained high,[1] and subsequent follow-up through medical school and on to national licensure examination (Medical Council of Canada [9] Qualifying Examination Parts I and II) revealed the MMI to be the best predictor for subsequent clinical performance,[5] [7] professionalism,[6] and ability to communicate with patients and successfully obtain national licensure.[7] [8] Since its formal inception at the Michael G. DeGroote School of Medicine at McMaster University in 2004, the MMI subsequently spread as an admissions test across medical schools, and to other disciplines. By 2008, the MMI was being used as an admissions test by the majority of medical schools in Canada, Australia and Israel, as well as other medical schools in the United States and Brunei. This success lead to the development of a McMaster spin-off company, APT Inc., to commercialize the MMI system. The MMI was branded as ProFitHR [10] and made available to both the academic and corporate sector.[11] By 2009, the list of other disciplines using the MMI included schools for dentistry, pharmacy, midwifery, physiotherapy and occupational therapy, veterinary medicine, ultrasound technology, nuclear medicine technology, X-ray technology, medical laboratory technology, chiropody, dental hygiene, and postgraduate training programs in dentistry and medicine.

MMI Procedure

1. Interview stations – the domain(s) being assessed at any one station are variable, and normally reflects the objectives of the selecting institution. Examples of domains include the "soft skills" - ethics, professionalism, interpersonal relationships, ability to manage, communicate, collaborate, as well as perform a task. An MMI interview station takes considerable time and effort to produce; it is composed of several parts, including the stem question, probing questions for the interviewer, and a scoring sheet.

2. Circuit(s) of stations – to reduce costs of the MMI significantly below that of most interviews,[12] the interview "stations" are kept short (eight minutes or less) and are conducted simultaneously in a circuit as a bell-ringer examination. The preferred number of stations depends to some extent on the characteristics of the candidate group being interviewed, though nine interviews per candidate represents a reasonable minimum.[3] The circuit of interview stations should be within sufficiently close quarters to allow candidates to move from interview room to interview room. Multiple parallel circuits can be run, each circuit with the same set of interview stations, depending upon physical plant limitations.

3. Interviewers – one interviewer per interview station is sufficient.[3] In a typical MMI, each interviewer stays in the same interview throughout, as candidates rotate through. The interviewer thus scores each candidate based upon the same interview scenario throughout the course of the test.

4. Candidates – each candidate rotates through the circuit of interviews. For example, if each interview station is eight minutes, and there are nine interview stations, it will take the nine candidates being assessed on that circuit 72 minutes to complete the MMI. Each of the candidates begins at a different interview station, rotating to the next interview station at the ringing of the bell.

5. Administrators – each circuit requires at least one administrator to ensure that the MMI is conducted fairly and on time.

Utility of the MMI

The MMI requires less expenditure of resources than standard interview formats.[11] Test security breaches tend not to unduly influence results.[13] Sex of candidate and candidate status as under-represented minority tends not to unduly influence results.[11] [14] Preparatory courses taken by the candidate tend not to unduly influence results.[15] The MMI has been validated and tested for over seven years and the product is now available "off the shelf."[8]

References

[1]   Eva KW, Reiter HI, Rosenfeld J, Norman GR. An admissions OSCE: the multiple mini-interview. Medical Education, 38:314-326 (2004).

[2]   Barrick MR, Mount MK. The Big 5 personality dimensions and job performance: a meta-analysis. Personnel Psychology 1991, 44:1-26.

[3]   Eva KW, Reiter HI, Rosenfeld J, Norman GR. The relationship between interviewer characteristics and ratings assigned during a Multiple Mini-Interview. Academic Medicine, 2004 Jun; 79(6):602.9.

[4]   Dodson M, Crotty B, Prideaux D, Carne R, Ward A, de Leeuw E. The multiple mini-interview: how long is long enough? Med Educ. 2009 Feb;43(2):168-74.

[5]   Eva KW, Reiter HI, Rosenfeld J, Norman GR. The ability of the Multiple Mini-Interview to predict pre-clerkship performance in medical school. Academic Medicine, 2004, Oct; 79(10 Suppl): S40-2.

[6]   Reiter HI, Eva KW, Rosenfeld J, Norman GR. Multiple Mini-Interview Predicts for Clinical Clerkship Performance, National Licensure Examination Performance. Med Educ. 2007 Apr;41(4):378-84.

[7]   Eva KW, Reiter HI, Trinh K, Wasi P, Rosenfeld J, Norman GR. Predictive validity of the multiple mini-interview for selecting medical trainees. Accepted for publication January 2009 in Medical Education.

[8]   Hofmeister M, Lockyer J, Crutcher R. The multiple mini-interview for selection of international medical graduates into family medicine residency education. Med Educ. 2009 Jun;43(6):573-9.

[9]   http://www.mcc.ca/

[10] http://www.profithr.com/

[11] www.ProFitHR.com

[12] Rosenfeld J, Eva KW, Reiter HI, Trinh K. A Cost-Efficiency Comparison between the Multiple Mini-Interview and Panel-based Admissions Interviews. Advanced Health Science Education Theory Pract. 2008 Mar;13(1):43-58

[13] Reiter HI, Salvatori P, Rosenfeld J, Trinh K, Eva KW. The Impact of Measured Violations of Test Security on Multiple-Mini Interview (MMI). Medical Education, 2006; 40:36-42.

[14] Moreau K, Reiter HI, Eva KW. Comparison of Aboriginal and Non-Aboriginal Applicants for Admissions on the Multiple Mini-Interview using Aboriginal and Non-Aboriginal Interviewers. Teaching and Learning in Medicine, 2006; 18:58-61.

[15] Griffin B, Harding DW, Wilson IG, Yeomans ND. Does practice make perfect? The effect of coaching and retesting on selection tests used for admission to an Australian medical school. Med J Aust. 2008 Sep 1;189(5):270-3

National Association of Colleges and Employers

The **National Association of Colleges and Employers** (**NACE**) is a nonprofit professional association established in 1956 in Bethlehem, Pennsylvania for college career services and recruiting practitioners and others interested in the employment of the college educated.

Currently, more than 5,200 college career services practitioners at nearly 2,000 colleges and universities and more than 3,000 HR professionals focused on college relations and recruiting hold membership in NACE.

Ethics and professional standards

NACE members operate under the association's *Principles for Professional Conduct*, its code of ethics. The association also provides its career services members with guidelines for their operations through the *Professional Standards for College & University Career Services*.

Research

NACE conducts research into four main areas: 1) benchmarks for members on their operations and professional practices; 2) the hiring outlook for new college graduates; 3) starting salary offers to new college graduates; and 4) student attitudes about careers, the job search, and employers.

Publications and events

NACE publishes a quarterly journal and biweekly newsletter for its members. It also publishes the annual *Job Choices* magazine series for college students and new graduates.

NACE hosts an annual conference, a five-day training management program for career services professionals (the Management Leadership Institute), workshops, and virtual seminars.

External links

- Official website [1]

References

[1] http://http://www.naceweb.org

New Jersey/Eastern Pennsylvania/Delaware HERC

The New Jersey/ Eastern Pennsylvania/Delaware Higher Education Recruitment Consortium (NJ/Eastern PA/DE HERC) is a job-placement and recruitment organization for institutions of higher education in New Jersey, Eastern Pennsylvania, and Delaware. It is a part of the National HERC network.

About NJ/Eastern PA/DE HERC

The NJ/Eastern PA/DE HERC was established in 2005 as the New Jersey HERC. It expanded into eastern Pennsylvania and Delaware in 2008, and currently serves 41 campuses across 3 states. It is one of eleven regional HERCs in the US, consisting of over 450 campuses in 19 states. The NJ/Eastern PA/DE HERC maintains a web based search engine [1] with listing for faculty and staff job openings at all member institutions along with dual career search option.

Member Institutions

The NJ/Eastern PA/DE HERC has 43 institutions of higher educations as members:

Albright College; Brookdale Community College; Bryn Mawr College; Bucknell University; Burlington County College; Caldwell College; The College of New Jersey; College of Saint Elizabeth; County College of Morris; Drew University; Drexel University; Fairleigh Dickinson University; Georgian Court University; Gettysburg College; Gloucester County College; Hudson County Community College; Lehigh University; Mercer County Community College; Middlesex County College; Monmouth University; Montclair State University; New Jersey City University; Passaic County Community College; Princeton University; Ramapo College of New Jersey; Richard Stockton College of New Jersey; Rider University; Rowan University; Rutgers University; Saint Peter's College; Seton Hall University; Susquehanna University; Temple University; Thomas Edison State College; Thomas Jefferson University; University of Delaware; University of Medicine and Dentistry of New Jersey; University of Pennsylvania; University of the Sciences in Philadelphia; Ursinus College; Widener University

References

National HERC Website [2]

NJ/Eastern PA/DE HERC website [2]

Rutgers University Job Seeker's Information [3]

State of New Jersey Commission on Education [4]

Princeton University Family Friendly Policies page [5]

External links

- *National HERC Website* [2]
- *NJ/Eastern PA/DE HERC website* [2]

References

[1] http://www.njepadeherc.org/c/search.cfm?site_id=685

[2] http://www.njepadeherc.org/home/index.cfm?site_id=685

[3] http://www.rutgers.edu/information/information-job-seekers

[4] http://www.state.nj.us/highereducation/More_HE_Resources/colljobs.htm

[5] http://www.princeton.edu/dof/policies/family_friendly/family_friendly/

NotchUp

NotchUp

URL	notchup.com [1]
Type of site	Crowdsourced Recruiting
Available language(s)	English
Launched	2008
Current status	Online

NotchUp, Inc. is a Silicon Valley based start-up that is first to offer an on-demand recruiting service that uses crowdsourcing combined with social media[2] and an advanced web-based technology platform. NotchUp is a privately held company headquartered in Palo Alto, California.

The company's service is based on the premise that the best people are already employed, but are open to exploring opportunities that offer a better value proposition than their current job. NotchUp finds passive candidates[3] [4] for job postings using a crowdsourced[5] group of independent contractors called Talent Scouts. NotchUp posts positions on their web site and the 2000+ Talent Scouts use NotchUp's proprietary software to match their personal and professional connections in social media such as LinkedIn, Facebook, MySpace and Twitter. Companies with job postings rate the candidates and either independently take the next steps or use NotchUp's services to make connections and do additional screening. Talent Scouts are then compensated based on how accurately they matched candidates to the position.

NotchUp's proprietary technology monitors Talent Scout performance and accuracy, and uses that information as part of a formula for computing candidate ratings, and also factors this data into the algorithms for assigning work to the scouts. Scouts are provided feedback they can use to improve their accuracy, and therefore their earnings, over time.

The company was started in 2008 by co-founders Jim Ambras and Rob Ellis and initially offered a Pay for Interview service[6] [7]. It was recently listed by Business Insider as one of the "20 Hot Silicon Valley Startups You Need To Watch" in 2010[8]. The company has seed funding from Floodgate[9], Nueva Ventures[10] and Steve Blank.

References

[1] http://notchup.com/

[2] Sharlyn Lauby. "Tips for Effective Recruiting on Social Media Sites" (http://mashable.com/2010/05/25/recruiting-social-media/), *Mashable*, 2010-05-25

[3] Lou Adler. "How to Recruit and Hire Passive Candidates" (http://www.adlerconcepts.com/resources/column/recruiting/how_to_recruit_and_hire_passiv.php)", 2004-12-17

[4] Balanced Recruiting. "Balanced Recruiting" (http://www.bostonglobe.com/uploadedFiles/advertiser/Data_Center/Marketing_Solutions/Whitepapers/Balanced_Recruiting.pdf), *Boston Globe Media*

[5] Sarah Kessler. "5 Creative Uses for Crowdsourcing" (http://mashable.com/2010/05/26/creative-crowdsourcing/), *Mashable*, 2010-05-27

[6] Erick Schonfeld. "Stealth Job Site NotchUp Makes Companies Pay To Interview You" (http://techcrunch.com/2008/01/22/stealth-job-site-notchup-makes-companies-pay-to-interview-you/), *TechCrunch*, 2008-01-22

[7] Helen Coster. "Pay to Play" (http://www.forbes.com/forbes/2008/0929/062.html), *Forbes Magazine*, 2008-09-29

[8] Nick Saint. "20 Hot Silicon Valley Startups You Need To Watch" (http://www.businessinsider.com/hot-silicon-valley-startups-2010-3#notchup-is-a-crowd-sourced-lead-generation-platform-13), *Business Insider*, 2010-04-02

[9] Floodgate http://www.floodgate.com/

[10] Nueva Ventures http://www.nuevaventures.com

of the

; his or

:ir new

i better

:able in

:ek out

obs.[15]

/www.notchup.com/)

1g

on and

nent by

ns, and

n as **organizational socialization**, refers to the

hich new employees acquire the necessary

behaviors to become effective organizational

Tactics used in this process include formal

leos, printed materials, or computer-based

ice newcomers to their new jobs and

has demonstrated that these socialization

e outcomes for new employees such as higher

job performance, greater organizational

ion in stress and intent to quit.[2] [3] [4] These

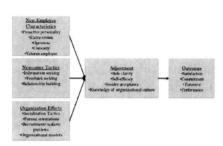

A model of onboarding (adapted from Bauer & Erdogan, 2011).

to learn

(1991)

itanding

vely the

rmation,

actively

ons and

nitoring

irmation

nitment,

important to an organization looking to retain a competitive advantage in an increasingly

vorkforce. In the United States, for example, up to 25% of workers are organizational

onboarding process.[5]

iccess

rs rather

e efforts

lback on

cial and

irn what

ien they

into the

high in

cultures

iceted operation influenced by a number of factors pertaining to both the individual

zation. Researchers have separated these factors into three broad categories: new employee

oyee behaviors, and organizational efforts.[6] New employee characteristics are individual

ing workers, ranging from personality traits to previous work experiences. New employee

ecific actions carried out by newcomers as they take an active role in the socialization

itional efforts help facilitate the process of acclimating a new worker to an establishment

orientation or mentoring programs.

icteristics

workers

a coffee

; shown

sfaction

ince that employees with certain personality traits and experiences adjust to an organization

a proactive personality, the "Big Five", curiosity, and greater experience levels.

refers to the tendency to take charge of situations and achieve control over one's

personality predisposes some workers to engage in behaviors such as information seeking

zation process, thus helping them to adapt more efficiently and become high-functioning

Empirical evidence also demonstrates that a proactive personality is related to increased

nd performance.[8] [9]

traits—openness, conscientiousness, extraversion, agreeableness, and neuroticism—have

success, as well. Specifically, new employees who are extraverted or particularly open to

y to seek out information, feedback, acceptance, and relationships with co-workers. They

if adjustment and tend to frame events more positively.[3]

istantial role in the newcomer adaptation process and is defined as the "desire to acquire

is individual exploration of an organization's culture and norms.[10] Individuals with a

frame challenges in a positive light and eagerly seek out information to help them make

ational surroundings and responsibilities, leading to a smoother onboarding experience.[11]

Employee experience levels also affect the onboarding process such that more experienced membe workforce tend to adapt to a new organization differently from, for example, a new college graduate star her first job. This is because seasoned employees can draw from past experiences to help them adjust to work settings and therefore may be less affected by specific socialization efforts because they have (a understanding of their own needs and requirements at work[12] and (b) are more familiar with what is acc the work context.[13] [14] Additionally, veteran workers may have used their past experiences to organizations in which they will be a better fit, giving them an immediate advantage in adapting to their new

New employee behaviors

Certain behaviors enacted by incoming employees, such as building relationships and seeking in form feedback, can help facilitate the onboarding process. Newcomers can also quicken the speed of their adju demonstrating behaviors that assist them in clarifying expectations, learning organizational values and n gaining social acceptance.[1]

Information seeking occurs when new employees ask questions of their co-workers and superiors in an effc about their new job and the company's norms, expectations, procedures, and policies. Miller and Jabl developed a typology of information sought after by new hires. These include referent information, unde what is required to function on the job (role clarity); appraisal information, understanding how effec newcomer is able to function in relation to job role requirements (self-efficacy); and finally, relational inf information about the quality of relationships with current organizational employees (social acceptance). B seeking information, employees can effectively reduce uncertainties about their new jobs and organiza make sense of their new working environments.[16] Newcomers can also passively seek information via n their surroundings or by simply viewing the company website or handbook.[1] Research has shown that in seeking by incoming employees is associated with social integration, higher levels of organizational con job performance, and job satisfaction in both individualistic and collectivist cultures.[17]

Feedback seeking is similar to information seeking, but it is focused on a new employee's particular behavi than on general information about the job or company. Specifically, feedback seeking refers to new employ to gauge how to behave in their new organization. A new employee may ask co-workers or superiors for fee how well he or she is performing certain job tasks or whether certain behaviors are appropriate in the s political context of the organization. In seeking constructive criticism about their actions, new employees l kinds of behaviors are expected, accepted, or frowned upon within the company or work group, and v incorporate this feedback and adjust their behavior accordingly, they begin to blend seamlessly organization.[18] Instances of feedback inquiry vary across cultural contexts such that individuals self-assertiveness and cultures low in power distance report more feedback seeking than newcomers i where self-assertiveness is low and power distance is high.[19]

Also called networking, relationship building involves an employee's efforts to develop camaraderie with c and even supervisors. This can be achieved informally through simply talking to their new peers during break or through more formal means such as taking part in pre-arranged company events. Research h relationship building to be a key part of the onboarding process, leading to outcomes such as greater job s and better job performance,[20] as well as decreased stress.[21]

Organization socialization efforts

Organizations also invest a great amount of time and resources into the training and orientation of new company hires. Organizations differ in the variety of socialization activities they offer in order to integrate productive new workers. Possible activities include their socialization tactics, formal orientation programs, recruitment strategies, and mentorship opportunities.

Socialization tactics

Socialization tactics, or orientation tactics, are designed based on an organization's needs, values, and structural policies. Some organizations favor a more systematic approach to socialization, while others follow a more "sink or swim" approach in which new employees are challenged to figure out existing norms and company expectations without guidance.

Van Maanen and Schein model (1979)

John Van Maanen and Edgar H. Schein have identified at least six major tactical dimensions that characterize and represent all of the ways in which organizations may differ in their approaches to socialization.

Collective versus Individual socialization

Collective socialization refers to the process of taking a group of recruits who are facing a given boundary passage and putting them through the same set of experiences together. Examples of this include: basic training/boot camp for a military organization, pledging for fraternities/sororities, education in graduate schools, and so forth. Socialization in the Individual mode allows newcomers to accumulate unique experiences separate from other newcomers. Examples of this process include: Apprenticeship programs, specific internships, "on-the-job" training, etc.[22]

Formal vs. Informal socialization

Formal socialization refers to those tactics in which newcomers are more or less segregated from others and trained of the job. These processes can be witnessed with such socialization programs as police academies, internships, and apprenticeships. Informal socialization processes, on the other hand, involve little separation between newcomers and the existing employees, nor is there any effort made to distinguish the newcomer's role specifically. Informal tactics provides a non-interventional environment for recruits to learn their new roles via trial and error. Examples of informal socialization include on-the-job training assignments, apprenticeship programs with no clearly defined role, and more generally, any situation in which a newcomer is placed into a work group with no recruit role.[22]

Sequential vs. Random socialization

Sequential socialization refers to the degree to which an organization or occupation specifies discrete and identifiable steps for the newcomers to know what phases they need to go through. Random socialization occurs when the sequences of steps leading to the targeted role are unknown, and the entire progression is quite ambiguous. In other words, while there are numerous steps or stages leading to specific organizational roles, there is necessarily no specific order in which the steps should be taken.[22]

Fixed vs. Variable socialization

This dimension refers to the extent to which the steps have a timetable developed by the organization and communicated to the recruit in order to convey when the socialization process is complete. Fixed socialization provides a recruit with the exact knowledge of the time it will take complete a given passage. For instance, some management trainees can be put on " fast tracks" where they are required to accept new rotational assignment on an annual basis despite their own preferences. Variable socialization processes gives a newcomer no specific timetable, but a few clues as to when to expect a given boundary passage. This type of socialization is commonly associated upwardly mobile careers within business organizations because of several uncontrolled factors such as the state of the economy or turnover rates which determine whether any given newcomer will be promoted to a higher level or not.[22]

Serial vs. Disjunctive socialization

A serial socialization process refers to experienced members of the organization grooming the newcomers who are about to occupy similar positions within the organization. These experience members essentially serve as role models for the inexperienced newcomers. A prime example of serial socialization would be a rookie police officer getting assigned patrol duties with an experienced veteran who has been in law enforcement for a lengthy period of time. Disjunctive socialization, in contrast, refers to when newcomers are not following the guidelines of their predecessors, and there are no role models to inform new recruits on how to fulfill their duties.[22]

Investiture vs. Divestiture socialization

This tactic refers to the degree to which a socialization process either affirms or disaffirms the identity of the newly entering recruit. Investiture socialization processes sanction and document for newcomers the viability and efficacy of the personal characteristics that they bring to the organization. When organizations use this socialization process it prefers that the recruit remains the exact way that he or she naturally behaves and the organization merely makes use of the skills, values, and attitudes that the recruit is believed to have in their possession. Divestiture socialization, on the other hand, is a process that organizations use to reject and remove the certain personal characteristics of a recruit. Many occupations and organizations require newcomers to sever previous ties, and forget old habits in order to create a new self-image based upon new assumptions.[22]

Thus, tactics influence the socialization process by defining the type of information newcomers receive, the source of this information, and the ease of obtaining it.[22]

Jones's model (1986)

Building upon the work of Van Maanen and Schein, Jones (1986) proposed that the previous six dimensions could be reduced to two categories: institutionalized and individualized socialization. Companies that use institutionalized socialization tactics implement structured step-by-step programs, enter into an orchestrated orientation as a group, and receive help from an assigned role model or mentor. Examples of organizations using institutionalized tactics include the military, in which new recruits undergo extensive training and socialization activities through a participative cohort, as well as incoming freshmen at universities, who may attend orientation weekends before beginning classes.

On the opposite end of the spectrum, other organizations use individualized socialization tactics in which the new employee immediately starts working on his or her new position and figures out company norms, values, and expectations along the way. In this orientation system, individuals must play a more proactive role in seeking out information and initiating work relationships.[23]

Formal orientations

Regardless of the socialization tactics utilized, formal orientation programs can facilitate understanding of company culture, and introduces new employees to their work roles and the organizational social environment. Formal orientation programs may consist of lectures, videotapes, and written material, while other organizations may rely on more usual approaches. More recent approaches such as computer-based orientations and Intranets have been used by organizations to standardize training programs across branch locations. A review of the literature indicates that orientation programs are successful in communicating the company's goals, history, and power structure.

Recruitment events

Recruitment events play a key role in identifying which prospective employees are a good fit with an organization. Recruiting events allow employees to gather initial information about an organization's expectations and company culture. By providing a realistic job preview of what life inside the organization is like, companies can weed out potential employees who are clearly a misfit to an organization and individuals can identify which employment agencies are the most suitable match for their own personal values, goals, and expectations. Research has shown that new employees who receive a great amount of accurate information about the job and the company tend to adjust better.[24] Organizations can also provide realistic job previews by offering internship opportunities.

Mentorship

Mentorship has demonstrated importance in the socialization of new employees.[25] [26] Ostroff and Kozlowski (1993) discovered that newcomers with mentors become more knowledgeable about the organization than did newcomers without mentors. Mentors can help newcomers better manage their expectations and feel comfortable with their new environment through advice-giving and social support.[27] Chatman (1991) found that newcomers are more likely to have internalized the key values of their organization's culture if they had spent time with an assigned mentor and attended company social events. Literature has also suggested the importance of demographic matching between organizational mentors and protégés.[25] Enscher & Murphy (1997) examined the effects of similarity (race and gender) on the amount of contact and quality of mentor relationships. Results indicate that liking, satisfaction, and contact were higher in conditions of perceived mentor-protégé similarity.[28]

Employee adjustment

In order to increase the success of an onboarding program, it is important for an organization to monitor how well their new hires are adjusting to their new roles, responsibilities, peers, supervisors, and the organization at large. Researchers have noted that role clarity, self-efficacy, social acceptance, and knowledge of organizational culture are particularly good indicators of well-adjusted new employees who have benefitted from an effective onboarding system.

Role clarity

Role clarity describes a new employee's understanding of his or her job responsibilities and organizational role. One of the goals of an onboarding process is to aid newcomers in reducing ambiguity and uncertainty so that it is easier for them to get their jobs done correctly and efficiently. A poor onboarding program, for example, may produce employees who exhibit sub-par productivity because they are unsure of their exact roles and responsibilities. On the other hand, a strong onboarding program would produce employees who are especially productive because they know exactly what is expected of them in their job tasks and their organizational role. Given this information, it is easy to see why an organization would benefit substantially from increasing role clarity for a new employee. Not only does role clarity imply greater productivity, but it has also been linked to both job satisfaction and organizational commitment.[29]

Self-efficacy

Self-efficacy is the degree to which new employees feel capable of successfully completing their assigned job tasks and fulfilling their responsibilities. It makes logical sense that employees who feel as though they can get the job done would fare better than those who feel overwhelmed in their new positions, and unsurprisingly, researchers have found that job satisfaction, organizational commitment, and turnover are all correlated with feelings of self-efficacy.[3]

Social acceptance

Social acceptance gives new employees the support needed to be successful. While role clarity and self-efficacy are important to a newcomer's ability to meet the requirements of a job, the feeling of "fitting in" can do a lot for one's perception of the work environment and has been demonstrated to increase commitment to an organization and decrease turnover.[3] If an employee feels well-received by his or her peers, a personal investment in the organization develops, and leaving becomes less likely.

Knowledge of organizational culture

Knowledge of organizational culture refers to how well a new employee understands a company's values, goals, roles, norms, and overall organizational environment. For example, some organizations may have very strict, yet unspoken, rules of how interactions with superiors should be conducted or whether overtime hours are the norm and an expectation. Knowledge of one's organizational culture is important for the newcomer looking to adapt to a new company, as it allows for social acceptance and aids in completing work tasks in a way that meets company standards. Overall, knowledge of organizational culture has been linked to increased satisfaction and commitment, as well as decreased turnover.[30]

Outcomes

Historically, organizations have overlooked the influence of business practices in shaping enduring work attitudes and thus have continually underestimated their impact on financial success.[31] Employees' job attitudes are particularly important from an organization's perspective because of their link to employee engagement and performance on the job. Employee engagement attitudes, such as satisfaction with one's job and organizational commitment or loyalty, have important implications for an employee's work performance and intentions to stay with or quit an organization. This translates into strong monetary gains for organizations as research has demonstrated that individuals who are highly satisfied with their jobs and who exhibit high organizational commitment are likely to perform better and remain in an organization, whereas individuals who have developed negative attitudes (are highly dissatisfied and unattached to their jobs) are characterized by low performance and high turnover rates.[32] [31] Unengaged employees are very costly to organizations in terms of slowed performance and rehiring expenses. Since, attitudinal formations begin from the initial point of contact with an organization, practitioners would be wise to take advantage of positive attitudinal development during socialization periods in order to ensure a strong, productive, and dedicated workforce.

Limits and criticisms of onboarding theory

Although the outcomes of socialization organization have been positively associated with the process of uncertainty reduction, they may not necessarily be desirable to all organizations. Jones (1986) as well as Allen and Meyer (1990) found that socialization tactics were related to commitment, but they were negatively correlated to role clarity.[23] [33] Because formal socialization tactics insulate the newcomer from their full responsibilities while "learning the ropes", there is a potential for role confusion once expected to fully enter the organization. In some cases though, organizations may even desire a certain level of person-organizational misfit in order to achieve outcomes via innovative behaviors.[6] Depending on the culture of the organization, it may be more desirable to increase ambiguity despite the potentially negative connection with organizational commitment.

Additionally, socialization researchers have had major concern over the length of time that it takes newcomers to adjust. There has been great difficulty determining the role that time plays, but once the length of the adjustment is determined, organizations can make appropriate recommendations regarding what matters most in various stages of the adjustment process.[6]

Further criticisms include the use of special orientation sessions to educate newcomers about the organization and strengthen their organizational commitment. While these sessions have been found to be often formal and ritualistic, several studies have found them unpleasant or traumatic.[34] Orientation sessions are a frequently used socialization tactic, however, employees have not found them to be helpful, nor has any research provided any evidence for their benefits.[35] [36] [37] [38] [39]

Executive onboarding

Executive onboarding is the application of general onboarding principles to helping new executives become productive members of an organization. Practically, executive onboarding involves acquiring, accommodating, assimilating and accelerating new executives.[40] Proponents emphasize the importance of making the most of the "honeymoon" stage of a hire, a period which has been described by various sources as either the first 90 to 100 days or the first full year.[41] [42] [43]

Effective onboarding of new executives can be one of the most important contributions any hiring manager, direct supervisor or human resources professional can make to long-term organizational success, because executive onboarding done right can improve productivity and executive retention, and build shared corporate culture. A study of 20,000 searches revealed that 40 percent of executives hired at the senior level are pushed out, fail, or quit within 18 months.[44]

Onboarding may be especially valuable for externally recruited executives transitioning into complex roles, because it may be difficult for those individuals to uncover personal, organizational, and role risks in complicated situations when they don't have formal onboarding assistance.[45] Onboarding is also an essential tool for executives promoted into new roles and/or transferred from one business unit to another.[46]

It is often valuable to have new executives start some onboarding activities in the "Fuzzy Front End" even before their first day.[47] This is one of ten steps executives can follow to accelerate their onboarding.[48]

1. Position yourself for success
2. Choose how to engage the context and culture
3. Embrace and leverage the Fuzzy Front End before day one
4. Take control of day one: Make a powerful first impression
5. Drive action by activating and directing ongoing communication
6. Embed a strong burning imperative
7. Exploit key milestones to drive team performance
8. Over-invest in early wins to build team confidence
9. Secure adept people in the right roles and deal with the inevitable resistance
10. Evolve people, plans, and practices to capitalize on changing circumstances.

Recommendations for practitioners

Ultimately, practitioners should seek to design an onboarding strategy that takes individual newcomer characteristics into consideration and encourages proactive behaviors, such as information seeking, that help facilitate the development of role clarity, self-efficacy, social acceptance, and knowledge of organizational culture. Research has consistently shown that doing so produces valuable outcomes such as high job satisfaction (the extent to which one enjoys the nature of his or her work), organizational commitment (the connection one feels to an organization), and job performance in employees, as well as lower turnover rates and decreased intent to quit.

In terms of structure, empirical evidence indicates that formal institutionalized socialization is the most effective onboarding method. New employees who complete these kinds of programs tend to experience more positive job attitudes and lower levels of turnover in comparison to those who undergo individualized tactics.[6] [49] Finally, it is also important to note that in-person onboarding techniques are more effective than virtual ones. Though it may initially appear to be less expensive for a company to use a standard computer-based orientation program to introduce their new employees to the organization, research has demonstrated that employees learn more about their roles and company culture through face-to-face orientation.[50]

References

[1] Bauer, T. N., & Erdogan., B. (2011). Organizational socialization: The effective onboarding of new employees. In S. Zedeck (Ed.), APA handbook of industrial and organizational psychology, Vol 3: Maintaining, expanding, and contracting the organization, APA Handbooks in Psychology (pp. 51–64). Washington, DC, US: American Psychological Association.

[2] Ashford, S. J., & Black, J. S. (1996). Proactivity during organizational entry: The role of desire for control. Journal of Applied Psychology, 81, 199–214.

[3] Kammeyer-Mueller, J. D., & Wanberg, C. R. (2003). Unwrapping the organizational entry process: Disentangling multiple antecedents and their pathways to adjustment. Journal of Applied Psychology, 88, 779–794.

[4] Fisher, C. D. (1985). Social support and adjustment to work: A longitudinal study. Journal of Management, 11, 39–53.

[5] Rollag, K., Parise, S., & Cross, R. (2005). Getting new hires up to speed quickly. MIT Sloan Management Review, 46, 35–41.

[6] Bauer, T. N., Bodner, T., Erdogan, B., Truxillo, D. M., & Tucker, J. S. (2007). Newcomer adjustment during organizational socialization: A meta-analytic review of antecedents, outcomes and methods. *Journal of Applied Psychology*, 92, 707–721.

[7] Saks, A. M., & Ashforth, B. E. (1996). Proactive socialization and behavioral self-management. Journal of Vocational Behavior, 48, 301–323.

[8] Erdogan, B., & Bauer, T. N. (2009). Perceived overqualification and its outcomes: The moderating role of empowerment. Journal of Applied Psychology, 94, 557–565.

[9] Crant, J. M. (2000). Proactive behavior in organizations. Journal of Management, 26, 274–276.

[10] Litman, J.A. (2005). Curiosity and the pleasures of learning: Wanting and liking new information. Cognition & Emotion, 19, 793–814.

[11] Ashford, S.J., & Cummings, L.L. (1983). Feedback as an individual resource: Personal strategies of creating information. Organizational Behavior and Human Performance, 32,370–398.

[12] Beyer, J. M., & Hannah, D. R. (2002). Building on the past: Enacting established personal identities in a new work setting. Organizational Science, 13, 636–652.

[13] Kirschenbaum, S. S., (1992). Influence of experience on information-gathering strategies. Journal of Applied Psychology, 77, 343–352.

[14] Meglino, B., DeNisi, A., & Ravlin, E. (1993). Effects of previous job exposure and subsequent job status on the functioning of a realistic job preview. Personnel Psychology, 46, 803–822.

[15] Carr, J. C., Pearson, A. W., West, M. J., & Boyar, S. L. (2006). Prior occupational experience, anticipatory socialization, and employee retention. Journal of Management, 32, 343–359.

[16] Miller, V. D., & Jablin, F. M., (1991). Information seeking during organizational entry: Influences, tactics, and a model of the process. Academy of Management Review, 16, 92–120.

[17] Menguc, B., Han, S. L., & Auh, S. (2007). A test of a model of new salespeople's socialization and adjustment in a collectivist culture. Journal of Personal Selling and Sales Management, 27, 149–167.

[18] Wanberg, C. R., & Kammeyer-Mueller, J. D. (2000). Predictors and outcomes of proactivity in the socialization process. Journal of Applied Psychology, 85, 373–385.

[19] Morrison, E. W., Chen, Y., & Salgado, S. R. (2004). Cultural differences in newcomer feedback seeking: A comparison of the United States and Hong Kong. Applied Psychology: An International Review, 53, 1–22.

[20] Ashford, S. J., & Black, J. S. (1996). Proactivity during organizational entry: The role of desire for control. Journal of Applied Psychology, 81, 199–214.

[21] Fisher, C. D. (1985). Social support and adjustment to work: A longitudinal study. Journal of Management, 11, 39–53.

[22] Van Maanen, J., & Schein, E. H. (1979). Toward a theory of organizational socialization. *Research in Organizational Behavior*, 1, 209–264.

[23] Jones, G. R. (1986). Socialization tactics, self-efficacy, and newcomers' adjustments to organizations. *Academy of Management Journal*, 29, 262–279.

[24] Klein, H. J., Fan, J., & Preacher, K. J. (2006). The effects of early socialization experiences on content mastery and outcomes: A mediational approach. Journal of Vocational Behavior, 68, 96–115.

[25] Chatman, J. A. (1991). Matching people and organizations: Selection and socialization in public accounting firms. Administrative Science Quarterly, 36, 459–484.

[26] Major, D. A., Kozlowski, S. W. J., Chao, G. T., & Gardner, P. D. (1995). A longitudinal investigation of newcomer expectations, early socialization outcomes, and the moderating effects of role development factors. Journal of Applied Psychology, 80, 418–431.

[27] Ostroff, C., & Kozlowski, S. W. J. (1993). The role of mentoring in the information gathering processes of newcomers during early organizational socialization. Journal of Vocational Behavior, 42, 170–183.

[28] Enscher, E. A., Murphy, S. E., (1997). Effects of race, gender, perceived similarity, and contact on mentor relationships. Journal of Vocational Behavior, 50, 460–481.

[29] Adkins, C. L. (1995). Previous work experience and organizational socialization: A longitudinal examination. Academy of Management Journal, 38, 839–862.

[30] Klein, H. J., & Weaver, N. A. (2000). The effectiveness of an organizational-level orientation training program in the socialization of new hires. Personnel Psychology, 53, 47–66.

[31] Saari, L. M. & Judge, T. A. (2004). Employee attitudes and job satisfaction. Human Resource Management, 43, 395–407.

[32] Ryan, A. M., Schmit, M. J., & Johnson, R. (1996). Attitudes and effectiveness: Examining relations at an organizational level. Personnel Psychology, 49, 853–882.

[33] Allen, N.J., & Meyer, J.P. (1990). Organizational socialization tactics: A longitudinal analysis of links to newcomers' commitment and role orientation. *Acadmeny of Management Journal*, 33, 847–858

[34] Rohlen, T.P. (1973). "Spiritual education" in a Japanese bank. *American Anthropologist*, 75, 1542–1562.

[35] Louis, M.R., Posner, B.Z., & Powell, G.N. (1983). The availability and helpfulness of socialization practices. *Personnel Psychology*, 36, 857–866.

[36] Nelson, D.L., & Quick, J.C. (1991). Social support and newcomer adjustment in organizations: Attachment theory at work? *Journal of Organizational Behavior*, 12, 543–554.

[37] Posner, B.Z., & Powell, G.N. (1985). Female and male socialization experiences: an initial investigation. Journal of Occupational Psychology, 70, 81–85.

[38] Saks, A.M. (1994). Moderating effects of self-efficacy for the relationship between training method and anxiety and stress reductions of newcomers. Journal of Organizational Behavior, 15, 639–654.

[39] Wanous, J.P. (1993). Newcomer orientation programs that facilitate organizational entry. In organizational perspectives (pp. 125–139). Hillsdale, NJ: Lawrence Erlbaum Associates.

[40] Bradt, George; Mary Vonnegut (2009). *Onboarding: How To Get Your New Employees Up To Speed In Half The Time*. John Wiley & Sons. ISBN 0470485817.

[41] Watkins, Michael (2003). *The First 90 Days*. Harvard Business School Publishing. ISBN 1591391105.

[42] "That tricky first 100 days". *The Economist*. July 15, 2006.

[43] Stein, Christiansen (2010). *Successful Onboarding: Strategies to Unlock Hidden Value Within Your Organization*. McGraw-Hill. ISBN 0071739378.

[44] Masters, Brooke (March 30, 2009). "Rise of a Headhunter". *Financial Times*.

[45] Bradt, George (2006, revised edition 2009). *The New Leader's 100-Day Action Plan*. J. Wiley and Sons. ISBN 0470407034.

[46] Watkins, Michael (2009). *Your Next Move*. Harvard Business School Publishing. ISBN 9781422147634.

[47] McGregor, Jena (February 5, 2007). "How to Take the Reins At Top Speed". *Business Week*.

[48] Bradt, George (February 16, 2011). "The New Leaders Playbook". *Forbes*.

[49] Saks, A. M., Uggerslev, K. L., & Fassina, N. E. (2007). Socialization tactics and newcomer adjustment: A meta-analytic review and test of a model. Journal of Vocational Behavior, 70, 413–446.

[50] Wesson, M. J., & Gogus, C. I. (2005). Shaking hands with a computer: An examination of two methods of organizational newcomer orientation. Journal of Applied Psychology, 90, 1018–1026.

Further reading

- Ashforth, B. E., & Saks, A. M. (1996). Socialization tactics: Longitudinal effects on newcomer adjustment. *Academy of Management Journal, 39,* 149–178.

- Gruman, J. A., Saks, A. M., & Zweig, D. L. (2006). Organizational socialization tactics and newcomer proactive behaviors: An integrative study. *Journal of Vocational Behavior, 69,* 90–104.

- Klein, H. J., Fan, J., & Preacher, K. J. (2006). The effects of early socialization experiences on content mastery and outcomes: A mediational approach. *Journal of Vocational Behavior, 68,* 96–115.

Online job fair

An **online job fair**, also known as a **virtual job fair** or **electronic job fair**, is an online version of a traditional job fair. They allow employers and job seekers to meet and discuss employment opportunities by way of specialised websites. Like a traditional job fair, online job fairs are live, fully interactive, and held at specific times.

There are several companies who offer these fairs. One specialist online job fair company is ejobfairs,[1] who have been operating online job fairs since 2005.[2] . There are also companies that do them as part of a larger offering of electronic trade shows such as inexpo,[3] ubivent,[4] and unisfair.[5]

Online job fairs have grown in popularity and use, now being utilised by some Colleges[6] and Fortune 500 companies.[7]

References

[1] Google search results for electronic job fairs (http://www.google.com/search?hl=en&safe=off&q="electronic+job+fairs"& btnG=Search)

[2] ejobfairs company profile (http://www.pr.com/company-profile/overview/29162)

[3] Inexpo homepage (http://www.inexpo.com)

[4] Ubivent - European provider for virtual events (homepage) (http://www.ubivent.com)

[5] Unisfair - Powering the World's Virtual Events (homepage) (http://www.unisfair.com)

[6] Oswego: State University of New York newsletter (http://www.oswego.edu/alumni/publications/newsletter/fl01.pdf)

[7] Recruiter Life Internet Magazine (http://preview.recruiterlife.com/index.php?/radio/radioview/action/shows_for_profile/frmProfileId/ 122/)

http://www.dataentrywork.net/ (http://www.dataentrywork.net/?id=346195)

Online vetting

Online vetting, also known as **cyber-vetting**[1] is increasingly being used by potential employers and other acquaintances to vet people's online presence or "internet reputation" ("*netrep*")[2] on social network services such as Facebook, MySpace, Twitter, Bebo, and LinkedIn. Employers may check profiles, posts, and photographs for indications that the candidate is unsuitable.

Views and practice

"Many young people are posting content online without thinking about the electronic footprint they leave behind.

The cost to a person's future can be very high if something undesirable is found by the increasing number of education institutions and employers using the internet as a tool to vet potential students or employees."

— David Smith, deputy commissioner for the Information Commissioner's Office.[3]

A survey in 2007 found that half of UK employees would be outraged if their employers looked up information about them on social networking sites, and 56% thought it would be unethical. Employer surveys found that between 1/5 and 2/3 of employers conduct internet searches, including of social networking sites, and that some have turned down applicants as a result of their searches.[1] 21% of colleges and universities surveyed said they looked at the social networking of prospective students, usually for those applying for scholarships and other limited awards and programmes.[4] Prospective political appointees to the Obama administration were asked to list all their blog posts, any emails, text messages, and instant messages that could suggest a conflict of interest or public source of embarrassment, the URLs of any sites that featured them in a personal or professional capacity, and all of their online aliases.[5]

Job applicants have been refused due to criticising previous employers and discussing company information online,[6] [7] as well as for posting provocative and inappropriate photographs, drinking or drug use, poor communication skills, making discriminatory comments, and lying about qualifications.[8] Several companies offer online reputation management services, including helping to remove embarrassing information from websites.[9]

Legal position

Legal experts have warned human resources departments about vetting prospective employees online, due to the possibility of discrimination and the unreliability of this information.[10] The chairman of the UK Children's Charities' Coalition on Internet Safety argued that it was "possibly illegal, but certainly unethical". While the Information Commissioner's Office advised that just looking at information on someone's social networking profiles would not be illegal, an employment law specialist noted that under the Data Protection Act 1998, processing and storing the information or using it to make discriminatory decisions could be.[11]

Age discrimination might result from such a practice, due to the age profile of users of social networking sites.[10] [12] Failed candidates may be able to use discrimination legislation to ask about vetting operations and even ask for IT records to check access to social networks.[6] In the US, vetting using social networking sites risks breaching the Fair Credit Reporting Act (FCRA), which requires employers to gain the consent of applicants before doing a background check, state laws that limit the consideration of off-duty conduct in making employment decisions, and any searches risk breaching prohibitions against commercial use contained in the terms of service of the social networking sites.[13]

In 2006, a trainee teacher at a high school in Pennsylvania was denied her teaching degree after her supervisor found a picture she posted on MySpace captioned "Drunken pirate" and deemed it "unprofessional". She sued, arguing that by acting on the basis of her legal out-of-hours behavior Millersville University had breached her First Amendment rights, but a federal district court ruled that the photograph was not "protected speech" under the First Amendment.[14]

References

[1] "Cyber-vetting managers face backlash" (http://www.management-issues.com/2007/10/18/research/cyber-vetting-managers-face-backlash.asp). *Management Issues*. 18 October 2007. . Retrieved 5 May 2010.

[2] Nesbitt, Sean; Camilla Marriott, Taylor Wessing (29 October 2007). "Caught in the net" (http://www.thelawyer.com/caught-in-the-net/129676.article). *The Lawyer*. . Retrieved 5 May 2010.

[3] Hope, Christopher (23 November 2007). "Facebook posts 'could threaten your career'" (http://www.telegraph.co.uk/technology/3355280/Facebook-posts-could-threaten-your-career.html). *Daily Telegraph*. . Retrieved 5 May 2010.

[4] Greenwood, Bill (September 2009). "Facebook: The Next Great Vetting Tool?" (http://www.infotoday.com/it/sep09/Greenwood.shtml). *Information Today*. . Retrieved 5 May 2010.

[5] Croll, Alistair (29 April 2010). "Promiscuous online culture and the vetting process" (http://radar.oreilly.com/2010/04/promiscuous-online-culture.html). *O'Reilly Radar*. . Retrieved 5 May 2010.

[6] Lynas, James (6 August 2007). "Social networking sites: friend or foe?" (http://www.personneltoday.com/articles/2007/08/06/41764/social-networking-sites-friend-or-foe.html). *Personnel Today*. . Retrieved 5 May 2010.

[7] Phelps, David (27 June 2009). "Before a job hunt, put a lid on tweets" (http://www.startribune.com/business/49213757.html?elr=KArks:DCiU1OiP:DiiUiD3aPc:_Yyc:aUU). *Star Tribune*. . Retrieved 5 May 2010.

[8] Eaton, Kim (19 August 2009). "If You're Applying for a Job, Censor Your Facebook Page" (http://www.fastcompany.com/blog/kit-eaton/technomix/if-youre-applying-job-censor-your-facebook-page). *Fast Company*. . Retrieved 5 May 2010.

[9] Langfitt, Frank (15 November 2006). "Startups Help Clean Up Online Reputations" (http://www.npr.org/templates/story/story.php?storyId=6462504). *NPR*. . Retrieved 5 May 2010.

[10] Wort, Jo (24 June 2008). "Vetting through social networking sites: weekly dilemma" (http://www.personneltoday.com/articles/2008/06/24/46448/vetting-through-social-networking-sites-weekly-dilemma.html). *Personnel Today*. . Retrieved 5 May 2010.

[11] Farmer, Ben (27 November 2007). "Facebook vetting 'could be illegal'" (http://www.telegraph.co.uk/news/uknews/3355337/Facebook-vetting-could-be-illegal.html). *Daily Telegraph*. . Retrieved 5 May 2010.

[12] "Workplace Twittering" (http://www.cambridge-news.co.uk/Business/Workplace-Twittering.htm). *Cambridge News*. 16 June 2009. . Retrieved 5 May 2010.

[13] Zeidner, Rita (1 October 2007). "How Deep Can You Probe?" (http://www.shrm.org/Publications/hrmagazine/editorialcontent/pages/
       1007sr-zeidner.aspx). *HR Magazine* (Society for Human Resource Management). . Retrieved 5 May 2010.

[14] Rosen, Jeffrey (19 July 2010). "The Web Means the End of Forgetting" (http://www.nytimes.com/2010/07/25/magazine/25privacy-t2.
       html?_r=2&pagewanted=1). *New York Times*. . Retrieved 27 July 2010.

Further reading

- Kennedy, Nicole; Matt Macko. "Social Networking Privacy and Its Affects on Employment Opportunities" (http:/
  /www.ethicapublishing.com/2CH12.htm). *Convenient or Invasive - The Information Age*. Boulder, Colorado:
  Ethica Publishing.
- Davis, Donald Carrington (2006-2007). "MySpace Isn't Your Space: Expanding the Fair Credit Reporting Act to
  Ensure Accountability and Fairness in Employer Searches of Online Social Networking Services" (http://www.
  law.ku.edu/publications/journal/pdf/v16n2/davis.pdf). *Kansas Journal of Law and Public Policy* **XVI** (2):
  237–256.

External links

- Employers Tap Web for Employee Information (http://www.npr.org/templates/story/story.
  php?storyId=5695383&ps=rs) – 2006 National Public Radio report

Overqualification

Overqualification is the state of being skilled or educated beyond what is necessary for a job. There can often be high costs for companies associated with training employees. This could be a problem for professionals applying for a job where they significantly exceed the job requirements because potential employers may feel they are using the position as a stepping stone.

Overqualified candidates may be seen as taking the position temporarily in order to obtain work experience for another position or taking the position temporarily until better employment can be found. Therefore it may be in a company's interest to reject job candidates that significantly exceed their job requirements because they are "overqualified" and not likely to be loyal to a position or company. An example would be an experienced high level manager who is overqualified for a low level management position.

As a euphemism

The concept of overqualification is often a euphemism used by employers when they do not want to reveal their true reasons for not hiring an applicant. The term "overqualified" can mask age discrimination, but it can also mask legitimate concerns of an employer, such as uncertainty of your ability to do the job, or concerns that you only want a job on a temporary basis, while you seek for another more desirable position.[1] Being overqualified also often means that a person was asking for too high a salary.[2] [3] "Overqualified" can also be used to describe a resistance to new technologies, or a pompous approach.[3]

In the United States the term "overqualified" has been found by the courts to sometimes be used as a "code word for too old" (i.e.: age discrimination) in the hiring process. Hamm v. New York City Office of theComptroller (D. Ct. NY, March 4, 1998).

Responses to being described as overqualified

Noluthando Crockett-Ntonga recommends that job applicants address potential concerns such as salary requirements in a cover letter and interview before the employer makes any comments about overqualification.[3] Barbara Moses advises applicants who are described as being overqualified to emphasize their willingness to mentor younger co-workers, and to focus on what attracts them about the position they are applying to rather than emphasizing their ambition or desire to be challenged.[2] Being overqualified can be an asset for employers, especially when the breadth of your experience enables you to take on additional responsibilities in ways that benefit the employer.[3]

The Ph.D. Degree

The Ph.D. degree can reflect overspecialization that manifests itself as a lack of perspective; for example, a Ph.D. might not adequately prepare one for careers in development, manufacturing, or technical management.[4]

In the corporate world, some Ph.D. graduates have been criticized as being unable to turn theories into useful strategies, and being unable to work on a team, although Ph.D.s are seen as desirable and even essential in many positions, such as supervisory roles in research, especially Ph.D.s in biomedical sciences.[5]

Even in some college jobs, people can associate negative factors with the Ph.D., including a lack of focus on teaching, overspecialization, and an undesirable set of professional priorities, often focusing on self-promotion. These forces have led both to an increase in some educational institutions hiring candidates without Ph.D.s as well as a focus on the development of other doctoral degrees, such as the D.A. or Doctor of arts.[6]

Some employers have reservations about hiring people with Ph.D.s in full-time, entry-level positions, but are eager to hire them in temporary positions.[7]

References

[1] "What does 'overqualified' mean?", *Atlanta Journal-Constitution*, Aug. 14, 2008. (http://www.ajc.com/hotjobs/content/hotjobs/careercenter/articles/2008/08/14/lindgren_overqualified.html)

[2] Anne Fisher, "'Overqualified' May Be A Smokescreen", *Fortune*, May 31, 2004. (http://money.cnn.com/magazines/fortune/fortune_archive/2004/05/31/370688/index.htm)

[3] Vickie Elmer, "Getting an 'Overqualified' Response", *Washington Post*, Dec. 21, 2008; Page K01. (http://www.washingtonpost.com/wp-dyn/content/article/2008/12/20/AR2008122000441.html)

[4] (http://units.aps.org/units/fiap/newsletters/nov95/03.cfm) John A. Armstrong, "Rethinking the Ph.D.", originally appeared in *Issues in Science and Technology*.

[5] Lee Anna Jackson, "Past the prestige: what career options does your Ph.D. offer?(Making Connections)", *Black Enterprise*, Aug. 1, 2004. (http://www.accessmylibrary.com/coms2/summary_0286-22107688_ITM)

[6] (http://web2.ade.org/ade/bulletin/n027/027004.htm) Edmond L. Volpe, "A Portrait of the Ph.D. as a Failure", *ADE Bulletin*, 027 (November 1970): 4-10.

[7] Susan Basalla May, "Behind the Ivory Tower: Breaking In as a Temp", *Chronicle of Higher Education*, May 2003. (http://chronicle.com/cgi2-bin/printable.cgi?article=http://chronicle.com/jobs/news/2003/05/2003053001c.htm)

Peak earning years

Peak earning years refers to the time in life when workers earn the most money per year.

US perspective

Given their initial lack of experience, workers' earnings start out low. Earnings peak when workers hit middle age, then begin to fall as retirement approaches. But peak earnings now occur later in life and reach a higher level.

Two decades ago, the **peak earning years** were between 35 and 44. Now they occur ten years later. Twenty years ago, those in their peak earning years took home about twice as much as workers between the ages of 20 and 24. Now they earn more than three times as much.

In the past, muscle power was an important factor in earnings, but that falters with age. Today, people are paid for working smarter and doing so for a longer period of time.

Performance-linked incentives

A **Performance Linked Incentive** (PLI) is a form of payment from an employer to an employee, which is directly related to the performance output of an employee and which may be specified in an employment contract. PLI may either be open ended (does not have a fixed ceiling) or close ended (has an upper ceiling which is normally stipulated in the employment contract)

Open ended incentives are normally applicable revenue generating activities (eg., Sales) and Close ended incentives are associated to support functions (eg., Operation, Human Resources, Administration etc)

PLI vs other financial remuneration

PLI vs salary

Salary is paid for the efforts that one puts in and PLI is paid for the results. Salary is paid in short, definitive cycles (e.g., weekly, monthly, fortnightly etc) while PLI is paid in a longer cycle of monthly, quarterly or half-yearly,yearly.

PLI vs bonus

Bonus is paid for the performance of the organization while PLI is paid for the individual's performance. Bonus is normally paid yearly or half-yearly. This is normally paid as a percentage of one's salary, or as a fixed amount, irrespective of the employee's individual performance.

PLI vs retention bonus

Some organizations give a retention bonus which is payable for the period that an employee stays back in the organization. This is paid for the value added by the employee by virtue of mere presence and not necessary for the efforts or work output. Normally retention bonus is paid yearly or half-yearly which will incentivise the employee to stay back in the organization for the payment.

Method of calculating PLI

PLI, by virtue of being sanctified in the employment contract, is paid for objective, measurable and visible results. Management by objectives is the generally used to define the output which determines the payment of PLI. Since PLI is paid for the results and not merely for the efforts, the objects should be chosen to reflect those activities whose results are visible immediately after the effort.

Also, in calculating PLI, only the performance and not the potential of the employee should be considered. Potential of the employee is normally subjective and can be contested. PLI should be based on metrics which are absolutely objective and clearly perceived as fair by both employee and employer.

PLI vs Appraisal

Appraisals, normally conducted half-yearly or annually is used to decide on the salary increments and promotions of the employee. This, being permanent increase, takes both performance and potential of the employee.

References

External links

- 17 Things (http://business.17things.com/what-are-salary-requirements.html) Explanation of salary requirements and how to establish these.

Permanent employment

Permanent employees or **regular employees** work for a single employer and are paid directly by that employer. In addition to their wages, they often receive benefits like subsidized health care, paid vacations, holidays, sick time, or contributions to a retirement plan. Permanent employees are often eligible to switch job positions within their companies. Even when employment is "at will", permanent employees of large companies are generally protected from abrupt job termination by severance policies, like advance notice in case of layoffs, or formal discipline procedures. They may be eligible to join a union, and may enjoy both social and financial benefits of their employment.

Rarely *permanent employment* means employment of an individual that is guaranteed throughout the employee's working life. In the private sector, such jobs are rare; permanent employment is far more common in the public sector, where profit and loss is not as important.

Examples of permanent employment

- Partner at a law firm
- Tenure of a senior academic

External links

- In Japan, Secure Jobs Have a Cost [1]

References

[1] http://www.nytimes.com/2009/05/20/business/global/20zombie.html?scp=72&sq=japan&st=cse

Person specification

The **person specification** is an extension of the job description. It is a profile of the type of person needed to do a job and is produced along with a job description following a job analysis.

Elements of a person specification include:

- Attainments (experience and qualifications)
- Specialized skills
- Interests
- Personality

References

- acas.gov.uk [1]
- businesslink.gov.uk [2]

References

[1] http://www.acas.gov.uk

[2] http://www.businesslink.gov.uk/bdotg/action/detail?type=RESOURCES&itemId=1073793806

Probation (workplace)

In a workplace setting, **probation** is a status given to new employees of a company or business. This status allows a supervisor or other company manager to closely evaluate the progress and skills of the newly hired worker, determine appropriate assignments and monitor other aspects of the employee – such as how they interact with co-workers, supervisors or customers.

A probationary period varies widely depending on the business, but usually lasts anywhere from 30 to 90 days. If the new employee shows promise and does well during the probationary time, they are usually removed from probationary status, and may be given a raise or promotion as well (in addition to other privileges, as defined by the business). Probation is usually defined in a company's employee handbook, which is given to workers when they first begin a job.

The probationary period also allows an employer to terminate an employee who is determined not to be doing well at their job or otherwise deemed not suitable for a particular position. Some companies have an *at will* policy, which allows a company manager to terminate an employee at any point during the probationary period.

Some companies may place employees on probationary status, particularly if their performance is below a set standard or for disciplinary reasons. In this instance, the employee is usually given a period of time to either improve their performance or modify their behavior before more severe measures are used. Similarly, students with unsatisfactory grades may also be placed on *academic probation* by their institution.

Realistic Job Preview

Realistic Job Previews (RJPs) are devices used in the early stages of personnel selection to provide potential applicants with information on both positive and negative aspects of the job (Premack & Wanous, 1985).

The employee exchange or psychological contract between employer and employee is at the heart of this concept (Shore & Tetrick, 1994). Being hired after use of the RJP, the employee enters into the contract with their eyes open, aware of what the organization will provide to them (pay, hours, schedule flexibility, culture, etc.) and also what will be expected from them (late hours, stress, customer interaction, high urgency, degree of physical risk, etc.).

High turnover of new hires can occur when they are unpleasantly surprised by an aspect of their job, especially if that aspect is especially important to them. For example, if they take the job with an understanding that they won't have to work weekends, then are immediately scheduled for Saturday night, it undermines trust and the psychological contract is breached. Better informed candidates who continue the application process are more likely to be a good fit with the position, and the ones who choose not to continue save themselves time pursuing a job or company that wasn't right for them. The hiring organization saves time on testing and interviewing only those candidates with a strong chance of success.

RJPs can take the form of videos (e.g., Home Depot; PetSmart), testimonials (www.retailology.com) or short tests (e.g., www.sheetz.com). Regardless of format, effective RJPs accurately foreshadow the culture that the candidate is signing up for, warts and all. Other critical components include: Candor and openness; specificity (while avoiding a deluge of information); representative visual depictions of the work environment, preferably with the employee actually performing common tasks; testimonials from real employees, not actors. Ideally, RJP information should be focused on the things that matter most to the candidate demographic, parts of the job or culture that correlate with engagement and turnover.

Empirical research suggests a fairly small effect size, even for properly designed RJPs ($d = .12$), with estimates that they can improve job survival rates ranging from 3% to 10%. For large organizations in retail or transportation that do mass hiring and experience new hire turnover above 200% in a large population, a 3-10% difference can translate to significant monetary savings. Some experts (e.g., Roth; Martin, 1996) estimate that RJPs screen out between 15% and 36% of applicants.

According to researchers there are four issues that challenge RJP:

1. Recruiters do not share RJPs during interviews. (Rynes, 1991)]
2. The nature of "realistic" information shared (in lab research or in the field) is unclear (Breaugh & Billings, 1988)
3. Not asking the right questions.
4. Applicants consistently report desiring more specific, job-relevant information than they commonly receive (Barber & Roehling, 1993; Maurer, Howe, & Lee,1992)

In addition to this there is a chance for Realistic Job Preview to become more effective in order to eliminate turnovers. The presentation format and timing of the RJP can be improved whether the real information is provided early on or later in the recruitment factor.Consequently more specific topic should be addressed and information sources used (e.g. job incumbent versus human resource staff person).

Notes

References

- Breaugh, J.A. (1983). Realistic Job Previews: A Critical Appraisal and Future Research Directions. *The Academy of Management Review*. October, 8 (4): 612-619.
- Breaugh, J.A. and J.A. Billings (1988). "The Realistic Job Preview: Five Key Elements and their Importance for Research and Practice. *Journal of Business and Psychology*. Summer, 24:291-305.
- Landy & Conte (2007). Work in the 21st Century. Blackwell.
- Meglino, B.M., A.S. DeNisi, S.A. Youngblood, and K.J. Williams (1988). "Effects of Realistic Job Previews: A Comparison Using an Enhancement and a Reduction Preview." Journal of Applied Psychology. 73 (2): 259-266.
- Premack, S.L. and J.P. Wanous (1985). A Meta-Analysis of Realistic Job Preview Experiments. *Journal of Applied Psychology*. 70 (4): 706-719.
- Roth and Roth (1995). Reduce turnover with realistic job previews. *The CPA Journal*.
- Shore and Tetrick (1994). The psychological contract as an explanatory framework in the employment relationship. Trends in organizational behavior, chapter 7, pp.91-109. Edited by Cooper and Rousseau.

Recession-proof job

A **recession-proof job** is a job that one is likely to be able to find even during hard economic times. Though these jobs are not truly "recession-proof," they have a continual demand for workers, thereby increasing the chances that one who has the skills will be likely to find employment.[1] [2]

What makes a job so-called recession-proof is society's perpetual need and heavy demand for the service provided by the field.[3] Certain fields, such as health care, education, law enforcement, and various computer-related occupations are thereby always in demand. But as to which specific jobs are the most recession-proof, this varies in different eras, as the times change, and each recession differs.[4] Also, the geographic locality may make a difference.

When a recession occurs, many people, especially those who have lost their jobs, those whose jobs have been threatened, or those who fear losing their jobs are motivated to seek education to be able to obtain recession-proof employment in their future.[5]

External links

- List of the 150 most recession-proof jobs from Time Magazine [6]

References

[1] "Recession-Proof Jobs in the Valley - 12/05/08 - Fresno News - abc30.com" (http://a.abclocal.go.com/kfsn/story?section=news/local& id=6539810). A.abclocal.go.com. 2008-12-05. . Retrieved 2010-03-19.

[2] "Ride Out Recession With Penny Pinching, Job Tips" (http://cbs2.com/consumer/money.jobs.recession.2.641620.html). cbs2.com. 2008-01-30. . Retrieved 2010-03-19.

[3] "Job Safety Explored" (http://www.jonesbahamas.com/news/45/ARTICLE/18708/2008-11-20.html). Jonesbahamas.com. 2008-11-20. . Retrieved 2010-03-19.

[4] Marcia Heroux Pounds. "Want Job Security? - KDAF" (http://www.the33tv.com/sns-health-jobs-recession-proof,0,7437899.story). The33tv.com. . Retrieved 2010-03-19.

[5] "Economic conditions motivate some to make career changes" (http://www.commercialappeal.com/news/2009/may/15/recession-proof/). The Commercial Appeal. . Retrieved 2010-03-19.

[6] http://www.time.com/time/business/article/0,8599,1858773,00.html

Recruitment advertising

Recruitment advertising, also known as **Recruitment Communications** and **Recruitment_Agency**, includes all communications used by an organization to attract talent to work within it.

Recruitment advertisements may be the first impression of a company for many people, and the first impression the firm makes goes a long way to determining interest in the job opening being advertised. Recruitment advertisements typically have a uniform layout and contain the following elements:

* the job title heading and location
* an explanatory paragraph describing the company, including the Employer Brand
* a description of the position
* entry qualifications
* the remuneration package (not always provided by the employer)
* further details and from where application forms may be sought

In the United Kingdom many recruitment advertisements fail to provide all the information listed above and this is frustrating for potential applicants.

When faced with hiring many roles, corporate employers have many channels and options to choose from. They may:

* A retained search firm
* A contingency search firm
* Retain a recruitment process outsourcing organization
* Use a candidate fulfillment service
* Retain a recruitment advertising agency
* Retain a specialist interactive recruitment advertising agency
* Leverage old media to advertise their openings (print, radio and television)
* Leverage job boards
* Leverage new media
* Invest in additional internal resources

Each of these channels has its benefits and many firms will use a mix of some or all of the above options.

The use of a specialist recruitment advertising agency enables organisations to receive professional advice on media, design and copywriting specifically related to the recruitment process. This enables their advertisement to stand out in the relevant publication and build an employment brand. Advertisers are now able to use micro-sites to put most of the job content and allowing the advert to be more creative with minimal copy. Recruitment advertising has now developed into a speciality service where most leading organisations use the services of a specialist agency.

The way companies hunt for talent is changing and this had led to sites that freelancers can sign up to and get to bid on jobs advertised; they are normally free to join but the agency will take between 10% and 25% of what you earn.

Recruitment in the Republic of Ireland

The recruitment service industry in Ireland is a flourishing commercial environment built on the strong and constant economic growth Ireland has experienced the last 10–15 years due to the Celtic Tiger, most prominently in Dublin. Specialized recruitment agencies (sometimes known as employment agencies or simply recruiters) across the country offer personnel consulting, specialist corporate recruiting, CV databasing, job-finding and headhunting, and temporary worker management services. These agencies usually work with larger business clients who are seeking qualified employees. There are approximately 600 recruitment agencies in Ireland, with an estimated 300 of those based in Dublin alone. Often large, growing businesses in Ireland prefer to outsource their recruitment and job advertising needs to an outside firm, and recruitment agencies offer these key services to these clients, usually in exchange for a percentage-based compensation matched from the new employee's earned salary. In this way, the client pays the recruitment agency for services rendered – the candidate (new employee) should not pay anything for being recruited.

Employment agencies in Ireland are licensed by the Department of Enterprise, Trade and Employment under the *Employment Agency Act 1971*. The main thrust of the act is to outlaw exploitation of jobseekers. Under the act an agency is permitted to charge a maximum of one pound (€1.27).

In recent times the Irish economy has slumped and the success of traditional recruitment agencies has begun to slide. Indeed a large number of Irish agencies have gone out of business altogether (300 in dublin falling to around 50), and there have been growing concerns about the future of the industry. This is due, in no small part, to the large fee's charged by traditional agencies (The industry average is 15% of the first years salary). In reaction to this more and more companies are rebranding themselves as Flat Fee recruiters[1] offering a slightly reduced service at heavily reduced fees, some under €1000 per placement.

References

[1] For example see www.easyrecruit.ie

Recruitment Process Insourcing

Recruitment Process Insourcing ("RPI") is a diversion from contemporary Recruitment Process Outsourcing (RPO) services, a subset of Business Process Outsourcing. RPI differs from RPO in its more intimate delivery, focusing on absorbing the client company's current state, culture, and alignment with special attention paid to the needs and demands of the fourth Generation candidate marketplace and its unique recruitment, retention and talent development challenges.

Key Differentiators of RPI

- Its delivery of services is onsite
- Recruitment campaigns should be branded in collaboration with the client's human resources operations
- Retainer/Fulfillment fee structure
- Scalable to Demand
- Addresses key stages of Organizational Maturity Model
- Cost effective, faster and higher rate of retention than Contingency Search
- Process maturity and execution cuts across company functions and industry disciplines.

Recruitment Process Outsourcing

Recruitment Process Outsourcing is a form of business process outsourcing (BPO) where an employer outsources or transfers all or part of its recruitment activities to an external service provider.

The Recruitment Process Outsourcing Association defines RPO as follows: "when a provider acts as a company's internal recruitment function for a portion or all of its jobs. RPO providers manage the entire recruiting/hiring process from job profiling through the onboarding of the new hire, including staff, technology, method and reporting. A properly managed RPO will improve a company's time to hire, increase the quality of the candidate pool, provide verifiable metrics, reduce cost and improve governmental compliance."[1]

The RPO Alliance, a group of the Human Resources Outsourcing Association (HROA), approved this definition in February 2009: "Recruitment Process Outsourcing (RPO) is a form of business process outsourcing (BPO) where an employer transfers all or part of its recruitment processes to an external service provider. An RPO provider can provide its own or may assume the company's staff, technology, methodologies and reporting. In all cases, RPO differs greatly from providers such as staffing companies and contingent/retained search providers in that it assumes ownership of the design and management of the recruitment process and the responsibility of results."[2]

Occasional recruitment support, for example temporary, contingency and executive search services is more analogous to out-tasking, co-sourcing or just sourcing. In this example, the service provider is "a" source for certain types of recruitment activity.[3] The biggest distinction between RPO and other types of staffing is *Process*. In RPO, the service provider assumes ownership of the process, while in other types of staffing the service provider is part of a process controlled by the organization buying their services.

History

While temporary, contingency and executive search firms have provided staffing services for many decades, the concept of an employer outsourcing the management and ownership of part or all of their recruiting process was not first realized on a consistent basis until the 1970s, in Silicon Valley's highly competitive high-tech labor market. Fast-growing high-tech companies were hard-pressed to locate and hire the technical specialists they required, and so had little choice but to pay large fees to highly specialized external recruiters in order to staff their projects. Over time, companies began to examine how they might reduce the growing expenses of recruitment fees while still hiring hard-to-find technical specialists. Toward this end, companies began to examine the various steps in the recruiting process with an eye toward outsourcing only those portions that they had the greatest difficulty with and that added the greatest value to them. Initial RPO programs typically consisted of companies purchasing lists of potential candidates from RPO vendors. This "search/research" function, as it was called, generated names of competitors' employees for a company and served to augment the pool of potential candidates from which that company could hire.

Over time, as business in general embraced the concept of outsourcing more and more, RPO gained favor among Human Resource management: not only did RPO reduce overhead costs from their budgets, but it also helped improve the company's competitive advantage in the labor market. As labor markets became more and more competitive, RPO became more of an acceptable option. Furthermore, through the advent in the 1980s and 1990s of human resources outsourcing (HRO) companies that began taking on the processes associated with benefits, taxes and payroll, companies began recognizing that recruiting—a significant cost of HR—should also be considered for outsourcing. In the early 2000s, more companies began considering the outsourcing of recruitment for major portions of their recruiting need.

There have been fundamental changes in the US labor market that serve to reinforce the use of RPO as well. The labor market has become increasingly dynamic: workers today change employers more often than in previous generations. De-regulated labor markets have also created a shift towards contract and part-time labor and shorter work tenures. These trends increase recruitment activity and may encourage the use of RPO. It should also be noted that even in slower economic times or higher unemployment, RPO is still considered by companies to assist in an increasing need to screen through a larger candidate pool.

Benefits

RPO's promoters claim that the solution offers improvement in quality, cost, service and speed.

- Quality and Cost - RPO providers claim that leveraging economies of scale enables them to offer recruitment processes at lower cost while economies of scope allow them to operate as high-quality specialists. Those economies of scale and scope arise from a larger staff of recruiters, databases of candidate resumes, and investment in recruitment tools and networks. RPO solutions are also claimed to change fixed investment costs into variable costs that flex with fluctuation in recruitment activity. Companies may pay by transaction rather than by staff member, thus avoiding under-utilization or forcing costly layoffs of recruitment staff when activity is low.

- Service and Speed - The commercial relationship between an RPO provider and a client is likely to be based on specific performance targets. With remuneration dependent on the attainment of such targets, an RPO provider will concentrate their resources in the most effective way - at times to the exclusion of non-core activity. Traditional internal recruitment teams are less likely to have such clearly defined performance targets.

Organizations with efficient hiring process that are viewed as employers of choice by potential staff may stand to gain benefits from an RPO process.

Risks

RPO can only succeed in the context of a well-defined corporate and staffing strategy. As with any program, a company must manage its RPO activities, providing initial direction and continued monitoring to assure the desired results.

- Loose Definition of RPO - As RPO is a commercial concept rather than a specific definition, there is little regulation to RPO providers. As such, a recruitment agency may brand their services as RPO without actually structuring them in a way that will provide the most benefit to their clients.

- Cost - The cost of engaging an RPO provider may be more than the cost of the internal recruitment department, as an RPO provider is likely to have higher business overheads.

- Effectiveness - Improperly implemented RPO could reduce the effectiveness of recruitment, should an RPO provider not understand or seek to understand the recruitment solution that they will be providing.

- Failure to Deliver - RPO service providers may fail to provide the quality or volume of staff required by their clients, especially when finding candidates in industry sectors where there are staff shortages.

- Lack of Competition - Placing all recruitment in the hands of a single outside provider may discourage the competition that would arise if multiple recruitment providers were used.

- Pre-Existing Issues - An RPO solution may not work if the company's existing recruitment processes are performing poorly, or if the service provider lacks appropriate recruitment processes or procedures to work with the client. In this situation, it is better for the company to undergo a recruitment optimisation programme.

- Employer Branding - RPO providers do not necessarily act as custodians of their clients' employer brand in the way that a strongly aligned retained search firm or internal recruiting resource would.

- Engagement - Many RPO organisations perform their staffing functions and service offsite or offshore, disconnecting the provider from the client company's growth and recruiting strategy. While this effect can be mitigated through strong relationship management, some of the momentum and energy associated with the rapid upscaling of a workforce through recruitment may dissipate.

References

[1] Rpoa Rfp (http://www.rpoassociation.org/index.php)

[2] HROA Special Interest Group Publishes Definition of RPO, Feb. 19, 2009 (http://www.marketwire.com/press-release/Hroa-952070.html)

[3] differentiating between RPO and other types of staffing (http://www.hrotoday.com/Magazine.asp?artID=1641)

Referral recruitment

Referral recruitment is the development of a recruitment strategy that is dependent on referrals by existing employees. This approach is usually favoured when the costs of recruiting needs to be reduced. As a result of the recession the amount of time and money invested in referral schemes has increased due to the perceived frivolousness of other method of recruiting.

There are disadvantages to putting too much emphasis on referral schemes, such as reduced workforce diversity and unfairness regarding other prospective candidates.[1] To combat these disadvantages some companies are opening up their referral schemes to external contributors. Not only does this help to combat the aforementioned issues, but it also increases the size of the network of potential referrers.

[1] Government, UK. "Employee Referral Schemes" (http://www.bis.gov.uk/policies/higher-education/access-to-professions/prg/recruitment-step-by-step/attracting-applications/employee-referral-schemes). *Employee Referral Schemes*. Department for Business Innovation and Skills. . Retrieved 28 March 2011.

recruitment

Résumé

A **résumé** (pronounced English pronunciation: /ˈrɛzjʊmeɪ/ *rez-ew-may* or /rɛzjʊˈmeɪ/; French: [ʁezyme]; sometimes spelled **resume**) is a document used by individuals to present their background and skillsets. Résumés can be used for a variety of reasons but most often to secure new employment.[1] A typical résumé contains a summary of relevant job experience and education. The résumé is usually one of the first items, along with a cover letter and sometimes job application packet, that a potential employer encounters regarding the job seeker and is typically used to screen applicants, often followed by an interview, when seeking employment. The résumé is comparable to a curriculum vitae in many countries, although in English Canada and the United States it is substantially different.

General

In many contexts, a résumé is short (usually one to three pages), and directs a reader's attention to the aspects of a person's background that are directly relevant to a particular position. Many résumés contain keywords that potential employers are looking for, make heavy use of active verbs, and display content in a flattering manner.

Since increasing numbers of job seekers and employers are using Internet-based job search engines to find and fill employment positions, longer résumés are needed for applicants to differentiate and distinguish themselves, and employers are becoming more accepting of résumés that are longer than two pages . Many professional résumé writers and human resources professionals believe that a résumé should be long enough so that it provides a concise, adequate, and accurate description of an applicant's employment history and skills . A résumé is a marketing tool in which the content should be adapted to suit each individual job application and/or applications aimed at a particular industry. The transmission of résumés directly to employers became

Resume outline for a college student

increasingly popular as late as 2002 . Jobseekers were able to circumvent the job application process and reach employers through direct email contact and résumé blasting, a term meaning the mass distribution of résumés to increase personal visibility within the job market. However the mass distribution of résumés to employers can often have a negative effect on the applicant's chances of securing employment as the résumés tend not to be tailored for the specific positions the applicant is applying for. It is usually therefore more sensible to adjust the résumé for each position applied for.

The complexity and simplicity of various résumé formats tend to produce results varying from person to person, for the occupation, and to the industry. It is important to note that résumés or CV's used by medical professionals, professors, artists and people in other specialized fields may be comparatively longer. For example, an artist's résumé, typically excluding any non-art-related employment, may include extensive lists of solo and group exhibitions.

Styles

A simple résumé is a summary typically limited to one or two pages of size A4 or Letter-size highlighting only those experiences and credentials that the author considers most relevant to the desired position. US academic CVs are typically longer.

Résumés may be organized in different ways. The following are some of the more common formats:

Reverse chronological résumé

A reverse chronological résumé enumerates a candidate's job experiences in reverse chronological order, generally covering the last 10 to 15 years. Positions are listed with start and end dates. Current active positions on a resume typically have the start date listed to present or the current year. Both are considered acceptable.

The reverse chronological résumé format is most commonly used by those who are not professional résumé writers. In using this format, the main body of the document becomes the Professional Experience section, starting from the most recent experience going chronologically backwards through a succession of previous experience. The reverse chronological résumé works to build credibility through experience gained, while illustrating career growth over time and filling all gaps in a career trajectory. A chronological résumé is not recommended in the event that the job seeker has gaps in his career summary. In the United Kingdom the chronological résumé tends to extend only as far back as the subject's GCSE/Standard Grade qualifications.

Functional résumé

A functional résumé lists work experience and skills sorted by skill area or job function.

The functional résumé is used to assert a focus to skills that are specific to the type of position being sought. This format directly emphasizes specific professional capabilities and utilizes experience summaries as its primary means of communicating professional competency. In contrast, the chronological résumé format will briefly highlight these competencies prior to presenting a comprehensive timeline of career growth via reverse-chronological listing with most recent experience listed first. The functional résumé works well for those making a career change, having a varied work history and with little work experience. A functional résumé is also preferred for applications to jobs that require a very specific skill set or clearly defined personality traits. A functional résumé is a good method for highlighting particular skills or experience, especially when those particular skills or experience may have derived from a role which was held some time ago. Rather than focus on the length of time that has passed, the functional résumé allows the reader to identify those skills quickly.

Hybrid résumé

The hybrid résumé balances the functional and chronological approaches. A résumé organized this way typically leads with a functional list of job skills, followed by a chronological list of employers. The hybrid résumé has a tendency to repeat itself and is therefore less widely used than the other two forms.

Online résumés

The Internet has brought about a new age for the résumé. As the search for employment has become more electronic, résumés have followed suit. It is common for employers to only accept résumés electronically, either out of practicality or preference. This electronic boom has changed much about the way résumés are written, read, and handled.

- Job seekers must choose a file format in which to maintain their résumé. Many employers, especially recruitment agencies on their behalf, insist on receiving résumés as Microsoft Word documents. The old Word (.doc 1997–2003) version is the preferred version.[2] Others will only accept résumés formatted in HTML, PDF, or plain ASCII text.
- Many potential employers now find candidates' résumés through search engines, which makes it more important for candidates to use appropriate keywords when writing a résumé.
- Many large employers use electronic résumé processing systems to handle large volumes of résumés. Job ads may direct applicants to email a résumé to their company or visit their website and submit a résumé in electronic format.

Some career fields include a special section listing the life-long works of the author. For computer-related fields, the softography; for musicians and composers, the discography; for actors, a filmography.

Keeping résumés online has become increasingly common for people in professions that benefit from the multimedia and rich detail that are offered by an HTML résumé, such as actors, photographers, graphic designers, developers, dancers, etc.

Job seekers are finding an ever increasing demand to have an electronic version of their résumé available to employers and professionals who use Internet recruiting at any time.

For job seekers, taking résumés online also facilitates distribution to multiple employers via Internet. Online résumé distribution services have emerged to allow job seekers to distribute their résumés to employers of their choices via email.

Another advantage to online résumés is the significant cost savings over traditional hiring methods. In the United States, the Employment Management Association has included Internet advertising in its cost-per-hire surveys for several years. In 1997, for example, it reported that the average cost-per-hire for a print ad was $3,295, while the average cost-per-hire with the Internet was $377.[3] This in turn has cut costs for many growing organizations, as well as saving time and energy in recruitment. Prior to the development of résumés in electronic format, employers would have to sort through massive stacks of paper to find suitable candidates without any way of filtering out the poor candidates. Employers are now able to set search parameters in their database of résumés to reduce the number of résumés which must be reviewed in detail in the search for the ideal candidate.

Finally, the Internet is enabling new technologies to be employed with résumés, such as video résumés—especially popular for multimedia job seekers. Another emerging technology is graphic-enabled résumés.[4]

References

[1] resume. (http://dictionary.reference.com/browse/resume) Dictionary.com Unabridged. Random House, Inc. 30 Oct. 2010.

[2] John Miller, MIT Academy research, "The resume in eyes of the business owner", Articles.org

[3] Career Development Articles – Career Planning Guide – Career Opportunities (http://www.careerjournal.com/hrcenter/weddlesguide/ 19990405-weddle.html)

[4] How an Older Worker Can Get the Interview – US News and World Report (http://www.usnews.com/articles/business/careers/2008/05/ 28/how-an-older-worker-can-get-the-interview.html)

Further reading

* Bennett, Scott A. *The Elements of Résumé Style: Essential Rules and Eye-Opening Advice for Writing Résumés and Cover Letters that Work.* AMACOM, 2005 ISBN 0-8144-7280-X.

* Whitcomb, Susan Britton. *Resume Magic: Trade Secrets of a Professional Resume Writer,* Third Edition. JIST Publishing, 2006. ISBN 978-1593573119.

* *Euro CV*, Jean-Pierre Thiollet, Paris, Top Editions, 1997. ISBN 2 87 73 1131 7

Role-based assessment

Modern psychological testing can be traced back to 1908 with the introduction of the first successful intelligence test, the Binet-Simon Scale.[1] From the Binet-Simon came the revised version, the Stanford-Binet, which was used in the development of the Army Alpha and Army Beta tests used by the United States military.[2] During World War I, Robert S. Woodworth developed the Woodworth Personal Data Sheet (WPDS), to determine which soldiers were better prepared to handle the stresses of combat. The WPDS signaled a shift in the focus of psychological testing from intellect to personality.[3]

By the 1940s, the quantitative measurement of personality traits had become a central theme in psychology, and it has remained so into the 2000s. During this time, numerous variations and versions of 'personality tests' have been created, including the widely used Myers-Briggs, DISC, and Cattell's 16PF Questionnaire.[4]

Role-Based Assessment (RBA) differs significantly from personality testing. Instead of quantifying individual personality factors, RBA's methodology was developed, from its very beginnings, to make qualitative observations of human interaction. In this sense, RBA is a form of behavioral simulation. Understanding the quality of a person's behavior on a team can be a valuable adjunct to other forms of evaluation (such as data on experience, knowledge, skills, and personality) because the ability to successfully cooperate and collaborate with others is fundamental to organizational performance.

Concepts

Coherence

In TGI Role-Based Assessment, 'Coherence' describes a positive and constructive orientation to working with others to achieve common goals, overcome obstacles, and meet organizational needs.

Role

A person's 'Role' describes their strongest affinity for, or attraction to, serving a certain type of organizational need, e.g., planning for the future vs. executing current tasks vs. preserving and sharing knowledge.

Teaming Characteristics

Each RBA report includes a detailed section on 'Teaming Characteristics', which are derived, in part, from the relationship between a person's level of Coherence and their unique Role (or Roles). As their name suggests, Teaming Characteristics can help managers and coaches to understand how well a person will 'fit' within a team and/or adapt to their job responsibilities.

Historical Development

Dr. Janice Presser began collaborating with Dr. Jack Gerber in 1988 to develop tools and methods for measuring the fundamental elements of human 'teaming' behavior, with a goal of improving individual and team performance. Their work began as a blending of Dr. Presser's earlier work in family and social relationships with Dr. Gerber's 'Mosaic Figures' test, which had been designed to produce qualitative information on how individuals view other people.

Three generations of assessments were developed, tested and used in the context of actual business performance. The initial Executive Behavior Assessment was focused on the behavior of persons with broad responsibility for organizational performance. The second iteration, called the Enhanced Executive Behavior Assessment, incorporated metrics on the behavior of executives working in teams. Drs. Presser and Gerber then successfully applied their testing methodology to team contributors outside of the executive ranks, and as development and testing efforts continued, Role-Based Assessment (RBA) emerged.

By 1999, RBA was established as a paper-based assessment, and was being sold for use in pre-hire screening and organizational development. Drs Presser and Gerber formed The Gabriel Institute in 2001, with the goal of making RBA available to a greater audience via the Internet. They knew that the effort would require years of development at unknown cost, but they believed that the potential benefits to people, teams, and organizations of every size and kind were too important to ignore.

Mid-year in 2009, TGI Role-Based Assessment[TM] became generally available as an online assessment instrument. Later in 2009, the Society for Human Resource Management (SHRM) published a two-part white paper by Dr. Presser, which introduced ground- breaking ideas on the measurement and valuation of human synergy in organizations, and an approach to the creation of a strong, positively-oriented human infrastructure.[5] [6]

Applications

The most common use of TGI Role-Based Assessment is in pre-hire screening evaluations. RBA's focus on 'teaming' behavior offers a different way to allegedly predict how an individual will fit with company culture, on a given team, and how they are likely to respond to specific job requirements.[7]

RBA is also claimed to have unique potential for strengthening a human infrastructure. Results from RBA reports can be aggregated, providing quantitative data that is used for analysis and resolution of team performance problems, and to identify and select candidates for promotion.[8]

References

[1] Santrock, John W. (2008) A Topical Approach to Life-Span Development (4th Ed.) Concept of Intelligence (283-284) New York: McGraw-Hill.

[2] Fancher, R. (1985). The Intelligence Men: Makers of the IQ Controversy. New York:W.W. Norton & Company

[3] Kaplan, Robert M.; Saccuzzo, Dennis P. (2009). *Psychological Testing: Principles, Applications, and Issues* (Seventh ed.). Belmont (CA): Wadsworth. pp. 17–18. ISBN 978-0-495-09555-2. Lay summary (http://www.cengagebrain.com/shop/en/US/storefront/ US?cmd=catProductDetail&ISBN=0495095559&cid=GB1) (9 November 2010).

[4] " Personality Theories, Types and Tests. (http://www.businessballs.com/personalitystylesmodels.htm)" Businessballs.com. 2009.

[5] SHRM - " The Measurement & Valuation of Human Infrastructure: An Introduction to CHI Indicators (http://www.shrm.org/Research/ Articles/Articles/Pages/InfrastructureCHI.aspx)"

[6] SHRM – " The Measurement & Valuation of Human Infrastructure: An Intro. To the 'New Way to Know' (http://www.shrm.org/Research/ Articles/Articles/Pages/New Way to Know.aspx)"

[7] Edmonds Wickman, Lindsay. " Role-Based Assessment: Thinking Inside the Box. (http://www.talentmgt.com/assessment_evaluation/ 2008/October/746/)" Talent Management Magazine (October 2008). Media Tec Publishing Inc.

[8] Edmonds Wickman, Lindsay. " Role-Based Assessment: Thinking Inside the Box. (http://www.talentmgt.com/assessment_evaluation/ 2008/October/746/)" Talent Management Magazine (October 2008). Media Tec Publishing Inc.

External links

- University of Pennsylvania Journal of Labor and Employment Law " Personality Tests in Jeopardy (https:// www.thegabrielinstitute.com/pdfget/? file=UPenn_JournalofLaborEmploymentLaw_Assessments.pdf)"
- Innovation America – " Put Your Money Where Your Team Is! (http://www.innovationamerica.us/index.php/ innovation-daily/3780-put-your-money-where- your-team-is-)"
- National Association of Seed and Venture Funds (NASVF) " Make Sure People Will Fit…Before You Hire Them. (http://www.nasvf.org/index.php?option=com_content&view=article& id=146:make-sure-people-will-fit-nbefore-you-hire-them&catid=5:features&Itemid=38)"

Salary

A **salary** is a form of periodic payment from an employer to an employee, which may be specified in an employment contract. It is contrasted with piece wages, where each job, hour or other unit is paid separately, rather than on a periodic basis.

From the point of a business, salary can also be viewed as the cost of acquiring human resources for running operations, and is then termed personnel expense or salary expense. In accounting, salaries are recorded in payroll accounts.

History

First paid salary

While there is no first pay stub for the first work-for-pay exchange, the first salaried work would have required a human society advanced enough to have a barter system to allow work to be exchanged for goods or other work. More significantly, it presupposes the existence of organized employers—perhaps a government or a religious body—that would facilitate work-for-hire exchanges on a regular enough basis to constitute salaried work. From this, most infer that the first salary would have been paid in a village or city during the Neolithic Revolution, sometime between 10,000 BCE and 6000 BCE.

A cuneiform inscribed clay tablet dated about BCE 3100 provides a record of the daily beer rations for workers in Mesopotamia. The beer is represented by an upright jar with a pointed base. The symbol for rations is a human head eating from a bowl. Round and semicircular impressions represent the measurements.[1]

By the time of the Hebrew Book of Ezra (550 to 450 BCE), salt from a person was synonymous with drawing sustenance, taking pay, or being in that person's service. At that time salt production was strictly controlled by the monarchy or ruling elite. Depending on the translation of Ezra 4:14 [2], the servants of King Artaxerxes I of Persia explain their loyalty variously as "because we are salted with the salt of the palace" or "because we have maintenance from the king" or "because we are responsible to the king."

The Roman word *salarium*

Similarly, the Roman word *salarium* linked employment, salt and soldiers, but the exact link is unclear. The least common theory is that the word soldier itself comes from the Latin *sal dare* (to give salt). Alternatively, the Roman historian Pliny the Elder stated as an aside in his Natural History's discussion of sea water, that "[I]n Rome. . .the soldier's pay was originally salt and the word salary derives from it. . ." *Plinius Naturalis Historia XXXI.* [3] Others note that *soldier* more likely derives from the gold solidus, with which soldiers were known to have been paid, and maintain instead that the *salarium* was either an allowance for the purchase of salt [4] or the price of having soldiers conquer salt supplies [5] and guard the Salt Roads [6] (*Via Salarium*) that led to Rome.

Payment in the Roman empire and medieval and pre-industrial Europe

Regardless of the exact connection, the *salarium* paid to Roman soldiers has defined a form of work-for-hire ever since in the Western world, and gave rise to such expressions as "being worth one's salt."

Yet within the Roman Empire or (later) medieval and pre-industrial Europe and its mercantile colonies, salaried employment appears to have been relatively rare and mostly limited to servants and higher status roles, especially in government service. Such roles were largely remunerated by the provision of lodging and food, and livery clothes, but cash was also paid. Many courtiers, such as valets de chambre in late medieval courts were paid annual amounts, sometimes supplemented by large if unpredictable extra payments. At the other end of the social scale, those in many forms of employment either received no pay, as with slavery (though many slaves were paid some money at least), serfdom, and indentured servitude, or received only a fraction of what was produced, as with sharecropping. Other common alternative models of work included self- or co-operative employment, as with masters in artisan guilds, who often had salaried assistants, or corporate work and ownership, as with medieval universities and monasteries.

Payment during the Commercial Revolution

Even many of the jobs initially created by the Commercial Revolution in the years from 1520 to 1650 and later during Industrialisation in the 18th and 19th centuries would not have been salaried, but, to the extent they were paid as employees, probably paid an hourly or daily wage or paid per unit produced (also called piece work).

Share in earnings as payment

In corporations of this time, such as the several East India Companies, many managers would have been remunerated as owner-shareholders. Such a remuneration scheme is still common today in accounting, investment, and law firm partnerships where the leading professionals are equity partners, and do not technically receive a salary, but rather make a periodic "draw" against their share of annual earnings.

The Second Industrial Revolution and salaried payment

From 1870 to 1930, the Second Industrial Revolution gave rise to the modern business corporation powered by railroads, electricity and the telegraph and telephone. This era saw the widespread emergence of a class of salaried executives and administrators who served the new, large-scale enterprises being created.

New managerial jobs lent themselves to salaried employment, in part because the effort and output of "office work" were hard to measure hourly or piecewise, and in part because they did not necessarily draw remuneration from share ownership.

As Japan rapidly industrialized in the 20th century, the idea of office work was novel enough that a new Japanese word (salaryman), was coined to describe those who performed it, and their remuneration.

Salaried employment in the 20th century

In the 20th century, the rise of the service economy made salaried employment even more common in developed countries, where the relative share of industrial production jobs declined, and the share of executive, administrative, computer, marketing, and creative jobs—all of which tended to be salaried—increased.

Salary and other forms of payment today

Today, the idea of a salary continues to evolve as part of a system of all the combined rewards that employers offer to employees. Salary (also now known as fixed pay) is coming to be seen as part of a "total rewards" system which includes bonuses, incentive pay, and commissions), benefits and perquisites (or perks), and various other tools which help employers link rewards to an employee's measured performance.

Salaries in the U.S.

Further information: Income in the United States

In the United States, the distinction between periodic salaries (which are normally paid regardless of hours worked) and hourly wages (meeting a minimum wage test and providing for overtime) was first codified by the Fair Labor Standards Act of 1938. At that time, five categories were identified as being "exempt" from minimum wage and overtime protections, and therefore salariable. In 1991, some computer workers were added as a sixth category but effective August 23, 2004 the categories were revised and reduced back down to five (executive, administrative, professional, computer, and outside sales employees). Salary is generally set on a yearly basis.

"The FLSA requires that most employees in the United States be paid at least the federal minimum wage for all hours worked and overtime pay at time and one-half the regular rate of pay for all hours worked over 40 hours in a workweek.

However, Section 13(a)(1) of the FLSA provides an exemption from both minimum wage and overtime pay for employees employed as bona fide executive, administrative, professional and outside sales employees. Section 13(a)(1) and Section 13(a)(17) also exempt certain computer employees. To qualify for exemption, employees generally must meet certain tests regarding their job duties *and* be paid on a salary basis at not less than $455 per week. Job titles do not determine exempt status. In order for an exemption to apply, an employee's specific job duties and salary must meet all the requirements of the Department's regulations." [7]

Of these five categories only Computer Employees has an hourly wage-based exemption ($27.63 per hour) while Outside Sales Employee is the only main category not to have the minimum salary ($455 per week) test though some sub categories under Professional (like teachers and practitioners of law or medicine) also do not have the minimum salary test.

A general rule for comparing periodic salaries to hourly wages is based on a standard 40 hour work week with 50 weeks per year (minus two weeks for vacation). (Example: $40,000/year periodic salary divided by 50 weeks equals $800/week. Divide $800/week by 40 standard hours equals $20/hour). Real median household income in the United States climbed 1.3 percent between 2006 and 2007, reaching $50,233 according to a report released by the U.S. census bureau. This is the third annual increase in real median household income.

Salaries in Japan

Further information: Salaryman

In Japan, owners would notify employees of salary increases through "jirei". The concept still exists and has been replaced with an electronic form, or email in larger companies.

Salaries in India

In India, salaries are generally paid on the last working day of the month (Government, Public sector departments, Multinational organizations as well as majority of other private sector companies). Several other companies pay after the month is over, but generally by the 5th of every month. However there are companies pay after this also. For instance, for companies under 'Godrej Group', salary is paid on 9th of month for the preceding month. In case 9th is a holiday, it is paid on 10th, and in case both 9th and 10th are holiday, it is paid on 8th.

The minimum wages in India are governed by the Minimum Wages Act, 1948. Details regarding the same can be seen at http://labourbureau.nic.in/wagetab.htm Employees in India are notified regarding their salary increase through a hard copy letters given to them.

References

[1] Early writing tablet recording the allocation of beer, British Museum. "BBC History of the World in 100 Objects" (http://www.britishmuseum.org/explore/highlights/highlight_objects/me/t/tablet,_allocation_of_beer.aspx). . Retrieved 2010 - 11 - 11.

[2] http://bible.cc/ezra/4-14.htm

[3] http://penelope.uchicago.edu/Thayer/L/Roman/Texts/Pliny_the_Elder/31*.html

[4] http://www.etymonline.com/index.php?search=salary

[5] http://www.salt.org.il/arch.html

[6] http://www.salt.org.il/turkey.html

[7] http://www.dol.gov/whd/regs/compliance/fairpay/main.htm DOL's FairPay Overtime Initiative

Screening Resumes

Screening resumes is the process of sorting resumes to disqualify candidates using successively more detailed examinations of the resumes. The objective is to locate the most qualified candidates for an open job.[1] While some of this can be done with the aid of automation and computers, there are still skills and techniques that help quickly eliminate unqualified candidates.

Introduction

One of the first meaningful decision points of a recruitment effort is the evaluation of skills, knowledge and abilities for a given job candidate. The most common form of this evaluation is the screening of resumes.

Process

The objective of screening resumes is to eliminate candidates that to not meet the job requirements. Today the act of screening a resume may generally be divided into three steps, the first pass or scanning for keywords, the second pass which includes reading the resume to evaluate the candidate against the job requirements and the final pass, a full review of the resume including a subjective qualitative review of the candidates job history. Each step requires a more detailed review of the resume.

Keywords

The resume screening process presumes a well written job description. From this job description, 3-5 carefully chosen keywords are selected. These keywords are used to narrow down a large pool of candidates to a more manageable set of resumes that will be read in more detail.

The keywords selected are derived from required skills or activities in the job description. To minimize the number of desirable candidates dropped in this first step, consider using synonyms and closely related terms in addition to the keywords selected.[2]

This step of the process can often be aided by computers. For example, if you have a resume database, these keywords are the search queries used to find potential candidates in the database.

Further, this step is sometimes delegated to a junior person who can be trained to look for keywords and perform the initial sort.

Evaluation

Once a resume has been initially screened for keywords, it needs a more careful review. This second pass is designed to verify some of the second order criteria of the job description are met. For instance, level of education, years of experience required by the position, salary range and current location. Other functions of this evaluation include a closer look at job functions performed by the candidate and comparing them to the job description.

This phase often requires a more in depth understanding of the job description and requirements. For instance to determine relevant years of experience, the reviewer must add the number of years at the relevant jobs to come up the years experience. It can often be a judgment call on which parts of a job history are relevant to a job search. This means the person performing this step must have a suitable depth of understanding about the job description and requirements for the position.

Qualitative Review

Resumes that reach this step of the process are from candidate that meet many of the requirements of the job description.[3] This final pass is to examine the more subtle subjective qualities of the candidate. The objective is remove candidates with red flags that could mean potential job fraud and to separate the top candidates from the remaining resumes.

Resume Red Flags

There are a number of red flags when looking at resumes that should, at the very least, be noted and questioned as part of any phone screen with the candidate. Some of these red flags are easy to spot such as gaps in employment, job hopping, multiple moves to different states, using years instead of months/years for employment history and noting a college and degree program without indicating graduation. Others still are more subtle, like a significant drop in responsibility or a completely new career direction. While there are many valid reasons for some of these red flags, it should generate follow up questions if all other qualities of the resume are suitable for moving to further contact with the candidate.

Other Factors

Other factors is a broad term that is somewhat subjective when it comes to reviewing resumes. Here are a couple of examples that may help give one candidate an edge over another in the review process.

* Does the candidate have a history of advancement including more responsibility and challenge in each subsequent position?
* Does the candidate have experience working at a company of similar size and resource?
* Does the candidate have the correct industry experience?
* If this person applied directly for the position, would it be a significant drop in responsibility or challenge?
* Is the person over qualified? Are they willing to accept a much lower salary?

These other factors are best used to further evaluate candidates already deemed to meet the basic qualification. They serve to initially prioritize the next phase of the recruitment process, which is to make initial contact with the candidates.

References

[1] Recruiting Essentials on How to Review a Resume (http://www.staffing-and-recruiting-essentials.com/How-To-Review-A-Resume.html)

[2] Resume Screening with Keywords (http://www.collegerecruiter.com/internships/2009/04/pass_the_first_round_of_resume.php)

[3] Steps in a resume review (http://humanresources.about.com/od/selectemployees/a/resume_review_2.htm)

Simultaneous Recruiting of New Graduates

Simultaneous Recruiting of New Graduates or **Periodic Recruiting of New Graduates** (新卒一括採用 *Shinsotsu-Ikkatsu-Saiyō*) is the custom that companies hire new graduates all at once and employ them; this custom is unique to Japan and South Korea. The Japanese post-war economic miracle spread this custom among many companies in order to produce steady employment every year.

In these countries, most students do job hunting during their period of attendance at universities or high schools to get informal offers of employment. Since companies like to hire only new graduates, some students who have not found a job as graduation approaches opt to stay in school another year. Most companies pay little attention to academic records or a student's university experiences, preferring to train new employees within the company. The prestige of the university students get into determines their success in life. The system is inherited from the Chinese Imperial Examination. In other countries, people tend to do job-hunting soon before or after graduation, and companies do not discriminate against those who did not graduate recently.

The practice is for big companies to hire school-leavers "in bulk" to replace retiring workers and groom in-house talent, and the numbers can vary widely from year to year. Employers hire a group of people in a mechanic fashion every year. Toyota, for example, hired more than 1,500 graduates in 2010, nearly halving the intake from the year before. Toyota plans to cut it further to 1,200 for 2011 hires. The company may offer more jobs later on, but those who missed out on the current round of hiring will have a slim chance to land one because they will get trumped by fresh graduates.

It leaves thousands of young Japanese sidelined in extended studies, part-time jobs, or on the dole instead of supporting the domestic economy as the confident consumers and productive workers aging Japan badly needs.

Criticism

In Japanese society, the value of degrees in higher education is extremely low. If one has a doctorate in science, he can't expect employment at a respectable job. Japan's idiosyncratic Simultaneous Recruiting of New Graduates is a large factor.

Nowadays this traditional custom causes many social problems in Japan. If a Japanese person does not make a decision on employment before his/her university graduation, he/she will be faced with enormous hardships eventually finding a job because most Japanese companies hire students scheduled to graduate in spring. In recent years, an increasing number of university seniors looking for jobs have chosen to repeat a year to avoid being placed in the "previous graduate" category by companies. In the system Japanese companies penalize students who study overseas or have already graduated. Some people think the convention is behind the times and no longer necessary.

There is a lot of criticism of this custom. One professor criticizes the process: "If business is in a slump at the point of one's graduation and he cannot get a job, this custom produces inequality of opportunity, and people in this age bracket tend to remain unemployed for a long time."[1] Another professor criticizes: "If this custom is joined to permanent employment, it produces closed markets of employment, where outplacement is hard, and the employees tend to obey any and all unreasonable demands made by their companies so as not to be fired."[2] Whether they get a job when they graduate decides their whole life," says Yuki Honda, a professor at the University of Tokyo's Graduate School of Education.

Japan ranks 19th among the 19 OECD countries regarding freedom of choice in life.

References

[1] Youth Employment in Japan's Economic Recovery:'Freeters' and 'NEETs' (http://www.japanfocus.org/-Kosugi-Reiko/2022) The Asia-Pacific Journal: Japan Focus, 11th May 2006

[2] Career Development under the Lifetime Employment System of Japanese Organizations (http://ir.nul.nagoya-u.ac.jp/dspace/bitstream/ 2237/3769/1/KJ00000137258.pdf) (PDF) Bulletin of the Faculty of Education, Nagoya University, 1988, Vol. 35, 1-20

External links

- Bleak Economy, Japanese Students Grow Frustrated With Endless Job Hunt (http://chronicle.com/article/ Japanese-Students-Abandon/64007/In)
- More universities allowing students to delay graduation due to job shortage (http://mdn.mainichi.jp/mdnnews/ news/20100315p2a00m0na017000c.html)
- Japanese Graduates Finding Few Jobs (http://www.nytimes.com/1994/06/25/business/ company-news-japanese-graduates-finding-few-jobs.html)
- Ph. D.'s in Japan can't find work: Little recognition for high expertise, says Mainichi Communications Survey (http://www.mutantfrog.com/2005/06/16/getting-a-doctorate-in-japan/)
- Economic and Social Data Rankings (Freedom of choice in life) (http://www.kisc.meiji.ac.jp/cgi-isc/ cgiwrap/~kenjisuz/country.cgi?LG=e&CO=15)
- Hiring practices in Japan (http://www.economist.com/business-finance/displaystory.cfm?story_id=15720585)
- Once drawn to U.S. universities, more Japanese students staying home (http://www.washingtonpost.com/ wp-dyn/content/article/2010/04/10/AR2010041002835.html)
- Japan offers a lifetime job, if hired right out of school (http://www.usatoday.com/money/world/ 2009-03-05-japan-lifetime-employment_N.htm)
- Japanese jobseekers hold Tokyo pep rally (http://www.ajc.com/news/nation-world/ japanese-jobseekers-hold-tokyo-831044.html)

Social recruiting

Social recruiting is a contested term[1] . It is a concept at the intersection of recruitment and the embryonic field of social media. There are several terms used interchangeably including social hiring, social recruitment and social media recruitment.

Competing definitions

The most common definition used for social recruiting is that it is the process of sourcing or recruiting candidates through the use of social platforms as promotional and/or advertising channels by employers and recruiters. Career placement offices at university campuses also use social recruiting since social media is familiar to and often embraced by students and graduates as a job searching medium.

Since late 2009 there has been some discussion in the recruitment and social media communities about whether simply using social media as a communication and marketing channel can be called "social recruiting"[2] . The argument is that for recruiting to be truly social, it needs to build a community, facilitate communication within that community, and rely on social connections between community members to recruit.

References

[1] http://recruitingfuture.com/2011/03/08/redefining-social-recruiting-for-2011/
[2] http://www.booleanblackbelt.com/2010/07/how-social-recruiting-has-not-changed-recruitment/

Sourcing (personnel)

Sourcing in personnel management work refers to the identification and uncovering of candidates (also known as talent) through proactive recruiting techniques.

Historical context

The evolution of recruiting has changed significantly over the last few decades. What started out as the responsibility of office managers to place job advertisements in newspapers or help wanted signs to attract potential employees has now grown into a multibillion-dollar industry, where the identification of talent requires internal corporate recruitment departments or employment agencies solely focused on this transaction through both proactive and reactive recruiting techniques.

Today the actual act of identifying candidates has even been split into dedicated roles and job functions, whereas historically sourcing was the sole and inclusive responsibility of the recruiter along with other job responsibilities (examples):

- Screen and interview candidates against the position requirements
- Work closely with the hiring manager on hiring activities
- Help with the "offer letter" and interview process

A third-party recruitment agency or corporate recruiting department can now be made up of individuals dedicated to just the sourcing of candidates while recruiters can either focus on more account management responsibilities or leverage sourcing experts to supplement an additional volume of potential candidates. An increasing number of agencies and corporate recruiting departments outsource this work to a Recruitment Process Outsourcing vendor.

Detailed definition

The actual act of sourcing for candidates is performed by either a recruiter (be it an internal corporate recruiter or agency recruiter) or a dedicated recruiter just focused on the sourcing function. The definition of sourcing needs to be clearly defined by what it is, as much as what it is not. Candidate sourcing activity typically ends once the name, job title, job function and contact information for the potential candidate is determined by the candidate sourcer. To further develop a list of names that were sourced some companies have a second person then reach out to the names on the list to initiate a dialogue with them with the intention of pre-screening the candidate against the job requirements and gauging the interest level in hearing about new job opportunitites. This activity is called "candidate profiling" or "candidate pre-screening". The term candidate sourcing should not be confused with candidate research.

In some situations a person that "sources" candidates can and will perform both 'primary' and 'secondary' sourcing techniques to identify candidates as well as the candidate profiling to further pre-screen candidates but there is a growing market for experts solely focused on "telephone sourcing", "internet sourcing/researching" and candidate profiling. The actual act to source candidates can usually be split out into two clearly defined techniques: primary sourcing and secondary sourcing.

Primary sourcing/phone sourcing

In recruiting and sourcing, this means the leveraging of techniques (primarily the phone) to identify candidates with limited to no presence of these individuals in any easily accessible public forum (the Internet, published list, etc). It requires the uncovering of candidate information via a primary means of calling directly into organizations to uncover data on people, their role, title and responsibilities.

The term "phone sourcers" or "phone name generator" or "telephone names sourcer" generally applies to the utilization of primary sourcing techniques.[1]

Secondary sourcing/Internet sourcing

In recruiting and sourcing, this means the using of techniques (primarily the Internet and utilizing advanced Boolean operators) to identify candidates. Individuals in the recruiting industry that have deep expertise in uncovering talent in the harder to reach places on the internet (forums, blogs, alumni groups, conference attendee lists, personal home pages, etc).

The term "internet sourcer", "Internet name generator" or "internet researcher" generally applies to the use of secondary sourcing techniques.[2] [3]

Examples of sourcing techniques

Sourcing for candidates refers to proactively identifying people who are either a) not actively looking for job opportunities (passive candidates) or b) candidates who are actively searching for job opportunities (active candidates), though the industry also recognizes the existence of 'active candidate sourcing' using candidate databases, job boards and the like.

Though there has been much debate within the staffing community as to how to accurately define an "active candidate" versus a "passive candidate" typically either term is irrelevant to a candidate sourcer as the status of any particular candidate can change from moment to moment or with a simple phone call from a recruiter that happenes to present a job opportunity that is perceived to be either better or worse than the job the person has now. The status of being an "active" or "passive" candidate is fluid and changing depending on the circumstances and position being offered.

Activities related to sourcing in Recruiting can also be categorized into Push Activities and Pull Activities. **Push Activities**: Are activities undertaken to reach out to the target audience. This generally includes, Head Hunting, HTML Mailers, Referral Follow-ups.

Pull Activities: Are activities that result in applicants coming to know of an opportunity on their own. Pull Activities may include the following: Advertising on a Microsite with Registration Process (This makes Search Engines Crawl the site and index it on various Search Results), Advertising (In Newspapers, Cable TVs, through Flyers/Leaflets in Malls etc.) with a phone number and email id clearly mention for SMSs and Inbound Calls and Mails. Posting a Job in Job Portals, which will be seen by candidates and applied against.

In summary, A push activity is akin to a direct marketing activity, whereas Pull activities are more of indirect marketing of the same concept. Both rest of the applicant getting interested and the interest triggering a response (Applying, Referring, Calling, Sending an SMS etc.). These action triggers are also sometimes referred to as **Call To Action (CTA)** steps.

Proactive techniques

1. Using Boolean operators on major search engine sites (Google, Live.com, Yahoo!, etc.) to identify potential candidates who might meet the criteria of the position to be filled based on targeted keywords. Example string in Google: "SAP consultant" (resume | CV | "curriculum vitae").[4]
2. Searching for candidates in job boards [5] (e.g. Monster.com) using keywords related to the position requirements.
3. Looking in own recruitment database.
4. Networking with individuals to uncover candidates. This includes the use of social networking tools and sites such as LinkedIn.
5. "Phone sourcing" or cold calling into companies that might contain individuals that match the key requirements of the position that needs to be filled.

Examples of what sourcing is not

Reactive techniques

1. Reviewing candidates who have applied to positions through the corporate/agency web site
2. Processing an employee referral
3. Corporate recruiter receiving candidates from employment agencies
4. Screening candidates at a career fair

Natural habitat

By nature of the position, recruiters do not have the time to conduct primary research and initial candidate development. A typical recruiter is bombarded with calls all day from vendors, busy processing candidates, meeting with hiring managers, and talking with employees. Those distractions can throw off an otherwise excellent Internet search or telephone sourcer. Sourcers must remain focused on the search and development of leads just as recruiters must remain focused on maintaining communication with candidates in process, enforcing HR policies, attending meetings, negotiating, and handling the hiring from initial offer to onboarding.

Specialization: internet researcher

Internet research is a highly specialized field that takes years to master. Many of the best sourcers started out as recruiters who found they enjoy the "thrill of the hunt" more than the rest of the process and became successful because of their heightened research skills and abilities. Another common origin for strong sourcers is from professions where research or investigative skills are an imperative (journalists, librarians, fact-checkers, academic researchers, etc.), which is a common skillset with the field of competitive intelligence.

Several recruiters can rely on the same sourcer to generate leads and fill the pipeline with pre-screened or pre-qualified candidates. Sourcers are often the initial point of contact with a candidate, qualifying whether they are a real job seeker or just a job shopper. As a result, sourcers are uniquely positioned to sell or "pre-close" candidates before the candidates enter the recruitment process.[6]

Specialization: diversity sourcing

Corporate recruiters specializing in the sourcing of candidates for inclusion in a diverse candidate pool. Methods include searching for specific keywords [7] found on resumes, sourcing from affinity groups and researching other communities.

References

[1] Recruiting Bloggers on 'Phone Sourcing' (http://www.recruitingbloggers.com/rbs/2007/01/phone_sourcing_.html)

[2] Career Journal (http://www.careerjournal.com/hrcenter/weddlesguide/20010215-weddle100.html)

[3] Recruiters Network (http://www.recruitersnetwork.com/articles/article.cfm?ID=1071)

[4] Google Boolean Result Link (http://www.google.com/search?sourceid=navclient&gfns=1&ie=UTF-8& rls=GGIC,GGIC:2006-25,GGIC:en&q="SAP+consultant"+(resume+l+CV+l+"curriculum+vitae"))

[5] http://fundoorecruiter.blogspot.com/2010/01/boolean-search-explained-for-recruiters.html

[6] Electronic Recruiting 101 (http://www.ere.net/electronicrecruiting101/)

[7] Keyword search in Job Portals (http://fundoorecruiter.blogspot.com/2010/01/boolean-search-explained-for-recruiters.html)

SourceCon Sourcing Conference (http://www.sourcecon.com/)

South West African Native Labour Association

The **South West African Native Labour Association** (SWANLA) was a labour recruitment organisation which recruited primarily Ovambo people from Ovamboland in northern Namibia to work in the diamond mines in Namibia's southern Karas Region. It was infamous for its use of contract labour and human rights abuses among those employed in the mines. It was established in 1943 during World War II to accommodate a rising demand for labour.[1] SWANLA was a driving force in the creation of opposition political movements, including future liberation movement and ruling party of Namibia South West Africa People's Organization (SWAPO).[1]

References

[1] The Institutionalization of Contract Labour in Namibia (http://www.jstor.org/pss/2637589) Journal of Southern African Studies, Vol. 25.1. March 1999

St. Louis Regional HERC

The Saint Louis Regional Higher Education Recruitment Consortium (St. Louis Regional HERC) is a job-placement and recruitment organization supporting institutions of higher education, research and healthcare (medical centers) in the greater Saint Louis area, Central Missouri and Central Illinois. It is a part of the National HERC network.

About Saint Louis Regional HERC

The Saint Louis Regional HERC was established in 2007, and currently serves 16 institutions in 2 states. It is one of eleven regional HERCs in the US, consisting of over 500 campuses in 23 states. The St. Louis Regional HERC maintains a free web based search engine [1] with comprehensive listings for faculty, research and staff job openings at all member institutions. It also has a linked search option for dual career couples looking for jobs in the region.

Member Institutions

The St. Louis Regional HERC has 16 institutions of higher educations as members:

Barnes Jewish Hospital; Central Methodist University, Adult Degree Program; Donald Danforth Plant Science Center; East Central College; Fontbonne University; Harris-Stowe State University; Lewis and Clark Community College; Lindenwood University; Maryville University; Saint Louis University; Southern Illinois University at Edwardsville; St. Charles Community College; St. Louis College of Pharmacy; St. Louis Community College; University of Illinois at Springfield; University of Missouri - St. Louis; Washington University in St. Louis

References

National HERC Website [2]

St. Louis Regional HERC website [2]

External links

- *National HERC Website* [2]
- *St. Louis Regional HERC website* [2]
- *Finding jobs as a dual career couple in Saint Louis* [3]

References

[1] http://www.stlrherc.org/c/search.cfm?site_id=1916
[2] http://www.stlrherc.org
[3] http://www.stltoday.com/business/article_b038198f-4b8f-5a5f-b9d7-3432025eb77b.html

Talent community

A talent community is a collection of social cliques (or talent networks) of people that are part of the job seeking process. These people may be seeking a job themselves, offering career advice to others, recruitment professionals, college campus recruiters, sourcers, and friends seeking jobs or advice. Talent communities operate through two-way interaction between community members. A talent community is not a list of candidates on a web page or in a spreadsheet, it is an environment consisting of people who can share ideas for the purpose of career networking or social recruiting of candidates. Employers can interact and communicate with prospective employees as well as inform candidates about employment opportunities, receive referrals, and handpick qualified individuals from inside the group. A talent community can include prospective candidates, past applicants, current employees, and past employees. Talent communities are managed by recruiters and/or hiring managers.

Description

A talent community is a network of candidates, contacts, alumni, employees and job seekers allowing productive two-way communication between contacts. A community facilitates collaboration and sharing of information. It involves people conversing and working together to solve problems, meet goals, share opinions, and ideas. This social engagement makes people feel included and compelled to contribute positively to the betterment of the community.

Cross-membership communication within a community encourages groups to form organically according to their similar shared values, interests, and opinions. People within the talent community stay engaged because of the value brought to them by participating in these groups and the content that is generated by open, relevant communication.

Kevin Wheeler, the President and Founder of Global Learning Resources, Inc. categorizes the distinguishable features of a Talent Community as: [1]

- Collaboration and sharing
- Feeling included
- Similar values
- Openness
- Engagement

The benefits of building a talent community:

- Qualified candidates at a recruiter's fingertips
- Less dependence on expensive, ineffective job boards
- Less money spent on job advertisements
- Increased interaction with potential candidates
- Better quality of applicants to job openings
- Creates a talent pipeline for future job openings
- Attracts passive candidates

How to build your own talent community:

Your careers page needs to be a central hub for current, past ("alumni"), and potential employees. Create more than just a list of job openings by encouraging communication and interaction. Show candidates what it's like to work for you, provide employee testimonials and encourage them to get in touch with people working at your organization. You can include a list of job openings, create different groups based on field or industry, install forums, and much more.

Talent Pool vs. Talent Community

A talent pool is a database of everyone that has ever applied to a recruiter's jobs, regardless of relevance.[2] It facilitates one-sided communication.

In a talent community relationships are key. Hiring managers connect to employees, candidates and their friends. Contacts are organized into relevant talent networks. Employee referral programs are enhanced as the focus is on quality, not quantity. Most importantly, they are social. Contacts are truly engaged through social media rather than just email, telephone and jobs boards.

References

[1] *Beyond Talent Pools: Building Dynamic Communities* by Kevin Wheeler — (http://www.ere.net/2010/06/10/
     beyond-talent-pools-building-dynamic-communities/)
[2] *Talent Community or Applicant Database* by Kevin Wheeler — (http://www.ere.net/2007/05/10/
     talent-community-or-applicant-database/)

The Select Family of Staffing Companies

The Select Family of Staffing Companies (Koosharem Corp.)

Type	Private
Industry	nationwide staffing, employee leasing, and workforce management
Founded	1985
Headquarters	Santa Barbara, CA, USA
Revenue	$1.748 billion (2010 revenues)
Subsidiaries	Select Staffing, Select Truckers Plus, Select Medical Staffing, Remedy Intelligent Staffing, RemX Financial Staffing, RemX IT Staffing, RemX OfficeStaff, RemX Engineering, RemX Scientific, RemX Search & Placement, Project Solvers
Website	www.selectfamily.com [1]

The Select Family of Staffing Companies is an American company that provides temporary and permanent staff.

A member of the American Staffing Association, The Select Family is ranked as the 9th-largest employment agency in the United States (3rd-largest for industrial staffing, and 6th-largest for office/clerical)[2] and the 17th largest in the world.[3] The company primarily offers services in human resources, and has over 400 offices in 45 states.

The company's major divisions include Select Staffing, Remedy Intelligent Staffing, RemX Financial Staffing, RemX IT Staffing, RemX OfficeStaff, RemX Search & Placement, RemX Engineering, RemX Scientific, Select Truckers Plus, Project Solvers (design), Westaff, Butler America, and Select Medical Staffing.[4]

With annual revenue at $1.498 billion for 2009 (a nearly 4% increase from 2008 in a year where the industry saw sharp declines), the company employs over 80,000 job seekers in assignments with 6,000+ client companies.[5] in a wide variety of industries, including manufacturing, industrial, clerical, ladministrative, accounting, finance, information technology, life sciences, construction, trucking, health care, engineering, and professional services.

Select Family History

Known originally as Select Temporaries, the company opened its first office in Santa Barbara, California in 1985. In the 1990s, the company began an acquisitive growth strategy, purchasing an average of two competitors a year. Since 2000, It has bought or merged with over 50 top staffing firms nationwide, including Checkmate Staffing, First Site Staffing, Staffing Services and Progressive Personnel Services[6], National Careers Corporation, PDQCareers.com and CT Engineering, Ablest Inc.,[7], Tandem Staffing Solutions,[8], and Westaff[9], among others.

The company's largest acquisition to date was of RemedyTemp, Inc. in 2006.[10] From this purchase, it received multiple new divisions and entered into new niche markets, including Remedy Intelligent Staffing (franchise) and RemX Specialty Staffing (finance and accounting, IT, high-end clerical, scientific, fashion/design, and engineering). As a result, The Select Family of Staffing Companies was chosen as the umbrella name for all divisions. As the same time, Select was briefly renamed SelectRemedy (it retains the SelectRemedy name in certain markets), before changing its name to Select Staffing in 2007.

By early 2008, the group continued to grow with the purchase of Resolve Staffing's assets.[11] Through this acquisition, the company ventured into new industries to now include support for health care (Select Medical Staffing), trucking (Select Truckers Plus), and fashion/design (Project Solvers) for clients nationwide.

Divisions

Select Staffing

Originally called Select Temporaries, Select acquired RemedyTemp, Inc. in 2006 and was renamed SelectRemedy briefly, before changing its name to Select Staffing in 2007.[12] Since then, Select Staffing has grown through the acquisition of several recruiting agencies that focus on clerical and light-industrial personnel in a wide range of industries. It still goes by the name SelectRemedy in the state of Illinois.

Prospective workers must go through a five-step screening process that includes integrity screening, formal application, behavioral interview, reference checks, employment eligibility verification, drug tests, and background checks. Applicants must also undergo skill assessments focused on their area of interest, as well as safety procedures.

Select Staffing has offices nationwide.

Select Truckers Plus

Born out of the company's buyout of Resolve Staffing in early 2008, Select Truckers Plus, as it was renamed, specializes in driver leasing. Truckers Plus drivers must pass 11 Department of Transportation requirements and maintain current and valid driver qualifications.[13]

Select Medical Staffing

Select Medical Staffing, formerly Resolve Staffing's Health Care Division, focuses primarily on travel and per diem nursing, as well as physician and allied health personnel placement.

Remedy Intelligent Staffing

Remedy Intelligent Staffing is one of the company's nationwide franchise networks,[14] and has more than four decades of recruiting experience. Remedy uses what it calls the "Intelligent Fit" process that was formulated to include a client needs assessment, a skills and behavioral evaluation of the candidate, and finally, performance management to match job candidates with positions.

Westaff

Westaff is the other one of the company's franchise networks[15] . It was acquired in March 2009 when Select's parent company acquired the 61-year-old California-based staffing firm.

RemX Specialty Staffing

The RemX Specialty Staffing division provides temporary and permanent placement solutions for accounting, financial, IT, administrative, fashion/design, biomedical, and engineering professionals. RemX Specialty Staffing comprises the following divisions: RemX Financial Staffing, RemX IT Staffing, RemX OfficeStaff, RemX Engineering, RemX Scientific, Project Solvers, and RemX Search & Placement. Each division has offices in major U.S. markets.

Power Training Institute

Power Training Institute offers professional development programs focused on such topics as enhancing skills for managers and supervisors, as well as customer service and sales representatives.

Management

- D. Stephen Sorensen, Chairman and Chief Executive Officer

Franchising

A franchising program was launched in 1998, resulting in franchises being granted to more than 100 licensees.[16]

With the acquisition of Westaff in 2009 came many more franchise offices, which still operate under the Westaff brand.

References

[1] http://www.selectfamily.com/
[2] 2010 List of Largest U.S. Staffing Firms — Staffing Industry Analysts, Inc., July 23, 2010
[3] 2010 List of Largest Global Staffing Firms — Staffing Industry Analysts, Inc., August 11, 2010
[4] http://www.selectfamily.com
[5] http://www.selectstaffing.com/SelectStaffing/main.cfm?nlvl1=4
[6] Crain's Detroit Business — May 6, 2006
[7] Reuters — April 4, 2007
[8] Yahoo! Finance — October 3, 2007
[9] Yahoo! Finance — March 20, 2009
[10] Reuters — May 11, 2006
[11] Reuters — Jan 30, 2008
[12] http://www.selectstaffing.com/SelectStaffing/main.cfm?nlvl1=4&nlvl2=82&nlvl3=63&pg=
[13] http://www.truckersplus.com/drivers.html
[14] http://www.remedystaff.com/RemedyStaff/main.cfm?nlvl1=4
[15] http://www.westaff.com
[16] http://www.remedyfranchise.com/faq.html

Times Ascent

Times Ascent

Type	Weekly Supplement (publishing)
Format	Broadsheet
Owner	Bennett, Coleman & Co. Ltd.
Publisher	Bennett, Coleman & Co Ltd.
Editor	Neha Sharma Sara
Language	English
Headquarters	Mumbai
Official website	Times Ascent [1]

Times Ascent

Times Ascent is a weekly supplement of The Times of India newspaper, that is focused on human resource development, employment and job opportunities.[2] The editorial covers future and current trends, and news features, for job seekers and HR professionals. The features are about the changing paradigm of work, the personal fulfillment that the employee seeks, the emotional engagement the employer expects, and the empowerment for both. Times Ascent has 10 editions in the following Indian cities - Mumbai, Pune, Hyderabad, Lucknow, Ahmedabad, Chennai, Kolkata, Bangalore, Delhi and Nagpur.

Content

The Times Ascent website [3] was launched in January 2007.[4] The website, is an extension of the print version. In the print version, the font of the headline is Myriad Roman, and that of the strapline and the main copy is Pointer OS Display Roman. The various sections of editorial content on the portal are as follows:

- **'Gyan Gurus'** are regular columnists who are is industry watchers and experts
- **Thought Pool** is a section written by student journalists
- **Ask the Expert** Questions are addressed to various experts on human resources and allied fields
- **Live chat sessions** are regularly scheduled on the website
- **Books Section** is where visitors can also recommend and read reviews of leading management books

Beyond the editorial content, the readers have access to research oriented content

- executive education options
- Corporate Social Responsibility activities of various organizations
- white papers

Marketing

The Ascent rebranding has been done in consultation with JWT Mindset. Times Ascent has also come out with an automated response tracking software called 'Ascent Matcher' for its clients. The sky blue color in the masthead and as a background shade in articles will capture the essence of the opportunities.[5]

References

[1] http://timesascent.in/

[2] "The Times Of India" (http://www.itopc.org/travel-requisite/newspapers/times-of-india.html). Indian Tour Operators Promotion Council.

[3] http://timesascent.com

[4] "Times Ascent" (http://www.reviewstream.com/reviews/?p=68217). Reviewstream. .

[5] "The new look Times Ascent has more content" (http://www.afaqs.com/perl/media/story.html?sid=23321). afaqs. 2009-02-13. .

External links

- Official Website (http://timesascent.in)
- ePaper (http://epaper.timesofindia.com/Daily/Skins/Ascent/section.asp)
- Times Of India (http://timesofindia.com)

Trends in pre-employment screening

A number of companies publish annual research into pre-employment screening, applicant fraud and its effect on business.

The market

Larger companies are more likely to outsource than their smaller counterparts – the average staff size of the companies who outsource is 3,313 compared to 2,162 for those who carry out in-house checks. Primary step will be to screen the resume from a list of prospective applicants. A preliminary telephonic or web based interview is held to identify the range of discrepancy within the resume and the interviewee. Such a move also helps to identify whether the resume is professionally written, elaborated or involve resume fraud. Further a series of resumes are shortlisted.

Financial services firms outsource the service the most, with over a quarter (26%) doing so, compared to an overall average of 16% who outsource vetting to a third party provider.

However, recent research by Powerchex shows a reverse in the trend. They found that in the 2006/7 period CV discrepancies had fallen by 31% to 13%.[1]

Background Verification

Pre-screening background verification and post-interview background checks are two strategies that are involved in pre-employment screening. Pre-screening background verification is deployed when the even the interview will contain data or information which are vital for the organization to disclose. Such a strategy is used mostly in the Military, strategic industries and higher levels of employees. While post-hiring background verification occurs once the resumes are shortlisted for pre-employment screening.

Third party background verification firms allow candidates to screen their own backgrounds on basis of identity, address, references, criminal background checks, drug test, financial records, court record checks and driving license verification and to verify the authenticity of their resume. Such a strategy allows candidates to gain a preferential advantage as it reduces background check expenses from the point of view of the recruiter. Such third party firms include Intelius and PeopleFinders.com are a few among them.

Male/female

It is alleged that men stand a higher chance of clearing the pre-employment screening than women. However equality of opportunity gives women an equal platform for employment as some firms like Facebook, Google insist the candidates not to disclose about their gender during pre-employment screening. This reduces gender bias during stages of pre-employment screening. Women are marginally more likely to have a discrepancy on their CV: 13% of applicants submitted by women have a discrepancy compared to only 10% of those for men

Impact of qualifications

Graduates have marginally less discrepancies: 13% of their CVs contain a discrepancy compared to 17% of non-graduates.

Impact of seniority and age

Since Equal Opportunity or Equality of Opportunity is considered important and ethical in the job market, seniority of age is left to question in the preliminary stages of pre-employment screening. However the age of the candidate can be verified from various documents that are mandatory to be submitted. However the recent trend is to follow the equality of opportunity to all the candidates at the preliminary stages of screening. Someone in a junior administrative position is 23% more likely to have a discrepancy on their CV than in a managerial role. An applicant aged under 20 is 26% more likely to have a discrepancy than a 51-60 year old.[2]

References

[1] Matt Keating (4 August 2007). "Boris Johnson seeks office, any office" (http://money.guardian.co.uk/workweekly/story/0,,2141051,00. html). *The Guardian*. . Retrieved 2010-03-25.

[2] dofonline (http://dofonline.co.uk/personnel/personnel-2007/drop-in-financial-job-applicant-frauds01807.html). Dofonline.co.uk

Versatilist

A **Versatilist** is someone who can be a specialist for a particular discipline, while at the same time be able to change to another role with the same ease.

The term "versatilist" was first coined in an article from Gartner, where it states:

> "Versatilists are able to apply a depth of skill to a progressively widening scope of situations and experiences, equally at ease with technical issues as with business strategy."

It is to the advantage of an organization to employ versatilists—because an enterprise will be able to easily redeploy this type of employee based on changes in business requirements or strategy.

To illustrate this using a mathematical concept, the versitilist has a higher area under the curve rating. Think of a person having some level of knowledge/experience in 15 knowledge areas. That person may have a very high competency (score 5) in 3 areas, a medium level of competency (score 3) in 5 areas an introductory level of competency (score 1) in 4 areas and no competency (score 0) in 3 areas. This creates an area under the curve of 34. This is different from a specialist who may score very high in 1 area and have no competency in others. This is also different from a generalist who may score a 1 or 3 in every area.

This breadth of knowledge and experience is what enables faster changes to other roles.

Also Known As

- Generalizing Specialist
- Technical Craftsperson
- Renaissance Developer
- T-shaped person: See The Ten Faces of Innovation by Tom Kelley
- Master Generalist

References

- Gartner Says Technical Aptitude No Longer Enough To Secure Future for IT Professionals, *Gartner Press Release*, 9 November 2005. [1]
- Friedman, Thomas L. The World Is Flat: A Brief History of the Twenty-First Century. New York: Farrar, Straus, and Giroux, 2005.
- Generalizing Specialists - Improving Your IT Skills [2]

References

[1] http://www.gartner.com/press_releases/asset_139314_11.html
[2] http://www.agilemodeling.com/essays/generalizingSpecialists.htm

Vetting

Vetting is a process of examination and evaluation, generally referring to performing a background check on someone before offering him or her employment, conferring an award, etc. In addition, in intelligence gathering, assets are vetted to determine their usefulness.

Origin

To *vet* was originally a horse-racing term, referring to the requirement that a horse be checked for health and soundness by a veterinarian before being allowed to race. Thus, it has taken the general meaning "to check".

It is a figurative contraction of *veterinarian*, which originated in the mid-17th century. The colloquial abbreviation dates to the 1860s; the verb form of the word, meaning "to treat an animal", came a few decades later—according to the *Oxford English Dictionary*, the earliest known usage is 1891—and was applied primarily in a horse-racing context. ("He vetted the stallion before the race", "You should vet that horse before he races", etc.) By the early 1900s, *vet* had begun to be used as a synonym for *evaluate*, especially in the context of searching for flaws. [1]

Finance

Vetting can refer to the process of analyzing stocks, bonds, and any other securities or financial instruments before committing money.

Media

In book publishing, the duty of fact-checking commonly falls to copy editors.

In the journalism field, newspaper, periodical, and television news articles or stories may be vetted by fact-checkers, whose job it is to check the correctness of factual assertions made in news copy. However, fact-checking is a time-consuming and costly process, so stories in daily publications are typically not fact-checked. Reporters are expected to check their own facts, sometimes with the aid of an in-house reference library. Information which is verified by two independent sources is commonly stated as fact.

Even when published or televised material is not specifically fact-checked, it is often vetted by a company's legal department to avoid committing slander or libel.

Political selection

Politicians are often thoroughly vetted. For example, in the United States, a party's presidential nominee must choose a vice-presidential candidate to accompany him or her on the ticket. Prospective vice-presidential candidates must undergo thorough evaluation by a team of advisers acting on behalf of the nominee.[2] In later stages of the vetting process, the team will examine such items as a prospective vice-presidential candidate's finances, personal conduct, and previous coverage in the media.[2]

[3]

Transitional Justice

Vetting is also a term used in the field of transitional justice. When countries undergo a process of transition—after a period of armed conflict or authoritarian rule—they must determine what to do with public employees who perpetrated human rights abuses. They also must examine and revise the institutional structures that allowed such abuses to occur. Vetting is the processes of assessing the integrity of individuals (such as their adherence to relevant human rights standards) in order to determine their suitability for public employment. Countries transitioning to democracy and peace often utilize such processes to ensure that abusive or incompetent public employees are excluded from public service.[4]

Ships

Ship/vessel vetting is the process by which a charterer determines whether a vessel is suitable to be chartered, based on the information available to it. Ports, terminals, insurers and other maritime industry operators also vet ships to identify and manage risks, and many shipowners and ship managers use ship vetting services to monitor information about their own vessels.

Unlike certification or classification, vetting is a private, voluntary system operators may opt to use to help them choose a particular vessel from among all of the certified vessels available, and to manage their risks.

Vetting in its current form first appeared in 1993, when the Ship Inspection Report (SIRE) database was created for use by oil companies. For each voyage, the vetting department assesses the vessel to be used, relying in particular on inspection results.

Oil tanker vetting

The results of inspections carried out by oil companies, who are members of the OCIMF (Oil Companies International Marine Forum), are shared via the joint SIRE database. Oil majors perform inspections according to a standard report format developed by the OCIMF. These reports are available to all OCIMF members via the SIRE database, which provides each company's vetting department with the information it needs to apply its own internal criteria without having to inspect each vessel itself. Tanker vetting inspections are usually carried out during commercial unloading operations, with the prior agreement of the shipowner and management company, the only organizations authorized to allow third parties onboard.

Vetting inspections do not include a survey of the vessel's structural elements, which is the responsibility of the classification society and the shipowner as part of the vessel's regular maintenance and of the process of ensuring that it complies with applicable rules and regulations. In any case, it would be technically impossible for a vetting department to carry out such a structural survey.

Vetting inspections also give the company access to confidential documents relating to the vessel's maintenance and classification, which can only be consulted by third parties onboard.

Dry vetting

Dry bulk and container ships can also be vetted. Systems for dry vetting were developed after SIRE had proved valuable for oil industry standards, and in recognition that substandard ships remained a major risk for the shipping industry. Vetting for dry vessels is less regulated than in the oil industry, remains less structured, and is not universally used, although acceptance has grown significantly, especially through the growth of accessible online vetting services including equasis and RightShip.

Dry bulk and container vetting can also incorporate vessel inspections, along similar lines to the oil industry processes described above, although systems for inspection requests, reports and the sharing of reports are again much less standardized.

Software

Vetting is also a reference to software development. The process of vetting code refers to ensuring a build of software meets a set of requirements before the build is passed to the quality control environment for further testing.

External links

- International Center for Transitional Justice (ICTJ); Pablo de Greiff and Alexander Mayer-Rieckh. (2007): "Justice as Prevention: Vetting Public Employees in Transitional Societies" [5]

References

[1] Juliet Lapidos, *Vetting Vet The origins of vet, verb tr.*. http://www.slate.com/id/2199254/(September 3, 2008).

[2] See, e.g., Ben Smith, *Richardson Defense Raises Questions*, Politico, March 8, 2007 (http://www.politico.com/news/stories/0307/3054. html)

[3] cocokol;o.12455/236

[4] The International Center for Transitional Justice (ICTJ) on Vetting (http://www.ictj.org/our-work/research/vetting)

[5] http://www.ictj.org/publication/justice-prevention-vetting-public-employees-transitional-societies

Video resume

A **video resume** is a way for job seekers to showcase their abilities beyond the capabilities of a traditional paper resume. The video resume allows prospective employers to see, hear and get a feel for how the applicant presents themselves.

History

Video resumes (called a Video CV in the United Kingdom) were first introduced in the 1980s for use and distribution via VHS tape, but the idea never took off beyond the video taping of interviews. However, with the modern capabilities of transmitting streaming video via the internet, video resumes have taken on new popularity.[1] Video resumes are now being widely accepted by companies throughout the world for varying professions and the need for objectivity in these videos is becoming a serious issue. Many copycat video resume companies have sites where people can upload their own videos, but companies are shying away from accepting homemade, webcam pieces.

Criticism

With the popularity of video hosting solutions there has been much debate in the usefulness of video resumes. Most recruiters feel that a video alone does not give an employer enough information about a candidate to make a proper evaluation of the applicant's potential and more importantly skills. One article suggests that

> "While a video resume introduces applicants on camera, the value such visual imagery adds is debatable. A text resume allows for specific pieces of information to be parsed out and compared across candidates. When the information is delivered verbally, recruiters need to glean the details themselves."[2]

Video resumes can serve to facilitate racial, ethnic, class-based and age discrimination, or lead to accusations of such discrimination.[3]

References

[1] "It's a Wrap. You're Hired!" (http://www.time.com/time/magazine/article/0,9171,1592860,00.html). *Time*. February 22, 2007. . Retrieved May 27, 2010.

[2] Time to Call Pause on Video Resumes (http://www.ere.net/articles/db/DDFA0ECCDE2C4005A476D53EEFEC18A7.asp)

[3] Lefkow, Dave. "What the Lawyers Think of Video Resumes"; directorofrecruiting.com, June 24, 2007 (http://www.directorofrecruiting.com/2007/06/what_the_lawyer.html)

External links

- Stephen J. Dubner, author of *Freakonomics* on video resumes (http://freakonomics.blogs.nytimes.com/2007/06/29/why-isnt-the-video-resume-more-popular)
- Job seekers show rather than tell (http://www.usatoday.com/tech/news/techinnovations/2007-04-24-video-resumes_N.htm) article from *USA Today*
- Video Resumes: Lights, Camera, Hire Me (http://abcnews.go.com/Business/CareerManagement/story?id=5526142&page=1) article from *ABC News*

Witwatersrand Native Labour Association

The **Witwatersrand Native Labour Association**, more usually known by its initials WNLA or more popularly as "Wenela" was set up by the gold mines in South Africa as a recruiting agency for migrant workers.

Eventually it comprised a large organisation, with its own depots, buses and aeroplanes[1] , spread over the whole of Southern Africa - South Africa, Basutoland, Swaziland, South West Africa, Bechuanaland, Northern Rhodesia, Southern Rhodesia, Nyasaland, Angola, Mocambique, extending into the Belgian Congo and Tanganyika.

Each depot had administrative and medical staff and a "barracks" to house recruits both before departure and on their return. Some had clinics and even schools, where the recruits were taught, first, Fanagalo, the lingua franca of Southern Africa (fifteen hours of tuition was enough to be useful), and then the rudiments of what mining was all about.

Tours were usually of six months duration, but many spent their entire working lives as migrant workers.

In Northern Rhodesia (now Zambia) the Government had instituted a "hut tax" of quite a small amount, payable annually for each hut. It was a form of "tribal initiation" for each teenager to go down to the mines for at least one tour, and would bring back enough money to pay the hut tax for the entire village.

Thus Fanagalo became the lingua franca of the whole of Southern Africa.

References

[1] http://eu.airliners.net/photo/Wenela/Douglas-DC-4/0038437&tbl=photo_info&photo_nr=1&sok=WHERE__%28airline_%3D_%27Wenela%27%29_&sort=_order_by_photo_id_DESC_&prev_id=&next_id=NEXTID

Sources

- http://www.jstor.org/pss/3002372
- http://www.queensu.ca/samp/Treaties/Wenela.htm
- http://www.sarpn.org.za/documents/d0001831/Migrant_labour_Kanyenze_March2004.pdf
- http://www.ncbi.nlm.nih.gov/pubmed/4620369

Work-at-home scheme

A **work-at-home scheme** is a get-rich-quick scheme in which a victim is lured by an offer to be employed at home, very often doing some simple task in a minimal amount of time with a large amount of income that far exceeds the market rate for the type of work. The true purpose of such an offer is for the perpetrator to extort money from the victim, either by charging a fee to join the scheme, or requiring the victim to invest in products whose resale value is misrepresented.[1]

An ad for a work-at-home scheme posted on a pole

Work-at-home schemes have been around for decades, with the classic "envelope stuffing" scam originating in the United States during the Depression in the 1920s.[2] In this scam, the worker is offered entry to a scheme where they can earn $2 for every envelope they fill. After paying a small $2 fee to join the scheme, the victim is sent a flyer template for the self-same work-from-home scheme, and told to post these advertisements around their local area - the victim is simply "stuffing envelopes" with flyer templates that perpetuate the scheme.[2] Originally found as ads in newspapers or magazines, equivalents of "envelope stuffing" have expanded into more modern media, such as television and radio ads, and on the Internet.

In some countries, law enforcement agencies work to fight work-at-home schemes. In 2006, the United States Federal Trade Commission established Project False Hopes, a federal and state law enforcement sweep that targets bogus business opportunity and work at home scams. The crackdown involved more than 100 law enforcement actions by the FTC, the Department of Justice, the United States Postal Inspection Service, and law enforcement agencies in eleven states.[1]

Legitimate work-at-home opportunities do exist, and many people do their jobs in the comfort of their own homes. But anyone seeking such an employment opportunity must be wary of accepting a home employment offer, as only about one in 42 such ads have been determined to be legitimate.[3] Most legitimate jobs at home require some form of post-high-school education, such as a college degree or certificate, or trade school, and some experience in the field in an office or other supervised setting. Additionally, many legitimate at-home jobs are not like those in schemes are portrayed to be, as they are often performed at least some of the time in the company's office, require more self discipline than a traditional job, and have a higher risk of firing.

Types of work

Common types of work found in work-at-home schemes include:

- Stuffing envelopes
- Assembly of items of some type, such as crafts, jewellery or medical equipment. The worker is required to pay up front for materials and construction kits, and when they attempt to sell the finished products back to the scheme's organiser, they are told that the products "don't meet our specifications", leaving the worker with assembled products and no buyer.[2]
- Data entry
- Processing medical claims. The worker pays several hundred dollars for medical billing software, but will later discover that most medical clinics process their own bills, outsource their billing to established firms rather than individuals, or have stricter requirements than the purchased software can provide.[2]
- Forum spamming. Usually advertised as some variant of "email processing", the worker is simply given instructions on spamming online forums, and told they can make money by selling these same instructions online.[2]
- Making phone calls
- Phone sex
- Online surveys
- Sales of a product or service that is difficult or impossible to sell. This is often done in the form of a pyramid scheme.
- Some ads claim to offer a device that makes passive sales calls, and the "employee" will be paid a commission of the sales.

Some ads offer legitimate forms of work that really do exist, but exaggerate the salary and understate the effort that will have to be put into the job, or the exaggerate amount of work that will be available. Many such ads do not even specify the type of work that will be performed.

Some similar schemes do not advertise work that would be performed at home, but may instead offer occasional, sporadic work away from home for large payments, paired with a lot of free time. Some common offers fitting this description are:

- Acting - seeking extras to perform in movies and television commercials.
- Mystery shopping - Getting paid to shop and dine. While mystery shopping actually does exist, it requires hard work, is paid close to minimum wage, and most importantly, does not require an up-front fee to join.
- Pay per click

Signs of a scam

Signs of a work-at-home scam versus a legitimate job may include:

- Payment of fee is required prior to starting employment. In the United States, the Federal Trade Commission states that *under no circumstances* should anyone be forced to pay a fee in order to obtain a job. In many countries, no legitimate employer will require a fee be paid as a condition of starting work (except perhaps a small amount for a criminal background check).
- Pay is too good to be true. Though there may be legitimate jobs in existence in which employees are paid to perform the particular task in question, even from home, in reality, they would be paid a wage that is fair for that type of work and level of education, not the $40 per hour or $3000 per week that is typically offered in a work-at-home scheme.
- Employer will seemingly hire anyone, with no experience necessary and no qualifications. Legitimate work-at-home employers will only be interested in those who have the proper experience, skills, certification, and other qualifying factors, and will give at least some scrutiny to an applicant seeking employment. But the

perpetrator of a work-at-home scheme is only interested in the payment required to join.

- Company is little known, and does not seemingly have a customer base bringing them revenue from which they can pay employees.
- Company does not appear to have a permanent location. Its address, phone number, and website appear to be centered around recruitment of employees, not customers.
- Company tries to show unnatural benefits of working in a very short period of time.
- Keeps on contacting you again and again until and unless you reply.

Victims

The typical victim of a work-at-home scheme may be:

- A burned out employee of a legitimate job seeking an exit to his/her stressful lifestyle
- An unemployed person seeking high-paying easy work
- An uneducated person with few or no skills looking for a job with a good salary
- An employed person wanting to make extra money to supplement his/her regular income.
- Senior citizens, disabled persons, stay-at-home parents, and others who cannot easily leave home in order to make a living.
- Those with busy schedules full of unpaid activities who wish to earn money in their spare time.
- Those with long or tiresome commutes looking to remain at home and eliminate their travel to work.
- Someone who doesn't take the time to carefully investigate the industry, job and company.
- A frustrated person who just wants to earn by any means.

Consequences

The consequences of falling for a work-at-home scheme may be as follows:[4]

- Loss of money: It may be only the initial fee to join, which may be a large or small amount. Some scammers will run after receiving just this fee. Others will continue to ask for more in order for the promise of high pay to be fulfilled. Some will act on a two-way street, actually issuing paychecks, all the while receiving payments of greater value in return, which in some cases have exceeded tens of thousands of US dollars. In other cases, the employer may obtain the victim's personal information for purposes of identity theft.
- Loss of legitimate job: Those with a real job may quit in hopes of a better one, only to find they cannot get their original job back after they discover their dream job was only a hoax.
- Damaged reputation: Those who engage in sales of a faulty or otherwise controversial product may be tarnishing their own name as the salesperson of such a worthless item.
- Trouble with law: Some victims may actually receive money. But at the same time, they may be unknowingly breaking the law, on behalf of the perpetrator of the scheme, but will be fully legally responsible. Such violations may be criminal or civil in nature. In other cases, they will not be committing any criminal acts, but they will end up framed in an investigation for the crimes of the perpetrator.
- Wasted time: Victims will often invest huge amounts of time with no pay in return. This is time that can be spent earning money at a legitimate job.

References

[1] Federal Trade Commission. / "Federal, State Law Enforcers Complete Bogus Business Opportunity Sweep" (http://www.ftc.gov/opa/ 2006/12/falsehopes.shtm). ftc.gov. /. Retrieved 2006-12-06.

[2] "Top 10 Work At Home and Home Based Business Scams" (http://www.scambusters.org/work-at-home.html). . Retrieved 8 December 2010.

[3] "Working From Home: Don't Get Scammed" (http://abcnews.go.com/GMA/TakeControlOfYourLife/story?id=3003833&page=1). ABC: Good Morning America. . Retrieved 2009-07-03.

[4] "BBB Alerts & News" (http://www.bbb.org/alerts/article.asp?ID=436). Bbb.org. 2003-03-25. . Retrieved 2009-07-03.

External links

- Better Business Bureau information on Work-at-home schemes (http://us.bbb.org/WWWRoot/SitePage. aspx?site=113&id=a9d5facf-8d95-4794-b575-d070a2704151&ctl05_gc1_s_rgNewsChangePage=12&art=408)
- AOL article about work-at-home schemes (http://jobs.aol.com/article/_a/ working-from-home-dont-get-scammed/20070410113709990001)
- Work-at-home job deals often are just a scam, AARP Bulletin, March 23, 2009 (http://bulletin.aarp.org/ yourmoney/work/articles/workathome_job_deals_often_are_just_a_scam.html)

LinkedIn

LinkedIn Corporation

Type	Public
Traded as	NYSE: LNKD [1]
Founded	Santa Monica, California (2003)
Founder	Reid Hoffman Allen Blue Konstantin Guericke Eric Ly Jean-Luc Vaillant
Headquarters	Mountain View, California, US
Area served	Worldwide
Key people	Reid Hoffman, (Chairman) Jeff Weiner, (CEO)
Revenue	US$161.4 million (Jan. – Sep. 2010)[2]
Net income	$1.85 million (2010)
Employees	1,000 (2010)
Slogan	Relationships Matter
Website	linkedin.com [3]
IPv6 support	No
Alexa rank	16 (July 2011)[4]
Type of site	Social network service
Advertising	Google, AdSense
Registration	Required
Users	100 million (March 2011)
Available in	English, French, German, Italian, Portuguese, Spanish, Romanian, Russian and Turkish.
Launched	May 5, 2003
Current status	Active

LinkedIn (pronounced /ˌlɪŋkt.ˈɪn/) (NYSE: LNKD [1]) is a business-related social networking site. Founded in December 2002 and launched in May 2003,[5] it is mainly used for professional networking. As of 22 March 2011, LinkedIn reports more than 100 million registered users, spanning more than 200 countries and territories worldwide.[6] [7] The site is available in English, French, German, Italian, Portuguese, Spanish, Romanian, Russian and Turkish.[8] [9] Quantcast reports Linkedin has 21.4 million monthly unique U.S. visitors and 47.6 million globally.[10] In June 2011, LinkedIn has 33.9 million unique visitors, up 63 percent from a year earlier and surpassed MySpace.[11]

LinkedIn filed for an initial public offering in January 2011 and traded its first shares on May 19, 2011, under the NYSE symbol "LNKD".[12]

Company background

LinkedIn's CEO is Jeff Weiner, previously a Yahoo! Inc. executive. The company was founded by Reid Hoffman and founding team members from PayPal and Socialnet.com (Allen Blue, Eric Ly, Jean-Luc Vaillant, Lee Hower, Konstantin Guericke, Stephen Beitzel, David Eves, Ian McNish, Yan Pujante, and Chris Saccheri).

Founder Reid Hoffman, previously CEO of LinkedIn, is now Chairman of the Board. Bhushan Kasvekar is Vice President of Products.[13] LinkedIn is headquartered in Mountain View, California, with offices in Omaha, Chicago, New York and London. It is funded by Sequoia Capital, Greylock, Bain Capital Ventures,[14] Bessemer Venture Partners and the European Founders Fund. LinkedIn reached profitability in March 2006[15] Through January 2011, the company had received a total of $103 million of investment.[16]

In 2003, Sequoia Capital led the Series A investment in the company.[17] In June 2008, Sequoia Capital, Greylock Partners, and other venture capital firms purchased a 5% stake in the company for $53 million, giving the company a post-money valuation of approximately $1 billion.[18]

In June 2010, LinkedIn announced it would be opening up a European headquarters in Dublin, Ireland.[19]

In July 2010, Tiger Global Management LLC purchased a 1% stake in the company for $20 million at a valuation of approximately $2 billion.[20]

In August 2010, LinkedIn announced the acquisition of Mspoke. It is the company's first acquisition for an undisclosed amount. This acquisition aims to help LinkedIn users do more than just find a job, increase users' activity[21] and improve its 1% premium subscription ratio.[22]

In October 2010 Silicon Valley Insider ranked the company No.10 on its Top 100 List of most valuable start ups.[23] As of December 2010, the company was valued at $1.575 billion in private markets.[24]

LinkedIn filed for an initial public offering on January 27, 2011.[25] The IPO occurred on May 19. Shares, initially priced at $45, rose to $122.70 in the first day of trading.[26] The stock closed up 109% in its first day of trading, making it the fifth-largest first day gainer in the post bubble era.[27]

Membership

With 100 million users, LinkedIn is ahead of its competitors Viadeo (30 million)[28] and XING (10 million).[29] The membership grows by a new member approximately every second. About half of the members are in the United States and 11 million are from Europe. With 3 million users, India has the fastest-growing network of users as of 2009. The Netherlands has the highest adoption rate per capita outside the US at 30%.[30] LinkedIn recently reached 4 million users in UK[31] and 1 million in Spain.[32]

As of March 2011 the service had 44 million users in the US and 56 million outside.[33]

Features

One purpose of the site is to allow registered users to maintain a list of contact details of people with whom they have some level of relationship, called *Connections*. Users can invite anyone (whether a site user or not) to become a connection. However, if the recipient of an invitation selects "I don't know", this counts against the person inviting them, and after five such "IDKs" a member cannot invite another to connect without first supplying their recipient mail address.

This list of connections can then be used in a number of ways:

- A contact network is built up consisting of their direct connections, the connections of each of their connections (termed *second-degree connections*) and also the connections of second-degree connections (termed *third-degree connections*). This can be used to gain an introduction to someone a person wishes to know through a mutual contact.

- It can then be used to find jobs, people and business opportunities recommended by someone in one's contact network.
- Employers can list jobs and search for potential candidates.
- Job seekers can review the profile of hiring managers and discover which of their existing contacts can introduce them.
- Users can post their own photos and view photos of others to aid in identification.
- Users can now follow different companies and can get notification about the new joining and offers available.
- Users can save (i.e. bookmark) jobs which they would like to apply for.

The "gated-access approach" (where contact with any professional requires either a preexisting relationship, or the intervention of a contact of theirs) is intended to build trust among the service's users. LinkedIn participates in the EU's International Safe Harbor Privacy Principles.[34]

LinkedIn also allows users to research companies with which they may be interested in working. When typing the name of a given company in the search box, statistics about the company are provided. These may include the ratio of female to male employees, the percentage of the most common titles/positions held within the company, the location of the company's headquarters and offices, or a list of present and former employees.

The feature LinkedIn Answers,[35] similar to Yahoo! Answers, allows users to ask questions for the community to answer. This feature is free and the main difference from the latter is that questions are potentially more business-oriented, and the identity of the people asking and answering questions is known.

Another LinkedIn feature is LinkedIn Polls.

A mobile version of the site was launched in February 2008 which gives access to a reduced feature set over a mobile phone. The mobile service is available in six languages: Chinese, English, French, German, Japanese and Spanish.[36]

In mid-2008, LinkedIn launched LinkedIn DirectAds as a form of sponsored advertising.[37]

In October, 2008, LinkedIn revealed plans to opening its social network of 30 million professionals globally as a potential sample for business-to-business research. It is testing a potential social-network revenue model-research that to some appears more promising than advertising.[38]

In October, 2008, LinkedIn enabled an "applications platform" that allows other online services to be embedded within a member's profile page. Among the initial applications were an Amazon Reading List that allows LinkedIn members to display books they are reading, a connection to Tripit, and a Six Apart, WordPress and TypePad application that allows members to display their latest blog postings within their LinkedIn profile.[39]

In November, 2010, LinkedIn allowed businesses to list products and services on company profile pages; it also permitted LinkedIn members to "recommend" products and services and write reviews.[40]

In January 2011, LinkedIn acquired CardMunch, a mobile app maker that scans business cards and converts into contacts. LinkedIn plans to integrate this functionality into their services in the near future.[41]

LinkedIn also supports the formation of interest groups, and as of March 24, 2011 there are 870,612 such groups whose membership varies from 1 to 377,000.[42] The majority of the largest groups are employment related, although a very wide range of topics are covered mainly around professional and career issues, and there are currently 128,000 groups for both academic and corporate alumni.

Groups support a limited form of discussion area, moderated by the group owners and managers. Since groups offer the ability to reach a wide audience without so easily falling foul of anti-spam solutions, there is a constant stream of spam postings, and there now exist a range of firms who offer a spamming service for this very purpose. LinkedIn has devised a few mechanisms to reduce the volume of spam, but recently took the decision to remove the ability of group owners to inspect the email address of new members in order to determine if they were spammers. [42]

Groups may be private, accessible to members only or may be open to Internet users in general to read, though they must join in order to post messages.

Reception

LinkedIn has received a generally positive reception from critics. Online trade publication TechRepublic claimed that "LinkedIn has become the de facto tool for professional networking."[43] Irish journalist James O'Sullivan commented in the *Evening Echo*, an award-winning regional newspaper in the Republic of Ireland, where the company has its European headquarters, that "LinkedIn.com, a business-orientated networking site, can be an ideal way for professionals to present an online profile of themselves...Unlike social networking sites, [with] LinkedIn you're outlining all your credentials; presenting the professional rather than the personal you. Considering the sheer vastness of the digital space, the potential for building up a solid base of contacts and fostering new business relationships is boundless."[44]

Restriction of access to some countries

In 2009 Syrian users reported that LinkedIn server stopped accepting connections originating from IP addresses assigned to Syria. As company's Customer Support stated, services provided by them are subject to US export and re-export control laws and regulations and *"As such, and as a matter of corporate policy, we do not allow member accounts or access to our site from Cuba, Iran, North Korea, Sudan, or Syria."*[45]

Cuba, Iran, Sudan and Syria are not available in the list of countries that LinkedIn users can select as one's location. However, as of April 2010, North Korea is still present there.

In February 2011 it was reported that LinkedIn was being blocked in China after calls for a "Jasmine Revolution". It was speculated to have been blocked because it is an easy way for dissidents to access Twitter, which had been blocked previously.[46] After a day of being blocked, LinkedIn access was restored in China.

SNA LinkedIn

The Search, Network, and Analytics team at LinkedIn has a web site[47] that hosts the open source projects built by the group. The most notable one is Project Voldemort,[48] a distributed key-value structured storage system with low-latency similar in purpose to Amazon's Dynamo and Google's BigTable.

References

[1] http://www.nyse.com/about/listed/quickquote.html?ticker=lnkd

[2] LinkedIn's IPO Filing: All The Long-Held Secrets You Want To Know (http://www.businessinsider.com/linkedin-s1)

[3] http://www.linkedin.com/

[4] "Linkedin.com Site Info" (http://www.alexa.com/siteinfo/linkedIn.com). Alexa Internet. . Retrieved 2011-07-12.

[5] "Linked-In — Profile" (http://www.thealarmclock.com/mt/archives/2004/08/linkedin_hq_mou.html). alarm:clock. August 6, 2004. . Retrieved January 17, 2008.

[6] LinkedIn – About Us (http://press.linkedin.com/about)

[7] LinkedIn Surpasses 100 Million Users [INFOGRAPHIC] (http://mashable.com/2011/03/22/linkedin-surpasses-100-million-users-infographic/)

[8] "Italians get a local flavour of LinkedIn" (http://press.linkedin.com/italy-launch-english). April 15, 2010. . Retrieved April 23, 2010.

[9] "Look who's talking Russian, Romanian and Turkish now!" (http://blog.linkedin.com/2011/06/21/russian-romanian-turkish). June 21, 2011. . Retrieved June 21, 2011.

[10] "LinedIn" (http://www.quantcast.com/linkedin.com). quantcast.com. . Retrieved December 17, 2010.

[11] http://www.bloomberg.com/news/2011-07-08/linkedin-tops-myspace-to-become-second-largest-u-s-social-networking-site.html

[12] Pepitone, Julianne (January 27, 2011). "LinkedIn files for IPO, reveals sales of $161 million" (http://money.cnn.com/2011/01/27/technology/linkedin_ipo/index.htm). CNN<pmey. . Retrieved January 28, 2011.

[13] "About LinkedIn: Management" (http://www.linkedin.com/static?key=management). Linkedin.com. . Retrieved December 7, 2009.

[14] "Press Release about Sequoia Capital Investing in LinkedIn" (http://www.linkedin.com/static?key=investors). . Retrieved November 14, 2007.

[15] "Press Releases: LinkedIn Premium Services Finding Rapid Adoption" (http://www.linkedin.com/static?key=press_releases_030706). LinkedIn. March 7, 2006. . Retrieved December 7, 2009.

[16] Swisher, Kara (January 27, 2011). "Here Comes Another Web IPO: LinkedIn S-1 Filing Imminent" (http://kara.allthingsd.com/20110127/here-comes-another-web-ipo-linkedin-s-1-filing-imminent/). *Boom Town*. . Retrieved January 27, 2011.

[17] LinkedIn Crunchbase Profile (http://www.crunchbase.com/company/linkedin)

[18] Guynn, Jessica (June 17, 2008). "LinkedIn networks way to $53-million investment" (http://www.latimes.com/business/la-fi-linkedin18-2008jun18,0,6631759.story). *The Los Angeles Times*. . Retrieved June 17, 2008.

[19] LinkedIn to open HQ in Dublin (http://www.insideireland.ie/index.cfm/section/news/ext/linkedin001/category/1091)

[20] "Tiger Global Said to Invest in LinkedIn at $2 billion Valuation" (http://www.businessweek.com/news/2010-07-28/tiger-global-said-to-invest-in-linkedin-at-2-billion-valuation.html). *Bloomberg BusinessWeek*. July 28, 2010. . Retrieved July 29, 2010.

[21] Hardy, Quentin (August 4, 2010). "LinkedIn Hooks Up" (http://www.forbes.com/2010/08/03/social-network-mspoke-technology-linkedin.html). *Forbes*. . Retrieved August 5, 2010.

[22] "Does local beat global in the professional-networking business?" (http://www.economist.com/node/14931599). *The Economist*. November 19, 2009. . Retrieved August 5, 2010.

[23] Fusfeld, Adam (September 23, 2010). "2010 Digital 100 Companies 1–100" (http://www.businessinsider.com/2010-digital-100-companies-1-100). businessinsider.com. . Retrieved December 17, 2010.

[24] Demos, Telis; Menn, Joseph (January 27, 2011). "LinkedIn looks for boost with IPO" (http://www.ft.com/cms/s/0/59e47ba4-2a54-11e0-b906-00144feab49a.html). *Financial Times*. . Retrieved January 28, 2011.

[25] LinkedIn establishes IPO terms (http://www.renaissancecapital.com/ipohome/news/LinkedIn-establishes-IPO-terms-9550.html) Renaissance Capital

[26] "LinkedIn's Stock Soars Amid Social Media Interest" (http://www.npr.org/2011/05/19/136466578/linkedins-stock-soars-amid-social-media-interest). Associated Press. May 19, 2011. .

[27] "LinkedIn has 5th largest first day gain in post bubble era" (http://www.renaissancecapital.com/ipohome/news/LinkedIn-has-5th-largest-first-day-gain-in-post-bubble-era-9647.html). *Renaissance Capital*. May 19, 2011. . Retrieved May 19, 2011.

[28] "LinkedIn competitor Viadeo hits 30 million members" (http://eu.techcrunch.com/2010/05/11/linkedin-competitor-viadeo-hits-30-million-members/). TechCrunch.com. May 11, 2010. . Retrieved July 25, 2010.

[29] "Facts and Figures" (http://corporate.xing.com/deutsch/investor-relations/basisinformationen/fakten-und-zahlen/). XING. September 1, 2010. . Retrieved November 26, 2010.

[30] "LinkedIn: 50 million professionals worldwide. LinkedIn. October 14, 2009. Retrieved November 3, 2009" (http://blog.linkedin.com/2009/10/14/linkedin-50-million-professionals-worldwide/). Blog.linkedin.com. . Retrieved December 7, 2009.

[31] "Four million UK professionals opt for a LinkedIn profile. Retrieved July 25, 2010" (http://www.bankingtimes.co.uk/11062010-four-million-uk-professionals-opt-for-a-linkedin-profile/). bankingtimes.com. . Retrieved July 25, 2010.

[32] "LinkedIn reaches 1 million users in Spain, competitors keep up the pressure. Retrieved July 25, 2010" (http://eu.techcrunch.com/2010/07/21/linkedin_reaches_1_million_users_in_spain_competition_keeps_up_the_pressure/). eu.techcrunch.com. . Retrieved July 25, 2010.

[33] Sid Yadav, venturebeat.com. " LinkedIn reaches 100 million users, but how many are coming back? (http://venturebeat.com/2011/03/22/linkedin-reaches-100-million-users-but-how-many-are-coming-back/)." March 22, 2011. Retrieved March 24, 2011.

[34] "Privacy Policy" (http://www.linkedin.com/static?key=pop_privacy_policy). LinkedIn. July 14, 2006. . Retrieved January 17, 2008.

[35] "LinkedIn Answers unlocks the world's best source of business knowledge: trusted professionals" (http://www.linkedin.com/static?key=press_releases_011607). Linkedin.com. January 16, 2007. . Retrieved December 7, 2009.

[36] "Social-networking site LinkedIN introduces mobile version" (http://life.tweakers.net/nieuws/52094/social-networkingsite-linkedin-introduceert-mobiele-versie.html). tweakers.net. . Retrieved February 25, 2008.

[37] *LinkedIn DirectAds launch* (http://shoutex.com/blog/linkedin-directads-google-adwords-ppc-1/), by Zaki Usman Nov 2008

[38] LinkedIn's promising new revenue model: sending you surveys. By: Neff, Jack, Advertising Age, 00018899, 10/27/2008, Vol. 79, Issue 40. Database: Business Source Complete

[39] *Facebook in a Suit: LinkedIn Launches Applications Platform* (http://www.businessweek.com/the_thread/techbeat/archives/2008/10/linkedin_launch.html), BusinessWeek, October 28, 2008

[40] "LinkedIn Adopts 'Recommend' Over 'Like'" (http://www.clickz.com/clickz/news/1866328/linkedin-adopts-recommend), Clickz.com, November 2, 2010

[41] *CardMunch acquired by LinkedIn* (http://shoutex.com/blog/cardmunch-iphone-app-for-business-users/), shoutEx.com Feb 2011

[42] Groups Directory | LinkedIn (http://www.linkedin.com/groupsDirectory?results=&pplSearchOrigin=GLHD&keywords=)

[43] "Five Benefits of LinkedIn for Organizations (and IT Pros) | TechRepublic." Web. May 9, 2011.

[44] O'Sullivan, James (2011), "Make the most of the networking tools that are available", Evening Echo, 09-May-11. Pg 32.

[45] "Syria: Linkedin Kicks Off Syrian Users!" (http://advocacy.globalvoicesonline.org/2009/04/18/syria-linkedin-kicks-off-syrian-users/). Global Voices Advocacy. April 18, 2009. . Retrieved April 30, 2010.

[46] Ungerleider, Neal (February 25, 2011). "China blocks access to LinkedIn" (http://www.cnn.com/2011/TECH/social.media/02/25/china.blocks.linkedin.fastco/index.html?iref=NS1). *Fast Company*. . Retrieved February 25, 2011.

[47] SNA-projects.com (http://sna-projects.com/)

[48] Project-voldemort.com (http://project-voldemort.com/)

External links

- Official website (http://http://www.linkedin.com/)
- SEC FORM S-1 REGISTRATION STATEMENT (http://sec.gov/Archives/edgar/data/1271024/000119312511016022/ds1.htm) – LinkedIn's IPO filing

Facebook

Facebook, Inc.

Type	Private
Founded	Cambridge, Massachusetts[1] (2004)
Founder	• Mark Zuckerberg • Eduardo Saverin • Dustin Moskovitz • Chris Hughes
Headquarters	Palo Alto, California, U.S., will be moved to Menlo Park, California, U.S. in June 2011
Area served	Worldwide
Key people	• Mark Zuckerberg (CEO) • Chris Cox (VP of Product) • Sheryl Sandberg (COO) • Donald E. Graham (Chairman)
Revenue	▲ US$2 billion (2010 est.)[2]
Net income	N/A
Employees	2000+ (2010)[3]
Website	[4]
IPv6 support	www.v6.facebook.com [5]
Alexa rank	2 (July 2011)[6]
Type of site	Social networking service
Advertising	Banner ads, referral marketing, casual games
Registration	Required
Users	750 million [7] (active in July 2011)
Available in	Multilingual
Launched	February 4, 2004
Current status	Active

Facebook is a social networking service and website launched in February 2004, operated and privately owned by Facebook, Inc.[1] As of July 2011, Facebook has more than 750 million active users.[8] [9] Users may create a personal profile, add other users as friends, and exchange messages, including automatic notifications when they update their profile. Facebook users must register before using the site. Additionally, users may join common-interest user groups, organized by workplace, school or college, or other characteristics. The name of the service stems from the colloquial name for the book given to students at the start of the academic year by university administrations in the United States to help students get to know each other better. Facebook allows any users who declare themselves to be at least 13 years old to become registered users of the website.

Facebook was founded by Mark Zuckerberg with his college roommates and fellow computer science students Eduardo Saverin, Dustin Moskovitz and Chris Hughes.[10] The website's membership was initially limited by the founders to Harvard students, but was expanded to other colleges in the Boston area, the Ivy League, and Stanford University. It gradually added support for students at various other universities before opening to high school students, and, finally, to anyone aged 13 and over, but based on ConsumersReports.org on May 2011, there are 7.5 million children under 13 with accounts, violating the site's terms.[11]

A January 2009 Compete.com study ranked Facebook as the most used social networking service by worldwide monthly active users, followed by MySpace.[12] *Entertainment Weekly* included the site on its end-of-the-decade "best-of" list, saying, "How on earth did we stalk our exes, remember our co-workers' birthdays, bug our friends, and play a rousing game of Scrabulous before Facebook?"[13] Quantcast estimates Facebook has 138.9 million monthly unique U.S. visitors in May 2011.[14] According to *Social Media Today*, in April 2010 an estimated 41.6% of the U.S. population had a Facebook account.[15] Nevertheless, Facebook's market growth started to stall in some regions, with the site losing 7 million active users in the United States and Canada in May 2011.[16]

History

Mark Zuckerberg wrote Facemash, the predecessor to Facebook, on October 28, 2003, while attending Harvard as a sophomore. According to *The Harvard Crimson*, the site was comparable to Hot or Not, and "used photos compiled from the online facebooks of nine houses, placing two next to each other at a time and asking users to choose the 'hotter' person".[17] [18]

Mark Zuckerberg co-created Facebook in his Harvard dorm room.

To accomplish this, Zuckerberg hacked into the protected areas of Harvard's computer network and copied the houses' private dormitory ID images. Harvard at that time did not have a student "facebook" (a directory with photos and basic information). Facemash attracted 450 visitors and 22,000 photo-views in its first four hours online.[17] [19]

The site was quickly forwarded to several campus group list-servers, but was shut down a few days later by the Harvard administration. Zuckerberg was charged by the administration with breach of security, violating copyrights, and violating individual privacy, and faced expulsion. Ultimately, however, the charges were dropped.[20] Zuckerberg expanded on this initial project that semester by creating a social study tool ahead of an art history final, by uploading 500 Augustan images to a website, with one image per page along with a comment section.[19] He opened the site up to his classmates, and people started sharing their notes.

The following semester, Zuckerberg began writing code for a new website in January 2004. He was inspired, he said, by an editorial in *The Harvard Crimson* about the Facemash incident.[21] On February 4, 2004, Zuckerberg launched "Thefacebook", originally located at thefacebook.com.[22]

Six days after the site launched, three Harvard seniors, Cameron Winklevoss, Tyler Winklevoss, and Divya Narendra, accused Zuckerberg of intentionally misleading them into believing he would help them build a social network called HarvardConnection.com, while

Chris Hughes

Dustin Moskovitz

Sean Parker

he was instead using their ideas to build a competing product.[23] The three complained to the *Harvard Crimson*, and the newspaper began an investigation. The three later filed a lawsuit against Zuckerberg, subsequently settling.[24]

Membership was initially restricted to students of Harvard College, and within the first month, more than half the undergraduate population at Harvard was registered on the service.[25] Eduardo Saverin (business aspects), Dustin Moskovitz (programmer), Andrew McCollum (graphic artist), and Chris Hughes soon joined Zuckerberg to help promote the website. In March 2004, Facebook expanded to Stanford, Columbia, and Yale.[26] It soon opened to the other Ivy League schools, Boston University, New York University, MIT, and gradually most universities in Canada and the United States.[27] [28]

Facebook incorporated in the summer of 2004, and the entrepreneur Sean Parker, who had been informally advising Zuckerberg, became the company's president.[29] In June 2004, Facebook moved its base of operations to Palo Alto, California.[26] It received its first investment later that month from PayPal co-founder Peter Thiel.[30] The company dropped *The* from its name after purchasing the domain name facebook.com in 2005 for $200,000.[31]

Cameron Winklevoss

Date	Users (in millions)	Days later	Monthly growth[32]
August 26, 2008	100[33]	1665	178.38%
April 8, 2009	200[34]	225	13.33%
September 15, 2009	300[35]	150	10%
February 5, 2010	400[36]	143	6.99%
July 21, 2010	500[37]	166	4.52%
January 5, 2011	600[38] [39]	168	3.57%
July 6, 2011	750[40]	182	2.54%

I+ Total active users[41] Facebook launched a high-school version in September 2005, which Zuckerberg called the next logical step.[42] At that time, high-school networks required an invitation to join.[43] Facebook later expanded membership eligibility to employees of several companies, including Apple Inc. and Microsoft.[44] Facebook was then opened on September 26, 2006, to everyone of age 13 and older with a valid email address.[45] [46]

On October 24, 2007, Microsoft announced that it had purchased a 1.6% share of Facebook for $240 million, giving Facebook a total implied value of around $15 billion.[47] Microsoft's purchase included rights to place international ads on Facebook.[48] In October 2008, Facebook announced that it would set up its international headquarters in Dublin, Ireland.[49] In September 2009, Facebook said that it had turned cash-flow positive for the first time.[50] In November 2010, based on SecondMarket Inc., an exchange for shares of privately held companies, Facebook's value was $41 billion (slightly surpassing eBay's) and it became the third largest US web company after Google and Amazon.[51] Facebook has been identified as a possible candidate for an IPO by 2013.[52]

Traffic to Facebook increased steadily after 2009. More people visited Facebook than Google for the week ending March 13, 2010.[53]

In March 2011 it was reported that Facebook removes approximately 20,000 profiles from the site every day for various infractions, including spam, inappropriate content and underage use, as part of its efforts to boost cyber security.[54]

In early 2011, Facebook announced plans to move to its new headquarters, the former Sun Microsystems campus in Menlo Park, California.[55] [56]

Company

Entrance to Facebook's current headquarters in the Stanford Research Park, Palo Alto, California.

Ownership

Mark Zuckerberg owns 24% of the company, Accel Partners owns 10%, Digital Sky Technologies owns 10%,[57] Dustin Moskovitz owns 6%, Eduardo Saverin owns 5%, Sean Parker owns 4%, Peter Thiel owns 3%, Greylock Partners and Meritech Capital Partners own between 1 to 2% each, Microsoft owns 1.3%, Li Ka-shing owns 0.75%, the Interpublic Group owns less than 0.5%, a small group of current and former employees and celebrities own less than 1% each, including Matt Cohler, Jeff Rothschild, Adam D'Angelo, Chris Hughes, and Owen Van Natta, while Reid Hoffman and Mark Pincus have sizable holdings of the company, and the remaining 30% or so are owned by employees, an undisclosed number of celebrities, and outside investors.[58] Adam D'Angelo, chief technology officer and friend of Zuckerberg, resigned in May 2008. Reports claimed that he and Zuckerberg began quarreling, and that he was no longer interested in partial ownership of the company.[59]

Management

Key management personnel comprise Chris Cox (VP of Product), Sheryl Sandberg (COO), and Donald E. Graham (Chairman). As of April 2011, Facebook has over 2,000 employees, and offices in 15 countries.[60]

Revenue

Most of Facebook's revenue comes from advertising. Microsoft is Facebook's exclusive partner for serving banner advertising,[61] and therefore Facebook serves only advertisements that exist in Microsoft's advertisement inventory.

Year	Revenue	Growth
2006	$52[62]	—
2007	$150[63]	188%
2008	$280[64]	87%
2009	$775[65]	177%
2010	$2000[2]	158%

|+ Revenues

(estimated, in millions US$)

Facebook generally has a lower clickthrough rate (CTR) for advertisements than most major websites. Banner advertisements on Facebook have generally received one-fifth the number of clicks compared to those on the Web as a whole.[66] This means that a smaller percentage of Facebook's users click on advertisements than many other large websites. For example, while Google users click on the first advertisement for search results an average of 8% of the time (80,000 clicks for every one million searches),[67] Facebook's users click on advertisements an average of 0.04% of the time (400 clicks for every one million pages).[68]

Sarah Smith, who was Facebook's Online Sales Operations Manager, confirmed that successful advertising campaigns can have clickthrough rates as low as 0.05% to 0.04%, and that CTR for ads tend to fall within two weeks.[69] Competing social network MySpace's CTR, in comparison, is about 0.1%, 2.5 times better than Facebook's but still low compared to many other websites. Explanations for Facebook's low CTR include the fact that Facebook's users are more technologically savvy and therefore use ad blocking software to hide advertisements, that users are younger and therefore better at ignoring advertising messages, and that MySpace users spend more time browsing through content, while Facebook users spend their time communicating with friends and therefore have their attention diverted away from advertisements.[70]

On pages for brands and products, however, some companies have reported CTR as high as 6.49% for Wall posts.[71] Involver, a social marketing platform, announced in July 2008 that it managed to attain a CTR of 0.7% on Facebook (over 10 times the typical CTR for Facebook ad campaigns) for its first client, Serena Software, managing to convert 1.1 million views into 8,000 visitors to their website.[72] A study found that, for video advertisements on Facebook, over 40% of users who viewed the videos viewed the entire video, while the industry average was 25% for in-banner video ads.[73]

Mergers and acquisitions

On November 15, 2010, Facebook announced it had acquired FB.com from the American Farm Bureau Federation for an undisclosed amount. On January 11, 2011, the Farm Bureau disclosed $8.5 million in "domain sales income", making the acquisition of FB.com one of the ten highest domain sales in history.[74]

Operations

A custom-built data center with substantially reduced ("38% less") power consumption compared to existing Facebook data centers opened in April 2011 in Prineville, Oregon.[75]

Website

Users can create profiles with photos, lists of personal interests, contact information, and other personal information. Users can communicate with friends and other users through private or public messages and a chat feature. They can also create and join interest groups and "like pages" (called "fan pages" until April 19, 2010), some of which are maintained by organizations as a means of advertising.[76]

Facebook's homepage features a login form on the top right for existing users, and a registration form directly underneath for new visitors.

To allay concerns about privacy, Facebook enables users to choose their own privacy settings and choose who can see specific parts of their profile.[77] The website is free to users, and generates revenue from advertising, such as banner ads.[78] Facebook requires a user's name and profile picture (if applicable) to be accessible by everyone. Users can control who sees other information they have shared, as well as who can find them in searches, through their privacy settings.[79]

The media often compare Facebook to MySpace, but one significant difference between the two websites is the level of customization.[80] Another difference is Facebook's requirement that users give their true identity, a demand that MySpace does not make.[81] MySpace allows users to decorate their profiles using HTML and Cascading Style Sheets (CSS), while Facebook allows only plain text.[82] Facebook has a number of features with which users may interact. They include the Wall, a space on every user's profile page that allows friends to post messages for the user to see;[83] Pokes, which allows users to send a virtual "poke" to each other (a notification then tells a user that they have been poked);[84] Photos, where users can upload albums and photos;[85] and Status, which allows users to inform their friends of their whereabouts and actions.[86] Depending on privacy settings, anyone who can see a user's profile can also view that user's Wall. In July 2007, Facebook began allowing users to post attachments to the Wall, whereas the Wall was previously limited to textual content only.[83]

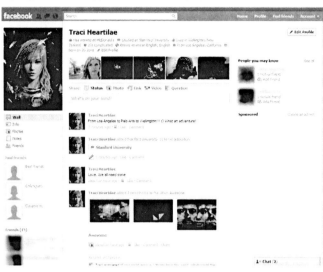

Profile shown on Facebook in 2011

Facebook profile shown in 2007

Profile shown on Thefacebook in 2005

On September 6, 2006, a News Feed was announced, which appears on every user's homepage and highlights information including profile changes, upcoming events, and birthdays of the user's friends.[87] This enabled spammers and other users to manipulate these features by creating illegitimate events or posting fake birthdays to attract attention to their profile or cause.[88] Initially, the News Feed caused dissatisfaction among Facebook users; some complained it was too cluttered and full of undesired information, others were concerned that it made it too easy for others to track individual activities (such as relationship status changes, events, and conversations with other users).[89]

In response, Zuckerberg issued an apology for the site's failure to include appropriate customizable privacy features. Since then, users have been able to control what types of information are shared automatically with friends. Users are now able to prevent user-set categories of friends from seeing updates about certain types of activities, including profile changes, Wall posts, and newly added friends.[90]

On February 23, 2010, Facebook was granted a patent[91] on certain aspects of its News Feed. The patent covers News Feeds in which links are provided so that one user can participate in the same activity of another user.[92] The patent may encourage Facebook to pursue action against websites that violate its patent, which may potentially include websites such as Twitter.[93]

Alli Hsieh **is singing the 20th century FOX song.**

Jen Taillon **added new photos.**

Dana Hornbeak **removed "piano" from her interests.**

Dave McClure **posted a video.**

Toronto Garage

Download not available The user has chosen not to allow download of this file. If you need it badly, send a request on his/her slidespace.

Facebook presentation by meagan marks @ Toronto FB Dev Garage. Interesting stats & metrics info. worth checking out.

Facebook mobile graphical user interface

One of the most popular applications on Facebook is the Photos application, where users can upload albums and photos.[94] Facebook allows users to upload an unlimited number of photos, compared with other image hosting services such as Photobucket and Flickr, which apply limits to the number of photos that a user is allowed to upload. During the first years, Facebook users were limited to 60 photos per album. As of May 2009, this limit has been increased to 200 photos per album.[95] [96] [97] [98]

Privacy settings can be set for individual albums, limiting the groups of users that can see an album. For example, the privacy of an album can be set so that only the user's friends can see the album, while the privacy of another album can be set so that all Facebook users can see it. Another feature of the Photos application is the ability to "tag", or label, users in a photo. For instance, if a photo contains a user's friend, then the user can tag the friend in the photo. This sends a notification to the friend that they have been tagged, and provides them a link to see the photo.[99]

Facebook Notes was introduced on August 22, 2006, a blogging feature that allowed tags and embeddable images. Users were later able to import blogs from Xanga, LiveJournal, Blogger, and other blogging services.[45] During the week of April 7, 2008, Facebook released a Comet-based[100] instant messaging application called "Chat" to several networks,[101] which allows users to communicate with friends and is similar in functionality to desktop-based instant messengers.

Facebook launched Gifts on February 8, 2007, which allows users to send virtual gifts to their friends that appear on the recipient's profile. Gifts cost $1.00 each to purchase, and a personalized message can be attached to each gift.[102] [103] On May 14, 2007, Facebook launched Marketplace, which lets users post free classified ads.[104] Marketplace has been compared to Craigslist by CNET, which points out that the major difference between the two is that listings posted by a user on Marketplace are seen only by users in the same network as that user, whereas listings posted on Craigslist can be seen by anyone.[105]

On July 20, 2008, Facebook introduced "Facebook Beta", a significant redesign of its user interface on selected networks. The Mini-Feed and Wall were consolidated, profiles were separated into tabbed sections, and an effort was made to create a "cleaner" look.[106] After initially giving users a choice to switch, Facebook began migrating all users to the new version beginning in September 2008.[107] On December 11, 2008, it was announced that Facebook was testing a simpler signup process.[108]

On June 13, 2009, Facebook introduced a "Usernames" feature, whereby pages can be linked with simpler URLs such as http:/ / www. facebook. com/ facebook [109] as opposed to http:/ / www. facebook. com/ profile. php?id=20531316728 [110].[111] Many new smartphones offer access to Facebook services through either their web-browsers or applications. An official Facebook application is available for the iPhone OS, the Android OS, and the WebOS. Nokia and Research In Motion both provide Facebook applications for their own mobile devices. More than 150 million active users access Facebook through mobile devices across 200 mobile operators in 60 countries.

On November 15, 2010, Facebook announced a new "Facebook Messages" service. In a media event that day, CEO Mark Zuckerberg said, "It's true that people will be able to have an @facebook.com email addresses, but it's not email". The launch of such a feature had been anticipated for some time before the announcement, with some calling it a "Gmail killer". The system, to be available to all of the website's users, combines text messaging, instant messaging, emails, and regular messages, and will include privacy settings similar to those of other Facebook services. Codenamed "Project Titan", Facebook Messages took 15 months to develop.[112] [113]

In February 2011, Facebook began to use the hCalendar microformat to mark up events, and the hCard microformat for the events' venues, enabling the extraction of details to users' own calendar or mapping applications.[114]

Since April 2011 Facebook users have had the ability to make live voice calls via Facebook Chat, allowing users to chat with others from all over the world. This feature, which is provided free through T-Mobile's new Bobsled service, lets the user add voice to the current Facebook Chat as well as leave voice messages on Facebook.[115]

On July 6th 2011, Facebook launched its video calling services using Skype as its technology partner. It allows one to one calling using a Skype Rest API.[116] For a brief period of time earlier that day, the URL "facebook.com" led to a Swedish website that was hosted through Google Sites. On July 14th Facebook wouldn't allow access.

Reception

According to comScore, Facebook is the leading social networking site based on monthly unique visitors, having overtaken main competitor MySpace in April 2008.[117] ComScore reports that Facebook attracted 130 million unique visitors in May 2010, an increase of 8.6 million people.[118] According to Alexa, the website's ranking among all websites increased from 60th to 7th in worldwide traffic, from September 2006 to September 2007, and is currently 2nd.[119] Quantcast ranks the website 2nd in the U.S. in traffic,[120] and Compete.com ranks it 2nd in the U.S.[121] The website is the most popular for uploading photos, with 50 billion uploaded cumulatively.[122] In 2010, Sophos's "Security Threat Report 2010" polled over 500 firms, 60% of which responded that they believed that Facebook was the social network that posed the biggest threat to security, well ahead of MySpace, Twitter, and LinkedIn.[123]

Facebook is the most popular social networking site in several English-speaking countries, including Canada,[124] the United Kingdom,[125] and the United States.[126] [127] [128] [129] In regional Internet markets, Facebook penetration is highest in North America (69 percent), followed by Middle East-Africa (67 percent), Latin America (58 percent), Europe (57 percent), and Asia-Pacific (17 percent).[130]

The website has won awards such as placement into the "Top 100 Classic Websites" by *PC Magazine* in 2007,[131] and winning the "People's Voice Award" from the Webby Awards in 2008.[132] In a 2006 study conducted by Student Monitor, a New Jersey-based company specializing in research concerning the college student market, Facebook was named the second most popular thing among undergraduates, tied with beer and only ranked lower than the iPod.[133]

On March 2010, Judge Richard Seeborg issued an order approving the class settlement in *Lane v. Facebook, Inc.*, the class action lawsuit arising out of Facebook's Beacon program.

In 2010, Facebook won the Crunchie "Best Overall Startup Or Product" for the third year in a row[134] and was recognized as one of the "Hottest Silicon Valley Companies" by Lead411.[135] However, in a July 2010 survey performed by the American Customer Satisfaction Index, Facebook received a score of 64 out of 100, placing it in the bottom 5% of all private-sector companies in terms of customer satisfaction, alongside industries such as the IRS e-file system, airlines, and cable companies. The reasons why Facebook scored so poorly include privacy problems, frequent changes to the website's interface, the results returned by the News Feed, and spam.[136]

In December 2008, the Supreme Court of the Australian Capital Territory ruled that Facebook is a valid protocol to serve court notices to defendants. It is believed to be the world's first legal judgement that defines a summons posted on Facebook as legally binding.[137] In March 2009, the New Zealand High Court associate justice David Gendall allowed for the serving of legal papers on Craig Axe by the company Axe Market Garden via Facebook.[138] [139] Employers (such as Virgin Atlantic Airways) have also used Facebook as a means to keep tabs on their employees and have even been known to fire them over posts they have made.[140]

By 2005, the use of Facebook had already become so ubiquitous that the generic verb "facebooking" had come into use to describe the process of browsing others' profiles or updating one's own.[141] In 2008, Collins English Dictionary declared "Facebook" as its new Word of the Year.[142] In December 2009, the New Oxford American Dictionary declared its word of the year to be the verb "unfriend", defined as "To remove someone as a 'friend' on a social networking site such as Facebook. As in, 'I decided to unfriend my roommate on Facebook after we had a fight.'"[143]

In April 2010, according to *The New York Times*, countries with the most Facebook users were the United States, the United Kingdom, and Indonesia.[144] Indonesia has become the country with the second largest number of Facebook users, after the United States, with 24 million users, or 10% of Indonesia's population.[145] Also in early 2010, Openbook was established, an avowed parody (and privacy advocacy) website[146] that enables text-based searches of those Wall posts that are available to "Everyone", i.e. to everyone on the Internet.

Writers for *The Wall Street Journal* found in 2010 that Facebook apps were transmitting identifying information to "dozens of advertising and Internet tracking companies". The apps used an HTTP referrer which exposed the user's identity and sometimes their friends'. Facebook said, "We have taken immediate action to disable all applications that violate our terms".[147]

Privacy

According to comScore, an internet marketing research company, Facebook collects as much data from its visitors as Google and Microsoft, but considerably less than Yahoo!.[148] In 2010, the security team began expanding its efforts to reduce the risks to users' privacy.[123] On November 6, 2007, Facebook launched Facebook Beacon, which was an ultimately failed attempt to advertise to friends of users using the knowledge of what purchases friends made.

Criticism

Facebook has met with controversies. It has been blocked intermittently in several countries including the People's Republic of China,[149] Vietnam,[150] Iran,[151] Uzbekistan,[152] Pakistan,[153] Syria,[154] and Bangladesh on different bases. For example, it was banned in many countries of the world on the basis of allowed content judged as anti-Islamic and containing religious discrimination. It has also been banned at many workplaces to prevent employees wasting their time on the site.[155] The privacy of Facebook users has also been an issue, and the safety of user accounts has been compromised several times. Facebook has settled a lawsuit regarding claims over source code and intellectual property.[156] In May 2011 emails were sent to journalists and bloggers making critical allegations about Google's privacy policies; however it was later discovered that the anti-Google campaign, conducted by PR giant Burson-Marsteller, was paid for by Facebook in what CNN referred to as "a new level skullduggery" and which Daily Beast called a "clumsy smear".[157]

In July 2011, German authorities began to discuss the prohibition of events marked the site. The decision is based on several cases of overcrowding or receipt of persons not invited to private events.[158] [159] In the event of the 16th anniversary of a girl in Hamburg, who was accidentally configured as an audience, 1500 "guests" attended the party and after reports of disturbances in overcrowding, more than a hundred policemen had to be deployed for crowd control. A policeman was injured and eleven participants were arrested for assault, property damage and resistance to authorities.[160] In another unexpected event with overcrowding, 41 young people were arrested and at least 16 injured.[161]

Media impact

In April 2011, Facebook launched a new portal for marketers and creative agencies to help them develop brand promotions on Facebook.[162] The company began its push by inviting a select group of British advertising leaders to meet Facebook's top executives at an "influencers' summit" in February 2010. Facebook has now been involved in campaigns for True Blood, American Idol, and Top Gear.[163]

Social impact

Facebook has affected the social life and activity of people in various ways. It can reunite lost family members and friends. One such reunion was between John Watson and the daughter he had been searching for 20 years. They met after Watson found her facebook profile.[164] Another father-daughter reunion was between Tony Macnauton and Frances Simpson, who had not seen each other for nearly 48 years.[165]

Some studies have named Facebook as a source of problems in relationships. Several news stories have suggested that using Facebook causes divorce and infidelity, but the claims have been questioned and refuted by other commentators.[166] [167]

Political impact

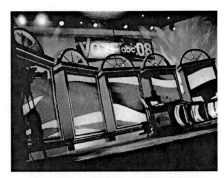

The stage at the Facebook – Saint Anselm College debates in 2008.

Facebook's role in the American political process was demonstrated in January 2008, shortly before the New Hampshire primary, when Facebook teamed up with ABC and Saint Anselm College to allow users to give live feedback about the "back to back" January 5 Republican and Democratic debates.[168] [169] [170] Charles Gibson moderated both debates, held at the Dana Center for the Humanities at Saint Anselm College. Facebook users took part in debate groups organized around specific topics, register to vote, and message questions.[171]

Over 1,000,000 people installed the Facebook application 'US politics' in order to take part, and the application measured users' responses to specific comments made by the debating candidates.[172] This debate showed the broader community what many young students had already experienced: Facebook was an extremely popular and powerful new way to interact and voice opinions. An article by Michelle Sullivan of Uwire.com illustrates how the "facebook effect" has affected youth voting rates, support by youth of political candidates, and general involvement by the youth population in the 2008 election.[173]

In February 2008, a Facebook group called "One Million Voices Against FARC" organized an event in which hundreds of thousands of Colombians marched in protest against the Revolutionary Armed Forces of Colombia, better known as the FARC (from the group's Spanish name).[174] In August 2010, one of North Korea's official government websites and the official news agency of the country, Uriminzokkiri, joined Facebook.[175]

In 2010 an English director of public health, whose staff was researching Syphilis, linked and attributed a rise in Syphilis cases in areas of Britain to Facebook. The reports of this research were rebuked by Facebook as "ignoring the difference between correlation and causation".[176]

Media

- At age 102, Ivy Bean of Bradford, England joined Facebook in 2008, making her one of the oldest people ever on Facebook. An inspiration to other residents of the care home in which she lived,[177] she quickly became more widely known and several fan pages were made in her honor. She visited Prime Minister Gordon Brown and his wife, Sarah, in Downing Street early in 2010.[178] Some time after creating her Facebook page, Bean also joined Twitter, when she passed the maximum number of friends allowed by Facebook. She became the oldest person to ever use the Twitter website. At the time of her death in July 2010, she had 4,962 friends on Facebook and more than 56,000 followers on Twitter. Her death was widely reported in the media and she received tributes from several notable media personalities.[179]
- "FriendFace", a December 2008 episode of the British sitcom, *The IT Crowd*, parodied Facebook and social networking sites in general.[180]
- American author Ben Mezrich published a book in July 2009 about Mark Zuckerberg and the founding of Facebook, titled *The Accidental Billionaires: The Founding of Facebook, A Tale of Sex, Money, Genius, and Betrayal*.[181]
- In response to the Everybody Draw Mohammed Day controversy and the ban of the website in Pakistan, an Islamic version of the website was created, called MillatFacebook.[182]
- "You Have 0 Friends", an April 2010 episode of the American animated comedy series, *South Park*, parodied Facebook.[183]
- *The Social Network*, a drama film directed by David Fincher about the founding of Facebook, was released October 1, 2010.[184] The film features an ensemble cast consisting of Jesse Eisenberg as Mark Zuckerberg,

Andrew Garfield as Eduardo Saverin, Justin Timberlake as Sean Parker, and Armie Hammer as Cameron and Tyler Winklevoss. The film was written by Aaron Sorkin and adapted from Ben Mezrich's 2009 book. The film was distributed by Columbia Pictures. No staff members of Facebook, including Zuckerberg, were involved with the project. However, one of Facebook's co-founders, Eduardo Saverin, was a consultant for Mezrich's book. Mark Zuckerberg has said that *The Social Network* is inaccurate.[185]

- On February 22, 2011, an Egyptian baby was named "Facebook" to commemorate the vital role Facebook and other social media played in Egypt's revolution.[186]
- On May 16, 2011, an Israeli couple named their daughter after the Facebook "like" feature. They explained that it wasn't to advertise for Facebook, but because they fancied the meaning behind the word.[187] [188]

Notes

[1] Eldon, Eric (December 18, 2008). "2008 Growth Puts Facebook In Better Position to Make Money" (http://venturebeat.com/2008/12/18/2008-growth-puts-facebook-in-better-position-to-make-money/). *VentureBeat* (San Francisco). . Retrieved December 19, 2008.

[2] Womack, Brian (December 16, 2010). "Facebook 2010 Sales Said Likely to Reach $2 Billion, More Than Estimated" (http://www.bloomberg.com/news/2010-12-16/facebook-sales-said-likely-to-reach-2-billion-this-year-beating-target.html). *Bloomberg* (New York). . Retrieved January 5, 2011.

[3] "Press Info" (http://www.facebook.com/press/info.php), Facebook. Retrieved May 27, 2010.

[4] https://www.facebook.com

[5] http://www.v6.facebook.com/

[6] "Facebook.com Site Info" (http://www.alexa.com/siteinfo/facebook.com). Alexa Internet. . Retrieved 2011-07-12.

[7] Facebook says membership has grown to 750 million - USATODAY.com (http://www.usatoday.com/tech/news/2011-07-06-facebook-skype-growth_n.htm)

[8] "Goldman to clients: Facebook has 600 million users" (http://www.msnbc.msn.com/id/40929239/ns/technology_and_science-tech_and_gadgets/). *MSNBC*. January 5, 2011. . Retrieved July January 15, 2011.

[9] "Facebook Has More Than 600 Million Users, Goldman Tells Clients" (http://www.businessinsider.com/facebook-has-more-than-600-million-users-goldman-tells-clients-2011-1). *Business Insider*. January 5, 2011. . Retrieved January 15, 2011.

[10] Carlson, Nicholas (March 5, 2010). "At Last — The Full Story Of How Facebook Was Founded" (http://www.businessinsider.com/how-facebook-was-founded-2010-3#we-can-talk-about-that-after-i-get-all-the-basic-functionality-up-tomorrow-night-1). *Business Insider*. .

[11] "Five million Facebook users are 10 or younger" (http://news.consumerreports.org/electronics/2011/05/five-million-facebook-users-are-10-or-younger.html). *ConsumerReports.org*. May 10, 2011. . Retrieved May 15, 2011.

[12] Kazeniac, Andy (February 9, 2009). "Social Networks: Facebook Takes Over Top Spot, Twitter Climbs" (http://blog.compete.com/2009/02/09/facebook-myspace-twitter-social-network/). *Compete Pulse blog*. . Retrieved February 17, 2009.

[13] Geier, Thom; Jensen, Jeff; Jordan, Tina; Lyons, Margaret; Markovitz, Adam; *et al.* (December 11, 2009). "THE 100 Greatest Movies, TV Shows, Albums, Books, Characters, Scenes, Episodes, Songs, Dresses, Music Videos, and Trends that entertained us over the 10 Years". *Entertainment Weekly* (New York) ((1079/1080):74-84).

[14] "facebook.com — Quantcast Audience Profile" (http://www.quantcast.com/facebook.com). Quantcast.com. April 29, 2011. . Retrieved May 15, 2011.

[15] Wells, Roy (August 8, 2010). "41.6% of the U.S. Population has a Facebook account" (http://www.socialmediatoday.com/roywells1/158020/416-us-population-has-facebook-account). *Social Media Today*. . Retrieved January 6, 2011.

[16] "Is Facebook growth stalling in North America?" (http://edition.cnn.com/2011/TECH/social.media/06/13/facebook.dropping.america/index.html). CNN. . Retrieved 2011-06-21.

[17] Locke, Laura (July 17, 2007). "The Future of Facebook" (http://www.time.com/time/business/article/0,8599,1644040,00.html). *Time* (New York). . Retrieved November 13, 2009.

[18] Tabak, Alan J. (February 9, 2004). "Hundreds Register for New Facebook Website" (http://web.archive.org/web/20050403215543/http://www.thecrimson.com/article.aspx?ref=357292). *The Harvard Crimson* (Cambridge, MA). Archived from the original (http://www.thecrimson.com/article.aspx?ref=357292) on April 3, 2005. . Retrieved November 7, 2008.

[19] McGirt, Ellen (May 1, 2007). "Facebook's Mark Zuckerberg: Hacker. Dropout. CEO." (http://www.fastcompany.com/magazine/115/open_features-hacker-dropout-ceo.html). *Fast Company* (New York). . Retrieved November 5, 2009.

[20] Kaplan, Katharine (November 19, 2003). "Facemash Creator Survives Ad Board" (http://www.thecrimson.com/article.aspx?ref=350143). *The Harvard Crimson* (Cambridge, MA). . Retrieved February 5, 2009.

[21] Hoffman, Claire (June 28, 2008). "The Battle for Facebook" (http://web.archive.org/web/20080703220456/http://www.rollingstone.com/news/story/21129674/the_battle_for_facebook/). *Rolling Stone* (New York). Archived from the original (http://www.rollingstone.com/news/story/21129674/the_battle_for_facebook/) on July 3, 2008. . Retrieved February 5, 2009.

[22] Seward, Zachary M. (July 25, 2007). "Judge Expresses Skepticism About Facebook Lawsuit" (http://online.wsj.com/article/SB118539991204578084.html?mod=googlenews_wsj). *The Wall Street Journal* (New York). . Retrieved April 30, 2008.

[23] Carlson, Nicolas (March 5, 2010). "In 2004, Mark Zuckerberg Broke Into A Facebook User's Private Email Account" (http://www. businessinsider.com/how-mark-zuckerberg-hacked-into-the-harvard-crimson-2010-3). *Business Insider*. . Retrieved March 5, 2010.

[24] Stone, Brad (June 28, 2008). "Judge Ends Facebook's Feud With ConnectU" (http://bits.blogs.nytimes.com/2008/06/26/ judge-ends-facebooks-feud-with-connectu/index.html). *New York Times blog*. .

[25] Phillips, Sarah (July 25, 2007). "A brief history of Facebook" (http://www.guardian.co.uk/technology/2007/jul/25/media.newmedia). *The Guardian* (London). . Retrieved March 7, 2008.

[26] Facebook (January 1, 2007). "Company Timeline" (http://www.facebook.com/press/info.php?timeline). Press release. . Retrieved March 5, 2008.

[27] Rosmarin, Rachel (September 11, 2006). "Open Facebook" (http://www.forbes.com/2006/09/11/ facebook-opens-up-cx_rr_0911facebook.html). *Forbes* (New York). . Retrieved June 13, 2008.

[28] Nguyen, Lananh (April 12, 2004). "Online network created by Harvard students flourishes" (http://www.tuftsdaily.com/2.5541/1. 600318). *The Tufts Daily* (Medford, MA). . Retrieved August 21, 2009.

[29] Rosen, Ellen (May 26, 2005). "Student's Start-Up Draws Attention and $13 Million" (http://www.nytimes.com/2005/05/26/business/ 26sbiz.html?_r=2&scp=1&sq=thefacebook+parker&st=nyt). *The New York Times*. . Retrieved May 18, 2009.

[30] "Why you should beware of Facebook" (http://www.theage.com.au/news/general/beware-facebook/2008/01/18/1200620184398. html?page=fullpage#contentSwap2). *The Age* (Melbourne). January 20, 2008. . Retrieved April 30, 2008.

[31] Williams, Chris (October 1, 2007). "Facebook wins Manx battle for face-book.com" (http://www.theregister.co.uk/2007/10/01/ facebook_domain_dispute/). *The Register* (London). . Retrieved June 13, 2008.|

[32] "Monthly growth" is the average percentage growth rate at which the total number of active users grows each month over the specified period.

[33] Zuckerberg, Mark (August 26, 2008). "Our First 100 Million" (http://blog.facebook.com/blog.php?post=28111272130). The Facebook Blog. . Retrieved June 26, 2010.

[34] Zuckerberg, Mark (April 8, 2009). "200 Million Strong" (http://blog.facebook.com/blog.php?post=72353897130). The Facebook Blog. . Retrieved June 26, 2010.

[35] Zuckerberg, Mark (September 15, 2009). "300 Million and On" (http://blog.facebook.com/blog.php?post=136782277130). The Facebook Blog. . Retrieved June 26, 2010.

[36] "New navigation for users and 400 million active users announcement" (http://www.facebook.com/notes/facebook-ads/ new-navigation-for-users-and-400-million-active-users-announcement/326050130129). Facebook. February 4, 2010. . Retrieved June 26, 2010.

[37] Zuckerberg, Mark (July 21, 2010). "500 Million Stories" (http://blog.facebook.com/blog.php?post=409753352130). The Facebook Blog. . Retrieved July 21, 2010.

[38] Carlson, Nicholas (January 5, 2011). "Goldman to clients: Facebook has 600 million users" (http://www.msnbc.msn.com/id/40929239/ ns/technology_and_science-tech_and_gadgets/). *MSNBC*. . Retrieved February 11, 2011.

[39] This value is from an investment document. The date is from when the document was revealed to the public, not the actual date that the website reached this many users.

[40] Nathan Olivarez-Giles and Jessica Guynn (July 6, 2011). "Facebook unveils video calling with Skype, has more than 750 million users" (http://latimesblogs.latimes.com/technology/2011/07/watch-facebooks-new-product-announcement-live.html). *L.A. Times*. . Retrieved July 6, 2011.

[41] An "active user" is defined by Facebook as a user who has visited the website in the last 30 days.

[42] Dempsey, Laura (August 3, 2006). "Facebook is the go-to Web site for students looking to hook up". *Dayton Daily News* (Ohio).

[43] Lerer, Lisa (January 25, 2007). "Why MySpace Doesn't Card" (http://classic-web.archive.org/web/20080602081817/http://www. forbes.com/security/2007/01/25/myspace-security-identity-tech-security-cx_ll_0124myspaceage.html). *Forbes* (New York). . Retrieved May 13, 2011.

[44] Lacy, Sarah (September 12, 2006). "Facebook: Opening the Doors Wider" (http://www.businessweek.com/technology/content/sep2006/ tc20060912_682123.htm?chan=top+news_top+news+index_technology). *BusinessWeek* (New York). . Retrieved March 9, 2008.

[45] Abram, Carolyn (September 26, 2006). "Welcome to Facebook, everyone" (http://blog.facebook.com/blog.php?post=2210227130). The Facebook Blog. . Retrieved March 8, 2008.

[46] "Terms of Use" (http://www.facebook.com/terms.php). Facebook. November 15, 2007. . Retrieved March 5, 2008.

[47] Microsoft (October 24, 2007). "Facebook and Microsoft Expand Strategic Alliance" (http://www.microsoft.com/Presspass/press/2007/ oct07/10-24FacebookPR.mspx). Press release. . Retrieved November 8, 2007.

[48] "Facebook Stock For Sale" (http://www.businessweek.com/magazine/content/08_33/b4096000952343. htm?chan=rss_topEmailedStories_ssi_5). *BusinessWeek* (New York). . Retrieved August 6, 2008.

[49] Facebook (October 2, 2008). "Facebook to Establish International Headquarters in Dublin, Ireland" (http://www.facebook.com/press/ releases.php?p=59042). Press release. . Retrieved November 30, 2008.

[50] "Facebook 'cash flow positive,' signs 300M users" (http://www.cbc.ca/technology/story/2009/09/16/tech-facebook-300-million-users. html). *CBC News* (Toronto). September 16, 2009. . Retrieved March 23, 2010.

[51] Womack, Brian (November 15, 2010). "Facebook Becomes Third Biggest US Web Company" (http://www.thejakartaglobe.com/ technology/facebook-becomes-third-biggest-us-web-company/406751). *The Jakarta Globe*. .

[52] "6 Reasons Groupon's Rejection Of Google Is Great For The Universe" (http://www.businessinsider.com/google-groupon-deal). *Business Insider*. December 10, 2010. . Retrieved January 13, 2011.

[53] Dougherty, Heather (March 15, 2010). "Facebook Reaches Top Ranking in US" (http://weblogs.hitwise.com/heather-dougherty/2010/03/facebook_reaches_top_ranking_i.html). *Experian Hitwise (blog)*. .

[54] "Facebook deletes 20,000 underage profiles daily" (http://ibnlive.in.com/news/facebook-deletes-20000-underage-profiles-daily/146972-11.html). *IBN Live*. Press Trust of India (Noida, Uttar Pradesh). March 24, 2011. . Retrieved March 24, 2011.

[55] Parr, Ben (February 7, 2011). " These Are Facebook's New Offices [PHOTOS] (http://mashable.com/2011/02/07/facebook-menlo-park-pics/)." *Mashable* (New York). Retrieved April 6, 2011.

[56] Brundage, Sandy (February 8, 2011). "Facebook moving headquarters to Menlo Park: Social-networking giant to move into former Sun/Oracle campus" (http://www.almanacnews.com/news/show_story.php?id=8270). *The Almanac* (Menlo Park, CA).

[57] "Facebook's friend in Russia" (http://tech.fortune.cnn.com/2010/10/04/facebooks-friend-in-russia/?source=cnn_bin&hpt=Sbin). *Fortune*. October 4, 2010. . Retrieved December 18, 2010.

[58] Kirkpatrick, David (2010). *The Facebook effect: the inside story of the company that is connecting the world* (http://books.google.com/books?id=RRUkLhyGZVgC&printsec=frontcover&dq=The+Facebook+Effect&hl=en&ei=IE-eTbSaDsTagQft0p3YDw&sa=X&oi=book_result&ct=result&resnum=1&ved=0CCwQ6AEwAA#v=onepage&q=outside investors&f=false). New York: Simon & Schuster. ISBN 9781439109809. .

[59] McCarthy, Caroline (May 11, 2008). "As Facebook goes corporate, Mark Zuckerberg loses an early player" (http://news.cnet.com/8301-13577_3-9941488-36.html). *CNET.com*. . Retrieved July 12, 2010.

[60] "Facebook Factsheet" (http://www.facebook.com/press/info.php?factsheet). . Retrieved April 10, 2011.

[61] "Product Overview FAQ: Facebook Ads" (http://www.facebook.com/press/faq.php#Facebook+Ads). Facebook. . Retrieved March 10, 2008.

[62] Arrington, Michael (April 26, 2006). "Facebook Goes Beyond College, High School Markets" (http://techcrunch.com/2006/04/26/facebook-goes-beyond-college-high-school-markets/). *TechCrunch*. . Retrieved July 13, 2010.

[63] Schonfeld, Erick (January 31, 2008). "Facebook Finances Leaked" (http://techcrunch.com/2008/01/31/facebook-finances-leaked/). *TechCrunch*. . Retrieved July 13, 2010.

[64] Arrington, Michael (May 19, 2009). "Facebook Turns Down $8 billion Valuation Term Sheet, Claims 2009 Revenues Will Be $550 million" (http://techcrunch.com/2009/05/19/facebook-turns-down-8-billion-valuation-term-sheet-claims-2009-revenues-to-be-550-million/). *TechCrunch*. . Retrieved July 13, 2010.

[65] Tsotsis, Alexia (January 5, 2011). "Report: Facebook Revenue Was $777 Million In 2009, Net Income $200 Million" (http://techcrunch.com/2011/01/05/report-facebook-revenue-was-777-million-in-2009-net-income-200-million/). *TechCrunch*. . Retrieved January 5, 2011.

[66] "Facebook May Revamp Beacon" (http://www.businessweek.com/technology/content/nov2007/tc20071128_366355_page_2.htm). *BusinessWeek*. New York. November 28, 2007. . Retrieved July 18, 2010.

[67] "Google AdWords Click Through Rates Per Position" (http://www.accuracast.com/seo-weekly/adwords-clickthrough.php). AccuraCast. October 9, 2009. . Retrieved July 18, 2010.

[68] Denton, Nick (March 7, 2007). "Facebook 'consistently the worst performing site'" (http://valleywag.gawker.com/242234/facebook-consistently-the-worst-performing-site). *Gawker*. . Retrieved July 18, 2010.

[69] "Facebook Says Click Through Rates Do Not Match Those At Google" (http://techpulse360.com/2009/08/12/facebook-says-its-click-through-rates-do-not-match-those-at-google/). *TechPulse 360*. August 12, 2009. . Retrieved July 18, 2010.

[70] Leggatt, Helen (July 16, 2007). "Advertisers disappointed with Facebook's CTR" (http://www.bizreport.com/2007/07/advertisers_disappointed_with_facebooks_ctr.html). *BizReport*. . Retrieved July 18, 2010.

[71] Klaassen, Abbey (August 13, 2009). "Facebook's Click-Through Rates Flourish ... for Wall Posts" (http://adage.com/digitalnext/post?article_id=138442). *Advertising Age* (New York). . Retrieved July 18, 2010.

[72] Involver (July 31, 2008). "Involver Delivers Over 10x the Typical Click-Through Rate for Facebook Ad Campaigns" (http://www.prweb.com/releases/2008/07/prweb1162804.htm). Press release. . Retrieved July 18, 2010.

[73] Walsh, Mark (June 15, 2010). "Study: Video Ads On Facebook More Engaging Than Outside Sites" (http://www.mediapost.com/publications/?fa=Articles.showArticle&art_aid=130217). *MediaPost* (New York). . Retrieved July 18, 2010.

[74] "FB.com acquired by Facebook" (http://namemon.com/news/1-latest-news/115-fbcom-acquired-by-facebook). *NameMon News*. January 11, 2011. .

[75] "Zuckerberg makes surprise appearance at new Prineville, Ore. Facebook data center" (http://www.washingtonpost.com/business/zuckerberg-makes-surprise-appearance-at-new-prineville-ore-facebook-data-center/2011/04/16/AFT4NamD_story.html). *The Washington Post*. Associated Press. April 16, 2011. . Retrieved April 16, 2011.

[76] ww.facebook.com/sitetour/profile.php "Edit Your Profile" (http://web.archive.org/web/20080227212605/http://w). Facebook. Archived from the original (http://www.facebook.com/sitetour/profile.php) on February 27, 2008. ww.facebook.com/sitetour/profile.php. Retrieved March 7, 2008.

[77] "Search Privacy" (http://www.facebook.com/privacy/?view=search). Facebook. . Retrieved June 13, 2009.

[78] Barton, Zoe (April 28, 2006). "Facebook goes corporate" (http://web.archive.org/web/20080526001748/http://news.zdnet.com/2100-9588_22-6066533.html). *ZDNet News*. Archived from the original (http://news.zdnet.com/2100-9588_22-6066533.html) on May 26, 2008. . Retrieved March 9, 2008.

[79] "Choose Your Privacy Settings" (http://www.facebook.com/settings/?tab=privacy). Facebook. . Retrieved September 10, 2009.

[80] Stone, Brad (May 25, 2007). "Facebook Expands Into MySpace's Territory" (http://www.nytimes.com/2007/05/25/technology/25social.html). *The New York Times*. . Retrieved March 8, 2008.

[81] Ciccone, David (May 7, 2009). "Facebook Connect fully integrated into Mobility Today" (http://mobilitytoday.com/news/009500/facebook_connect_mt). Mobility Today Fitness. . Retrieved September 10, 2010.

[82] Sullivan, Mark (July 24, 2007). "Is Facebook the New MySpace?" (http://www.pcworld.com/article/id,134635-c,categories/article.html). *PC World* (San Francisco). . Retrieved April 30, 2008.

[83] Der, Kevin. "Facebook is off-the-wall" (http://blog.facebook.com/blog.php?post=3532972130). The Facebook Blog. . Retrieved July 30, 2007.

[84] "Inbox, Messages and Pokes" (http://www.facebook.com/help.php?page=20). Facebook. . Retrieved March 9, 2008.

[85] "The Facebook Gifts" (http://blog.facebook.com/blog.php?post=2406207130). Facebook. . Retrieved March 5, 2008.

[86] Ramadge, Andrew (November 26, 2007). "Facebook is ... reconsidering the word "is"" (http://www.news.com.au/technology/story/0,25642,22822400-5014108,00.html). *news.com.au Technology blog* (Sydney). . Retrieved March 8, 2008.

[87] Sanghvi, Ruchi (September 6, 2006). "Facebook Gets a Facelift" (http://blog.facebook.com/blog.php?post=2207967130). The Facebook Blog. . Retrieved February 11, 2008.

[88] "Facebook: Celebrate Your Birthday Every Day" (http://blog.colnect.com/2010/03/facebook-celebrate-your-birthday-every.html). Colnect blog. . Retrieved March 9, 2010.

[89] Lacy, Sarah (September 8, 2006). "Facebook Learns from Its Fumble" (http://www.businessweek.com/technology/content/sep2006/tc20060908_536553.htm?campaign_id=rss_tech). *BusinessWeek* (New York). . Retrieved June 28, 2008.

[90] Gonsalves, Antone (September 8, 2006). "Facebook Founder Apologizes In Privacy Flap; Users Given More Control" (http://www.informationweek.com/news/internet/ebusiness/showArticle.jhtml?articleID=192700574). *InformationWeek* (New York). . Retrieved June 28, 2008.

[91] US patent 7669123 (http://v3.espacenet.com/textdoc?DB=EPODOC&IDX=US7669123)

[92] "US Patent No. 7669123" (http://themelis-cuiper.com/22/us-patent-no-7669123.html). Social Media. March 1, 2010. . Retrieved March 9, 2010.

[93] "Facebook's news-feed patent could mean lawsuits" (http://www.cnn.com/2010/TECH/02/26/facebook.patent/index.html). *CNN*. February 26, 2010. . Retrieved July 12, 2010.

[94] Arrington, Michael (May 24, 2007). "Facebook Launches Facebook Platform; They are the Anti-MySpace" (http://www.techcrunch.com/2007/05/24/facebook-launches-facebook-platform-they-are-the-anti-myspace/). *TechCrunch*. . Retrieved June 28, 2008.

[95] "Share More Memories with Larger Photo Albums" (http://blog.facebook.com/blog.php?post=87157517130). . Retrieved January 4, 2010.

[96] "Upload: 60 or 200 photos in the same album?" (http://www.facebook.com/topic.php?uid=2305272732&topic=7363). Facebook. . Retrieved January 25, 2009.

[97] "How can I add more than 60 photos to an album?" (http://www.facebook.com/topic.php?uid=2305272732&topic=4947). Facebook. . Retrieved January 25, 2009.

[98] "Example of album from a regular user with a 200-photo limit" (http://www.facebook.com/album.php?aid=2003726&l=5f3c8&id=1352160452). Facebook. . Retrieved January 25, 2009.

[99] "Photos" (http://www.facebook.com/help.php?page=7). Facebook. . Retrieved March 15, 2008.

[100] Eugene (May 14, 2008). "Facebook Chat" (http://www.facebook.com/note.php?note_id=14218138919&id=9445547199&index=0). Facebook. . Retrieved June 2, 2008.

[101] Facebook (April 6, 2008). "Announcement: Facebook Launches Facebook Chat" (http://www.facebook.com/press/releases.php?p=27681). Press release. . Retrieved April 11, 2008.

[102] "Give gifts on Facebook!" (http://blog.facebook.com/blog.php?post=2234372130). Facebook. . Retrieved March 15, 2008.

[103] "Gifts" (http://www.facebook.com/help.php?page=16). Facebook. . Retrieved March 15, 2008.

[104] Morgenstern, Jared (May 14, 2007). "The Marketplace Is Open..." (http://blog.facebook.com/blog.php?post=2383962130). The Facebook Blog. . Retrieved March 15, 2008.

[105] McCarthy, Caroline (May 13, 2007). "Hands-on with Facebook Marketplace" (http://www.news.com/8301-10784_3-9718779-7.html). *CNET*. . Retrieved March 15, 2008.

[106] Havenstein, Heather (July 21, 2008). "Facebook Facelift Targets Aging Users and New Competitors" (http://www.nytimes.com/idg/IDG_852573C4006938800025748D0064C292.html?ref=technology). *The New York Times*. .

[107] Slee, Mark (September 10, 2008). "Moving to the new Facebook" (http://blog.new.facebook.com/blog.php?post=30074837130). The Facebook Blog. . Retrieved September 12, 2008.

[108] "Facebook Testing Even Simpler Sign Up; Closing The Gap With MySpace In The U.S." (http://www.techcrunch.com/2008/12/11/facebook-testing-even-simpler-sign-up-closing-the-gap-with-myspace-in-the-us/). *TechCrunch*. December 11, 2008. .

[109] http://www.facebook.com/facebook

[110] http://www.facebook.com/profile.php?id=20531316728

[111] DiPersia, Blaise (June 9, 2009). "Coming Soon: Facebook Usernames" (http://blog.facebook.com/blog.php?post=90316352130). The Facebook Blog. . Retrieved June 13, 2009.

[112] Gabbatt, Adam; Arthur, Charles (November 15, 2010). "Facebook mail: it might kill Gmail, but 'it's not email'" (http://www.guardian.co.uk/technology/2010/nov/15/facebook-mail-gmail-killer-email). *The Guardian* (London). .

[113] "Facebook adds 'social inbox' – with E-mail" (http://www.mercurynews.com/top-stories/ci_16619072). *San Jose Mercury News* (California). November 16, 2010. . Retrieved January 13, 2011.

[114] Protalinski, Emil (February 18, 2011). "Facebook adds hCalendar and hCard microformats to Events" (http://www.zdnet.com/blog/facebook/facebook-adds-hcalendar-and-hcard-microformats-to-events/266). *ZDNet blog*. . Retrieved March 24, 2011.

[115] Swartz, Jon. "Facebook hops aboard T-Mobile's Bobsled Service" (http://content.usatoday.com/communities/technologylive/post/2011/04/facebook-hops-aboard-t-mobiles-voip-service/1). *USA Today* (Washington DC). . Retrieved 20 April 2011.

[116] "Facebook starts video calling service to compete with Google+ hangouts" (http://digitalanalog.in/2011/07/07/facebook-starts-video-calling-service-to-compete-with-google-hangout/). . Retrieved 6 July 2011.

[117] "Facebook: Largest, Fastest Growing Social Network" (http://www.techtree.com/India/News/Facebook_Largest_Fastest_Growing_Social_Network/551-92134-643.html). *Techtree.com*. August 13, 2008. . Retrieved August 14, 2008.

[118] "Privacy, Schmivacy: Facebook Is Attracting Near-Record Numbers Of New Visitors" (http://techcrunch.com/2010/06/07/privacy-facebook-visitors/). *TechCrunch*. June 7, 2010. . Retrieved September 8, 2010.

[119] "Related info for: facebook.com/" (http://www.alexa.com/data/details/traffic_details/facebook.com?q=facebook). Alexa Internet. . Retrieved March 8, 2008.

[120] "Facebook.com Web Site Audience Profile" (http://www.quantcast.com/facebook.com). Quantcast. . Retrieved September 9, 2010.

[121] "We're Number Two! Facebook moves up one big spot in the charts" (http://blog.compete.com/2010/02/17/weâre-number-two-facebook-moves-up-one-big-spot-in-the-charts/). Compete.com. . Retrieved September 9, 2010.

[122] McGrath, Kristin (July 22, 2010). "Status update: Facebook logs 500 million members" (http://www.usatoday.com/tech/news/2010-07-21-facebook-hits-500-million-users_N.htm). *USA Today* (Washington DC). . Retrieved September 9, 2010.

[123] Cluley, Graham (February 1, 2010). "Revealed: Which social networks pose the biggest risk?" (http://www.sophos.com/blogs/gc/g/2010/02/01/revealed-social-networks-pose-biggest-risk/). Sophos. . Retrieved July 12, 2010.

[124] Yum, Kenny (May 18, 2007). "Facebook says 'Thanks, Canada'" (http://network.nationalpost.com/np/blogs/posted/archive/2007/05/18/facebook-says-thanks-canada.aspx). *National Post* (Toronto). . Retrieved April 30, 2008.

[125] Malkin, Bonnie (September 26, 2007). "Facebook is UK's biggest networking site" (http://www.telegraph.co.uk/news/main.jhtml?xml=/news/2007/09/25/nface125.xml). *The Daily Telegraph* (London). . Retrieved April 30, 2008.

[126] Caverly, Doug (June 16, 2009). "comScore: Facebook Catches MySpace in U.S." (http://www.webpronews.com/topnews/2009/06/16/comscore-facebook-catches-myspace-in-us). *WebProNews* (iEntry Network). . Retrieved September 24, 2009.

[127] "Facebook grows as MySpace cuts back" (http://atlanta.bizjournals.com/atlanta/stories/2009/06/15/daily47.html). *Atlanta Business Chronicle*. June 17, 2009. . Retrieved September 24, 2009. "The Conference Board report on first quarter online users in the U.S. showed Facebook with an even larger lead, with 78 percent of social network participants, followed by MySpace (42 percent), LinkedIn (17 percent) and Twitter (10 percent)."

[128] Hasselback, Drew (June 17, 2009). "Comscore says Facebook has surpassed MySpace for U.S. users" (http://network.nationalpost.com/np/blogs/fpposted/archive/2009/06/17/comscore-says-facebook-has-surpassed-myspace-for-u-s-users.aspx). *National Post* (Toronto). . Retrieved September 24, 2009. "Comscore says Facebook surpassed MySpace among U.S. users in May, while Nielsen figures that actually happened back in January."

[129] Wood, Cara (August 31, 2009). "Keeping pace with mainstream social media" (http://www.dmnews.com/keeping-pace-with-mainstream-social-media/article/147429/). *Direct Marketing News* (New York). . Retrieved September 24, 2009. "The giant in the space remains Facebook, which gets 87.7 million unique viewers per month, according to ComScore. MySpace, with nearly 70 million unique monthly visitors, has seen growth stagnate over the past year."

[130] McCarthy, Caroline (July 21, 2010). "Who will be Facebook's next 500 million?" (http://news.cnet.com/8301-13577_3-20011158-36.html). *CNET* (New York). . Retrieved September 23, 2008.

[131] "Social Networking" (http://www.pcmag.com/article2/0,2817,2169354,00.asp). *PC Magazine*. August 13, 2007. . Retrieved May 9, 2008.

[132] "12th Annual Webby Awards Nominees" (http://www.webbyawards.com/webbys/current.php?season=12). International Academy of Digital Arts and Sciences. . Retrieved May 6, 2008.

[133] "Survey: College Kids Like IPods Better Than Beer" (http://www.foxnews.com/story/0,2933,198632,00.html). *Fox News*. June 8, 2006. . Retrieved March 10, 2008.

[134] Kincaid, Jason (January 8, 2010). "Facebook Takes Best Overall For The Hat Trick" (http://techcrunch.com/2010/01/08/crunchies-winner/). *Techcrunch*. . Retrieved July 8, 2010.

[135] "Lead411 launches "Hottest Silicon Valley Companies" awards" (http://www.lead411.com/silicon-valley-companies.html). Lead411.com. May 25, 2010. . Retrieved July 8, 2010.

[136] Fowler, Geoffrey A. (July 20, 2010). "Users Rate Facebook Slightly Above the Tax Man" (http://blogs.wsj.com/digits/2010/07/20/users-rate-facebook-slightly-above-the-tax-man/). *Digits (Wall Street Journal technology blog)*. . Retrieved July 21, 2010.

[137] Towell, Noel (December 16, 2008). "Lawyers to serve notices on Facebook" (http://www.theage.com.au/articles/2008/12/16/1229189579001.html). *The Age* (Melbourne). . Retrieved March 23, 2010.

[138] "Kiwi judge follows Australian Facebook precedent" (http://www.theage.com.au/news/technology/web/kiwis-follow-australian-facebook-precedent/2009/03/16/1237054723620.html). *The Age*. Agence France-Presse (Melbourne). March 16, 2009. .

[139] Peters, Melanie (April 5, 2009). "Facebook trap criminals in its web" (http://www.iol.co.za/index.php?set_id=1&click_id=13& art_id=vn20090405104820309C778226&newslett=1&em=197599a6a20090405ah). *Independent Online* (Cape Town). .

[140] Cochran, Jason (November 6, 2008). "Watch out! Bosses are saving money by firing employees over Facebook posts" (http://www. walletpop.com/blog/2008/11/06/watch-out-bosses-are-saving-money-by-firing-employees-over-face/). *WalletPop.com*. . Retrieved May 6, 2010.

[141] McDonald, Soraya Nadia (July 4, 2005). "Facebooking, the rage on college campuses" (http://community.seattletimes.nwsource.com/ archive/?date=20050704&slug=btfacebook04). *The Seattle Times*. . Retrieved September 14, 2009.

[142] Nicole, Kristen (December 21, 2007). "I Can So "Facebook" You Now (and be gramatically correct)" (http://mashable.com/2007/12/ 21/facebook-noun-verb-collins-english-dictionary/). *Mashable*. . Retrieved March 23, 2010.

[143] "Unfriend is New Oxford dictionary's Word of the Year" (http://content.usatoday.com/communities/ondeadline/post/2009/11/ unfriend-is-new-oxford-dictionarys-word-of-the-year-/1). *USA Today* (Washington DC). November 17, 2009. . Retrieved July 12, 2010.

[144] Onishi, Norimitshu (April 19, 2010). "Debate on Internet's Limits Grows in Indonesia" (http://www.nytimes.com/2010/04/20/world/ asia/20indonet.html?ref=asia). *The New York Times*. . Retrieved April 19, 2010.

[145] "ACFTA: It Certainly Sounds Better Without the 'C', Doesn't It?" (http://heydiaspora.com/ acfta-it-certainly-sounds-better-without-the-c-doesnt-it/). Hey Diaspora!. . Retrieved November 7, 2010.

[146] "Openbook – Connect and share whether you want to or not" (http://youropenbook.org/about.html). Youropenbook.org. May 12, 2010. . Retrieved June 26, 2010.

[147] Steel, Emily; Fowler, Geoffrey A. (October 18, 2010). "Facebook in Privacy Breach" (http://online.wsj.com/article/ SB10001424052702304772804575558484075236968.html). *The Wall Street Journal* (New York). . Retrieved October 18, 2010.

[148] Story, Louise (March 10, 2008). "To Aim Ads, Web Is Keeping Closer Eye on You" (http://www.nytimes.com/2008/03/10/ technology/10privacy.html). *The New York Times*. . Retrieved March 9, 2008.

[149] "China's Facebook Status: Blocked" (http://blogs.abcnews.com/theworldnewser/2009/07/chinas-facebook-status-blocked.html). *ABC News blog*. July 8, 2009. . Retrieved July 13, 2009.

[150] Stocking, Ben (November 17, 2009). "Vietnam Internet users fear Facebook blackout" (http://news.smh.com.au/ breaking-news-technology/vietnam-internet-users-fear-facebook-blackout-20091117-iki0.html). *The Sydney Morning Herald*. Associated Press. . Retrieved January 9, 2011.

[151] Shahi, Afshin (July 27, 2008). "Iran's Digital War" (http://dailystaregypt.com/article.aspx?ArticleID=15313). *Daily Star* (Cairo). . Retrieved August 16, 2008.

[152] **(Russian)** "Uzbek authorities have blocked access to Facebook" (http://www.ferghana.ru/news.php?id=15794&mode=snews). *Ferghana News*. . Retrieved October 21, 2010.

[153] Cooper, Charles (May 19, 2010). "Pakistan Bans Facebook Over Muhammad Caricature Row – Tech Talk" (http://www.cbsnews.com/ 8301-501465_162-20005388-501465.html). *CBS News*. . Retrieved June 26, 2010.

[154] "Red lines that cannot be crossed" (http://www.economist.com/world/mideast-africa/displaystory.cfm?story_id=11792330). *The Economist* (London). July 24, 2008. . Retrieved August 17, 2008.

[155] Benzie, Robert (May 3, 2007). "Facebook banned for Ontario staffers" (http://www.thestar.com/News/article/210014). *Toronto Star*. . Retrieved August 16, 2008.

[156] Stone, Brad (April 7, 2008). "Facebook to Settle Thorny Lawsuit Over Its Origins" (http://bits.blogs.nytimes.com/2008/04/07/ facebook-to-settle-thorny-lawsuit-over-its-origins/). *The New York Times (blog)*. . Retrieved November 5, 2009.

[157] Pepitone, Julianne (May 12, 2011). "Facebook vs. Google fight turns nasty" (http://money.cnn.com/2011/05/12/technology/ facebook_google/index.htm). *CNN Money*. .

[158] Alemanha: Festas convocadas pelo Facebook são "ameaça à ordem pública" (http://www.ptjornal.com/201107041737/mundo/ alemanha-festas-convocadas-pelo-facebook-sao-ameaca-a-ordem-publica.html)

[159] Alemanha pode proibir festas combinadas pelo Facebook (http://www.destakjornal.com.br/readContent.aspx?id=10,101638)

[160] Alemanha quer proibir festas através do Facebook (http://www.dn.pt/especiais/interior.aspx?content_id=1896579&especial=Revistas de Imprensa&seccao=TV e MEDIA)

[161] Alemanha pretende acabar com eventos via Facebook (http://mtv.uol.com.br/memo/ alemanha-pretende-acabar-com-eventos-via-facebook), MTV

[162] "Facebook sets up site for ad creatives" (http://www.ft.com/cms/s/0/d508bcfc-589c-11e0-9b8a-00144feab49a. html#axzz1K4b20wrT). *Financial Times* (London). March 27, 2011. . Retrieved May 15, 2011.

[163] Wells, Emma K. (April 19, 2011). "Move Over Twitter: Facebook Wants a Piece of Social TV, Too" (http://www.tvgenius.net/blog/ 2011/04/19/4-ways-facebook-social-tv-1-video/). *tvgenius: TV Trends Blog*. . Retrieved May 15, 2011.

[164] "Father finds daughter on Facebook after 20 years apart" (http://abclocal.go.com/wabc/story?section=news/local&id=7739245). *WABC* (New York). October 23, 2010. . Retrieved May 15, 2011.

[165] "Facebook reunites father, daughter after 48 years" (http://news.in.msn.com/international/article.aspx?cp-documentid=3570509&=). *MSN India* (Delhi). January 27, 2010. .

[166] Gardner, David (December 2, 2010). "The marriage killer: One in five American divorces now involve Facebook" (http://www.dailymail. co.uk/news/article-1334482/The-marriage-killer-One-American-divorces-involve-Facebook.html). *Mail Online* (London). .

[167] Harwood, Jonathan (December 22, 2009). "Facebook causes one in five divorces, says law firm" (http://www.thefirstpost.co.uk/ 57742,news-comment,technology,facebook-causes-one-in-five-divorces-says-law-firm). *The First Post* (London). .

[168] "ABC News Joins Forces With Facebook" (http://abcnews.go.com/Technology/Politics/story?id=3899006&page=1). *ABC News*. December 18, 2007. . Retrieved March 23, 2010.

[169] Minor, Doug (November 29, 2007). "Saint Anselm to Host ABC Debates Jan. 5" (http://blogs.saintanselmcollege.net/2007/11/29/abcdebates/). Saint Anselm College blog. . Retrieved July 18, 2010.

[170] Bradley, Tahman (December 12, 2007). "Republicans Lead off ABC News, WMUR-TV and Facebook Back-To-Back Debates in New Hampshire" (http://blogs.abcnews.com/politicalradar/abc_wmur_and_facebook_debates/index.html). *Political Radar (blog)* (ABC News). . Retrieved March 23, 2010.

[171] Callahan, Ezra (January 5, 2008). "Tune in to the ABC News/Facebook Debates, Tonight 7 pm/6c on ABC" (http://blog.facebook.com/blog.php?post=8183627130). Facebook Blog. . Retrieved March 23, 2010.

[172] Goldman, Russell (January 5, 2007). "Facebook Gives Snapshot of Voter Sentiment" (http://abcnews.go.com/Politics/story?id=4091460&page=1). *ABC News*. . Retrieved March 23, 2010.

[173] Sullivan, Michelle (November 3, 2008). "'Facebook Effect' Mobilizes Youth Vote" (http://www.cbsnews.com/stories/2008/11/04/politics/uwire/main4568563.shtml). *CBS News*. . Retrieved March 23, 2010.

[174] Brodzinsky, Sibylla (February 4, 2008). "Facebook used to target Colombia's FARC with global rally" (http://www.csmonitor.com/World/Americas/2008/0204/p04s02-woam.html). *Christian Science Monitor* (Boston). . Retrieved August 1, 2010.

[175] Roberts, Laura (August 21, 2010). "North Korea joins Facebook" (http://www.telegraph.co.uk/technology/facebook/7957222/North-Korea-joins-Facebook.html). *The Daily Telegraph* (London). . Retrieved August 22, 2010.

[176] "Facebook 'linked to rise in syphilis'" (http://www.telegraph.co.uk/technology/facebook/7508945/Facebook-linked-to-rise-in-syphilis.html). *The Daily Telegraph* (London). March 24, 2010. .

[177] "Oldest Tweeter talks cuppas and casserole on Twitter at 104" (http://www.telegraph.co.uk/technology/twitter/5327822/Oldest-Tweeter-talks-cuppas-and-casserole-on-Twitter-at-104.html). *The Daily Telegraph* (London). May 15, 2009. .

[178] Millson, Alex (July 28, 2010). "Stars pay tribute to world's oldest Twitter user Ivy Bean after she dies aged 104" (http://www.dailymail.co.uk/tvshowbiz/article-1298433/Stars-pay-tribute-worlds-oldest-Twitter-user-Ivy-Bean-dies-aged-104.html?ITO=1490). *Daily Mail* (London). .

[179] Gray, Melissa (July 28, 2010). "Ivy Bean, 'world's oldest Twitter user,' dead at 104" (http://edition.cnn.com/2010/TECH/social.media/07/28/obit.ivy.bean/index.html?hpt=T2#fbid=txV8eA_Nah8). *CNN*. . Retrieved July 31, 2010.

[180] "The IT Crowd series 3 DVD review" (http://www.denofgeek.com/Reviews/222991/the_it_crowd_series_3_dvd_review.html). *Den Of Geek.com*. March 22, 2009. . Retrieved June 7, 2010. "Anyone who passes more than 15% of their working day on Facebook will love the 'Friendface' episode in series 3, which gently suggests that the likes of Friends Reunited and Facebook have a tendency to dig up situations – and people – that were buried with good reason"

[181] Hempel, Jessi (June 25, 2009). "The book that Facebook doesn't want you to read" (http://money.cnn.com/2009/06/25/technology/founding_of_facebook.fortune/). *CNN*. . Retrieved July 3, 2010.

[182] Hussain, Waqar (May 27, 2010). "Pakistanis create rival Muslim Facebook" (http://www.google.com/hostednews/afp/article/ALeqM5iOAHXhFHXrWMDdtAajYAxmypKT2w). Agence France-Presse. . Retrieved June 9, 2010.

[183] "South Park parodies Facebook" (http://www.guardian.co.uk/media/mediamonkeyblog/2010/apr/08/south-park-season-4-episode-14-facebook). *Guardian media blog* (London). April 8, 2010. . Retrieved June 7, 2010.

[184] "The Social Network (2010)" (http://www.imdb.com/title/tt1285016/). Internet Movie DataBase. . Retrieved July 3, 2010.

[185] Racheff, Jeffery (October 20, 2010). "Mark Zuckerberg Calls The Social Network Inaccurate" (http://www.limelife.com/blog-entry/Mark-Zuckerberg-Calls-The-Social-Network-Inaccurate-VIDEO/77351.html). *Limelife*. .

[186] Trenholm, Rich (February 22, 2011). "Egyptian names baby 'Facebook'" (http://news.cnet.com/8301-1023_3-20034931-93.html). *CNET News*. .

[187] Ehrlich, Brenna (May 17, 2011). "Parents name child after Facebook 'Like' button" (http://www.cnn.com/2011/TECH/social.media/05/16/baby.like.name.mashable/index.html). *CNN*. .

[188] Olivarez-Giles, Nathan (May 16, 2011). "Israeli newborn named 'Like' in tribute to Facebook" (http://latimesblogs.latimes.com/technology/2011/05/israeli-couple-names-daughter-like-in-tribute-to-facebook.html). *Los Angeles Times*. .

References

Further reading

- Kirkpatrick, David, "Why Facebook matters: It's not just for arranging dates. And it's not just another social network. Facebook offers sophisticated tools for maintaining social relationships" (http://money.cnn.com/ 2006/10/06/magazines/fortune/fastforward_facebook.fortune/index.htm), Fortune magazine, October 6, 2006

External links

- Official website (http://https://www.facebook.com)
- Facebook (http://twitter.com/facebook) on Twitter
- Facebook (http://www.guardian.co.uk/technology/facebook) collected news and commentary at *The Guardian*
- Collected news and commentary (http://topics.nytimes.com/top/news/business/companies/facebook_inc/ index.html) at *The New York Times*
- Facebook news and reviews (http://www.telegraph.co.uk/technology/facebook/) at *The Daily Telegraph* (London)
- Hits chart between Facebook and Google (http://www.ft.com/cms/s/2/ 67e89ae8-30f7-11df-b057-00144feabdc0.html#axzz1BfiyklYU)

Twitter

Twitter

	twitter
Type	Private
Founded	San Francisco, California, United States
Founder	Jack Dorsey Noah Glass Evan Williams Biz Stone
Headquarters	795 Folsom Street, Suite 600, San Francisco, CA 94107, United States[1]
Area served	Worldwide
Key people	Jack Dorsey (Executive chairman, head of product development) Dick Costolo (Chief executive officer) Evan Williams (Director) Biz Stone (Creative director)
Revenue	US $140 million (projected 2010)[2]
Employees	450 (2011)[3]
Slogan	I
Website	twitter.com [4]
Alexa rank	9 (July 2011)[5]
Type of site	Mobile social-network service, microblogging
Registration	Required (to post)
Users	200 million (March 2011)[6]
Available in	Multilingual, including English, French, German, Italian, Japanese, Korean, Russian, Spanish and Turkish
Launched	July 15, 2006[7]

Twitter is a website, owned and operated by Twitter Inc., which offers a social networking and microblogging service, enabling its users to send and read messages called *tweets*. Tweets are text-based posts of up to 140 characters displayed on the user's profile page.

The website is based in San Francisco. Twitter also has servers and offices in San Antonio and Boston. Twitter, Inc. was originally incorporated in California, but as of 2011 is incorporated in Delaware.[8]

Twitter was produced in March 2006 by Jack Dorsey and launched in July. Since then Twitter has gained popularity worldwide and is estimated to have 200 million users,[6] generating 200 million tweets a day and handling over 1.6 billion search queries per day.[9] It is sometimes described as the "SMS of the Internet".[10]

History

Creation

Twitter's origins lie in a "daylong brainstorming session" held by board members of the podcasting company Odeo. Dorsey introduced the idea of an individual using an SMS service to communicate with a small group.[11] The original project code name for the service was **twttr**, an idea that Williams later ascribed to Noah Glass,[12] inspired by Flickr and the five-character length of American SMS short codes. The developers initially considered "10958" as a short code, but later changed it to "40404" for "ease of use and memorability".[13] Work on the project started on March 21, 2006, when Dorsey published the first Twitter message at 9:50 PM Pacific Standard Time (PST): "just setting up my twttr".[14]

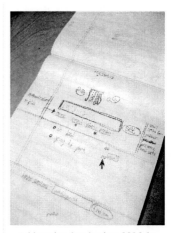

A blueprint sketch, circa 2006, by Jack Dorsey, envisioning an SMS-based social network.

> "...we came across the word 'twitter', and it was just perfect. The definition was 'a short burst of inconsequential information,' and 'chirps from birds'. And that's exactly what the product was." – Jack Dorsey[15]

The first Twitter prototype was used as an internal service for Odeo employees and the full version was introduced publicly on July 15, 2006.[7] In October 2006, Biz Stone, Evan Williams, Dorsey, and other members of Odeo formed Obvious Corporation and acquired Odeo and all of its assets—including Odeo.com and Twitter.com—from the investors and shareholders.[16] Williams fired Glass who was silent about his part in Twitter's startup until 2011.[17] Twitter spun off into its own company in April 2007.[18]

Reaction

The tipping point for Twitter's popularity was the 2007 South by Southwest (SXSW) festival. During the event, Twitter usage increased from 20,000 tweets per day to 60,000.[19] "The Twitter people cleverly placed two 60-inch plasma screens in the conference hallways, exclusively streaming Twitter messages," remarked *Newsweek*'s Steven Levy. "Hundreds of conference-goers kept tabs on each other via constant twitters. Panelists and speakers mentioned the service, and the bloggers in attendance touted it."[20]

Reaction at the festival was highly positive. Blogger Scott Beale said that Twitter "absolutely rul*[ed]*" SXSW. Social software researcher Danah Boyd said Twitter "own*[ed]*" the festival.[21] Twitter staff received the festival's Web Award prize with the remark "we'd like to thank you in 140 characters or less. And we just did!"[22]

The first unassisted off-Earth Twitter message was posted from the International Space Station by NASA astronaut T. J. Creamer on January 22, 2010.[23] By late November 2010, an average of a dozen updates per day were posted on the astronauts' communal account, @NASA_Astronauts. See also NASA Tweetup.

Previous Twitter logo, used until September 14, 2010.

In August 2010, the company appointed Adam Bain as President of Revenue from News Corp.'s Fox Audience Network.[24]

On September 14, 2010, Twitter launched a redesigned site including a new logo.[25]

Leadership

As chief executive officer, Dorsey saw the startup through two rounds of capital funding by the venture capitalists who backed the company.[26]

On October 16, 2008,[27] Williams took over the role of CEO, and Dorsey became chairman of the board.[28]

On October 4, 2010, Williams announced that he was stepping down as CEO. Dick Costolo, formerly Twitter's chief operating officer, became CEO. According to a Twitter blog, dated October 4, 2010, Williams was to stay with the company and "be completely focused on product strategy."[29]

According to *The New York Times*, "Mr. Dorsey and Mr. Costolo forged a close relationship" when Williams was away.[30] According to *PC Magazine*, Williams was "no longer involved in the day-to-day goings on at the company". He is focused on developing a new startup, but he became a member of Twitter's board of directors, and promised to "help in any way I can". Stone is still with Twitter but is working with AOL as an "advisor on volunteer efforts and philanthropy".[31]

Dorsey rejoined Twitter in March 2011, as executive chairman focusing on product development. His time is split with Square where he is CEO, and whose offices are within walking distance of Twitter's in San Francisco.[30]

Growth

The company experienced rapid growth. It had 400,000 tweets posted per quarter in 2007. This grew to 100 million tweets posted per quarter in 2008. In February 2010, Twitter users were sending 50 million tweets per day.[32] By March 2010, the company recorded over 70,000 registered applications.[33] As of June 2010, about 65 million tweets were posted each day, equaling about 750 tweets sent each second, according to Twitter.[34] As noted on Compete.com, Twitter moved up to the third-highest-ranking social networking site in January 2009 from its previous rank of twenty-second.[35]

Twitter's usage spikes during prominent events. For example, a record was set during the 2010 FIFA World Cup when fans wrote 2,940 tweets per second in the thirty-second period after Japan scored against Cameroon on June 14, 2010. The record was broken again when 3,085 tweets per second were posted after the Los Angeles Lakers' victory in the 2010 NBA Finals on June 17, 2010,[36] and then again at the close of Japan's victory over Denmark in the World Cup when users published 3,283 tweets per second.[37] When American singer Michael Jackson died on June 25, 2009, company servers crashed after users were updating their status to include the words "Michael Jackson" at a rate of 100,000 tweets per hour.[38]

Twitter acquired application developer Atebits on April 11, 2010. Atebits had developed the Apple Design Award-winning Twitter client Tweetie for the Mac and iPhone. The application, now called "Twitter" and distributed free of charge, is the official Twitter client for the iPhone, iPad and Mac.[39]

From September through October 2010, the company began rolling out "New Twitter", an entirely revamped edition of twitter.com. Changes included the ability to see pictures and videos without leaving Twitter itself by clicking on individual tweets which contain links to images and clips from a variety of supported websites including YouTube, Flickr, as well as a complete overhaul of the interface, which shifted links such as '@mentions' and 'Retweets' above the Twitter stream, while 'Messages and 'Log Out' became accessible via a black bar at the very top of twitter.com. As of November 1, 2010, the company confirmed that the "New Twitter experience" had been rolled out to all users.

On April 5, 2011, Twitter tested a new homepage, as well as phasing out the "Old Twitter."[40] However, a glitch came about after the page was launched, so the previous "retro" homepage was still in use until the issues were resolved.[41] On April 20, 2011, the new homepage was reintroduced, though the "Switch to Old Twitter" option is still available to users.[42]

Features

Twitter has been compared to a web-based Internet Relay Chat (IRC) client.[43]

Tweets are publicly visible by default; however, senders can restrict message delivery to just their followers. Users can tweet via the Twitter website, compatible external applications (such as for smartphones), or by Short Message Service (SMS) available in certain countries.[44] While the service is free, accessing it through SMS may incur phone service provider fees.

Users may subscribe to other users' tweets – this is known as *following* and subscribers are known as *followers*[45] or *tweeps* (Twitter + peeps).[46]

Twitter allows users the ability to update their profile by using their mobile phone either by text messaging or by apps released for certain smartphones / tablets.[47]

In a 2009 *Time* essay, technology author Steven Johnson described the basic mechanics of Twitter as "remarkably simple:"[48]

> As a social network, Twitter revolves around the principle of followers. When you choose to follow another Twitter user, that user's tweets appear in reverse chronological order on your main Twitter page. If you follow 20 people, you'll see a mix of tweets scrolling down the page: breakfast-cereal updates, interesting new links, music recommendations, even musings on the future of education.

Messages

Users can group posts together by topic or type by use of hashtags – words or phrases prefixed with a " # " sign. Similarly, the " @ " sign followed by a username is used for mentioning or replying to other users.[49] To repost a message from another Twitter user, and share it with one's own followers, the retweet function is symbolized by "RT" in the message.

In late 2009, the "Twitter Lists" feature was added, making it possible for users to follow (as well as mention and reply to) lists of authors instead of individual authors.[45] [50]

Through SMS, users can communicate with Twitter through five gateway numbers: short codes for the United States, Canada, India, New Zealand, and an Isle of Man-based number for international use. There is also a short code in the United Kingdom which is only accessible to those on the Vodafone, O2[51] and Orange[52] networks. In India, since Twitter only supports tweets from Bharti Airtel,[53] an alternative platform called smsTweet[54] was set up by a user to work on all networks.[55] A similar platform called GladlyCast[56] exists for mobile phone users in Singapore, Malaysia and the Philippines.

The messages were initially set to 140-character limit for compatibility with SMS messaging, introducing the shorthand notation and slang commonly used in SMS messages. The 140-character limit has also increased the usage of URL shortening services such as bit.ly, goo.gl, and tr.im, and content-hosting services, such as Twitpic, memozu.com and NotePub to accommodate multimedia content and text longer than 140 characters. Twitter uses bit.ly for automatic shortening of all URLs posted on its website.[57]

Tweet contents

San Antonio-based market-research firm Pear Analytics analyzed 2,000 tweets (originating from the US and in English) over a two-week period in August 2009 from 11:00 AM to 5:00 PM (CST) and separated them into six categories:[58]

- Pointless babble – 40%
- Conversational – 38%
- Pass-along value – 9%
- Self-promotion – 6%
- Spam – 4%
- News – 4%[58]

Social networking researcher Danah Boyd responded to the Pear Analytics survey by arguing that what the Pear researchers labelled "pointless babble" is better characterized as "social grooming" and/or "peripheral awareness" (which she explains as persons "want[ing] to know what the people around them are thinking and doing and feeling, even when co-presence isn't viable").[59]

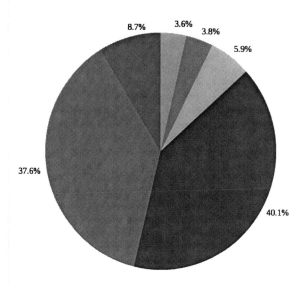

Content of Tweets according to Pear Analytics.Kelly, Ryan, ed (August 12, 2009). "Twitter Study – August 2009" (PDF format; Adobe Reader required). Twitter Study Reveals Interesting Results About Usage. San Antonio, Texas: Pear Analytics. . Retrieved Jun 3, 2010 News Spam Self-promotion Pointless babble Conversational Pass-along value

Rankings

Twitter is ranked as one of the ten-most-visited websites worldwide by Alexa's web traffic analysis.[60] Daily user estimates vary as the company does not publish statistics on active accounts. A February 2009 Compete.com blog entry ranked Twitter as the third most used social network based on their count of 6 million unique monthly visitors and 55 million monthly visits.[61] In March 2009, a Nielsen.com blog ranked Twitter as the fastest-growing website in the Member Communities category for February 2009. Twitter had annual growth of 1,382 percent, increasing from 475,000 unique visitors in February 2008 to 7 million in February 2009. It was followed by Zimbio with a 240 percent increase, and Facebook with a 228 percent increase.[62] However, Twitter has a user retention rate of forty percent.[63]

Adding and following content

There are numerous tools for adding content, monitoring content and conversations including Tweetdeck, Salesforce.com, HootSuite, and Twitterfeed.[64] Less than half of tweets are posted using the web user interface with most users using third-party applications (based on analysis of 500 million tweets by Sysomos).[65]

Authentication

As of August 31, 2010, third-party Twitter applications are required to use OAuth, an authentication method that does not require users to enter their password into the authenticating application. Previously, the OAuth authentication method was optional, it is now compulsory and the user-name/password authentication method has been made redundant and is no longer functional. Twitter stated that the move to OAuth will mean "increased security and a better experience."[66]

Demographics

Twitter.com Top5 Global Markets by Reach (%)[67] [68]	
COUNTRY	Percent
Indonesia Jun-2010	20.8%
Indonesia Dec-2010	19.0%
Brazil Jun-2010	20.5%
Brazil Dec-2010	21.8%
Venezuela Jun-2010	19.0%
Venezuela Dec-2010	21.1%
Netherlands Jun-2010	17.7%
Netherlands Dec-2010	22.3%
Japan Jun-2010	16.8%
Japan Dec-2010	20.0%

Note: Visitor Age 15+ Home and Work Locations. Excludes visitation from public computers such as Internet cafes or access from mobile phones or PDAs.

Twitter is mainly used by older adults who might not have used other social sites before Twitter, said Jeremiah Owyang, an industry analyst studying social media. "Adults are just catching up to what teens have been doing for years," he said.[69] According to comScore only eleven percent of Twitter's users are aged twelve to seventeen.[69] comScore attributes this to Twitter's "early adopter period" when the social network first gained popularity in business settings and news outlets attracting primarily older users. However, comScore as of late, has stated that Twitter has begun to "filter more into the mainstream", and "along with it came a culture of celebrity as Shaq, Britney Spears and Ashton Kutcher joined the ranks of the Twitterati."[70]

According to a study by Sysomos in June 2009, women make up a slightly larger Twitter demographic than men — fifty-three percent over forty-seven percent. It also stated that five percent of users accounted for seventy-five percent of all activity, and that New York has the most Twitter users.[71]

According to Quancast, twenty-seven million people in the US used Twitter as of September 3, 2009. Sixty-three percent of Twitter users are less than thirty-five years old; sixty percent of Twitter users are Caucasian, but a higher than average (compared to other Internet properties) are African American (sixteen percent) and Hispanic (eleven percent); fifty-eight percent of Twitter users have a total household income of at least $60,000.[72]

Finances

Twitter raised over US$57 million from venture capitalist growth funding, although exact numbers are not publicly disclosed. Twitter's first A round of funding was for an undisclosed amount that is rumored to have been between $1 million and $5 million.[73] Its second B round of funding in 2008 was for $22 million[74] and its third C round of funding in 2009 was for $35 million from Institutional Venture Partners and Benchmark Capital along with an undisclosed amount from other investors including Union Square Ventures, Spark Capital and Insight Venture Partners.[73] Twitter is backed by Union Square Ventures, Digital Garage, Spark Capital, and Bezos Expeditions.[75]

Twitter's San Francisco headquarters located at 795 Folsom St.

In May 2008, *The Industry Standard* remarked that Twitter's long-term viability is limited by a lack of revenue.[76] Twitter board member Todd Chaffee forecast that the company could profit from e-commerce, noting that users may want to buy items directly from Twitter since it already provides product recommendations and promotions.[77]

On April 13, 2010, Twitter announced plans to offer paid advertising for companies that would be able to purchase "promoted tweets" to appear in selective search results on the Twitter website, similar to Google Adwords' advertising model. As of April 13, Twitter announced it had already signed up a number of companies wishing to advertise including Sony Pictures, Red Bull, Best Buy, and Starbucks.[78] [79]

In July 2009, some of Twitter's revenue and user growth documents were published on *TechCrunch* after being illegally obtained by the hacker Croll Hacker. The documents projected 2009 revenues of $400,000 in the third quarter and $4 million in the fourth quarter along with 25 million users by the end of the year. The projections for the end of 2013 were $1.54 billion in revenue, $111 million in net earnings, and 1 billion users.[2] No information about how Twitter planned to achieve those numbers was published. In response, Twitter co-founder Biz Stone published a blog post suggesting the possibility of legal action against the hacker.[80]

Though the company only started selling ads midway through 2010 (late spring), it still managed to generate $45 million in annual revenue. Even operating at a loss through most of 2010, an addition of $200 million in new venture capital in December 2010 and a forecast $100 million to $110 million in revenue for 2011 rose the company's valuation to approximately $3.7 billion as of February 2011.[81] In March 2011, 35,000 Twitter shares sold for $34.50 each on Sharespost, an implied valuation of $7.8 billion.[82]

Twitter has been identified as a possible candidate for an initial public offering by 2013.[83]

In June of 2011, Twitter announced it would offer small businesses a self serve advertising system.[84]

Technology

Implementation

The Twitter Web interface uses the Ruby on Rails framework,[85] deployed on a performance enhanced Ruby Enterprise Edition implementation of Ruby.[86]

From the spring of 2007 until 2008 the messages were handled by a Ruby persistent queue server called Starling,[87] but since 2009 implementation has been gradually replaced with software written in Scala.[88] The service's application programming interface (API) allows other web services and applications to integrate with Twitter.[89] [90]

Interface

On April 30, 2009, Twitter adjusted its web interface, adding a search bar and a sidebar of "trending topics" — the most common phrases appearing in messages. Biz Stone explains that all messages are instantly indexed and that "with this newly launched feature, Twitter has become something unexpectedly important — a discovery engine for finding out what is happening right now."[91]

Outages

When Twitter experiences an outage, users see the "fail whale" error message image created by Yiying Lu,[92] illustrating eight orange birds using a net to hoist a whale from the ocean captioned "Too many tweets! Please wait a moment and try again."[93]

Twitter had approximately ninety-eight percent uptime in 2007 (or about six full days of downtime).[94] The downtime was particularly noticeable during events popular with the technology industry such as the 2008 Macworld Conference & Expo keynote address.[95] [96]

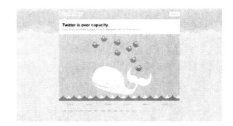

The Twitter fail whale error message.

- May 2008 – Twitter's new engineering team made architectural changes to deal with the scale of growth. Stability issues resulted in down time or temporary feature removal.
- August 2008 – Twitter withdrew free SMS services from users in the United Kingdom[97] and for approximately five months instant messaging support via a XMPP bot was listed as being "temporarily unavailable".[98]
- October 10, 2008 – Twitter's status blog announced that instant messaging (IM) service was no longer a temporary outage and needed to be revamped. It was announced that Twitter aims to return its IM service pending necessary major work.[99]
- June 12, 2009 – In what was called a potential "Twitpocalypse", the unique numerical identifier associated with each tweet exceeded the limit of 32-bit signed integers (2,147,483,647 total messages).[100] While Twitter itself was not affected, some third-party clients could no longer access recent tweets. Patches were quickly released, though some iPhone applications had to wait for approval from the App Store.[101]
- June 25, 2009 – Twitter crashed at least once and ran very slowly for some time after It recorded over 50,000 tweets about Michael Jackson's death in just one hour.[102] Michael Jackson was ranked on seven of the top ten trending topics.
- September 22, 2009 – The identifier exceeded the limit for 32-bit *unsigned* integers (4,294,967,296 total messages) again breaking some third-party clients.[103]
- August 6, 2009 – Twitter and Facebook suffered from a denial-of-service attack, causing the Twitter website to go offline for several hours.[104] It was later confirmed that the attacks were directed at one pro-Georgian user around the anniversary of the 2008 South Ossetia War, rather than the sites themselves.[105]
- December 17, 2009 – A hacking attack replaced the website's welcoming screen with an image of a green flag and the caption "This site has been hacked by Iranian Cyber Army" for nearly an hour. No connection between the hackers and Iran has been established.[106]
- November 2010 – A number of accounts encountered a fault that resulted in them seeing the "fail whale" when they tried to login to their accounts. The accounts themselves were not locked out as account holders could still see their "mentions" page and post from there. But the timeline and a number of other features were unavailable during this outage.

Privacy and security

Twitter messages are public but users can also send private messages.[107] Twitter collects personally identifiable information about its users and shares it with third parties. The service reserves the right to sell this information as an asset if the company changes hands.[108] While Twitter displays no advertising, advertisers can target users based on their history of tweets and may quote tweets in ads[109] directed specifically to the user.

A security vulnerability was reported on April 7, 2007, by Nitesh Dhanjani and Rujith. Since Twitter used the phone number of the sender of an SMS message as authentication, malicious users could update someone else's status page by using SMS spoofing.[110] The vulnerability could be used if the spoofer knew the phone number registered to their victim's account. Within a few weeks of this discovery Twitter introduced an optional personal identification number (PIN) that its users could use to authenticate their SMS-originating messages.[111]

On January 5, 2009, 33 high-profile Twitter accounts were compromised after a Twitter administrator's password was guessed by a dictionary attack.[112] Falsified tweets — including sexually explicit and drug-related messages — were sent from these accounts.[113]

Twitter launched the beta version of their "Verified Accounts" service on June 11, 2009, allowing famous or notable people to announce their Twitter account name. The home pages of these accounts display a badge indicating their status.[114]

In May 2010, a bug was discovered by İnci Sözlük users that allowed Twitter users to force others to follow them without the other users' consent or knowledge. For example, comedian Conan O'Brien's account, which had been set to follow only one person, was changed to receive nearly 200 malicious subscriptions.[115]

In response to Twitter's security breaches, the Federal Trade Commission brought charges against the service which were settled on June 24, 2010. This was the first time the FTC had taken action against a social network for security lapses. The settlement requires Twitter to take a number of steps to secure users' private information, including maintenance of a "comprehensive information security program" to be independently audited biannually.[116]

On December 14, 2010, the United States Department of Justice issued a subpoena directing Twitter to provide information for accounts registered to or associated with WikiLeaks.[117] Twitter decided to notify its users and said in a statement, "...it's our policy to notify users about law enforcement and governmental requests for their information, unless we are prevented by law from doing so".[107]

A "MouseOver" exploit occurred on September 21, 2010, when an XSS Worm became active on Twitter. When an account user held the mouse cursor over blacked out parts of a tweet, the worm within the script would automatically open links and re-post itself on the reader's account.[118] The exploit was then re-used to post pop-up ads and links to pornographic sites. The origin is unclear but Pearce H. Delphin (known on Twitter as @zzap) and a Scandinavian developer, Magnus Holm, both claim to have modified the exploit of a user, possibly Masato Kinugawa, who was using it to create coloured Tweets.[119] Kinugawa, a Japanese developer, reported the XSS vulnerability to Twitter on August 14. Later, when he found it was exploitable again, he created the account 'RainbowTwtr' and used it to post coloured messages.[119] Delphin says he exposed the security flaw by tweeting a JavaScript function for "onMouseOver",[119] and Holm later created and posted the XSS Worm that automatically re-tweeted itself.[118] Security firm Sophos reported the virus was spread by people doing it for "fun and games", but noted it could be exploited by cybercriminals.[118] Twitter issued a statement on their status blog at 13:50 UTC that "*The exploit is fully patched*".[118] [120] Twitter representative Carolyn Penner said no charges would be pressed.[121]

In May 2011, a claimant known as "CTB" (subsequently identified as Ryan Giggs) in the case of *CTB v Twitter Inc., Persons Unknown* took legal action at the High Court of Justice in London against Twitter.[122] , requesting that Twitter release details of account holders. This followed gossip posted on Twitter about Giggs' private life, causing conflict relating to privacy injunctions.[123] [124]

On May 29, 2011, it was reported that South Tyneside council in England had successfully taken legal action against Twitter in a court in California, which forced Twitter to reveal the details of five user accounts. The council was trying to discover the identity of a blogger called "Mr Monkey"[125] who allegedly posted libellous statements about three local councillors.[126]

Open source

Twitter released several open source projects developed while overcoming technical challenges of their service.[127] Notable projects are the Gizzard Scala framework for creating distributed datastores and the distributed graph database FlockDB.

URL shortener

t.co is a URL shortening service created by Twitter.[128] It is only available for links posted to Twitter and not available for general use.[128] Eventually all links posted to Twitter will use a t.co wrapper.[129] Twitter hopes that the service will be able to protect users from malicious sites,[128] and will use it to track clicks on links within tweets.[128] [130]

Having previously used the services of third parties TinyURL and bit.ly,[131] Twitter began experimenting with its own URL shortening service for direct messages in March 2010 using the twt.tl domain,[129] before it purchased the t.co domain. The service was tested on the main site using the accounts @TwitterAPI, @rsarver and @raffi.[129] On September 2, 2010, an email from Twitter to users said they would be expanding the roll-out of the service to users. On June 7, 2011, Twitter announced that it was rolling out the feature.[132]

Integrated Photo-sharing service

On June 1, 2011, Twitter announced its own integrated photo-sharing service that enables users to upload a photo and attach it to a Tweet right from Twitter.com.[133]

Decentralized architecture

The traditional centralized client-server architecture has not scaled with user demand, leading to server overload and significant loss of availability. There is some decentralized architecture to enhance the scalability of Twitter including Fethr[134] and Cuckoo. [135]

Uses

Twitter has been used for a variety of purposes in many different industries and scenarios. For example, it has been used to organize protests, sometimes referred to as "Twitter Revolutions" and which include the 2011 Egyptian protests, 2010–2011 Tunisian protests, 2009–2010 Iranian election protests, and 2009 Moldova civil unrest.[137] The service has also been used in emergencies and political campaigning.

It is also used for direct communication among social groups and organizations, with the use of "hashtags." For instance, #edchat, used at the end of a tweet, means that the communication will be viewed by all users who follow the topic which refers to an ongoing chat among educators.

Dorsey (left) said after a Twitter Town Hall held in July 2011, that Twitter received over 110,000 #AskObama tweets.[136]

Twitter is also increasingly used for making TV more interactive and social.[138] This effect is sometimes referred to as the "virtual watercooler" or social television. Twitter has been used successfully to encourage people to watch live TV events, such as the Oscars, the Super Bowl[139] and the MTV Video Music Awards; this strategy has however proven less effective with regularly scheduled TV shows.[140] Such direct cross-promotions have been banned from French television due to regulations against secret advertising.[141]

Reception

In 2006, when Twitter launched under the name "Twttr", Michael Arrington of *TechCrunch* commented that although he liked the service, he also noted that he felt uncomfortable with the fact that every user's Twitter page is available to the public.[142]

Change of focus

Twitter emphasized its news and information-network strategy in November 2009 by changing the question asked to users for status updates from "What are you doing?" to "What's happening?"[143] [144] *Entertainment Weekly* put it on its end-of-the-decade, "best-of" list, saying, "Limiting yourself to 140 characters—the maximum for messages on this diabolically addictive social-networking tool—is easy."[145]

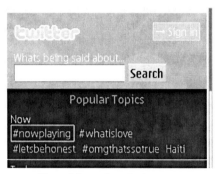

The mobile version of twitter.com

On November 22, 2010, Biz Stone, a cofounder of the company, expressed for the first time the idea of a **Twitter news network**,[146] a concept of wire-like news service he has been working on for years.[147]

Criticism

In May 2008, *The Wall Street Journal* wrote that social networking services such as Twitter "elicit mixed feelings in the technology-savvy people who have been their early adopters. Fans say they are a good way to keep in touch with busy friends. But some users are starting to feel 'too' connected, as they grapple with check-in messages at odd hours, higher cellphone bills and the need to tell acquaintances to stop announcing what they're having for dinner."[148]

"Using Twitter for literate communication is about as likely as firing up a CB radio and hearing some guy recite the *Iliad*", said tech writer Bruce Sterling.[149] "For many people, the idea of describing your blow-by-blow activities in such detail is absurd," hypothesized writer Clive Thompson in September 2008. "Why would you subject your friends to your daily minutiae? And conversely, how much of their trivia can you absorb? The growth of ambient intimacy can seem like modern narcissism taken to a new, supermetabolic extreme—the ultimate expression of a generation of celebrity-addled youths who believe their every utterance is fascinating and ought to be shared with the world."[150]

On the other hand Steve Dotto opined that part of Twitter's appeal is the challenge of trying to publish such messages in tight constraints.[151] "The qualities that make Twitter seem inane and half-baked are what makes it so powerful," says Jonathan Zittrain, professor of Internet law at Harvard Law School.[152]

In 2009, Nielsen Online reported that Twitter has a user retention rate of forty percent. Many people stop using the service after a month therefore the site may potentially reach only about ten percent of all Internet users.[153] In 2009, Twitter won the "Breakout of the Year" Webby Award.[154] [155]

During a February 2009 discussion on National Public Radio's *Weekend Edition*, the journalist Daniel Schorr stated that Twitter accounts of events lacked rigorous fact-checking and other editorial improvements. In response, Andy Carvin gave Schorr two examples of breaking news stories that played out on Twitter and said users wanted first-hand accounts and sometimes debunked stories.[156]

In an episode of *The Daily Show* on February 26, 2009, guest Brian Williams, a journalist, described tweets as only referring to the condition of the author. Williams implied that he would never use Twitter because nothing he did was interesting enough to publish in Twitter format.[157] During another episode of *The Daily Show* on March 2, 2009, host Jon Stewart negatively portrayed members of Congress who chose to "tweet" during President Obama's address to Congress (on February 24, 2009) rather than pay attention to the content of the speech. The show's Samantha Bee satirized media coverage of the service saying "there's no surprise young people love it − according to reports of young people by middle-aged people."[158]

Time magazine acknowledged growing level of influence in its 2010 Time 100 most influential people. To determine the influence of people it used a formula based on famous social networking sites, Twitter and Facebook. The list ranges from Barack Obama and Oprah Winfrey to Lady Gaga and Ashton Kutcher. The formula was (Twitter followers) x 2 + (Facebook connections) divided by 2.[159]

In March 2009, the comic strip *Doonesbury* began to satirize Twitter. Many characters highlighted the triviality of tweets although one defended the need to keep up with the constant-update trend.[160] SuperNews! similarly satirized Twitter as an addiction to "constant self-affirmation" and said tweets were nothing more than "shouts into the darkness hoping someone is listening".[161]

In May 2011 concerns have risen about Twitter restricting the reuse of its data by researchers.[162]

Social impact

Data from over 800,000 users of OkCupid show that, across all ages, daily posters to Twitter had shorter relationships than everyone else.[163] A recent study also shows that 13% of the Americans on the web used Twitter making it one of the most popular services in the United States.[164]

Censorship

Censorship of Twitter

Censorship of Twitter has occurred in Iran,[165] China, Egypt,[166] and South Korea.

Alleged censorship of WikiLeaks by Twitter

In December 2010, allegations have been made by several IT-news websites and other media reporting that Twitter appeared to engage in censorship activities by impeding WikiLeaks related tweets from becoming trending topics, despite high numbers of tweets concerning WikiLeaks due to activities such as the United States diplomatic cables leak.[167] [168] [169] However, Twitter has denied any involvement with altering Trend results explaining that "WikiLeaks and cablegate have trended worldwide or in specific locations."[170]

References

[1] "Contact Us" (http://twitter.com/about/contact). .

[2] Staff writer (July 15, 2009). "Hacker Exposes Private Twitter Documents" (http://bits.blogs.nytimes.com/2009/07/15/hacker-exposes-private-twitter-documents/?hpw.). *Bits* (blog of *The New York Times*). . Retrieved February 23, 2011.

[3] Shiels, Maggie (March 28, 2011). "Twitter co-founder Jack Dorsey rejoins company" (http://www.bbc.co.uk/news/business-12889048). *BBC News*. . Retrieved March 28, 2011.

[4] http://twitter.com/

[5] "Twitter.com Site Info" (http://www.alexa.com/siteinfo/twitter.com). Alexa Internet. . Retrieved 2011-07-12.

[6] "bbc.co.uk" (http://www.bbc.co.uk/news/business-12889048). BBC. . Retrieved 28 March 2011.

[7] Arrington, Michael (July 15, 2006). "Odeo Releases Twttr" (http://techcrunch.com/2006/07/15/is-twttr-interesting/). *TechCrunch*. . Retrieved September 18, 2010.

[8] California Secretary of State (18 February 2011). "California Secretary of State, Business Entities - Business Entity Detail" (http://kepler.sos.ca.gov/cbs.aspx). . Retrieved 23 February 2011.

[9] Twitter Search Team (2011-05-31). "The Engineering Behind Twitter's New Search Experience" (http://engineering.twitter.com/2011/05/engineering-behind-twitters-new-search.html). *Twitter Engineering Blog* (blog of Twitter Engineering Division). . Retrieved 2011-06-10.

[10] D'Monte, Leslie (April 29, 2009). "Swine Flu's Tweet Tweet Causes Online Flutter" (http://www.business-standard.com/india/news/swine-flu\s-tweet-tweet-causes-online-flutter/356604/). *Business Standard*. . Retrieved February 4, 2011. "Also known as the 'SMS of the internet', Twitter is a free social networking and micro-blogging service"

[11] **(registration required)** Miller, Claire Cain (October 30, 2010). "Why Twitter's C.E.O. Demoted Himself" (http://www.nytimes.com/2010/10/31/technology/31ev.html). *The New York Times.* . Retrieved October 31, 2010.

[12] Williams, Evan (April 13, 2011). "It's true..." (https://twitter.com/#!/ev/status/58275072011542529). Twitter. . Retrieved April 26, 2011.

[13] Sagolla, Dom (January 30, 2009). "How Twitter Was Born" (http://www.140characters.com/2009/01/30/how-twitter-was-born/). *140 Characters − A Style Guide for the Short Form.* 140 Characters. . Retrieved February 4, 2011.

[14] Dorsey, Jack (March 21, 2006). "just setting up my twttr" (http://twitter.com/jack/status/20). Twitter. . Retrieved February 4, 2011.

[15] Sano, David (February 18, 2009). "Twitter Creator Jack Dorsey Illuminates the Site's Founding Document" (http://latimesblogs.latimes.com/technology/2009/02/twitter-creator.html). *Los Angeles Times.* . Retrieved June 18, 2009.

[16] Malik, Om (October 25, 2006). "Odeo RIP, Hello Obvious Corp" (http://gigaom.com/2006/10/25/odeo-rip-hello-obvious-corp/). *GigaOM.* . Retrieved June 20, 2009.

[17] Madrigal, Alexis (April 14, 2011). "Twitter's Fifth Beatle Tells His Side of the Story" (http://www.theatlantic.com/technology/archive/2011/04/twitters-fifth-beatle-tells-his-side-of-the-story/237326/). *The Atlantic.* . Retrieved April 26, 2011.

[18] Lennon, Andrew. "A Conversation with Twitter Co-Founder Jack Dorsey" (http://www.thedailyanchor.com/2009/02/12/a-conversation-with-twitter-co-founder-jack-dorsey/). *The Daily Anchor.* . Retrieved February 12, 2009.

[19] Douglas, Nick (March 12, 2007). "Twitter Blows Up at SXSW Conference" (http://gawker.com/tech/next-big-thing/twitter-blows-up-at-sxsw-conference-243634.php). *Gawker.* . Retrieved February 21, 2011.

[20] Levy, Steven (April 30, 2007). "Twitter: Is Brevity The Next Big Thing?" (http://www.newsweek.com/id/35289). *Newsweek.* . Retrieved February 4, 2011.

[21] Terdiman, Daniel (March 10, 2007). "To Twitter or Dodgeball at SXSW?" (http://news.cnet.com/8301-17939_109-9696264-2.html). *CNET.* . Retrieved February 4, 2011.

[22] Stone, Biz (February 4, 2011). "We Won!" (http://blog.twitter.com/2007/03/we-won.html). Blog on Twitter. . Retrieved May 7, 2008.

[23] Press release (January 22, 2010). "Media Advisory M10-012 − NASA Extends the World Wide Web Out into Space" (http://www.nasa.gov/home/hqnews/2010/jan/HQ_M10-011_Hawaii221169.html). NASA. Retrieved February 5, 2011.

[24] Arrington, Michael (August 23, 2010). "Twitter Hires Adam Bain Away from News Corp. as President of Revenue" (http://techcrunch.com/2010/08/23/twitter-hires-adam-bain-away-from-news-corp-as-president-of-revenue/). *TechCrunch.* . Retrieved February 5, 2011.

[25] Cashmore, Pete (review essay) (September 16, 2010). "'New Twitter' Shows the Web Isn't Dead" (http://www.cnn.com/2010/TECH/social.media/09/16/cashmore.twitter.web/index.html). *CNN.* . Retrieved February 5, 2011.

[26] Miller, Claire Cain; Goel, Vindu (October 16, 2008). "Twitter Sidelines One Founder and Promotes Another" (http://bits.blogs.nytimes.com/2008/10/16/ttwitter-sidelines-one-founder-and-promotes-another/#more-1642). *Bits* (blog of *The New York Times*). . Retrieved February 5, 2011.

[27] **(registration required)** Miller, Claire Cain (October 20, 2008). "Popularity or Income? Two Sites Fight It Out" (http://www.nytimes.com/2008/10/21/technology/start-ups/21twitter.html). *The New York Times.* . Retrieved November 5, 2008.

[28] McCarthy, Caroline (October 16, 2008). "Twitter CEO Jack Dorsey Steps Down" (http://news.cnet.com/8301-13577_3-10068368-36.html). *CNET News.* . Retrieved November 5, 2008.

[29] Staff writer (October 4, 2010). "#newtwitterceo" (http://blog.twitter.com/2010/10/newtwitterceo.html). Blog of Twitter. . Retrieved February 5, 2011.

[30] Miller, Claire Cain (March 28, 2011). "Two Twitter Founders Trade Places" (http://bits.blogs.nytimes.com/2011/03/28/twitter-founders-trade-places/). *The New York Times.* . Retrieved March 28, 2011.

[31] Albanesius, Chloe (March 29, 2011). "Twitter's Evan Williams Confirms Departure" (http://www.pcmag.com/article2/0,2817,2382782,00.asp). *PC Magazine* (Ziff Davis). . Retrieved March 29, 2011.

[32] Beaumont, Claudine (February 23, 2010). "Twitter Users Send 50 Million Tweets Per Day − Almost 600 Tweets Are Sent Every Second Through the Microblogging Site, According to Its Own Metrics" (http://www.telegraph.co.uk/technology/twitter/7297541/Twitter-users-send-50-million-tweets-per-day.html). *The Daily Telegraph.* . Retrieved February 7, 2011.

[33] Staff writer (March 4, 2010). "Twitter Registers 1,500 Per Cent Growth in Users" (http://www.newstatesman.com/digital/2010/03/twitter-registered-created). *New Statesman.* . Retrieved February 7, 2011.

[34] Garrett, Sean (June 18, 2010). "Big Goals, Big Game, Big Records" (http://blog.twitter.com/2010/06/big-goals-big-game-big-records.html). *Twitter Blog* (blog of Twitter). . Retrieved February 7, 2011.

[35] Kazeniac, Andy (February 9, 2009). "Social Networks: Facebook Takes Over Top Spot, Twitter Climbs" (http://blog.compete.com/2009/02/09/facebook-myspace-twitter-social-network/). *Compete Pulse* (blog of compete.com). . Retrieved February 7, 2011.

[36] Miller, Claire Cain (June 18, 2010). "Sports Fans Break Records on Twitter" (http://bits.blogs.nytimes.com/2010/06/18/sports-fans-break-records-on-twitter/). *Bits* (blog of *The New York Times*). . Retrieved February 7, 2011.

[37] Van Grove, Jennifer (June 25, 2010). "Twitter Sets New Record: 3,283 Tweets Per Second" (http://mashable.com/2010/06/25/tps-record/). *Mashable.* . Retrieved February 7, 2011.

[38] Shiels, Maggie (June 26, 2009). "Web Slows After Jackson's Death" (http://news.bbc.co.uk/2/hi/technology/8120324.stm). *BBC News.* . Retrieved February 7, 2011.

[39] Miller, Claire Cain (April 11, 2010). "Twitter Acquires Atebits, Maker of Tweetie" (http://bits.blogs.nytimes.com/2010/04/09/twitter-acquires-atebits-maker-of-tweetie/). *Bits* (blog of *The New York Times*). . Retrieved February 7, 2011.

[40] "Twitter Users Report Twitter.com Has A New Homepage (SCREENSHOTS)" (http://www.huffingtonpost.com/2011/04/05/new-twitter-homepage_n_845110.html). Huffingtonpost.com. 2011-05-04. . Retrieved 2011-05-22.

[41] Dunn, John E (2011-04-06). "Twitter Delays Homepage Revamp After Service Glitch" (http://www.pcworld.com/article/224410/ twitter_delays_homepage_revamp_after_service_glitch.html). PCWorld. . Retrieved 2011-05-22.

[42] Crum, Chris (April 20, 2011). "New Twitter Homepage Launched" (http://www.webpronews.com/new-twitter-homepage-2011-04). . Retrieved April 25, 2011.

[43] Stutzman, Fred (April 11, 2007). "The 12-Minute Definitive Guide to Twitter" (http://dev.aol.com/article/2007/04/ definitive-guide-to-twitter). AOL Developer Network. . Retrieved November 12, 2008.

[44] "Using Twitter with Your Phone" (http://help.twitter.com/entries/14226-how-to-find-your-twitter-short-long-code). Twitter Support. . Retrieved June 1, 2010. "We currently support 2-way (sending and receiving) Twitter SMS via short codes and 1-way (sending only) via long codes."

[45] Stone, Biz (October 30, 2009). "There's a List for That" (http://blog.twitter.com/2009/10/theres-list-for-that.html). blog.twitter.com. . Retrieved February 1, 2010.

[46] Brown, Amanda (March 2, 2011). "The tricky business of business tweeting" (http://www.irishtimes.com/newspaper/features/2011/ 0302/1224291133449.html). *The Irish Times*. . Retrieved April 28, 2011.

[47] "Mobile Apps" (https://twitter.com/#!/download). .

[48] Johnson, Steven (June 5, 2009). "How Twitter Will Change the Way We Live" (http://www.time.com/time/printout/0,8816,1902604,00. html). *Time*. . Retrieved February 13, 2011.

[49] Strachan, Donald (February 19, 2009). "Twitter: How To Set Up Your Account" (http://www.telegraph.co.uk/travel/4698589/ Twitter-how-to-set-up-your-account.html). *The Daily Telegraph*. . Retrieved February 13, 2011.

[50] Staff writer (undated). "Twitter Lists!" (http://help.twitter.com/forums/10711/entries/76460). Support forum at help.twitter.com. . Retrieved February 13, 2011.

[51] Andrews, Robert (March 27, 2009). "Twitter Brings Back UK SMS; Vodafone First, Others To Follow" (http://www.guardian.co.uk/ media/pda/2009/mar/27/twitter-socialnetworking1). *The Guardian*. . Retrieved June 7, 2009.

[52] "Blog.Twitter.com" (http://blog.twitter.com/2009/11/another-first-in-uk.html). Blog.Twitter.com. November 16, 2009. . Retrieved March 28, 2010.

[53] Kutty, Darpana (October 15, 2009). "Twitter, Bharti Airtel Tie-Up To Activate Twitter SMS Service in India" (http://www.topnews.in/ twitter-bharti-airtel-tieup-activate-twitter-sms-service-india-2224961). *TopNews*. . Retrieved February 23, 2011.

[54] "SMStweet :: Send Twitter Message sing SMS in India" (http://www.smstweet.in/). India. . Retrieved April 3, 2010.

[55] Balanarayan, N.T. (December 17, 2009). "Tweeting Via SMS Is In, the Way It Should Be" (http://www.dnaindia.com/scitech/ report_tweeting-via-sms-is-in-the-way-it-should-be_1324562). *Daily News and Analysis*. . Retrieved February 23, 2011.

[56] "Update Twitter or Plurk by sending an SMS to a Singapore or Malaysia local number" (http://gladlycast.com/). Singapore. . Retrieved April 3, 2010.

[57] Wauters, Robin (May 6, 2009). "URL Shortening Wars: Twitter Ditches TinyURL for bit.ly" (http://www.techcrunch.com/2009/05/06/ url-shortening-wars-twitter-ditches-tinyurl-for-bitly). *TechCrunch*. . Retrieved March 28, 2010.

[58] Kelly, Ryan, ed (August 12, 2009). "Twitter Study – August 2009" (http://www.pearanalytics.com/blog/wp-content/uploads/2010/05/ Twitter-Study-August-2009.pdf) (PDF format; Adobe Reader required). *Twitter Study Reveals Interesting Results About Usage*. San Antonio, Texas: Pear Analytics. . Retrieved Jun 3, 2010

[59] Boyd, Danah (August 16, 2009). "Twitter: "pointless babble" or peripheral awareness + social grooming?" (http://www.zephoria.org/ thoughts/archives/2009/08/16/twitter_pointle.html). . Retrieved September 19, 2009.

[60] "Twitter.com – Traffic Details from Alexa" (http://www.alexa.com/siteinfo/twitter.com). Alexa Internet. August 26, 2010. . Retrieved August 26, 2010.

[61] Kazeniac, Andy (February 9, 2009). "Social Networks: Facebook Takes Over Top Spot, Twitter Climbs" (http://blog.compete.com/2009/ 02/09/facebook-myspace-twitter-social-network/). Compete.com. . Retrieved February 17, 2009.

[62] McGiboney, Michelle (March 18, 2009). "Twitter's Tweet Smell of Success" (http://blog.nielsen.com/nielsenwire/online_mobile/ twitters-tweet-smell-of-success/). Nielsen. . Retrieved April 5, 2009.

[63] Hoffman, Stefanie (April 29, 2009). "Twitter Quitters Outnumber Those Who Stay, Report Finds" (http://www.crn.com/security/ 217200834;jsessionid=0AQSMPNH52QRQQSNDLOSKHSCJUNN2JVN). United Business Media. . Retrieved April 29, 2009.

[64] "Publishing web content to Twitter" (http://www.gossinteractive.com/twitterfeed). Goss Interactive. February 16, 2010. . Retrieved February 16, 2010.

[65] "Inside Twitter Clients – An Analysis of 500 Million Tweets" (http://www.sysomos.com/insidetwitter/clients). Sysomos. November 2009. . Retrieved August 23, 2010.

[66] "Twitter Applications and OAuth" (http://blog.twitter.com/2010/08/twitter-applications-and-oauth.html). Twitter. August 30, 2010. . Retrieved September 13, 2010.

[67] "comScore Report: Twitter Usage Exploding in Brazil, Indonesia and Venezuela" (http://www.billhartzer.com/pages/ comscore-twitter-latin-america-usage/). Bill Hartzer. 2010-08-11. . Retrieved 2011-05-22.

[68] "The Netherlands lead Global Markets in Twitter.com reach" (http://www.comscoredatamine.com/2011/02/ the-netherlands-leads-global-markets-in-twitter-reach/). Comscoredatamine.com. 2011-02-10. . Retrieved 2011-05-22.

[69] Miller, Claire Cain (August 25, 2009). "Who's Driving Twitter's Popularity? Not Teens" (http://www.nytimes.com/2009/08/26/ technology/internet/26twitter.html). *The New York Times*. . Retrieved September 18, 2009.

[70] Lipsman, Andrew (September 2, 2009). "What Ashton vs. CNN Foretold About the Changing Demographics of Twitter" (http://blog. comscore.com/2009/09/changing_demographics_of_twitter.html). *comScore*. . Retrieved September 18, 2009.

[71] Cheng, Alex; Evans, Mark (June 2009). "Inside Twitter – An In-Depth Look Inside the Twitter World" (http://www.sysomos.com/ insidetwitter/). Sysomos. . Retrieved February 23, 2011.

[72] Bluff, Brian (May 2010). "Who Uses Twitter?" (http://www.site-seeker.com/_blogs/who-uses-twitter-demographic/). site-seeker.com. . Retrieved September 22, 2010.

[73] Staff writer (February 16, 2009). "Twitter Raises over $35M in Series C" (http://www.marketingvox.com/ twitter-raises-over-35m-in-series-c-043192//). *MarketingVOX*. . Retrieved February 23, 2011.

[74] Womack, Brian (November 12, 2008). "Twitter Shuns Venture-Capital Money as Startup Values Plunge" (http://www.bloomberg.com/ apps/news?pid=20601109&sid=afu06n0L7LZ4). *Bloomberg*. . Retrieved February 23, 2011.

[75] Miller, Claire Cain (October 16, 2008). "Twitter Sidelines One Founder and Promotes Another" (http://bits.blogs.nytimes.com/2008/10/ 16/ttwitter-sidelines-one-founder-and-promotes-another/#more-1642). *Bits* (blog of *The New York Times*). . Retrieved February 23, 2011.

[76] Snyder, Bill (March 31, 2008). "Twitter: Fanatical Users Help Build the Brand, But Not Revenue" (http://www.thestandard.com/news/ 2008/03/28/twitter-fanatical-users-help-build-brand-not-revenue). *The Industry Standard* (via Infoworld). . Retrieved February 23, 2011.

[77] Miller, Claire Cain (June 19, 2009). "Twitter Plans To Offer Shopping Advice and Easy Purchasing" (http://bits.blogs.nytimes.com/ 2009/06/19/twitter-plans-to-offer-shopping-advice-and-easy-purchasing/). *Bits* (blog of *The New York Times*). . Retrieved February 23, 2011.

[78] Arthur, Charles (April 13, 2010). "Twitter Unveils 'Promoted Tweets' Ad Plan – Twitter To Let Advertisers Pay for Tweets To Appear in Search Results" (http://www.guardian.co.uk/technology/2010/apr/13/twitter-advertising-google). *The Guardian*. . Retrieved February 23, 2011.

[79] Kimberley, Sara (April 13, 2010). "Twitter Debuts 'Promoted Tweets' Ad Platform" (http://www.mediaweek.co.uk/news/996226/ Twitter-debuts-Promoted-Tweets-ad-platform/). *MediaWeek* (U.K. edition). . Retrieved February 5, 2011.

[80] Stone, Biz (July 15, 2007). "Twitter, Even More Open Than We Wanted" (http://blog.twitter.com/2009/07/ twitter-even-more-open-than-we-wanted.html). *Twitter Blog* (blog of Twitter). . Retrieved February 23, 2011.

[81] Ante, Spencer E.; Efrati, Amir; Das, Anupretta (February 10, 2011). "Twitter as Tech Bubble Barometer" (http://online.wsj.com/article/ SB10001424052748703716904576134543029279426.html?KEYWORDS=twitter). *The Wall Street Journal*. . Retrieved February 23, 2011.

[82] Carlson, Nicholas (March 4, 2011). "Twitter Valued At $7.8 Billion In Private Market Auction" (http://www.sfgate.com/cgi-bin/article. cgi?f=/g/a/2011/03/04/businessinsider-twitter-valued-at-78-billion-in-private-market-auction-2011-3.DTL). *Business Insider via San Francisco Chronicle* (Hearst). . Retrieved March 26, 2011.

[83] Althucher, James (December 10, 2010). "6 Reasons Groupon's Rejection of Google Is Great for the Universe" (http://www. businessinsider.com/google-groupon-deal). *The Altucher Confidential* (blog of James Altucher via *Business Insider*). . Retrieved February 23, 2011.

[84] http://mashable.com/2011/06/09/twitter-ad-buying/

[85] Gomes, Lee (June 22, 2009). "The Pied Piper of Pay" (http://www.forbes.com/forbes/2009/0622/ software-internet-innovation-digital-tools.html). *Forbes*. . Retrieved June 16, 2009.

[86] ryan king (September 25, 2009). "Twitter on Ruby" (http://blog.evanweaver.com/articles/2009/09/24/ree/). . Retrieved October 31, 2009. "We recently migrated Twitter from a custom Ruby 1.8.6 build to a Ruby Enterprise Edition release candidate, courtesy of Phusion. Our primary motivation was the integration of Brent's MBARI patches, which increase memory stability."

[87] Payne (January 16, 2008). "Announcing Starling" (http://web.archive.org/web/20080120141113/http://dev.twitter.com/2008/01/ announcing-starling.html). Twitter. Archived from the original (http://dev.twitter.com/2008/01/announcing-starling.html) on January 20, 2008. . Retrieved January 11, 2009.

[88] Venners, Bill (April 3, 2009). "Twitter on Scala" (http://www.artima.com/scalazine/articles/twitter_on_scala.html). Artima Developer. . Retrieved June 17, 2009.

[89] "API Documentation" (http://groups.google.com/group/twitter-development-talk/web/api-documentation). Google Groups. . Retrieved May 8, 2008.

[90] "Twitter API Wiki / FrontPage" (http://apiwiki.twitter.com/). Apiwiki.twitter.com. . Retrieved September 18, 2010.

[91] Stone, Biz (April 30, 2009). "Twitter Search for Everyone!" (http://blog.twitter.com/2009/04/twitter-search-for-everyone.html). Twitter. . Retrieved May 7, 2008.

[92] **(registration required)** Walker, Rob (February 15, 2009). "Consumed – Fail Whale" (http://www.nytimes.com/2009/02/15/ magazine/15wwln_consumed-t.html?_r=2). *The New York Times Magazine*: p. 17. . Retrieved February 15, 2009.

[93] Whyte, Murray (June 1, 2008). "Tweet, Tweet – There's Been an Earthquake" (http://www.thestar.com/News/Ideas/article/434826). *Toronto Star*. . Retrieved February 23, 2011.

[94] Staff writer (December 19, 2007). "Twitter Growing Pains Cause Lots of Downtime in 2007" (http://royal.pingdom.com/2007/12/19/ twitter-growing-pains-cause-lots-of-downtime-in-2007/). *Royal Pingdom* (blog of Pingdom). . Retrieved February 23, 2011.

[95] Dorsey, Jack (January 15, 2008). "MacWorld" (http://blog.twitter.com/2008/01/macworld.html). *Twitter Blog* (blog of Twitter). . Retrieved February 23, 2011.

[96] Kuramoto, Jake (January 15, 2008). "MacWorld Brings Twitter to its Knees" (http://theappslab.com/2008/01/15/ macworld-brings-twitter-to-its-knees/). Oracle AppsLab. . Retrieved May 7, 2008.

[97] "Changes for Some SMS Users—Good and Bad News" (http://blog.twitter.com/2008/08/changes-for-some-sms-usersgood-and-bad.
      html). Twitter (blog). August 13, 2008. . Retrieved June 14, 2009.

[98] Dorsey, Jack (May 23, 2008). "Twitter IM Down May 23rd–May 24th" (http://getsatisfaction.com/twitter/topics/
      twitter_im_down_may_23rd_may24th). Get Satisfaction. . Retrieved July 29, 2008.

[99] Williams, Evan (October 10, 2008). "IM: Not Coming Soon" (http://status.twitter.com/post/53978711/im-not-coming-soon). *Twitter
      status blog*. . Retrieved December 31, 2008.

[100] Siegler, MG (June 12, 2009). "Twitter Moves Up The Twitpocalypse. All Hell May Break Loose Today." (http://www.techcrunch.com/
      2009/06/12/all-hell-may-break-loose-on-twitter-in-2-hours/). *TechCrunch*. . Retrieved July 18, 2009.

[101] O'Brien, John (June 24, 2009). "MacChat: 2009 – The Age of the Twitpocalypse" (http://blogs.news.com.au/techblog/index.php/
      news/comments/macchat_2009_the_age_of_the_twitpocalypse/56653). *Tech Blog* (blog of news.com.au). . Retrieved February 23, 2011.

[102] Google & Twitter crash at news of Jackson's death (http://news.icm.ac.uk/technology/
      google-twitter-crash-at-news-of-jacksonâs-death/2322/)

[103] Parr, Ben (September 21, 2009). "Twitpocalypse II: Twitter Apps Might Break Tomorrow" (http://mashable.com/2009/09/21/
      twitpocalypse-ii-update/). *Mashable*. . Retrieved February 23, 2011.

[104] Claburn, Thomas (August 6, 2009). "Twitter Downed by Denial of Service Attack" (http://www.informationweek.com/news/security/
      attacks/showArticle.jhtml?articleID=219100308). *InformationWeek*. . Retrieved August 6, 2009.

[105] Staff writer (August 7, 2009). "Web Attack 'Aimed at One Blogger'" (http://news.bbc.co.uk/1/hi/technology/8189162.stm). *BBC
      News*. . Retrieved February 23, 2011.

[106] Staff writer (December 18, 2009). "Twitter Hackers Appear To Be Shiite Group" (http://edition.cnn.com/2009/TECH/12/18/twitter.
      hacked/index.html). *CNN*. . Retrieved February 23, 2011.

[107] Rushe, Dominic (January 8, 2011). "Icelandic MP Fights US Demand for Her Twitter Account Details" (http://www.guardian.co.uk/
      media/2011/jan/08/us-twitter-hand-icelandic-wikileaks-messages). *The Guardian*. . Retrieved January 10, 2011.

[108] "Twitter Privacy Policy" (http://twitter.com/privacy/). Twitter. May 14, 2007. . Retrieved March 11, 2009.

[109] Hansell, Saul (July 16, 2009). "Advertisers Are Watching Your Every Tweet" (http://bits.blogs.nytimes.com/2009/07/16/
      advertisers-are-watching-your-every-tweet/). *The New York Times*. . Retrieved July 17, 2009.

[110] Gilbertson, Scott (June 11, 2007). "Twitter Vulnerability: Spoof Caller ID To Take Over Any Account" (http://www.webmonkey.com/
      2007/04/twitter_vulnerability_spoof_caller_id_to_take_over_any_account/). Webmonkey. . Retrieved February 5, 2011.

[111] Leyden, John (March 6, 2009). "Twitter SMS Spoofing Still Undead" (http://www.theregister.co.uk/2009/03/06/
      twitter_sms_spoofing_risk/). *The Register*. . Retrieved June 17, 2009.

[112] Stone, Biz (January 5, 2009). "Monday Morning Madness" (http://blog.twitter.com/2009/01/monday-morning-madness.html). .
      Retrieved June 17, 2009.

[113] Bellantoni, Christina; Stephen Dinan (January 5, 2009). "Obama's Twitter Site Hacked?" (http://www.washingtontimes.com/news/
      2009/jan/05/obamas-twitter-site-hacked/). *The Washington Times*. . Retrieved January 5, 2009.

[114] McCarthy, Caroline (June 12, 2009). "Twitter Power Players Get Shiny 'Verified' Badges" (http://news.cnet.com/
      8301-13577_3-10263759-36.html). *The Social* (blog of cNET.com). . Retrieved February 23, 2011.

[115] Ostrow, Adam (May 10, 2010). "Twitter Bug Lets You Control Who Follows You" (http://mashable.com/2010/05/10/
      twitter-follow-bug/). *Mashable*. . Retrieved May 11, 2010.

[116] Gonsalves, Antone (June 25, 2010). "Twitter, Feds Settle Security Charges – Twitter Must Establish and Maintain a 'Comprehensive
      Information Security Program' and Allow Third-Party Review of the Program Biannually for the 10 Years" (http://www.informationweek.
      com/news/security/privacy/showArticle.jhtml?articleID=225701450&subSection=Privacy). *InformationWeek*. . Retrieved February 23,
      2011.

[117] "Twitter Subpoena" (http://www.salon.com/news/opinion/glenn_greenwald/2011/01/07/twitter/subpoena.pdf) (PDF; requires
      Adobe Reader). *Salon.com*. . Retrieved January 10, 2011.

[118] Fildes, Jonathan (September 21, 2010). "Twitter Scrambles To Block Worms" (http://www.bbc.co.uk/news/technology-11382469).
      BBC News. . Retrieved February 23, 2011.

[119] Schroeder, Stan (September 22, 2010). "17-Year-Old Australian Boy, Japanese Developer Take Blame for Twitter Meltdown" (http://
      mashable.com/2010/09/22/twitter-meltdown-17-year-old/). *Mashable*. . Retrieved February 23, 2011.

[120] "Twitter Status – XSS Attack Identified and Patched" (http://status.twitter.com/post/1161435117/xss-attack-identified-and-patched).
      status.twitter.com. . Retrieved September 21, 2010.

[121] Staff writer (September 22, 2010). "Kiwi Link To Twitter 'Mouseover' Chaos" (http://www.nzherald.co.nz/technology/news/article.
      cfm?c_id=5&objectid=10675311). *The New Zealand Herald*. . Retrieved February 23, 2011.

[122] Twitter Inc., Unknown Posters Sued by Athlete Known as 'CTB' at U.K. Court (http://www.bloomberg.com/news/2011-05-20/
      twitter-inc-unknown-posters-sued-by-athlete-known-as-ctb-at-u-k-court.html) *From:* bloomberg.com *Date:* May 20, 2011

[123] "Twitter users served with privacy injunction" (http://www.politics.co.uk/news/culture-media-and-sport/
      twitter-users-served-with-privacy-injunction-$21388933.htm). Politics.co.uk. . Retrieved 2011-05-22.

[124] Parker, Nick. "Imogen footie rat in bid to gag Twitter site" (http://www.thesun.co.uk/sol/homepage/news/3593093/
      Imogen-footie-rat-in-bid-to-gag-Twitter-site.html). The Sun. . Retrieved 2011-05-22.

[125] "Mr Monkey" (http://mrmonkeysblog.wordpress.com/) accessed 30 May 2011

[126] "South Tyneside Council takes Twitter to court in US" (http://www.bbc.co.uk/news/uk-england-tyne-13588284). BBC News. 29 May 2011. .

[127] "Twitter / OpenSource" (http://twitter.com/about/opensource). Twitter.com. . Retrieved June 1, 2010.

[128] Staff writer (undated). "About Twitter's Link Service <http://t.co>" (http://support.twitter.com/entries/109623). Twitter Help Center (module of Twitter). . Retrieved February 23, 2011.

[129] Garrett, Sean (June 8, 2010). "Links and Twitter: Length Shouldn't Matter" (http://blog.twitter.com/2010/06/links-and-twitter-length-shouldnt.html). *Twitter Blog* (blog of Twitter). . Retrieved February 23, 2011.

[130] Metz, Cade (September 2, 2010). "Twitter Tightens Grip on Own Firehose" (http://www.theregister.co.uk/2010/09/02/twitter_ipad_app_and_url_shortener/). *The Register*. . Retrieved February 23, 2011.

[131] Weisenthal, Joe (May 6, 2009). "Twitter Switches from TinyURL to Bit.ly" (http://www.businessinsider.com/twitter-switches-from-tinyurl-to-bitly-2009-5). *Business Insider*. . Retrieved February 23, 2011.

[132] Penner, Carolyn (2011-06-07). "Link Sharing Made Simple" (http://blog.twitter.com/2011/06/link-sharing-made-simple.html). *Twitter Blog* (blog of Twitter). . Retrieved 2011-06-09.

[133] "Twitter now with integrated photo-sharing service and completely new twitter search" (http://techshrimp.com/2011/06/01/twitter-now-with-integrated-photo-sharing-service-and-completely-new-twitter-search/). Techshrimp. June 1, 2011. . Retrieved June 1, 2011.

[134] D. R. Sandler and D. S. Wallach (April 2009). "Birds of a FETHR: Open, decentralized micropublishing" (http://www.iptps.org/papers-2009/sandler.pdf) (PDF). Proc. of the 8th International Workshop on Peer-to-Peer Systems (IPTPS'09). .

[135] Tianyin Xu, Yang Chen, Xiaoming Fu, Pan Hui (October 2010). "Twittering by cuckoo: decentralized and socio-aware online microblogging services" (http://conferences.sigcomm.org/sigcomm/2010/papers/sigcomm/p473.pdf) (PDF). *ACM SIGCOMM Computer Communication Review* **40** (4): 473–474. .

[136] Jack Dorsey. (July 8, 2011). *Impressions on the White House Twitter Townhall* (http://www.whitehouse.gov/photos-and-video/video/2011/07/08/impressions-white-house-twitter-townhall). The White House. . Retrieved July 10, 2011.

[137] "Could Tunisia Be the Next Twitter Revolution?" (http://andrewsullivan.theatlantic.com/the_daily_dish/2011/01/could-tunisia-be-the-next-twitter-revolution.html). *The Atlantic*. January 13, 2011. . Retrieved January 15, 2011.

[138] "What Shows Are Viewers Tweeting About and What Does this Mean for Operators?" (http://www.tvgenius.net/blog/2011/03/31/shows-viewers-tweeting-operators/). Tvgenius.net. 2011-03-31. . Retrieved 2011-05-22.

[139] "Twitter Blog: Super Data" (http://blog.twitter.com/2010/02/super-data.html). Blog.twitter.com. 2010-02-10. . Retrieved 2011-05-22.

[140] http://www.tvgenius.net/blog/2011/05/25/twitter-drive-tv-live-ratings/

[141] http://www.france24.com/en/20110606-business-technology-france-regulators-ban-facebook-twitter-promotion-on-tv#

[142] Arrington, Michael (July 15, 2006). "Odeo Releases Twttr" (http://techcrunch.com/2006/07/15/is-twttr-interesting/). *TechCrunch*. . Retrieved February 23, 2011.

[143] Nuttall, Chris (November 20, 2009). "What's Happening? A Lot, Says Twitter" (http://blogs.ft.com/techblog/2009/11/whats-happening-a-lot-says-twitter-coo/). *FT Tech Hub* (blog of *Financial Times*). . Retrieved February 23, 2011.

[144] "Twitter Blog: What's Happening?" (http://blog.twitter.com/2009/11/whats-happening.html). Blog.twitter.com. November 19, 2009. . Retrieved March 28, 2010.

[145] Geier, Thom; Jensen, Jeff; Jordan, Tina; Lyons, Margaret; Markovitz, Adam; Nashawaty, Chris; Pastorek, Whitney; Rice, Lynette; Rottenberg, Josh; Schwartz, Missy; Slezak, Michael; Snierson, Dan; Stack, Tim; Stroup, Kate; Tucker, Ken; Vary, Adam B.; Vozick-Levinson, Simon; Ward, Kate (December 11, 2009), "The 100 Greatest Movies, TV Shows, Albums, Books, Character, Scenes, Episodes, Songs, Dresses, Music Videos, and Trends That Entertained Us over the Past 10 Years". *Entertainment Weekly*. Issue 1079/1080; pp. 74–84.

[146] Berkow, Jameson (November 23, 2010). "FP Tech Desk: The Coming Twitter News Network" (http://business.financialpost.com/2010/11/23/fp-tech-desk-the-coming-twitter-news-network/). *FPPosted* (blog of *Financial Post*). . Retrieved February 23, 2011.

[147] "Twitter As News-wire" (http://blog.twitter.com/2008/07/twitter-as-news-wire.html). blog.twitter.com. July 29, 2008. . Retrieved November 23, 2010.

[148] Lavallee, Andrew (March 16, 2007). "Friends Swap Twitters, and Frustration – New Real-Time Messaging Services Overwhelm Some Users with Mundane Updates from Friends" (http://online.wsj.com/public/article/SB117373145818634482-ZwdoPQ0PqPrcFMDHDZLz_P6osnl_20080315.html). *The Wall Street Journal*. . Retrieved February 22, 2011.

[149] **(registration required)** Pontin, Jason (April 22, 2007). "From Many Tweets, One Loud Voice on the Internet" (http://www.nytimes.com/2007/04/22/business/yourmoney/22stream.html). *The New York Times*. . Retrieved June 21, 2009.

[150] **(registration required)** Thompson, Clive (September 5, 2009). "I'm So Totally, Digitally Close to You" (http://www.nytimes.com/2008/09/07/magazine/07awareness-t.html?_r=1&pagewanted=all). *The New York Times Magazine*. . Retrieved August 22, 2009.

[151] Lewis, Nick (April 16, 2009). "Tweet This: It's the Year of the Twitter" (http://www.vancouversun.com/Entertainment/Tweet+this+year+Twitter/1470046/story.html). *The Vancouver Sun*. . Retrieved April 13, 2009.

[152] **(registration required)** Cohen, Noam (June 20, 2009). "Twitter on the Barricades: Six Lessons Learned" (http://www.nytimes.com/2009/06/21/weekinreview/21cohenweb.html?_r=1&hp). *The New York Times*. . Retrieved June 21, 2009.

[153] Goldsmith, Belinda (April 29, 2009). "Many Twitters Are Quick Quitters: Study" (http://www.reuters.com/article/deborahCohen/idUSTRE53S1A720090429). *Reuters*. . Retrieved February 22, 2011.

[154] Staff writer (undated). "13th Annual Webby Special Achievement Award Winners" (http://www.webbyawards.com/webbys/specialachievement13.php/#twitter). The Webby Awards. . Retrieved February 22, 2011.

[155] Paul, Ian (May 5, 2009). "Jimmy Fallon Wins Top Webby: And the Winners Are..." (http://www.pcworld.com/article/164374/ jimmy_fallon_wins_top_webby_and_the_winners_are.html). *PC World*. . Retrieved February 22, 2011.

[156] Carvin, Andy (February 28, 2009). "Welcome to the Twitterverse" (http://www.npr.org/templates/story/story. php?storyId=101265831). National Public Radio. . Retrieved February 22, 2011.

[157] Video (7+ minutes; requires Adobe Flash) (February 26, 2009). "Daily Show: Brian Williams – Whatever Brian Williams Is Doing at Any Moment of the Day Isn't Interesting Enough to Twitter" (http://www.thedailyshow.com/video/index.jhtml?videoId=219509& title=Brian-Williams). *The Daily Show* (via Comedy Central). . Retrieved February 22, 2011.

[158] Video (5+ minutes; requires Adobe Flash) (March 2, 2009). "Daily Show: Bee – Twitter Frenzy —Sam Bee Says Twitter Has Become Such a Big Deal Because It's Awesome and Our Rotting Corpses Are Grabbing for Its Glimmer" (http://www.thedailyshow.com/watch/ mon-march-2-2009/twitter-frenzy). *The Daily Show* (via Comedy Central. . Retrieved February 22, 2011.

[159] Vidyarthi, Neil (April 30, 2010). "Time Magazine's Social Influence Index Led by Obama, Gaga, Kutcher" (http://www.socialtimes. com/2010/04/time-magazines-social-influence-index-led-by-obama-gaga-kutcher/). socialtimes.com. . Retrieved February 22, 2011.

[160] Trudeau, Garry (March 2, 2009). "Doonesbury@Slate Daily Dose 3 March 2009" (http://www.doonesbury.com/strip/archive/2009/03/ 02). doonesbury.com (a website maintained by *Slate/The Washington Post*). . Retrieved February 22, 2011.

[161] Faure-Brac, Josh (March 16, 2009). "Twouble with Twitters" (http://current.com/items/89891774_twouble-with-twitters.htm) (Video (4+ minutes; requires Adobe Flash)). *SuperNews!* (via Current TV). . Retrieved February 22, 2011.

[162] Stuart Shulman, Twitter and History March On (http://blog.texifter.com/index.php/2011/05/07/twitter-and-history-march-on/), May 7, 2011

[163] Rudder, Christian (April 19, 2011). "10 Charts about Sex" (http://blog.okcupid.com/index.php/10-charts-about-sex/). .

[164] Twitter Popular in USA (http://axetue.com/2011/06/02/twitter-popularity-americans/)Article at Mashable

[165] Rebecca Santana (15 June 2009). "Iran Election, Uprising Tracked On Twitter As Government Censors Media" (http://www. huffingtonpost.com/2009/06/15/iran-election-uprising-tr_n_215914.html). . Retrieved 29 June 2011.

[166] **(registration required)** Fahim, Kareem (January 26, 2011). "Protesters in Egypt Defy Ban as Government Cracks Down" (http:// www.nytimes.com/2011/01/27/world/middleeast/27egypt.html?pagewanted=1&_r=1&hp). *The New York Times*. .

[167] Bell, Melissa (December 6, 2010). "WikiLeaks Left Off Twitter Trends?" (http://voices.washingtonpost.com/blog-post/2010/12/ wikileaks_left_off_twitter_tre.html). *BlogPost* (blog of *The Washington Post*). Retrieved February 22, 2011.

[168] Loli-Queru, Eugenia (December 6, 2010). "Twitter Appears to Censor WikiLeaks-Related Trends" (http://www.osnews.com/story/ 24100/Twitter_Appears_to_Censor_Wikileaks-Related_Trends?jkhyh=g). *OSNews*. Retrieved February 22, 2011.

[169] Twitter May be Censoring WikiLeaks (http://osdir.com/Article10586.phtml) osdir.com on 2010 12 06

[170] "To Trend or Not to Trend..." (http://blog.twitter.com/2010/12/to-trend-or-not-to-trend.html). blog.twitter.com. December 8, 2010. . Retrieved January 17, 2011.

External links

- Official website (http://http://twitter.com/) (Mobile (http://http://mobile.twitter.com/))
- Twitter (http://twitter.com/twitter) on Twitter
- Twitter Demographics and Audience Profile (http://www.quantcast.com/twitter.com#demographics) at Quantcast
- Twitter in Depth Archive (http://www.telegraph.co.uk/technology/twitter/) by *The Daily Telegraph*
- The Library of Congress is Archiving Your Tweets (http://www.npr.org/templates/story/story. php?storyId=126086325) – audio report by *NPR*
- Twittermania sweeps Russia's politicians (http://rt.com/Top_News/2010-08-31/ russia-politicians-twitter-mania.html) (RT article)
- Outrageous Tweets: A Short History (http://www.life.com/gallery/61741/ outrageous-tweets-a-short-history#index/0) - slideshow by *Life magazine*

Social media

The term **social media** refers to the use of web-based and mobile technologies to turn communication into interactive dialogue. Social media are media for social interaction, as a superset beyond social communication, but mainly still communicating just interactively using ubiquitously accessible and scalable communication techniques.

Shaping

Social media can take on many different forms, including Internet forums, weblogs, social blogs, microblogging, wikis, podcasts, photographs or pictures, video, rating and social bookmarking. By applying a set of theories in the field of media research (social presence, media richness) and social processes (self-presentation, self-disclosure) Kaplan and Haenlein created a classification scheme for different social media types in their Business Horizons article published in 2010. According to Kaplan and Haenlein there are six different types of social media: collaborative projects (e.g. Wikipedia),

An example of the share buttons common to many social web pages.

blogs and microblogs (e.g. Twitter), content communities (e.g. Youtube), social networking sites (e.g. Facebook), virtual game worlds (e.g. World of Warcraft), and virtual social worlds (e.g. Second Life). Technologies include: blogs, picture-sharing, vlogs, wall-postings, email, instant messaging, music-sharing, crowdsourcing, and voice over IP, to name a few. Many of these social media services can be integrated via social network aggregation platforms.

Patents

There has been rapid growth in the number of US patent applications that cover new technologies related to social media. The number of published applications has been growing rapidly over the past five years. There are now over 250 published applications.[2] Only about 10 of these applications have issued as patents, however, largely due to the multi-year backlog in examination of business method patents[3]

Purpose

Andreas Kaplan and Michael Haenlein define social media as "a group of Internet-based applications that build on the ideological and technological foundations of Web 2.0, which allows the creation and exchange of user-generated content."[4]

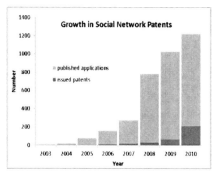

Number of US social network patent applications published per year and patents issued per year[1]

Distinction from industrial media

Businesses may refer to social media as consumer-generated media (CGM). A common thread running through all definitions of social media is a blending of technology and social interaction for the co-creation of value.

People obtain information, education, news and other data from electronic media and print media. Social media are distinct from industrial or traditional media, such as newspapers, television, and film. They are relatively inexpensive and accessible to enable anyone (even private individuals) to publish or access information, compared to industrial media, which generally require significant resources to publish information.

One characteristic shared by both social media and industrial media is the capability to reach small or large audiences; for example, either a blog post or a television show may reach no people or millions of people. Some of the properties that help describe the differences between social media and industrial media are:

1. Reach - both industrial and social media technologies provide scale and are capable of reaching a global audience. Industrial media, however, typically use a centralized framework for organization, production, and dissemination, whereas social media are by their very nature more decentralized, less hierarchical, and distinguished by multiple points of production and utility.
2. Accessibility - the means of production for industrial media are typically government and/or privately owned; social media tools are generally available to the public at little or no cost.
3. Usability - industrial media production typically requires specialized skills and training. Conversely, most social media production does not require specialized skills and training, or requires only modest reinterpretation of existing skills; in theory, anyone with access can operate the means of social media production.
4. Immediacy - the time lag between communications produced by industrial media can be long (days, weeks, or even months) compared to social media (which can be capable of virtually instantaneous responses; only the participants determine any delay in response). However, as industrial media begin adopting aspects of production normally associated with social media tools, this feature may not prove distinctive over time.
5. Permanence - industrial media, once created, cannot be altered (once a magazine article is printed and distributed changes cannot be made to that same article) whereas social media can be altered almost instantaneously by comments or editing.

Community media constitute an interesting hybrid of industrial and social media. Though community-owned, some community radios, TV and newspapers are run by professionals and some by amateurs. They use both social and industrial media frameworks.

Building "social authority" and vanity

Business metrics (revenues, reputation...)

Social media analytics (share of voice, resonation, support response...)

Engagement Data (clicks, fans, followers, views, check-ins...)

Social media ROI pyramid[5]

One of the key components in successful social media marketing implementation is building "social authority". Social authority is developed when an individual or organization establishes themselves as an "expert" in their given field or area, thereby becoming an influencer in that field or area.[6]

It is through this process of "building social authority" that social media becomes effective. That is why one of the foundational concepts in social media has become that you cannot completely control your message through social media but rather you can simply begin to participate in the "conversation" expecting that you can achieve a significant influence in that conversation.[7]

However, this conversation participation must be cleverly executed because while people are resistant to marketing in general, they are even more resistant to direct or overt marketing through social media platforms. This may seem counter-intuitive but is the main reason building social authority with credibility is so important. A marketer can generally not expect people to be receptive to a marketing message in and of itself. In the Edleman Trust Barometer report [8] in 2008, the majority (58%) of the respondents reported they most trusted company or product information coming from "people like me" inferred to be information from someone they trusted. In the 2010 Trust Report [9], the majority switched to 64% preferring their information from industry experts and academics. According to Inc. Technology's Brent Leary, "This loss of trust, and the accompanying turn towards experts and authorities, seems to be coinciding with the rise of social media and networks."[10] [11]

Internet usage effects

A study by the University of Maryland suggested that social media services may be addictive,[12] and that users of social media services leads to a "fear of missing out".[13] It has been observed that Facebook is now the primary method for communication by college students in the U.S.[14] [15]

There are various statistics that account for social media usage and effectiveness for individuals worldwide. Some of the most recent statistics are as follows:

- Social networking now accounts for 22% of all time spent online in the US.[16]
- A total of 234 million people age 13 and older in the U.S. used mobile devices in December 2009.[17]
- Twitter processed more than one billion tweets in December 2009 and averages almost 40 million tweets per day.[17]
- Over 25% of U.S. internet page views occurred at one of the top social networking sites in December 2009, up from 13.8% a year before.[17]
- Australia has some of the highest social media usage in the world. In usage of Facebook Australia ranks highest, with over 9 million users spending almost 9 hours per month on the site.[18] [19]
- The number of social media users age 65 and older grew 100 percent throughout 2010, so that one in four people in that age group are now part of a social networking site.[20]
- As of June 2011 Facebook has 750 Million users.[21]

According to a report by Nielson[22]

"In the U.S. alone, total minutes spent on social networking sites has increased 83 percent year-over-year. In fact, total minutes spent on Facebook increased nearly 700 percent year-over-year, growing from 1.7 billion minutes in April 2008 to 13.9 billion in April 2009, making it the No. 1 social networking site for the month."

The main increase in social media has been Facebook. It was ranked as the number one social networking site. Approximately 100 million users access this site through their mobile phone. According to Nielsen, global consumers spend more than 6 hours on social networking sites.

Probable historic impact

Social media may have been integral to the Arab revolutions and revolts of 2011.[23] [24] As one Cairo activist succinctly put it, [25] However, there is some debate about the extent to which social media facilitated this kind of change[26].

Criticisms

Andrew Keen criticizes social media in his book *The Cult of the Amateur*, writing, "Out of this anarchy, it suddenly became clear that what was governing the infinite monkeys now inputting away on the Internet was the law of digital Darwinism, the survival of the loudest and most opinionated. Under these rules, the only way to intellectually prevail is by infinite filibustering."[27]

Tim Berners-Lee contends that the danger of social networking sites is that most are silos and do not allow users to port data from one site to another. He also cautions against social networks that grow too big and become a monopoly as this tends to limit innovation.[28]

Economic impact by social marketing

Thus, using social media as a form of *marketing* has taken on whole new challenges. As the 2010 Trust Study [29] indicates, it is most effective if marketing efforts through social media revolve around the *genuine* building of authority. Someone performing a "marketing" role within a company **must** *honestly* convince people of their *genuine* intentions, knowledge, and expertise in a specific area or industry through providing valuable and accurate information on an ongoing basis without a marketing angle overtly associated. If this can be done, trust with, and of, the recipient of that information – and that message itself – begins to develop naturally. This person or organization becomes a thought leader and value provider - setting themselves up as a trusted "advisor" instead of marketer. "Top of mind awareness" develops and the consumer naturally begins to gravitate to the products and/or offerings of the authority/influencer.[10] [30]

Of course, there are many ways authority can be created – and influence can be accomplished – including: participation in Wikipedia which actually verifies user-generated content and information more than most people may realize; providing valuable content through social networks on platforms such as Facebook and Twitter; article writing and distribution through sites such as Ezine Articles and Scribd; and providing fact-based answers on "social question and answer sites" such as EHow and Yahoo! Answers.

As a result of social media – and the direct or indirect influence of social media marketers – today, consumers are as likely – or more likely – to make buying decisions based on what they read and see in platforms we call "social" but only if presented by someone they have come to trust. Additionally, reports have shown organizations have been able to bring back dissastisfied customers and stakeholders through social media channels.[31] This is why a purposeful and carefully designed social media strategy has become an integral part of any complete and directed marketing plan but must also be designed using newer "authority building" techniques.[32]

In his 2006 book, *The Wealth of Networks: How Social Production Transforms Markets and Freedom*, Yochai Benkler analyzed many of these distinctions and their implications in terms of both economics and political liberty. However, Benkler, like many academics, uses the neologism network economy or "network information economy" to describe the underlying economic, social, and technological characteristics of what has come to be known as "social media". The basic assumption with social media is there will be a demand for the information published using such media. The quantity of subscribers to the various providers seems to prove that assumption. However, the quality of the contents casted by individuals may be subject of a more distant view, regarding the multicast or even broadcast distribution as powered by vanity of the issuers. In contrast the reception of contents published by organisations shows the curiosity of the subscribers to learn more about the ever renewing world they are part of. Both aspects may generate economic value beyond the providers sake for the issuers of the contents.

However, building reputation and becoming recognised as an expert with a high yield in "social authority" may remind the fact that there is no quality assessment for the issued contents but the acclamation or applause by the readers or the opposite, deprecation or disapproval. That does not guaranteee for a reasonable value of the messages.

Ownership of Social Media Content

Social Media content is generated through social media interactions done by the users through the site. There has always been a huge debate on the ownership of the content on social media platforms since it is generated by the users and hosted by the company. Critics contend that the companies are making huge amount of money by using the content that does not belong to them[33] . Hence the challenge for ownership is lesser with the communicated content, but with the personal data disclosed by the subscribed writers and readers and the correlation to chosen types of content. The security danger beyond is the parasitic conveying, diffunding or leaking of agglomerated data to third parties with certain economic interest[34] .

Application examples

Communication

- **Blogs**: Blogger, ExpressionEngine, LiveJournal, Open Diary, TypePad, Vox, WordPress, Xanga
- **Microblogging**: FMyLife, Foursquare, Jaiku, Plurk, Posterous, Tumblr, Twitter, Qaiku, Google Buzz, Identi.ca Nasza-Klasa.pl
- **Location-based social networks**: Foursquare, Geoloqi, Gowalla, Facebook places, The Hotlist, Google Latitude
- **Social networking**: ASmallWorld, Bebo, Cyworld, Diaspora, Facebook, Google+, Tuenti, Hi5, Hyves, LinkedIn, MySpace, Ning, Orkut, Plaxo, Tagged, XING , IRC, Yammer
- **Events**: Eventful, The Hotlist, Meetup.com, Upcoming
- **Information Aggregators**: Netvibes, Twine (website)
- **Online Advocacy and Fundraising**: Causes, Kickstarter
- **Engagement Advertising & Monetization**: SocialVibe

Collaboration/authority building

- **Wikis**: PBworks, Wetpaint, Wikia, Wikimedia, Wikispaces
- **Social bookmarking** (or social tagging):[35] CiteULike, Delicious, Diigo, Google Reader, StumbleUpon, folkd
- **Social Media Gaming**: Empire Avenue[36]
- **Social news**: Digg, Mixx, NowPublic, Reddit, Newsvine
- **Social navigation**: Trapster, Waze [37]
- **Content Management Systems**: Wordpress, Drupal, Plone, Siteforum
- **Document Managing and Editing Tools**: Google Docs, Syncplicity, Docs.com, Dropbox.com
- **Collaboration**: Central Desktop

Multimedia

- **Photography and art sharing**: deviantArt, Flickr, Photobucket, Picasa, SmugMug, Zooomr
- **Video sharing**: sevenload, Viddler, Vimeo, YouTube, Dailymotion, Metacafe, Nico Nico Douga, Openfilm
- **Livecasting**: Justin.tv, Livestream, OpenCU, Skype, Stickam, Ustream, blip.tv, oovoo, Youtube
- **Music and audio sharing**: ccMixter, Pandora Radio, Spotify, Last.fm, MySpace Music, ReverbNation.com, ShareTheMusic, The Hype Machine, Groove Shark, SoundCloud, Bandcamp, Soundclick, imeem, Turntable.fm
- **Presentation sharing**: scribd, SlideShare, Prezi

Reviews and opinions

- **Product reviews**: epinions.com, MouthShut.com
- **Business reviews**: Customer Lobby, Yelp, Inc.
- **Community Q&A**: Askville, EHow, Stack Exchange, WikiAnswers, Yahoo! Answers, Quora, ask.com

Entertainment

- **Media and entertainment platforms**: Cisco Eos
- **Virtual worlds**: Active Worlds, Forterra Systems, Second Life, The Sims Online, World of Warcraft, RuneScape
- **Game sharing**: Kongregate, Miniclip, Newgrounds, Armor Games

Brand monitoring

- **Social media measurement**: Attensity, General Sentiment, Radian6, Statsit, Sysomos, Vocus

Leisure example

The Dutch man Ramon Stoppelenburg traveled around the world for free, without spending any money, from 2001 to 2003, thanks to his blog on Letmestayforaday.com [38]. His website was his profile with which he created his own necessary network of online offered places to stay for the night. This made Stoppelenburg one of the first people online who used the online media in a social and effective manner.

References

[1] Mark Nowotarski, "Don't Steal My Avatar! Challenges of Social Network Patents, IP Watchdog, January 23, 2011. (http://ipwatchdog.com/2011/01/23/donât-steal-my-avatar-challenges-of-social-networking-patents/id=14531/)

[2] USPTO search on published patent applications mentioning "social media" (http://appft.uspto.gov/netacgi/nph-Parser?Sect1=PTO2&Sect2=HITOFF&u=/netahtml/PTO/search-adv.html&r=0&p=1&f=S&l=50&Query=spec/"social+media"&d=PG01)

[3] USPTO search on issued patents mentioning "social media" (http://patft.uspto.gov/netacgi/nph-Parser?Sect1=PTO2&Sect2=HITOFF&u=/netahtml/PTO/search-adv.htm&r=0&p=1&f=S&l=50&Query=spec/"social+media"&d=PTXT)

[4] Kaplan, Andreas M.; Michael Haenlein (2010). "Users of the world, unite! The challenges and opportunities of Social Media" (http://www.sciencedirect.com/science/article/B6W45-4XFF2S0-1/2/600db1bd6e0c9903c744aaf34b0b12e1). *Business Horizons* 53 (1): 59–68. doi:10.1016/j.bushor.2009.09.003. ISSN 0007-6813. . Retrieved 2010-09-15.

[5] Framework: The Social Media ROI Pyramid (http://www.web-strategist.com/blog/2010/12/13/framework-the-social-media-roi-pyramid/)

[6] European Journal of Social Psychology (http://onlinelibrary.wiley.com/doi/10.1002/ejsp.355/abstract)

[7] Research Survey (http://mprcenter.org/blog/2010/08/04/research-survey-launched-social-media-and-influence-of-photos-on-body-image/)

[8] http://www.edelman.com/trust/2008/

[9] http://www.edelman.co.uk/trustbarometer/files/edelman-trust-barometer-2010.pdf

[10] Inc. Technology Brent Leary Article (http://technology.inc.com/internet/articles/201003/leary.html)

[11] Edelman 2010 Trust Barometer Study (http://www.edelman.com/trust/2010/)

[12] "Students Addicted to Social Media - New UM Study" (http://www.newsdesk.umd.edu/sociss/release.cfm?ArticleID=2144). . Retrieved 23 May 2011.

[13] "FOMO: The Unintended Effects of Social Media Addiction" (http://www.nbcnewyork.com/news/local/Social-Media-Is-Causing-Anxiety-and-Depression-122260279.html). . Retrieved 23 May 2011.

[14] Harris, Kandace (2008). "Using Social Networking Sites as Student Engagement Tools". *Diverse Issues in Higher Education* 25 (18).

[15] "Statistics" (http://www.facebook.com/press/info.php?statistics). Facebook. . Retrieved 23 May 2011.

[16] http://blog.nielsen.com/nielsenwire/global/social-media-accounts-for-22-percent-of-time-online/

[17] http://digital.venturebeat.com/2010/02/10/54-of-us-internet-users-on-facebook-27-on-myspace/trackback/

[18] . http://www.socialmedianews.com.au/social-media-stats-in-australia-facebook-blogger-myspace/.

[19] . http://www.socialmedianews.com.au/.

[20] "Boomers Joining Social Media at Record Rate" (http://www.cbsnews.com/stories/2010/11/15/national/main7055992.shtml). *CBS News.* 2010-11-15. .

[21] http://techcrunch.com/2011/06/23/facebook-750-million-users//

[22] "Time Spent on Facebook up 700 Percent, but MySpace.com Still Tops for Video, According to Nielsen" (http://www.nielsen.com/us/en/insights/press-room/2009/time_on_facebook.html). .

[23] http://www.wired.com/threatlevel/2011/01/tunisia/

[24] Kirkpatrick, David D. (2011-02-09). "Wired and Shrewd, Young Egyptians Guide Revolt" (http://www.nytimes.com/2011/02/10/world/middleeast/10youth.html?_r=1). *The New York Times.* .

[25] http://www.miller-mccune.com/politics/the-cascading-effects-of-the-arab-spring-28575/

[26] Malcolm Gladwell and Clay Shirky on Social Media and Revolution, Foreign Affairs March/April 2011 (http://www.foreignaffairs.com/articles/67325/malcolm-gladwell-and-clay-shirky/from-innovation-to-revolution)

[27] Keen, Andrew. *The Cult of the Amateur*. Random House. p. 15. ISBN 9780385520812.

[28] http://www.scientificamerican.com/article.cfm?id=long-live-the-web

[29] http://www.edelman.com/trust/2010/

[30] Search Engine Watch (http://searchenginewatch.com/3640221)

[31] http://www.marketingforecast.com/archives/10548

[32] Business Expert Brent Leary on Inc Technology Website (http://technology.inc.com/internet/articles/201003/leary.html)

[33] "How much is your content worth?" (http://digitalanalog.in/2011/06/28/how-much-is-your-content-worth/). .

[34] Jones, Soltren, Facebook: Threats to Privacy, MIT 2005 (http://groups.csail.mit.edu/mac/classes/6.805/student-papers/fall05-papers/facebook.pdf)

[35] Golder, Scott; Huberman, Bernardo A. (2006). "Usage Patterns of Collaborative Tagging Systems" (http://www.hpl.hp.com/research/idl/papers/tags/tags.pdf). *Journal of Information Science* **32** (2): 198–208. doi:10.1177/0165551506062337. .

[36] "Empire Avenue, the stockmarket where YOU'RE for sale" (http://thenextweb.com/apps/2010/07/26/empire-avenue-the-stockmarket-where-youre-for-sale-invites/). . Retrieved 22 March 2011.

[37] 10 Ways Geolocation is Changing the World (http://www.tonic.com/article/10-ways-geolocation-is-changing-the-world/)

[38] http://www.letmestayforaday.com

Further reading

- Benkler, Yochai (2006). *The Wealth of Networks*. New Haven: Yale University Press. ISBN 0300110561. OCLC 61881089.

- Gentle, Anne (2009). *Conversation and Community: The Social Web for Documentation*. Fort Collins, Colo: XML Press. ISBN 9780982219119. OCLC 464581118.

- Johnson, Steven Berlin (2005). *Everything Bad Is Good for You*. New York: Riverhead Books. ISBN 1573223077. OCLC 57514882.

- Li, Charlene; Bernoff, Josh (2008). *Groundswell: Winning in a World Transformed by Social Technologies*. Boston: Harvard Business Press. ISBN 9781422125007. OCLC 423555651.

- Scoble, Robert; Israel, Shel (2006). *Naked Conversations: How Blogs are Changing the Way Businesses Talk with Customers*. Hoboken, N.J: John Wiley. ISBN 047174719X. OCLC 61757953.

- Shirky, Clay (2008). *Here Comes Everybody*. New York: Penguin Press. ISBN 9781594201530. OCLC 458788924.

- Surowiecki, James (2004). *The Wisdom of Crowds*. New York: Anchor Books. ISBN 0385721706. OCLC 156770258.

- Tapscott, Don; Williams, Anthony D. (2006). *Wikinomics*. New York: Portfolio. ISBN 1591841380. OCLC 318389282.

- Powell, Guy R.; Groves, Steven W.; Dimos, Jerry (2011). *ROI of Social Media: How to improve the return on your social marketing investment*. New York: John Wiley & Sons. ISBN 9780470827413. OCLC 0470827416.

Article Sources and Contributors

Recruitment *Source*: http://en.wikipedia.org/w/index.php?oldid=439075757 *Contributors*: 16@r, AaronY, Acroterion, AdjustShift, AlasdairBailey, Alilliedekro, Allday Recruitment Ltd, Allstarrecruitmentgroup, Ameering, Amillar, Andycjp, Angr, Answerfish, Arjun024, Art LaPella, Arthena, Aruntm, BD2412, BMT, Belovedfreak, Ben Morton, Bender235, Betterusername, Bhaskarancm, Biker Biker, Billbt, Bluezone101, Bluiee, Bob Cooper, BostonRed, Brickweb, Bruce78, Btomasel, CWenger, Callcentrerecruit, Camw, Chester Markel, Chilli 2170, Chris the speller, Compaqevo, CorbinSimpson, DARTH SIDIOUS 2, DanielRigal, Dannygutknecht, Davalyn1, Dawn Bard, Dbee, Ddlj95, Dekisugi, Delifive, Denise Priestman, Deskana, Dina, Dmwgroup, EH74DK, EJLPP, Edward, Eeekster, Ehheh, Emijrp, Eujobcentre, Ewlyahoocom, Excirial, FS61, Faisaltradeimpex, Falconjh, Favonian, Filcro, Finalius, Flint McRae, Frame25, FutuRecruit, Fæ, Gail, Gbradt, Gilliam, Ginamarie1954, Glennlist, Gogo Dodo, Gohul s, GoodmanMasson, Govt Recruiter, GraemeL, Gutmach, Hsuffyan, Hu12, Hughcharlesparker, Hugheshk, Hut 8.5, Ian-ren-1987, Indon, Infotothemasses, Infrogmation, Inter, Ioparty, Iridescent, J.delanoy, JHunterJ, JRisdale, Jaa02vts, Jaranda, Java Kingpin, Jaymanlb, Jazza9, Jdsimmons81, Jeff G., Jennifer0503, Jglobalview, Jlanno, JoanneB, Joelong1313, Johnsav, Jojhutton, Jonathan.s.kt, JordanGekko, Juanscott, Kaihsu, Kakoui, Karenjc, KaySL, Kellyjoy, Killing Vector, Killivt03, Kinu, Krickhahn, Kuru, Lambardo, Laser813, Laudak, Lauracooper, Learnee, Linkspamremover, Lradrama, Lynnmit, Manderson198, Mangotree, Mas 18 dl, Mattador79, Mean as custard, Mentifisto, Michal Kubinec, MisfitToys, Mjennings123, Mnmngb, Mobrimer, Monkeyman, MrOllie, Msaout, Mufka, Mull Higgins, Nate1481, Naveed.r.khan, NerdyNSK, NicholasJones, Nickismith, Nikkimaria, Non-dropframe, Not Moony, Nurg, Ohnoitsjamie, OnBeyondZebrax, Onlineresourcing, Outfitrecruitment, PTJoshua, Pankajlhg, Pascal.Tesson, Paul hills, Petmal, Portgame, Proofreader77, Qwyrxian, R'n'B, Radicalsubversiv, Raven4x4x, Reaper Eternal, Recruit-England, Recruitlondon, Reevesby, Reyk, Richard Mosley, Rince 1969, Rossami, Rspeer, RyanCross, Samuel123adams, Sarahjansen, Seaphoto, Sennen goroshi, Shivprasd1986utkarsh, Sidhekin, Slowisz, SmartGRS, Somearemoreequal, SteveUT31, Stevenwmccrary58, Sumitwirc, Sunilk123, THB, TamsinKelly, TasTasniem, TastyPoutine, Teachtosing, Teamadams, Tftaz, The Recruit England, The Thing That Should Not Be, TheDude2006, Ticketservice, Tide rolls, Tlrmq, Tmol42, Tonnic, Trident13, Unlimitednadia, Versageek, Vesal, Vfandco, Vianello, Viny.krishn, Vlad.rotariu, Vrenator, Wavelength, Wayne Riddock, WeatherFug, Wiki-vr, Woudloper, Wtstoffs, Zzuuzz, 395 anonymous edits

Selection ratio *Source*: http://en.wikipedia.org/w/index.php?oldid=431494740 *Contributors*: Falcon8765, Jonkerz, Mycatharsis

Application for employment *Source*: http://en.wikipedia.org/w/index.php?oldid=439260733 *Contributors*: BD2412, Benben799, CharlesColemanjr, Chartier12, Fictionaddition, J.delanoy, JaGa, Jmencisom, Justme89, Lectonar, Nenyedi, Nikkimaria, PhilKnight, Stickee, Vsh3r, YUL89YYZ, 22 anonymous edits

Audition *Source*: http://en.wikipedia.org/w/index.php?oldid=428937133 *Contributors*: Absalom89, AdamJWahlberg, AdamViola, AgentPeppermint, Alpha Quadrant (alt), Biscuittin, Bobo192, Brianmacian, ByeByeBaby, Carol D, Cate, Cigarette, CommonsDelinker, Craneclassical, Crazygurl123, Daniel Case, Danyoung, David Shankbone, Davigdori, DocWatson42, Drpickem, Eaglet, Edward, El C, Ganymead, Gilliam, Girolamo Savonarola, Gogo Dodo, Ingolfson, J.delanoy, JLaTondre, January, Jdwyatt10, Jezhotwells, Jni, Kleinzach, Knavesdied, Lambtron, Lowellian, Lradrama, Manop, MiltonT, Mosmof, NawlinWiki, Nike787, Obankston, Ohnoitsjamie, Olegkr, OnBeyondZebrax, Pinky1lee, Redheylin, Rrburke, Samanthawright, ShelfSkewed, SiobhanHansa, Skier Dude, Starface01, StaticGull, SteinbDJ, TicketMan, Twice25, U54222, Viper1613, Volker89, WJTan123, Wavelength, Woohookitty, Wuttt, 61 anonymous edits

Background check *Source*: http://en.wikipedia.org/w/index.php?oldid=438572383 *Contributors*: 790, ATLBeer, Acegikmo1, Alansohn, Alexanderosias, Alphachimp, Andy stirling, Astgtciv, BD2412, BadSeed, Barek, Barkeep, Becks48, Bgo34, Bigdrv, Birdswitharms, Bonadea, Boozinf, BorgQueen, Briguy52748, Businessman1212, Captain-tucker, Caulde, Celrex, Chuckiesdad, CliffC, Combuchan, Conti, Coolcaesar, Corporate fudiciary, Courcelles, Crhoey, Crimcheck, Cvos, DS1953, Dawnseeker2000, Dezbryant, Differentview, Dinomite, Discospinster, Dmol, DoctorW, Drpickem, Edward, Efeller, Elockid, Enviroboy, Epetersen0506, Ericbwood, Eschulma, Ethan PLUMMER, Eyalbc, Fences and windows, Fieldday-sunday, FirstPrinciples, Firstamendment, Flalom, Fluzwup, FoolsWar, Fti74, Gjjr, GraemeL, Graham87, Grey Matter, Halmstad, HelenGray100, Hooperbloob, I already forgot, J.Simom, J.delanoy, JHMM13, Jameson001, Jennnyyyp, Jennybunns12, Jgianoglio, Johanvonhuber, Jordanperry, Jparenti, JuliannS, Kariteh, Kbh3rd, Koskim, Kthartley, Kubigula, LNMagic, Lilpinoy 82, Littlecheese41, Longhair, Lovingchocolate, Lowellian, Luvgrindcore, Mais oui!, Makhyan, Matt.T, Mattb112885, Mauls, MaxEnt, Medhavib, Mike Serfas, Minna Sora no Shita, Mkmtbk, Mlspriest, Mojoxrisen, Moonriddengirl, MrOllie, Msmithhrp, N-Man, Neil916, Nick, Nuujinn, ONeill, OfficeGirl, OzLink, PBP, Pakaran, Powerchap, Powerchex, Quotidinanity, Radagast83, RainbowOfLight, Resident Mario, Rich Farmbrough, Riggwelter, Rillian, Rjjelley, Robert Capwell, RobertV76, Robocoder, Ronz, RxS, Sapphic, Seancasey00, Searchinfo, Siddhant, Smooth O, Socilaz, Spiderwriter, Star Mississippi, Texacali3d, Texture, The Thing That Should Not Be, The Vandal Warrior, The.4thestate, TheProject, Thebluedrg, Themfromspace, Thorne, Thugdog Nasty, Thx2, Tide rolls, Trident13, UB65, Vaheterdu, Wavelength, Wayne Slam, Weyes, Whisky drinker, Wiki-expert-edit, Wikieditor06, Wsiinc, Yelyos, Zoom-Arrow, 289 anonymous edits

Campus placement *Source*: http://en.wikipedia.org/w/index.php?oldid=424901775 *Contributors*: Blue Haze, Ironholds, Malcolma, Mild Bill Hiccup, Post2akjain, Shalinjames, 9 anonymous edits

Candidate submittal *Source*: http://en.wikipedia.org/w/index.php?oldid=433814610 *Contributors*: BD2412, Cerebellum, Dbee, Fabrictramp, Kuru, Mandarax, Mild Bill Hiccup, Trident13, 1 anonymous edits

Careers In The Outdoors *Source*: http://en.wikipedia.org/w/index.php?oldid=436373656 *Contributors*: JustAGal, Trident13, 1 anonymous edits

Common Recruitment Examination *Source*: http://en.wikipedia.org/w/index.php?oldid=436498557 *Contributors*: Giraffedata, HenryLi, Prince Max (scientist), R'n'B, Trident13, Woohookitty, 2 anonymous edits

Competency-based job description *Source*: http://en.wikipedia.org/w/index.php?oldid=403320632 *Contributors*: Canis Lupus, Fabrictramp, Frap, Hazharry, Katharineamy, Malcolma, Skysmith, Toddmheine, Trident13, 4 anonymous edits

Cover letter *Source*: http://en.wikipedia.org/w/index.php?oldid=439069080 *Contributors*: Adoyle500, Aleenf1, Arthena, Av28, Avoided, Azuleagle, BD2412, Beezhive, Berean Hunter, Bibliomaniac15, Brandy Frisky, CWii, Calltech, Caltas, Captain Zyrain, CareerJimmy-1, Careerjob, Cflm001, Chuckd333, Classiko, CocoBa, Complete letter writing system, Corpx, Corwinstephen, Cover-letter-world.com, Discospinster, Dmscvan, Doctor rfp, EdenDD, Eire123, Examplesof, Fadikaouk, FatM1ke, FelipeVargasRigo, Fetchcomms, Flerion, Flewis, Frap, Gamer007, Gino76, Gogo Dodo, Greensburger, Harry, Hellno2, HomoUniversalis, Hu12, Iceman0311, Ithizar, JediChris1138, Jfingers88, Jonathandolce, Jpgordon, Just zis Guy, you know?, KCinDC, Kkx123, Kingjeff, Kiwi8, Koavf, Kutnpaste, Lcarscad, Leo R, LogicDictates, M.L, MER-C, MarSch, Mathinker, Matthew0028, Mitch Ames, Moira222, Monkeyman, Munay09, MyOwnLittlWorld, NawlinWiki, Nick Worth, Ohlcv, Ohnoitsjamie, Pabix, Pacemanscoop, Personman, Pinethicket, Piotrus, Polyppo, Qwyrxian, Ratherhaveaheart, Reaper Eternal, Richi, Rolandirwin, Ronz, Roughan123, SECProto, Salexe, Samanthamanning, Schoneth, Sfawcett, Shasho1, Shritwod, SiobhanHansa, Smalljim, Smiln32, Sourceline, Sparklejunkie, Stevev007, Stifle, TGilmour, Takeaway, Tatianamc, Templater, The Thing That Should Not Be, TheArmadillo, TheDJ, Themfromspace, Tide rolls, Trident13, Twigman1200, Usefultips, Veinor, Versageek, Vgranucci, Vinsfan368, Wadems, Wikidemon, WillardRobinson, Wolf2822, Workbloom, Xanthis, 245 anonymous edits

Cravath System *Source*: http://en.wikipedia.org/w/index.php?oldid=437402188 *Contributors*: Adam sk, Ademkader, Eastlaw, Gwern, Hmains, Ingolfson, Od Mishehu, R'n'B, SUL, Tangurena, Thumperward, 7 anonymous edits

e-recruitment *Source*: http://en.wikipedia.org/w/index.php?oldid=439075651 *Contributors*: Amillar, Bearian, Bluiee, Cerebellum, Edgar181, Fabrictramp, Goldenrowley, Killing Vector, Materialscientist, McSly, Mobile Snail, MrOllie, Naveed.r.khan, Olivergibbs, Schluessel, Timstrachan, WissensDürster, Youseagangsta, 12 anonymous edits

Employability *Source*: http://en.wikipedia.org/w/index.php?oldid=430948924 *Contributors*: Abdull, Antonielly, Avatar, Beanie2009, Bequw, Blathnaid, Bobauthor, Bodhisattvaspath, Bongwarrior, Cfailde, DoubleBlue, Elapsed, Flauto Dolce, Josen, KrakatoaKatie, Lgallindo, Mandarax, Mattg82, MiFeinberg, Mild Bill Hiccup, Monty845, Mynameisnotpj, Pearle, Plmoknijb, Rich Farmbrough, Rjanag, Sdisston, THD001UKBIS, Thumperward, Timtregenza, TobyJ, Trident13, Wimt, 45 anonymous edits

Employee referral *Source*: http://en.wikipedia.org/w/index.php?oldid=438493909 *Contributors*: Ameering, Aruntm, AvicAWB, BurntSox, DragonflySixtyseven, ErikHaugen, Fourthords, Hu12, NAHID, Nickismith, Orangemike, Pcrockford, R'n'B, ST47, Sunisthasingh, Tom Morris, Trident13, Wikijure, 11 anonymous edits

Employee value proposition *Source*: http://en.wikipedia.org/w/index.php?oldid=427311263 *Contributors*: Deepraj, Gene Nygaard, Jonik, Lenerd, M3taphysical, R W Mosley, Rbhill58, Simoncwalker, Woohookitty, 23 anonymous edits

Employer of last resort *Source*: http://en.wikipedia.org/w/index.php?oldid=346162563 *Contributors*: Christopher Parham, Nbarth, Notmyrealname, Peregrinmac, Trident13

Employment agency *Source*: http://en.wikipedia.org/w/index.php?oldid=432326300 *Contributors*: Adi4094, Amillar, Andycjp, Badagencies, Beland, Bjarki S, C777, Cliffb, Daryl.keeley, DreamGuy, Ewlyahoocom, Faisaltradeimpex, Femto, Glenn Chapman, Gosselin1964, Immunize, JamesAWood, Jnestorius, Joewski, Jojhutton, Judge999, Kubigula, Kuru, Maninderwalia, Mereda, Mhockey, Mild Bill Hiccup, Mnmngb, OverlordQ, Paulherron, Quintote, Rich257, Rrburke, Rwyrwa, Saviour1981, Scarabe21, Search4Lancer, Secretlondon, Snowmanradio, Snowolf, Sonyhamster, Stefanomione, Sydney180, T PeopleNet, T@nn, THB, Tlrmq, Trident13, TruthbringerToronto, Vegaswikian, Whalloper, Wikidea, Wndola, Yoongkheong, 79 anonymous edits

Employment contract *Source*: http://en.wikipedia.org/w/index.php?oldid=437303453 *Contributors*: 5 albert square, Ajayshirma, Arabani, BMF81, Baronnet, Bento00, Bluerasberry, Bpiereck, Bullzeye, Bwilkins, Capricorn42, Clark89, CliffC, Dargen, David efc, Dendrolo, E Shelkova, Edcolins, Embiggens, Ensign beedrill, GordonUS, Grutness, Gvanrossum, Gx872op, Hairhorn,

Hectorthebat, Hellno2, Ingram, IrishHR, J Dezman, Jake Wartenberg, JamesBWatson, Jimmy Fleischer, Jklamo, Jobshoppinfool, Joelr31, Julesd, Jusdafax, Justdignity, Kingpin13, Lapaz, LeCire, Levineps, Light current, Limideen, Lofor, Longhair, Maelnuneb, MarkBrooks, Martarius, Matty-chan, Misterx2000, Mwanner, Nagika, Ni'jluuseger, Nixeagle, Orange Suede Sofa, Pakaran, Pearle, Peteark, Poppy, Postdlf, Quercus basaseachicensis, Rob72, Robaker, Robertdriver, Ronz, Rwil02, Sheeana, Skarebo, Smalljim, Snowmanradio, Taffenzee, Templater, TerriersFan, The bellman, Tide rolls, Trident13, Versageek, Vlad, Vt-aoe, WikHead, Wikidea, Wolf530, 80 anonymous edits

Employment counsellor *Source*: http://en.wikipedia.org/w/index.php?oldid=430107585 *Contributors*: Barticus88, BrainyBabe, Denni, Dodoandthetoymaker, EricLexie, Fortdj33, Gumerski, HollyAm, Icairns, Intelligentsium, Mlazarchick, Ohnoitsjamie, PhilreCareered, R'n'B, Refsworldlee, Samipjobs, TastyPoutine, Tmol42, Trident13, Usb10, Wadems, Walshga, 3 anonymous edits

Europass *Source*: http://en.wikipedia.org/w/index.php?oldid=433201221 *Contributors*: Alphachimp, Bicko2008, BigHaz, Boy in the bands, Cchantep, Cel 84, Chowbok, Cikicdragan, Courcelles, CultureDrone, Eurocv, Europass-support, Hemlock Martinis, Jakob Suckale, Jerome Charles Potts, JoanneB, Johann1870, Killing Vector, Korg, Lachambre, MarcVanCoillie, Margaperez, Nabeth, National Europass Centre, Netvor, Oeadlro, Omicronpersei8, Patrick, Pburka, RL0919, Raguleader, Svetovid, Trident13, Versageek, Wiki-vr, Wshakespeare, Xionbox, Ybelov, АлександрВв, 98 anonymous edits

Executive pay *Source*: http://en.wikipedia.org/w/index.php?oldid=429042170 *Contributors*: Aitias, Alai, Alan16, Albie34423, Auminski, Barek, Barrylb, Beland, Bjpremore, Black Swan01, Bsohmers, Candacecheng, CardinalDan, Chivista, Chris the speller, Ckatz, Ckhartman, Cmprince, Conrad.pramboeck, CreativeGPX, Cynthia B., Cyrius, Danheac, Dave chun, Deltabeignet, Djr xi, Dlawbailey, Dnsalary, Doswell36, Download, Dr.enh, DreamGuy, Dub617, EditorTM, Edward, Emoticon, Equilarmchen, Eugene-elgato, Excirial, Fredbauder, Fusioneer, Glebchik, Gogo Dodo, Graham87, Ground Zero, Hjstern, Hu12, IButterfield, Ian Pitchford, Iccr, ImperfectlyInformed, JHMM13, Jamespoky, Jerryseinfeld, Jonpro, Jsernest, KaBlookie, Krj373, Kuru, LawsonJD, Lbook52, Li68910, Likeminas, Linkracer, Lwalt, Markosullivan93, Martyestel, Maurreen, MementoVivere, Mydogategodshat, Nbarth, Nezzo, Nminow, Ohconfucius, Ohnoitsjamie, Owen, Paolocioppa, Paul foord, Phiwum, Pm master, Pmcconnell426, Pnm, Quarma, R'n'B, Rd232, Rees11, Requestion, Rigadoun, Rmarghi, RossPatterson, Rrburke, RufusmanII, SMC, Sadads, SaliqKhan, Shajolly, SiobhanHansa, Sottolacqua, Sox First, Squids and Chips, StaticGull, Student7, SuperDaveMusic, Swliv, TastyPoutine, Tedder, The Rhymesmith, Themfromspace, Thincat, Thomasmack8, Thunder77, Trident13, VanCity99, Veinor, Vslashg, Wikidea, Wndola, Woohookitty, X96lee15, 153 anonymous edits

Executive search *Source*: http://en.wikipedia.org/w/index.php?oldid=438464954 *Contributors*: AC Boy, ArglebargleIV, Beetstra, Bhatiaj, Bigredpen, Bluecircle, Bulbouscell, Carbonix, Carmelhighlander09, Cchaplin82, Chris.smailes, Cybercobra, Davitul, Ddlj95, Dina, Discospinster, Donaldlaw, Elielion, Elizabeth Stuart, Execsearch, Ezequielconesa, FS61, Fadikaouk, Filcro, Finngall, Frankawa, Grafen, GratefulJahn, Infonet100, Ioannes Pragensis, Irene Kruger, J.delanoy, Jacekwi, Jeodesic, Jlbbean, Kathyb11, Kuru, Learnee, Lucasgroup2010, Mattthompsett, Middlebult, Mufka, NicholasJr, Patman, Piano non troppo, Pryzbilla, Psihealth, Rickvaughn, Robinalyson, Scarabe21, SmoochRepovichReynolds, Sonyhamster, Sterlingeason, SueHay, Supertouch, Swampy365, Theopt, Tlrmq, Trident13, Triworthsolutions, Versageek, Wattsey, Wikidweb, Wingsofglory, Zumiloko, 89 anonymous edits

ForceSelect *Source*: http://en.wikipedia.org/w/index.php?oldid=436570132 *Contributors*: Chzz, Johnpacklambert, Kuru, Mervyn, Milly1977, Semperlibre, Yoninah, 10 anonymous edits

Free agent (business) *Source*: http://en.wikipedia.org/w/index.php?oldid=385630187 *Contributors*: CRKingston, Dolovis, FisherQueen, JeffG92772, Macaonghus, NSK Nikolaos S. Karastathis, Trident13, Vanessakcarr, 2 anonymous edits

Global Career Development Facilitator *Source*: http://en.wikipedia.org/w/index.php?oldid=437238196 *Contributors*: DMParedes, Etaras1, Hnsjrgnweis, Jpmonroe, Katharineamy, Rjwilmsi, SMasters, Scarykitty, SlipperyHippo, Sultec, 1 anonymous edits

Golden hello *Source*: http://en.wikipedia.org/w/index.php?oldid=373050748 *Contributors*: BenFrantzDale, Grafen, JaGa, Jef-Infojef, Manjukirans, Mrmuk, PatrickFlaherty, Robofish, Smileyducks, Trident13, 3 anonymous edits

Graduate recruitment *Source*: http://en.wikipedia.org/w/index.php?oldid=411820797 *Contributors*: Bender235, BifferBlog, Clicketyclack, Dr Gangrene, Mr Sheep Measham, Pnm, Reevesby, Robofish, SchuminWeb, Seidenstud, Trident13, Woohookitty, 11 anonymous edits

Greater Chicago HERC *Source*: http://en.wikipedia.org/w/index.php?oldid=430083822 *Contributors*: Charnocat, GCMHERC, Mean as custard, Simbrex, 1 anonymous edits

Haigui *Source*: http://en.wikipedia.org/w/index.php?oldid=438117226 *Contributors*: ASDFGH, Heroeswithmetaphors, LLTimes, Metal.lunchbox, MrOllie, Nasmtih, R'n'B, Takamaxa, Viriditas, Yeezhg, 8 anonymous edits

Higher Education Recruitment Consortium *Source*: http://en.wikipedia.org/w/index.php?oldid=430085135 *Contributors*: Charnocat, Dirneherc, GCMHERC, Giraffedata, Grey Wanderer, JHunterJ, Leszek Jańczuk, Lionelt, Sganl, Simbrex, Socalherc, Umwherc, 6 anonymous edits

Hipsty *Source*: http://en.wikipedia.org/w/index.php?oldid=404890082 *Contributors*: Malcolma, Nick Number, Rich Farmbrough, Smurdah, Urizzato, 1 anonymous edits

Homeworker *Source*: http://en.wikipedia.org/w/index.php?oldid=397484137 *Contributors*: Andycjp, Bazzargh, Chriswaterguy, Davidsumnersmith, Deborah Eade, Gurch, GymDavis, Mrcheese007, Someguy1221, Superbass, Tedder, Trident13, 4 anonymous edits

hResume *Source*: http://en.wikipedia.org/w/index.php?oldid=425310169 *Contributors*: Abu badali, Editor2020, FredTubale, Indon, Jm34harvey, Mindmatrix, Pegship, Pigsonthewing, Ronz, Trident13, Unforgiven24, 36 anonymous edits

Independent contractor *Source*: http://en.wikipedia.org/w/index.php?oldid=439167760 *Contributors*: 1099reporter, Alan McBeth, AndrewHowse, Andrewsurtees, ArglebargleIV, Arminius, BD2412, Barek, Beland, Bluemoose, BruceHoag, Comet Tuttle, D-Rock, DTM, David91, DocWatson42, Edgar181, Erianna, Ewlyahoocom, Famspear, Fred Bauder, Grandia01, Grapedad, Grumpyyoungman01, Hellno2, Hixteilchen, Homepro, Ialsoagree, Imnotminkus, Jctrux, JeffBillman, Jobshoppinfool, Jojhutton, LeeG, Legis, Levineps, MarkBrooks, Maurreen, Mondez Durden, Mwanner, Netsnipe, Packer9037, Patrick2480, PhilKnight, PleaseStand, Postdlf, Queenmomcat, Rajwans, Remodeling101, Rlsheehan, Rsmcphail, SONORAMA, Saintjimmy777, Search4Lancer, Serveux, Squids and Chips, Swanepoel, TheBackpack, Trident13, Viriditas, Viva-Verdi, Wickifrank, Wikieditor1988, Woohookitty, Xyzzyplugh, Yenier, Z.E.R.O., Zzuuzz, 71 anonymous edits

Induction (teachers) *Source*: http://en.wikipedia.org/w/index.php?oldid=393370228 *Contributors*: Aiken drum, TDAnewmedia, Tafkam, Tassedethe, Trident13, 2 anonymous edits

Induction programme *Source*: http://en.wikipedia.org/w/index.php?oldid=400479826 *Contributors*: AbsolutDan, Brodger3, Carl.bunderson, Cloak Reaver, Cnbrb, Eryxhn, Fram, Fuhghettaboutit, Gbradt, HarryHenryGebel, Htctestar, Hu12, Isonomia, Ladybirdintheuk, Mariza1, Metta Bubble, MrOllie, NorthernThunder, Pearle, R'n'B, Rjwilmsi, Soopermuse, Tafkam, Themoose8, Tmol42, Tohd8BohaithuGh1, Tregoweth, Trident13, Wardy 24, Woohookitty, 33 anonymous edits

INGRADA *Source*: http://en.wikipedia.org/w/index.php?oldid=388078130 *Contributors*: Bearcat, BifferBlog, Dinarphatak, Dr Gangrene, Malcolma, Pegship, Reevesby

Integrity Inventory *Source*: http://en.wikipedia.org/w/index.php?oldid=433691868 *Contributors*: Eli.Begoun, Fredrafilson, Stuartyeates

Internal labor market *Source*: http://en.wikipedia.org/w/index.php?oldid=439237685 *Contributors*: Avibaby44035, Barkeep, Gaius Cornelius, Gilliam, Ithrowcheese, JayDVa, Kjkolb, Malcolma, Marcusaralias, Melesse, Optigan13, Pearle, Rich Farmbrough, Richard Arthur Norton (1958-), The Thing That Should Not Be, Trident13, 6 anonymous edits

Internet recruiting *Source*: http://en.wikipedia.org/w/index.php?oldid=379361442 *Contributors*: Bridgeplayer, Calltech, Chrisr2, Drewzhrodague, Frap, Gutmach, HeinzzzderMannn, Hu12, Ioannes Pragensis, Kquaas, Lingstar, Lojong, PM Poon, Requestion, Shadowjams, Trident13, WeatherFug, 10 anonymous edits

Interview suit *Source*: http://en.wikipedia.org/w/index.php?oldid=322534541 *Contributors*: ...adam..., 17Drew, 201075m, A.K.A.47, A.R., ASB1983, Ac101, Adambiswanger1, Admaletz, After Midnight, Ala.foum, Alai, AlanDJ, Aldis90, Ale jrb, Alison, Alngrdz, Altzinn, Alxndr, American Billionaire, Anarchangel23, Anthony Appleyard, Apichai007, Arici4, Artemis-Arethusa, Arthur Holland, Artimusoid, Atthewindow, Audrey, Axaladl, Aymatth2, Azer Red, B. Wolterding, Bardsandwarriors, Bart133, Bco321, Bejnar, Beland, Belovedfreak, Berkut, Binarybits, BlancaNFalbo, Blue520, Bobo192, Bongwarrior, Bubbleboys, Burltone, Calliopejen, CambridgeBayWeather, CanisRufus, Capesplit, Caspar esq., Cathleenk, Chiper26789, Chooper, Cmdrjameson, Coemgenus, CommonsDelinker, Cptnono, Crazyvas, Cybercobra, DWaterson, Damac, David Trumbull, Dblevins2, Delirium, Deltabeignet, DerHexer, Desk Jockey, DocWatson42, Dunnsworth, East718, EdH, Egon Eagle, Elcobbola, Elendil's Heir, Eleos, Epiphanysolutions, Esn, Esperant, Esrever, Everyking, ExLibre, Ezeu, FlamingSilmaril, FrancoGG, FredrikT, GB fan, Gadfium, Gaius Cornelius, Garrison Savannah, Gentgeen, George100, GeorgeFormby1, Gimboid13, Glloq, Godfrey Daniel, Greenlead, Ground Zero, Grundle2600, Gsp, Hages69, Hajhouse, Harry Sakal, Harrythered, Hede2000, HeilBush, Hellomynameis88, Herman Downs, Herrick, Hmains, Huw Powell, Ideletealot2, Iiii2333, Indiancorrection, JREL, JaGa, Jabc123, JacobJHWard, Janiepuentes, Jason Recliner, Esq., Jenmoa, Jhlynes, Jiang, Jiodarseo, Jiodarwiki1, Jiodarwiki2, Joan Rocaguinard, John Anderson, JohnRonald, Johnuniq, Jonkerz, Jooler, Josh Parris, Jotapianus, Joyceroakman, Jpbowen, Jpbrenna, Jpgordon, Julian Grybowski, Jusdafax, JzG, Kan8eDie, KarenSutherland, Keeshu, Kellymoberg, Kenyon, Koavf, Kristinwillis, Lambiam, Lbertybell, Liyster, Loggie, Lollerskates, LorenzoB, Lradrama, Lumarv, MER-C, Mandingoesque, Marcus Bowen, Matthew Proctor, Matthewrbowker, Mav, Max rspct, Mboverload, Meelar, Meika, Michael Hardy, Michaelbusch, Mkruijff, Mnc4t, Mobius, Moleskiner, Monkeyfishbird, Mqa, Mrpotatohead121, Mucket, MuffledThud, MuzikJunky, Mwanner, Mwzeller, MyButthole619, NathanoNL, NawlinWiki, Newsaholic, Nick Number, No more bongos, Nomist, OP41, Od001, Onecatowner, Open-collar, Owen, P. S. Burton, PKM, Paddae, Patiwat, Patrick, Paul Ittoop, PaulIttoop1990, Pedant17, PhilyG, Plainsong, Polimerek, Poppapo, Preslethe, PrincessWortheverything, Przepla, Psychiker, PubliusFL, Quill, Racconish, Rafael Campos, Rashad9607, Ray-Ginsay, Reflex Reaction, Requestion, Retrac.noremac, Ricemiller, Rich Farmbrough, Rigadoun, Rjwilmsi, Robert K S, Ronhjones, Rsimmonds01, Rubseb, SB Johnny,

SDC, Salanax, Sam Hocevar, Sandstein, Sator, Saxifrage, SchuminWeb, Scoutersig, Sdason, Sdrinkwater, Seraphimblade, Shanes, Shaul avrom, Shenme, Shirt58, Shoaler, SilkTork, Simarjitsinghsuri, Sniffandgrowl, Starwiz, Stevage, Strongbad1982, Summer Song, SummerWithMorons, Suzanne willson, Swpb, Tachyon01, TamCaP, TastyPoutine, Tatterfly, Taxman, TengoDas, Terwilliger, Textangel, That Baller, The Chef, The Collector, The Epopt, The Mummy, TheCormac, TheEditrix, TheGrimReaper NS, Themightyquill, Thiste, Thryduulf, TigerShark, TjoeC, Tobi, TomB123, Tonync, Uirauna, VAwebteam, Victoriashild, Vox latina, Vpfritz, Wac01, Walshga, Wayne Miller, Wechselstrom, Weierstraß, Wiseup26, Woohookitty, Woscafrench, Xdenizen, Xxanthippe, Yill577, Yuriz, Zachzab2, Zantastik, Zoicon5, Zundark, Zzuuzz, 605 anonymous edits

Jeopardy! audition process *Source*: http://en.wikipedia.org/w/index.php?oldid=438825144 *Contributors*: Aervanath, Anarchangel, Biggspowd, Booshakla, Chris the speller, ChrisP2K5, Chrislk02, Fish and karate, Fryede, Gary King, Gilliam, Goldrushcavi, Headbomb, Iner22, Katieh5584, Khatru2, King of Hearts, Lisa0012, Michal Nebyla, NOLA504ever, Nightscream, Njr75003, OntarioQuizzer, PKT, Poshua, Ridernyc, Rjwilmsi, Robert K S, Schmloof, Sjones23, Sottolacqua, Stifle, TenPoundHammer, Thatjeopardygirl, Tinlinkin, TrbleClef, Us441, 33 anonymous edits

Job description *Source*: http://en.wikipedia.org/w/index.php?oldid=439021604 *Contributors*: A3RO, Acceleratorhams, Alansohn, AlexJFox, AlexS0907, Amorymeltzer, AvicAWB, Benben799, Bernburgerin, Bhadani, BigDunc, Bobrayner, Bonadea, Bryanbgsu, Captain-n00dle, Ckob2, CliffC, Ctjf83, D10hitman, DARTH SIDIOUS 2, DMacks, Dawn Bard, Dianahidalgo, Dockfish, Epbr123, Eraserhead1, Immunize, Jujutacular, Kajervi, Kuru, MBisanz, Macy, Maksym Pomerko, Mannafredo, Mauler90, Max Naylor, Maxim, Mike Restivo, MithrandirAgain, Mjanulaitis, MrRadioGuy, N419BH, Naraht, NewEnglandYankee, Oxymoron83, Paduch, Phgao, Piano non troppo, PigFlu Oink, Possum, Recognizance, Red, Rumping, Ruy Pugliesi, S3000, SchuminWeb, Shadowjams, Sicco Jan Bier, Slakr, SoSaysChappy, Suffusion of Yellow, Tftaz, The Thing That Should Not Be, The Utahraptor, TheTrojanHought, Thomas Blomberg, Tide rolls, TimClicks, Tnxman307, Trident13, Tuxish, Washburnmav, Waterfox, Wavelength, WillMcC, Wjemather, Woohookitty, Yukida-R, 288 anonymous edits

Job fair *Source*: http://en.wikipedia.org/w/index.php?oldid=437765395 *Contributors*: Bobo192, Buschaot, Csodennc, Dneelon, Eslamsameh, Everyking, Gwernol, Happyam, IamTheFinder, Iceblock, JAYMEDINC, Jjron, Jobsforall, Jonathan Hall, Mastrchf91, Metropolitan90, Minisu, Mr.crabby, Nikkimaria, OxymoronNBG, PiracyFundsTerrorism, Prolog, Rich Farmbrough, Ronz, Sherurcij, TastyPoutine, TexasAndroid, Thadius856AWB, Uprightcomm, Velella, Woohookitty, 26 anonymous edits

Job fraud *Source*: http://en.wikipedia.org/w/index.php?oldid=438969065 *Contributors*: Aleksander Zawitkowski, BD2412, Caramelldansener, Dlrohrer2003, Edcolins, Emarsee, Heimstern, Hellno2, Jsnx, Keenan Pepper, Leebo, Mentifisto, Milsgnome, Pajamaknotts, Pegship, Powerchex, Pularoid, Reli source, Schaefer, Sid1138, Srich32977, Tim Parenti, Trident13, Vader Terence, 27 anonymous edits

Job interview *Source*: http://en.wikipedia.org/w/index.php?oldid=439105854 *Contributors*: 5 albert square, Adoyle500, Adrianodl, Ahmadmashhour, Alansohn, Alblineb, Amirreza, Anand2027, Andycjp, Andyjsmith, Ansonreed, Aude, Audriusa, Auntof6, Banetbi, Barthandelus, Beetstra, BellaBellaPrincess, Belovedfreak, Betterusername, Bloomster, Blotwell, Bluemoose, Bon508, Brideshead, BryanHolland, Bullseyeresumes, Bvanrossum, ByeByeBaby, Calltech, Cam munoz, Careerjob, Chedorlaomer, Ciphers, Closedmouth, Clrfh3, Coemgenus, Condem, Cornince, Courcelles, Cubejockey, Cunninla, Cusp98007, DVdm, Dancter, David Shay, Dd4w2000, Dekimasu, Dthomsen8, Duststar4, Dwarf Kirlston, Dwilso, Dysepsion, EdenDD, Elipongo, Elm-39, Ender3057, Falcon8765, Favonian, FelixWriter, FlamingSilmaril, Floquenbeam, Freedomusa, Gbradt, Gilliam, Gogo Dodo, Gr1st, GraemeL, Greensburger, Gsmodi, Hamtechperson, Hellno2, Hu12, Ida Shaw, Inchiquin, InterviewGuy, JYolkowski, JaGa, Jamesooders, Jenna814, JeremyA, Jeugeorge, JobInterviewCoach, John Broughton, Jschreib, KCinDC, Kigali1, Kingpin13, Kingturtle, Kku, Krwanam, Kulandai, Kuru, Kutnpaste, Lansing Kakazu, LeftClicker, Legendarylindsay, Levineps, Liao, LilHelpa, Limblessjack, MER-C, Mackus, Mal4mac, Massiveray, MattKeegan, Mitch Ames, Mlayl, MoRsE, Monterey Bay, Mr.marccortez, MrOllie, NERIC-Security, NameIsRon, NawlinWiki, Neutrality, Nissimziv, Nubiatech, Ohnoitsjamie, Owenjonesuk, Oxymoron83, Paxse, Petr Kopač, Pevernagie, Philx9771, Piano non troppo, Pinkadelica, Pkgadala, Pm master, Poseidon123, Qac 3, Qwerty800, Qwyrxian, RHM22, Ralu55, Rawkinrich, Red dwarf, Reynolds329, Rich257, Robby100, Robert J Nagle, Ronhjones, Ronz, Roughan123, Rwgiesel, Sandboxadvisors, Sander123, Satori Son, SimonP, SiobhanHansa, Skkuumar, Sladetrent, Smalbright6, SmartGuy, South Bay, SpaceFlight89, Sparklejunkie, SquidSK, StefanieSnag, Stev0, Stevegallery, Stevensherlock, Stevey7788, Stifle, Struway, Sunsetcleaningservice, Technopat, Teknic, Tenrub, Texture, Tftaz, Thebluedrg99999, Thecheesykid, Thegoldresume, Tifoso2, Tinton5, Tmol42, Toddfugere, Tommy2010, Trelawnie, Trident13, Tsmith2314, Usavisa webmaster, Vakathy, Versageek, Versus22, Vsh3r, Walshga, Wavelength, Websitesaccounts, Weeboab, Willcasserley, Woohookitty, Workbloom, Xag, Yamara, Yandman, Zondor, 320 anonymous edits

Job wrapping *Source*: http://en.wikipedia.org/w/index.php?oldid=403389789 *Contributors*: Bearcat, CutOffTies, Malcolma, MatthewVanitas, Nsuggs, Rich Farmbrough, Richard2009, T@nn

Labour hire *Source*: http://en.wikipedia.org/w/index.php?oldid=437931269 *Contributors*: Caiaffa, Davidmwilliams, Edward, Eliz81, Qwert1984, Surfing bird, Trident13, Unforgettableid, 14 anonymous edits

Military recruitment *Source*: http://en.wikipedia.org/w/index.php?oldid=426583664 *Contributors*: Alphachimp, Andrew0921, Andy Marchbanks, Arthena, BMF81, Billwilson5060, Buckshot06, Cazemier, Cliffb, DKalkin, Diaa abdelmoneim, Dp462090, Eltrain34, Eubulides, Frap, Gilgongo, Globosoft, Gwax331, Hmains, Hossen27, Howcheng, Inter16, Jonathanriley, JukoFF, Kaihsu, Kurieeto, Kuru, La goutte de pluie, Laudak, MarmadukePercy, Maxis ftw, Moustachioed Womanizer, Mr Taz, Mrg3105, Msaout, N-Lange.de, Nauticashades, NavyCS, NerdyNSK, Nevilledidit, Nick-D, NorthernThunder, Ohconfucius, Philip Trueman, Puddhe, PunkKillsFascists, Quarl, RadioBroadcast, Rjwilmsi, Rockybiggs, Rollo44, ScottBuckley, Str1977, SwordSmurf, Synthe, Tmaull, Transylvanus, Trident13, Van helsing, Vinay84, Work permit, 37 anonymous edits

Multiple mini interview *Source*: http://en.wikipedia.org/w/index.php?oldid=381732418 *Contributors*: 1ForTheMoney, Airplaneman, Celique, Gilula, Il Andr3w Il, Industryliaison, JHunterJ, Jungcam, Katharineamy, Ll Andr3w ll, RHaworth, Valentinejoesmith

National Association of Colleges and Employers *Source*: http://en.wikipedia.org/w/index.php?oldid=408546929 *Contributors*: 4mscollins, Cybercobra, D6, KathrynLybarger, Malcolma, NuclearWarfare, R'n'B, 5 anonymous edits

New Jersey/Eastern Pennsylvania/Delaware HERC *Source*: http://en.wikipedia.org/w/index.php?oldid=415277825 *Contributors*: LilHelpa, Mlpearc, Simbrex, 2 anonymous edits

NotchUp *Source*: http://en.wikipedia.org/w/index.php?oldid=386943885 *Contributors*: R'n'B, Skikirkwood, SocialRec, 9 anonymous edits

Onboarding *Source*: http://en.wikipedia.org/w/index.php?oldid=433058654 *Contributors*: Ademkader, Artoasis, BarbaraLond, Biscuittin, Boris1, Brianrangell, ChuckRos, Collect, Davewild, David.Monniaux, Dorissims, Eklamont, Fabrictramp, Fram, Gbradt, Heatherbreslin, Ioparty, Jason Butler, Lbook52, LindaAthans, Mandsford, MartinPoulter, Megaman en m, Megvon, Momoricks, MrOllie, Nasrani, Ohnoitsjamie, Orangemike, OsamaSajid, Phoenixarizona, Psiphiorg, R'n'B, Rich Farmbrough, Ricky Martinez, Robertpersaud, Saia5053, Sandstein, Suckaduck, Svick, TastyPoutine, Tmol42, Wberman, Woohookitty, Zumiloko, 65 anonymous edits

Online job fair *Source*: http://en.wikipedia.org/w/index.php?oldid=438045563 *Contributors*: Addshore, D6, Jafeluv, Jjron, Katieh5584, Mcalob, Nikkimaria, The Monster, WikHead, 9 anonymous edits

Online vetting *Source*: http://en.wikipedia.org/w/index.php?oldid=420246560 *Contributors*: Akerans, Auntyleona, Cybercobra, Decltype, Fences and windows, Shimeru, TheDude2006, Timneu22

Overqualification *Source*: http://en.wikipedia.org/w/index.php?oldid=434476319 *Contributors*: BullRangifer, Cazort, Cgingold, Closedmouth, DMBradbury, Dennis714, Evansad, Garik, HappyInGeneral, Hq3473, Jahredtobin, Jeffpw, Magioladitis, Mboverload, Ngebendi, Peregrine Fisher, Salad Days, Shaliya waya, Skomorokh, Trident13, Wavelength, Wildspell, Woohookitty, 20 anonymous edits

Peak earning years *Source*: http://en.wikipedia.org/w/index.php?oldid=267724027 *Contributors*: Goodwin-Brent, Hooperbloob, Multeitygirl, Night Gyr, Pleclech, Trident13, Trollderella, Vulture19

Performance-linked incentives *Source*: http://en.wikipedia.org/w/index.php?oldid=421298848 *Contributors*: Capt muthukrishnan, Mandarax, Mild Bill Hiccup, Nawat, 3 anonymous edits

Permanent employment *Source*: http://en.wikipedia.org/w/index.php?oldid=429603117 *Contributors*: Addshore, Anon004, Chocoholic2007, Cybercobra, Erechtheus, Espoo, Fadikaouk, Hellno2, Heroeswithmetaphors, Iridescent, Jimbo.a.jones, Nasugirl, Naval Scene, R'n'B, Radagast83, RichardVeryard, Skittleys, THF, Trident13, Versageek, 5 anonymous edits

Person specification *Source*: http://en.wikipedia.org/w/index.php?oldid=413724761 *Contributors*: Ahoerstemeier, Aitias, Ali pedram, D99figge, Gec118, Hazharry, Jason127, Kingturtle, LilHelpa, Malcolma, NebY, Philip Trueman, Trident13, 22 anonymous edits

Probation (workplace) *Source*: http://en.wikipedia.org/w/index.php?oldid=390300644 *Contributors*: 16@r, Andycjp, Briguy52748, Choster, Curps, Josh477, NeonMerlin, Patman, Penbat, Punctured Bicycle, Samuell, SorryGuy, Trident13, 9 anonymous edits

Realistic Job Preview *Source*: http://en.wikipedia.org/w/index.php?oldid=420096891 *Contributors*: Abrech, Avalon, Aymatth2, DGG, J04n, Judicatus, Kateshortforbob, Katladiv, Mamorrisjcp, Reynolds329, Tabletop, Trident13, 7 anonymous edits

Recession-proof job *Source*: http://en.wikipedia.org/w/index.php?oldid=417187302 *Contributors*: Alp101, Hellno2, Heroeswithmetaphors, PamD, R'n'B, Tpbradbury, Xanzzibar, Yaksar, 2 anonymous edits

Recruitment advertising *Source*: http://en.wikipedia.org/w/index.php?oldid=438392550 *Contributors*: Biscuittin, Bulwersator, Duvedal, Fabrictramp, HaeB, Jordioni, Krickhahn, Kuru, Mild Bill Hiccup, Neilcosta, Nesyhltn, Phil Bridger, Samuel123adams, StephenSwain, Trident13, Zzuuzz, 14 anonymous edits

Recruitment in the Republic of Ireland *Source*: http://en.wikipedia.org/w/index.php?oldid=329999811 *Contributors*: Cnbrb, Guliolopez, John Ellis Ireland, Krivak, Laudak, Mboverload, Million Little Gods, Mobrimer, MusicInTheHouse, Qqqqqq, Sarah777, Skier Dude, Snappy, Trident13, 10 anonymous edits

Recruitment Process Insourcing *Source*: http://en.wikipedia.org/w/index.php?oldid=280348223 *Contributors*: Avalon, Fabrictramp, Gary King, Pyrospirit, Rjannone, Spike Wilbury, Trident13

Recruitment Process Outsourcing *Source*: http://en.wikipedia.org/w/index.php?oldid=428781061 *Contributors*: Abenning.4, Acroterion, Apparition11, Arjen Dijksman, Bierzart, Bms15, Bryan Derksen, Cgayner, Chandraponneganti, Cnbrb, Emailmarios, Engage NZ, Fuadahasan, Grafen, Gregmmorrow, Gutmach, Hallsteven, Humanatek, Infotothemasses, JASpencer, Jamiequint, Jimbo.a.jones, KathrynLybarger, Kellyjoy, Kuru, Lady space, Mercurydimeguy, Mike.lifeguard, Mlouns, MrOllie, Nd grad, Nrcjersey, Pankajlhg, PatrickFlaherty, PedroPalhoto, Prari, R'n'B, Rillian, Rohandmathews, Ronhjones, Ronz, Rorry, Rpo epistle, Rwhitley, Saganaki-, SmartGRS, TF0001, Tejvir.chaudhary, Tmol42, Tnts, Trident13, Will Beback Auto, 107 anonymous edits

Referral recruitment *Source*: http://en.wikipedia.org/w/index.php?oldid=421128306 *Contributors*: Ebe123, Naturalselection01

Résumé *Source*: http://en.wikipedia.org/w/index.php?oldid=438955235 *Contributors*: 06bluntc, 159753, 16@r, 1chinaall, 2fierce4u, 2help, A. B., ABF, Aaronbrick, Abigor, Adambro, Adigun OJ, Aerosapien, Aeusoes1, Ahmadmashhour, Ajboho, Akarkera, Akindler90, Alansohn, Alex43223, AlexWangombe, Alexius08, Allanbrownrbi, Allstarecho, Aminrm, Amir syria, AndrewWilson-IanKelly, Andycjp, Angus Lepper, Animaterra1, Anneshawtv, AnonymousUser5, Antar37, Ardicius Greenknight, Astral, Audriusa, Awsoma, Axeman89, Axewiki, BD2412, BMF81, Babyjane101, BadCRC, Barista, Bart133, Bassbonerocks, Bdeshayes, Beaver, Bedgee, Beetstra, BenKovitz, Benboubker, Bens, Berean Hunter, Bernie74, Billboyer, Blanchardb, Bloodshedder, Bloomsden, Blotwell, Bmitchelf, Bonadea, Boy in the bands, BrOnXbOmBr21, Brentusa, Brianga, Briantw, Brick Thrower, Brighterorange, Broadway321, Btball, Btmaisel, Bucephalus, BullRangifer, Bwritings, Calabraxthis, Cameron Nedland, Camw, Can't sleep, clown will eat me, CanadianLinuxUser, Canley, Capricorn42, CareerOrigin, Careerjob, Careerjobs, Careerjoy, Careerlady, CareersOnLine, Carlm, Causa sui, Cbutler1467, Cdfkrf, Cellcv, Celly, Ceoil, Chaser, Cheesepuffs531, Chetan0203, Choster, Chrisminter, Christian List, Christopher Parham, Cikicdragan, Ck lostsword, Ckatz, Cleanupman, Clickedon, Clover345, Cls14, Cnanursing, CoJaBo, Complete letter writing system, ConformistDeviant, Coolth, Coralmizu, Corinnemansfield, Correogsk, Correon, Cosmos111, Courcelles, Crculver, Cspan64, Curps, Cybercobra, Cyp, D.Worthington, DARTH SIDIOUS 2, DRosenbach, Da monster under your bed, Daniel C. Boyer, Dantheman531, David from Downunder, David.Monniaux, Davidmi79, Dehaas99, DemonThing, Deor, DerHexer, Diligent Terrier, Discospinster, Diverman, Dixonredbud, Dkjfjsj, Doctormatt, Don4g, Donald Albury, Dong-gook, Dorvaq, Dtrielli, Dunxd, EEMIV, Earle Martin, Edalton, Egorre, Eire123, El C, El Cubano, Eli86juelz, Empoor, Enigmaman, EonBlueApocalypse, Ericgarcia17, Erik the Red 2, Eurobikermcdog, Euryalus, Excirial, Exefire, F-451, F15 sanitizing eagle, FJPB, Fabricationary, Faradayplank, Farhan Murtaza, FelixWriter, Fenice, Fernando S. Aldado, FisherQueen, Flewis, Flowanda, Frap, Fredrick day, Fubar Obfusco, Fuji268, Furrykef, GK, Gene Nygaard, Geoffsauer, Getresume, Gibsonan, Gilliam, Gneer, Gogo Dodo, Goras., Gordonfu, GraemeL, Graham87, Greenlead, Gregregregre, Greudin, Gsherry, Haakon, Halloweenman1971, Hankayla, Harryboyles, Harshmellow, Hbdywx, Heatseaker1, Hellno2, Helpontap, Heman, HenryLi, Heron, Hettyt1, Hmrox, Hobartimus, Holizz, Hu12, Huntscorpio, IAlex, Ianweller, Icairns, Iceberg123, Ieverhart, Igoldste, Incnis Mrsi, Insiriusdenial, Intershark, Ioeth, Iranway, Iridescent, Irrelevant, Islandman670, Isnow, J toffoli, JForget, Ja 62, Jacj, JackLumber, Jackson.hammond, Jacobdegree, Jamalex, Jarcher88, Jaredhawk, Jauerback, Jaw959, Jaysweet, Jeffmcneill, Jennica, Jerome Charles Potts, Jez9999, Jiang, Jifletch, Jihiro, Jimbob1630, Jjj7777, Jlao04, Jncraton, Jobbin, Jobsdblogsg, Joelholdsworth, John Hofmeyr, John Quincy Adding Machine, John2000, JohnOwens, Jonathandolce, Josephmalb, Joshgreen08, Josisb, Joule36e5, Jpgordon, Jstbeinme, Jtdirl, Jtomlin1, Judsonbc, Jujutacular, Jukcoder, Jwkpiano1, Kaden89064, Kane5187, Karam.Anthony.K, Kci.advisory, Khendon, Khoikhoi, Khoj badami, Khukri, Kindall, Kinneyboy90, Kitsune17717, Klorpet, Kolakandeee, Kubigula, Kuru, Kutnpaste, Kwamikagami, Kwertii, Kwev2rz, Kwicholhayes, LARS, La goutte de pluie, Lancerecruit2002, Laogeodritt, Lar, Lasfrain32, Laurel, Law, LeeG, Lenoxus, Libcub, Liberlogos, Lightmouse, Lingstar, Linkspamremover, LittleOldMe, Logictheo, Lord Pistachio, Lord Roem, LostLeviathan, Lostrealist, Lotje, LtPowers, M1ss1ontomars2k4, MER-C, Maartsen, Madeleine Price Ball, Magog the Ogre 2, Majorbrainy, Malia46, Man vyi, Mandarax, Mani1, Maralia, Marc paliotti, Mariotime95, Mark Renier, Marysunshine, Mashood khan, Mathinker, Mavigogun, Max Naylor, Max rspct, MaxVeers, Mdalums, Mderrick15, Meand, Meelar, Mekong Bluesman, Memming, Mentifisto, Michael Devore, Michael Hardy, Midgrid, Mihadoremi, Mikelleu, Mil97036, Milton Stanley, Mmustafa, Moira222, Mondriansky, Monkeyman, Monobi, Mordicai, Moulder, Mr Adequate, Mrchaotica, Mushroom, Musicalantonio, Mwtoews, Myresumaker, Natl1, NawlinWiki, NellieBly, Neo-Jay, Nerdygeek101, Netspy, Neucleon, Neverquick, NewEnglandYankee, Newlay, Newmanbe, Nghawes, Nickshanks, NigelR, Nightscream, Njh@bandsman.co.uk, Node ue, Nohat, Noisejunky, Nsaa, Nsahglen, Nufy8, OhanaUnited, Ohlcv, Ohnoitsjamie, Oli Filth, Onorem, Owen214, Oyp, PamD, Paul 012, Paul August, Paul Erik, Pavel Vozenilek, Pbwilson, Peterdjones, Pfahlstrom, Pfc432, Phgao, Philip Baird Shearer, Philip Trueman, PhilipO, Piano non troppo, Pigsonthewing, Pinaki ghosh, PinchasC, Plumpy, Pmsyyz, Poochy, Prashanthns, Puchiko, Quinsareth, QuiteUnusual, R6MaY89, Radiojon, Rajjhand, RandomXYZb, Raredavid, Rawkinrich, Rebel0610, Reinyday, Resumesbyscott, RetiredWikipedian789, Revth, Rhobite, Rillian, Ripmeester, Rivertorch, RobSullivan444, Robber93, RobertG, Robertgreer, Rohanrob, Rolandirwin, Ronhjones, Ronz, Rossenglish, Roundhouse0, Roux, Rukaribe, Ryubread, SDY, SJP, Salz789, Sam Vimes, Samanthamanning, Sandboxadvisors, Santhuosh, Scarian, SchfiftyThree, Schwnj, Sdalmonte, Seaphoto, Search4Lancer, Senator2029, Serag4000, Seraphim, Shadow dragonking, SheeEttin, Sheffernan, Sherbajoe, Shiner76, Shritwod, Shwir, Skendus, Skew-t, Sl, Smiln32, Son of More, Sophiedb, Sottolacqua, Sourceline, Sp, Spacefruit, SpamBilly, Sparklejunkie, Splintax, Sroc, Starkid, Starwiz, Steve Bob, Stevejobswashere, Steven Zhang, StoneWorks, Stoni, Sunsfan1797, Svick, Tanner Swett, Techman224, Templater, Tetzcatlipoca, Texture, The Magnificent Clean-keeper, The Person Who Is Strange, The Thing That Should Not Be, The wub, Thegoldresume, Themfromspace, Thingg, ThinkingTwice, Tide rolls, Tim Cunningham, TippTopp, Tomnelson17, Tregoweth, TrendResumes, Trident13, Trivialist, Trotter, Trovatore, Trusilver, Turk brown, Twas Now, Twp, Ulric1313, Uni-qdocs, Unionhawk, Unixer, Vedantm, Vegaswikian, Veinor, Velpaedia Jenkuklordanus, Vette330, Video tape, VigilancePrime, VodkaJazz, Vrenator, Vzbs34, WWC, WatermelonPotion, Wavelength, Wayiran, WeaselADAPT, Webf1n, Weeboab, Welshleprechaun, Wernty, Wes!, Wevi3, Whicky1978, WhisperToMe, Wii Wiki, Wik3private, Wiki alf, Wiki-vr, WikiSkeptic, Wikioogle=world take over, Wikiped12345, Willcasserley, Willyman79, Wimt, WoodElf, Workbloom, Wshakespeare, Xdenizen, Xenus, Yamla, Zandperl, Zellfaze, Zoe, Zondor, ZooFari, Zzuuzz, 1098 anonymous edits

Role-based assessment *Source*: http://en.wikipedia.org/w/index.php?oldid=434281652 *Contributors*: DragonflySixtyseven, HRman01, JoeBrennan, Jperiquito, Rich Farmbrough, WeijiBaikeBianji, 1 anonymous edits

Salary *Source*: http://en.wikipedia.org/w/index.php?oldid=434857457 *Contributors*: (aeropagitica), Acceleratorhams, Adam McMaster, Ahmad.ghamdi.24, Aibdescalzo, Alexf, Alreadybored, Animum, Anthonyc0472, Awesomewar, Bensin, Blathering1, BruceGrubb, CalendarWatcher, Calltech, Capricorn42, Casperdc, Celardore, Celarnor, Closedmouth, Coders4hire, Conrad.pramboeck, Daniel Case, Datastat, Delicious carbuncle, Discospinster, Dreadstar, EastTN, Elizabeyth, Empty Buffer, Enigmatical, Eras-mus, Eratina1979, Erossetti, Everyking, Farcical, Fenice, Fish and karate, Fratrep, Frederickmercury, Generacy, Gogo Dodo, Goldom, Goodwin-Brent, Grafen, Grick, HGB, HansomeRunnerBri, Hemanshu, Heyzeuss, Hlucky, Hmains, Hot200245, Hu12, IQ289, Igiffin, Ilyushka88, Insanity Incarnate, Invisifan, IvanLanin, JHMM13, JPD, Jackmilne, Johnbod, Joshisachin79, Julesd, Jwoodger, K.Nevelsteen, Kcoutu, Kenyon, Keryst, KevinCuddeback, Khushru kanga, KnowledgeOfSelf, Ksyrie, Kurieeto, Legion fi, Lewis1996wasere, LibLord, Lneal001, MER-C, MacGyverMagic, Macrakis, Malik Shabazz, Marquez, Martarius, Mathinker, Mattbrundage, Meenuarora, Michael Hardy, Mikael Häggström, MoodyGroove, MrVibrating, Mwanner, Ncsportsgirl626, NeonMerlin, Nick Number, Nicolas1981, Nirvana2013, Nixeagle, Nricardo, Odysses, Ohnoitsjamie, Oli Filth, Olivierchaussavoine, Palkaman34, Pasho1995, Patman, Philip Trueman, Phyxius, Piwko120, Polylerus, Poweroid, RadioActive, RanchoRosco, Rapidfire squad, RazorICE, Reconsider the static, Remni40, Requestion, ReyBrujo, Rich Farmbrough, Richmond96, Richoncode, Ricklaman, Rintrah, Rollo44, Ron2009, Ronz, Sachindole, Sarranduin, Scotty130995, Seregelly, Shamus44, Shanes, Shantavira, SickTwist, SkyWalker, Snek01, Soad123, SpuriousQ, Starwiz, Tbarr60, Tedder, Tellyaddict, Texture, The Land, TiMike, Timpo, Tomas e, Trident13, Ucanlookitup, ViddyViddy, Vt-aoe, Vuo, Wafulz, What123, Wiki alf, WikiSkeptic, Will Beback, Willking1979, Xanxz, Xaosflux, Xtiansimon, Zondor, 260 anonymous edits

Screening Resumes *Source*: http://en.wikipedia.org/w/index.php?oldid=372189307 *Contributors*: Malcolma, Tftaz

Simultaneous Recruiting of New Graduates *Source*: http://en.wikipedia.org/w/index.php?oldid=414186452 *Contributors*: Anon004, Babbage, Fotoske, Heroeswithmetaphors, Ngebendi, Oskilian, PC78, 29 anonymous edits

Social recruiting *Source*: http://en.wikipedia.org/w/index.php?oldid=432809214 *Contributors*: Bearcat, Feezo, JHunterJ, Jfelipe33, Jpjacobs.00, Malcolma, Malcolmxl5, Sarahjansen, 1 anonymous edits

Sourcing (personnel) *Source*: http://en.wikipedia.org/w/index.php?oldid=419351100 *Contributors*: 100110100, Ameering, Anticipation of a New Lover's Arrival, The, Atw1996, BostonRed, Carps, Clicketyclack, Cybercobra, Deor, Dmanaster, Evlekis, FrummerThanThou, Gbradt, Gogo Dodo, Gutmach, Infotothemasses, J04n, JHunterJ, Jobmachine, Kalypxo, Leslie61, Leviel, Lingstar, MrOllie, Nurg, Ohnoitsjamie, Pascal.Tesson, Qwyrxian, Rajeshkmr7, Rob McIntosh, Sebras, StefanieSnag, Tabletop, Tassedethe, Tpock11, Trident13, 40 anonymous edits

South West African Native Labour Association *Source*: http://en.wikipedia.org/w/index.php?oldid=428121582 *Contributors*: Namiba

St. Louis Regional HERC *Source*: http://en.wikipedia.org/w/index.php?oldid=396207463 *Contributors*: Rheyn, SBaker43, Sganl

Talent community *Source*: http://en.wikipedia.org/w/index.php?oldid=431605160 *Contributors*: Amorrison2010, Feezo, Giraffedata, Jfelipe33, Ldicolli, Malcolma, Melaen, NawlinWiki, Sarahjansen, 2 anonymous edits

The Select Family of Staffing Companies *Source*: http://en.wikipedia.org/w/index.php?oldid=423062377 *Contributors*: AndrewHowse, BD2412, Cameronella, Cjmclark, DGG, Deely, DoxTxob, Excirial, FreeRangeFrog, Jabrams-writer, R'n'B, Selectfamily, Themfromspace, Woohookitty, 19 anonymous edits

Times Ascent *Source*: http://en.wikipedia.org/w/index.php?oldid=367947473 *Contributors*: Auntof6, Kvivek05, Mokshjuneja

Trends in pre-employment screening *Source*: http://en.wikipedia.org/w/index.php?oldid=421888151 *Contributors*: Dawnseeker2000, Fences and windows, Flowanda, Gary King, Haribhagirath, Joeg524, Kthartley, Powerchap, Trident13, 1 anonymous edits

Versatilist *Source*: http://en.wikipedia.org/w/index.php?oldid=416980626 *Contributors*: A.M., Danishfurniture, David Koller, Dominoconsultant, Johnjgriffin, Pharos, Rich Farmbrough, Ronz, ScottWAmbler, Shire Reeve, TheRingess, Vinko, Wikinstone, Xyzzyplugh, 10 anonymous edits

Vetting *Source*: http://en.wikipedia.org/w/index.php?oldid=436064358 *Contributors*: Aerogami, AlexandraFiliaKelly, Commsintern2, Cossde, DCico, Evb-wiki, Excirial, Father Goose, Fences and windows, Froid, Gregfitzy, Grjm, Hawkaris, Ivorybow, J.delanoy, Jeodesic, Keithbob, Kubigula, Lensovet, Mporterf, Oden, Olwen Griffiths, Palanq, Pugluver94, Reinyday, Shadowjams, Sirussss, Stefanomione, Swat671, Trident13, Ulric1313, Vegaswikian, Where next Columbus?, YUL89YYZ, 49 anonymous edits

Video resume *Source*: http://en.wikipedia.org/w/index.php?oldid=428801225 *Contributors*: Amg2345, Avalon, Axlq, Bomaroon, Bonadea, Brentusa, Chanceous, Doctortodd113, Dpedersel, Drexell, ERcheck, ErikBowman, Frap, Granburguesa, JackLumber, Jkorbes, Jmaddalone, Jobtac, John254, Jonathanhartley, Knvb1123, Mark Renier, Mish9, NCraike, NMANMA, NURESUME, Nick123, Orangemike, PeopleScreening, Randal Graby, Reginmund, Sam.naes, Shalom Yechiel, Shortlistvideo, Simonholdings, Sohailmher, Someguy1221, Sp, Squids and Chips, Tabletop, TastyPoutine, Tregoweth, Trident13, Versageek, Wmae, Workblast, 70 anonymous edits

Witwatersrand Native Labour Association *Source*: http://en.wikipedia.org/w/index.php?oldid=428149382 *Contributors*: MSGJ, Namiba, Tabletop, 2 anonymous edits

Work-at-home scheme *Source*: http://en.wikipedia.org/w/index.php?oldid=439407275 *Contributors*: 1execl, Anneshawtv, Barek, Bart133, Bonadea, Bwpach, CKA3KA, Cashkate, Clsin, DanielEng, Dcoetzee, Ebyabe, Entrich, Falcon8765, Frivvy89, Fun2fun, Guthrie, Hellno2, Huey45, J.delanoy, Jeff Silvers, Jnestorius, Justinluu, Kalivd, Keraunos, Kittins floating in the sky yay, Leesteve1981, Lolinder, Lotje, Marco23554, McGeddon, Mdeets, Mitch Ames, NeilN, Neophoenixkun, Netsnipe, Nihonjoe, Ohnoitsjamie, Open to Wealth, Optics233, Oureffort, Owen214, Penbat, R'n'B, Rrburke, Salmank120, Sarataste, Sceptre, Sebwite, THEN WHO WAS PHONE?, Trident13, Versageek, Vinodtn, Websitesediting, Why Not A Duck, Wiikipedian, Work-from-home-job, Workathomejobs, Xyzzyplugh, Zoose1983, Zzuuzz, 68 anonymous edits

LinkedIn *Source*: http://en.wikipedia.org/w/index.php?oldid=439262300 *Contributors*: 16x9, 2bar, 50Stars, A3RO, AAAAA, Aaronba, Adyourservice.biz, Ageekgal, Ahmad87, Akonews, Alex Kosorukoff, Alexf, Altenmann, Amccall821, Amilator, Amire80, AnOddName, Angelthuylinh, Ark25, Arkim, Arran31, AspectusPR, Auto469680, Avouac, Axelschultze, Badgernet, Barek, Bbatsell, Beemer69, Bender235, Bongwarrior, Bubba73, Bubbabubba68, CDT007, CambridgeBayWeather, Cameron Scott, Camoz87, Canadian, Carlos Rosa PT, CecilWard, ChangChienFu, Cheong Kok Chun, ChrisUK, Classical geographer, CliffC, Commit charge, Computerjoe, Cosmoskramer, Countmac01, Csaccheri, Cunnington A, Cwooten71, Cxz111, Czj, DMCer, Dangerousnerd, Danholmesdxb, Danlev, Darrell Greenwood, DataWraith, Dbiel, Ddxc, Derboq, Dia^, Diannaa, DickieTruncheon, Dingar, Dirtpenguin, Discospinster, DisillusionedBitterAndKnackered, Dmama, Docket42, DominicConnor, Double.a.19, Download, DrSlump, Dreamyshade, Dreminemike, Drpickem, Dtobias, DuLithgow, Dwacon, ESkog, Eabuhadi, EagleOne, Edgar181, ElKevbo, Elisabethod, Elisor, Emesik, Engineman, Enoent, Enricopulatzo, EricWesBrown, Estebancortez, Eustress, Falcon8765, Fan-1967, Faznar, Fetchcomms, Ftiercel, Funjhunjhunwala, FunkyCanute, Fyrael, Gabi S., Gary King, Generic Player, Gidonb, Goalloverhere, Googol plex, GraemeL, GregorB, Gsarwa, H005, Hu12, I3142p168, Iamcookiemonster, Ida Shaw, Iggypin, Ilcheste, Instant Noodle Soup, Isyoucrazyson, IvanLanin, JFG, JackLumber, Jaltcoh, Jancikotuc, Jannecke h, Jay Gatsby, Jean-Marie Favre, Jedania, Jeromewiley, Johnuniq, Jonathanleblang, Josh.hoggan, JoshXF, Joshdhaliwal, Jovianeye, Jperfettini, Julielaurent, Jungle-Tile, K ideas, KFP, Kamnatijohn, Kbh3rd, Kcren, Kgopotsoj, Khalid hassani, Kidburla, Kidlittle, Kkleinberg, Kkm010, Kwamikagami, L Kensington, LarRan, Laserprinter, LasseVartiainen, Lindaeo, LisaKatz, Locris, Logan, Lotje, MMuzammils, Mac, Madhero88, Magentabanana, Mahoff, Marcireynolds, Marcus Qwertyus, MattTM, Matthewrlee, Me Three, Mephistophelian, Mets501, Michael Jahn, Michaelbarr123, Midlakewinter, Milfordwoman, MrOllie, Mrand, MsChristinaAdams, Munkyxtc, Mxn, NCSS, Netboy2005, Nickdella, Nposner, Nsaa, Ohconfucius, Ohnoitsjamie, Pationl, Paul Soomers, Pavel Vozenilek, Pcap, Ph.eyes, Philipwhiuk, PiRSquared17, Pingveno, Piotrus, Pjotr2, Poison Oak, Privatechef, Psantora, R'n'B, RJFJR, Rajesh4091989, Rd321, Rgbroitman, Rhombus, Rich Farmbrough, Richardswier, Richswier, Rjwilmsi, RobbertVisser, Robchogo, Robinson weijman, Ronz, Ross Burgess, Runner628, Sales Community, SamJohnston, Samejreltub, Samtheboy, Sandolsky, Sbonacorsi, Sciurinæ, Seancarlos, Sentity, Sha721, Shirulashem, Shortride, Slightsmile, SmartGuy, Smmgeek, SoKashira, Spyhawk, SqueakBox, Ssj5perfect cell, Stephen Gilbert, Stepheng3, Stev0, SummerWithMorons, Supermarco, SusanLesch, Syrthiss, THEunique, TJRC, TYelliot, TenPoundHammer, The wub, Thumperward, TitanOne, Tkynerd, Tlesher, Tonkie67, Treekids, Tregoweth, Treyblog, Trident13, Twerbrou, Uba33, UkPaolo, Ukexpat, Ultraexactzz, Unbound, UnitedStatesian, Universimmedia, Uucp, VArakawa, Vegetator, VenusianCat, Vieuxloup, VirtualSteve, Vlad, Volomed, W T L, Waldir, Wayne Slam, Weldon Keys, WhisperToMe, Wikiamd, Wikidemon, Wikinewguy, Wikipedian06, Wikiritter, Willking1979, Wjousts, Wulfe, Xeno, Xompanthy, Zencv, ZooFari, Zoran1986, Zscout370, आशीष भटनागर, 391 anonymous edits

Facebook *Source*: http://en.wikipedia.org/w/index.php?oldid=439445302 *Contributors*:)3uthead, -ross616-, 1111tomica, 123Hedgehog456, 12afser12, 16@r, 1ForTheMoney, 1tweed3, 1wolfblake, 2tothe4, 6bongo6, 81dollar, 88mphsss, 9014user, A Toyota's A Toyota, A. B., A.Ward, A1sapat, A3camero, A8UDI, A930913, ACBest, ACupOfCoffee, ADM, ADNghiem501, AMK1211, ANB, AROY411, AThing, Abasia, Abesam, Abhinav777, Academic Challenger, Acalamari, Acasson, Ace the bunny, Adam1213, AdamClarke, Adamb0223, Adambro, Adashiel, Adeelbutt88, Adeez, AdelaMae, Adguide, Aditya Gautam, AdmRose, Adriaan, Adrian J. Hunter, Aerotheque, Aervanath, Aezram, Afrowildo, Afterwriting, Agel to alive, AgentFade2Black, Ahmednh, Ahuskay, Aid85, Aidan129, Aido2002, Aim Here, Airplaneman, Akaala, Akamad, Al Fecund, Alansohn, Alarics, Albany NY, Alex Klotz, AlexHammer, Alexandru Stanoi, Alexjohnc3, Alextrevelian 006, Alexy527, Ali, AliRoolz, Alissa98cp, All Is One, All in, Allansteel, Allsaints23, Allstarecho, AlsoTrue, Altzinn, Amazins490, Ambrosia-, Amdma2003, Americanhero, Amjad z4, Amniarix, Amphytrite, Ams627, AnArchivist, Anabus, Anas Salloum, Andeep3450, Andonic, Andreakir, Andrevruas, AndrewWTaylor, Andrewlp1991, Andrewrutherford, Andy, Andy Marchbanks, AndyAgr, Anetode, Anewpester, Angel caboodle, Angela, Angelbo, Angelic Wraith, Angelocariati, Angleterre, Anikingos, Animal91X, Animum, Aniten21, Anna Frodesiak, Anurag golipkar, Apokrif, Appl3zealot, Arbero, Arbon42, Archdeceiver, Archiveman, Areeb cool, Arifhidayat, Arnabdas, Arstchnca, Arthur2045, Artichoker, Ash063, AshAloy, Ashellray, Ashershow1, Ashfree 13, Ashleyy osaurus, Asigiam213, Asklepiades, AtionSong, Atmospherica, Austinfidel, Av28, AxG, AxelBoldt, Aydin00, Aydinceri, Ayudante, Az1568, Azizasif, Aznxdarkricex, B Fizz, BHSMEtubaboy, BStarky, BaRiMzI, Babar54, Bandperson21, Barek, BarryTheUnicorn, Bart133, Baseballbaker23, Basement12, Bashereyre, Bassbasketball03, Bath116, Batmancj7, Bboy123, Bbqturtle, Bbriggs1, Bbruchs, Bcm5059, Bdesham, Beano, Beao, Bear199, Bearcat, Bearingafish, Beefcake32, Beetstra, Beghrato, Behun, Belekvor, Belikedurkheim, Bellagio99, Ben Arnold, Ben Tera, Bendavidu, Bender235, Benjistern, Betacommand, Betdud, Betterusername, Beyondparadise, Bgold, Bhadani, Bhaggs, Bianca1130, Bifgis, Big Bird, BigaZon, Bigbluefish, Bigd14631, Biggymo6, Bigtimepeace, Biivii, Bikri, Bill37212, Billim1, BillyMoses, Biruitorul, Bizjournals, Bjankuloski06en, Bjjjjj, Blackjack48, Blanchardb, Blehfu, BlueAg09, BlueSoxSWJ, Bluefoxicy, Bluerasberry, Bluetoast, BnaiBrithChai, Boaltmag, Bob bobato, Bobamnertiopsis, Bobo192, Bobsaget69, BogdanM02, Bonadea, Bonelayer12864, Bongwarrior, Bony devil, Bookofjude, Booyabazooka, Boreas74, Born Gay, Boston2austin, Bouklyloo, Bozonessinc, Bradv, Brahmanknight, Brandon, Brandon5485, Brazucs, BrekekekexKoaxKoax, Bretbenz, Bretter90, Brianga, Brianreading, Briansince1988, Brideshead, BroadSt Bully, BrokenSphere, Brokenbells, Brossow, BrotherE, Browardpat, Brucefry, Brusegadi, BryanG, Bsf436, Bstepp99, Bubba hotep, Bueller 007, Bugalugs13, Bull Market, Bullet234, Bungle, Burgessm, Burntsauce, Buteo lineatus, Buttermichi, Butterscotch, Bwithh, C.Fred, C628, CCRoxtar, CDThieme, CFM865, CHBMch05, CIS, CIreland, CJ Ramsay, CLW, CPColin, Cacofonie, Cafzal, Calabraxthis, Calliopejen1, Caltas, Camoz87, Can't sleep, clown will eat me, Canadian-Bacon, Canido11, Canterbury Tail, CanuckViking, Carachi, Cardinalngold, CaribDigita, Carlos boca, Carlosguitar, Caroline.duble, Cartoon Boy, CaseyPenk, Casper2k3, Caspertheghost, CassandraGemini, Catskul, Caulde, Cazort, Cbare, Cbuckley, Cclear44, CecilWard, Cedars, Cedrus-Libani, Cenarium, Cephal-odd, Ceyockey, Cgingold, Cguido, Chairlunchdinner, Chanlyn, Chantessy, Charismatic123, Chatfecter, Chendy, Chengdi, Chensiyuan, Cheong Kok Chun, Chesschampion, Chessphoon, Chester polarbear, Childzy, Chinamandan, Chloeobrian, Chocolate Dandelions, Chrhardy, Chris is me, Chris the speller, Chris14679, Chrislk02, Christopher Parham, Christopherlin, ChronicallyUninspired, Chzz, Ciaccona, Cindamuse, Cinéma C, Ckatz, Cleo20, Cmfusco53515, Cmoney05x, CobraBK, Coburnpharr04, Cocoaguy, Coemgenus, CokeBear, Colfulus, Colipon, Colleenthegreat, Colonies Chris, Columba livia, CommonsDelinker, Cool1097, CoolGuy, Coolcaesar, Coolmile88, Coop1128, Copana2002, Corbett3000, Cormacalian, Cornisle, Corpx, Corvus cornix, Corwinlw, Cowbellallen, Cprompt, Crackerjack, CrazyLegsKC, Crazycomputers, CredoFromStart, Cresix, Cretanforever, Crockspot, Crosby87, Crossmr, Crosstemplejay, Crystallina, Crzrussian, Csrempert, CuBiXcRaYfIsH, Cubbie1783, Cube b3, Curb Chain, CurranH, Curtmolloy, CutOffTies, Cutcopy, Cutter, Cwolfsheep, Cybercobra, Cyfal, Cyktsui, CypherXero, Cyrus XIII, Czj, D, D-Day, D.montero.melis, D2lraXBlZGlh, D9qhd8, DAMurphy, DC, DDmylesy, DGuey, DHN, DJAlik, DMCer, DMTayag, DMacks, DMurphy, DVD R W, DVdm, DVoit, DXBari, DaMenace123, Daa89563, Dabomb87, Daftpunkboy93, Dakin700, Dale Arnett, Damiens.rf, Dancter, DandanxD, Danhw052289, Daniel, Daniel Christensen, Daniel5127, DanielCD, DanielNuyu, Danlev, Danno uk, DannyDaWriter, DannyMac, Dansiman, Danski14, Dante Alighieri, Darb02, DarkFalls, DarkPrincess128, Darkage7, Darp-a-parp, Darrenhusted, Darth Panda, Dasani, Dasium, Davedonohue, Daveeburke, Davemathis, Daverocks, Daveswagon, Davex1000, David, David Biddulph, David Edgar, David the Aspie, DavidFarmbrough, DavidWBrooks, Davidlive, Davidyjeong, Dbloom, Dcamp314, De Katten, DeadEyeArrow, Deamon138, DeathNomad, Debresser, Dedtr9, Delband, Delivery:435, Dem393, Dendodge, DennisDallas, DerHexer, DerekHe, Deskana, Dethme0w, Detruncate, Dexter Nextnumber, Dextertittil, Dfrg.msc, Dhaluza, Dheppens, Dhimwit, DiRocco, DiVANSH, Dianebobk, Dickreuter, Didilorillard, Diego Grez, Dilbert307, Dim386, Dina, Dipsy12, Disavian, Discospinster, Dismas, Dispenser, Dittaeva, DividedByNegativeZero, Diving2010, DixonD, Djc wi, Djej1, Djgreen101, Djlollyb, Djmckee1, Djnicholson, Djottercreek, Djsasso, Dklizz, Dlavender45, DoC352, DocWatson42, Dodi.Blow, Dollarq, Dom Kaos, Don Vito Corleone, DonVincenzo, Donaldd23, Donama, Dondilly, Doradus, DoubleBlue, Doubleluckster, Dougbast, Douglasr007, Download, Downtown dan seattle, Dr. Blofeld, Dr.alf, Dr.finkelstein09, DrDisco, Dragoburaggo, Drappel, Dratman, DraxusD, Dread Specter, Dreaded Walrus, Dream out loud, Drinkadrink, Drmagnon, Drmaik, Drmies, Drur93, Dsemaya, Dstiling, Dt128, Dtremblay, Dubbya9, Dubtown11, Duckbill, Dudesleeper, Dunqn, Duoraven, DustinJunior, Dwayne, Dwight666, Dwilso, Dwo, Dyaa, Dynesclan, Dyolf, Dysepsion, DéRahier, EALacey, EGorodetsky, EJF, ESkog, EVula, Eags, Earldelawarr, EarthPerson, Eball, Ecopetition, Ed g2s, EddieMoore2008, Eddron, Edison, Edmondmuirocks, Edmundwoods, Edward655, EdwinHJ, Eedlee, Efe, Efeinberg, Eh1821, Ehlkej, Eionm, Eivmeidwl, Ejk81, Ekedolphin, Ekhcsub, ElKevbo, ElSaxo, Elawen, Elcarmean, Elcobbola, Electricbassguy, Elementrocks, Eleuther, ElfWord, Elhector, Eli81993, EliasAlucard, Elmer Clark, Elpezmuerto, Emcee, Emeraldcityserendipity, Emma23 K, Emx, Enchanter, EnderHegemony, Entoaggie09, Epbr123, Epeefleche, Eplack, Epson291, Erasoft24, Erencexor, EricWesBrown, Ericci8996, Erik503, Ermawiki, Erpingham, Esperant, Esprit15d, Esrogs, Estevoaei, Esthertaffet, Eternal Pink, Eternalsleeper, Euphrosyne, EurekaLott, Ev149, EventHorizon, Everlast1910, EveryDayJoe45, Everyguy, Everything counts, Evil saltine, Excirial, Exeunt, Expletivization, EyeRmonkey, Eysen, FCYTravis, FDR, FF2010, Facebookghost, Falcon8765, Falsetto, Fancypants09, Farine, FatalError, Favonian, Fbv65edel, Feasoron, Felixboy, Fennec, FeralDruid, Ferdiaob, Fetchcomms, FetchcommsAWB, Ffgamera, Fielding42, Filippowiki, FireBlizzard, FirefoxRocks, Firsfron, Fishman17, Fixer1234, FlamingFlamingo, FlamingSilmaril, Flamurai, Flashflash;, Flatterworld, Flewis, Flibbert, Florentino floro, Flyguy649, Flyingember, Fmccown, Fooladin, Foosh, Foregone conclusion, Format, Former user 2, Fortdj33, Frank1470, Franz-kafka, Frap, Frecklefoot, FrenchIsAwesome, FreplySpang, Frexes, Friendocity, Froid, Fromgermany, Frosted14, Fstutzman, FullMetal Falcon, Funandtrvl, Fuzheado, FxckNelson, Fæ, G7yunghi, GB fan, GBVrallyCI, GRRE, GRuban, GSchjetne, Gabe1972, Gaia Octavia Agrippa, Gakusha, Galforfia, Galileo99, Garethhamilton, Garik, Gary King, Gatewaycat, Gavzey, Gcr 2007, Gdo01, GeZe, Geary, Geneffects, GeneralBelly, GeneralCheese, Genkizkhan2004, Geo19 4, Geoking66, Geometry guy, George Pelltier, GeorgeBuchanan, Georgebrown92, Ger4llt, Geraldpringle, Gert7, Gertie1999, Gianfranco, Giganotosaurus Fan12345, Gilliam, Gioto, Girlwithgreeneyes, Gizmoleeds, GlassCobra, Glassgowkiss, Glen, Glenn Magus Harvey, Glennh70, Gltimmons, Goalloverhere, Gogo Dodo, Gogomkd123, GoldenGoose100, Golopoi23, Gonzonoir, Goob, Goodmanjaz, Goodnightmush, Gordi555, Goujas1979, Gphoto, Gpwhld, Gracenotes, Graham87, GrahameS, Grampion76, Grant McKenna, Grapetonix, Green-eyed girl, Greeves, Greg Comlish, Gregfitzy, GregorB, Gregorydavid, Grendles modor, Grundig, Gsarwa, Gscshoyru, Gtstricky, Gtsully, Gugubeans, Gunmetal Angel, Gunnar Larsson, Gupraabishek, Gurch, Guroadrunner, Gus Polly, Guyinblack25, Guyjohnston, Gwernol, H2g2bob, HTIDPH, HYC, Ha us 70, Hacker2000, Hackstar18, Hadal, Haha169, Halsteadk, Hamidejaz, Hammer Raccoon, Hammer15, Hammer1980, Hamsterlopithecus, Hans3778, Haon, Happyisenough, Happyme22, Hardeharhar, Harel, Harionlad, Harrydevoil, Hartewyu, HarveyHenkelmann, Haven40, Havocrazy, Hawkhkg11, Hbdragon88, Headit 3523, Hectorhector, HeinzzzderMannn, Heliostellar, Henrymrx, Hera1aphrodite, Hermione is a dude, Heroeswithmetaphors, HershlayDammit!, Hertz1888, Herwest, Hhi0901, Hhtfdomhki, HiLo48, Hildanknight, Hinchu, Hippo43, Historylover9893, Hleder, Hlm Z., Hmains, Hmwith, Hoary, Hobbsface2000, Holder, Homologeo, Hordaland, Hosszuka, Hotpinkshoes, HowardRob, Hschmid1, Htang3085, Htanna, Hu12, Hunter95, Husond, Hv, Hyleslie, Hypnosadist, I lyk breathing, I'mDown, I5bala, I8ASHOE, IHaresh, IJA, Ianjdickson2, Iankap99, Icecradle, Icedog, Icetall, Icetea8, Ida Shaw, Idetik, Igorberger, Ihope127, IlSoge, Ilkeston1990, Illinois2011, Ilovespears, Imcanadian69, InShaneee, Infinitum17, Ingenious14, Ingolfson, Instantnematode, Intelliot, Interchange88, Interscan, Iokerapid, Iph, Ipodfanz, Iran.azadi, Iridescent, Irish Souffle, Irishguy, IronGargoyle, Ironmagma, Irrypride, Isaac, Isatemple, Ishwasafish, Ismashed, Isnow, It's-is-not-a-genitive, Its time for time, IvanLanin, Ixfd64, J Di, J-beda, J. Nguyen, J.delanoy, JARSInc, JCDenton2052, JEN9841, JForget, JGXenite, JHP, JHunterJ, JJJJust, JJLatWiki, JaGa, Jackdyson, Jacobnut, Jacobolus, Jacono, Jaizovic, Jakub Vrána, Jamcib, James Roberts, JamesBWatson, Jameshfisher, Jamestaylor121, JamminBen, Jammy Tan, Jampearls, Jandalhandler, JanusK, Jaranda, Jared Hunt, Jareha, Jarjarbinks10, Jarsta, Java13690, Jay Gatsby, JaysOnMyFeet190, Jbmurray, Jburge, Jdw4jesus, Jean-Marie Favre, Jeanenawhitney, Jedcore, Jeff G., Jeffwang, Jeffykan, JeiTana, Jek339, Jem76, Jengirl1988, Jennyfer b, Jeremy Banks, Jeremy Visser, JeremyMcCracken, Jerickson314, Jerroleth, Jersey Devil, Jersyko, JetBlast, Jethro 82, Jetong, Jezarnold, Jfade, Jgalt23, Jharris700, Jiffles1, Jim Douglas, Jim McKeeth, Jimmy, Jimmy19, JimmyMac82, Jj137, Jjb52, Jjflex, Jjmanoman, Jlee1973, Jmfavre, JoeSmack, JoeyJoJoShabbaduJr, John, John Broughton, John Nevard, JohnKlax, Johnc69, Johningardia, Johnjosephbachir, Johnuniq, Jojit fb, Jonathan Barrett, JonathonReinhart, Jonny-mt, Jonpin, Jonthon, Jopo sf, Joschuaz, Jose8397, Josh99666, Joshua Issac, Joshuagross, Joshuapaquin, Joshw, Jossi, Jpunzel, Jrgilmore, Jryfle, Jschwa1, Jsplegge, Jtneill, JuJube, Jubileeclipman, Juledi, Julesd, Junhua Chang, Junkcops, Jusdafax, Justinboden86, Justinmmitchell, Jvcdude, Jwking, K. Takeda, K.O.T., KPH2293, KVDP, Kai svenson, Kakofonous, Kalyan3, Kamokazi, Kamoranakrre T. Eyaelitenan, Kane5187, Kansan, Kanyelover2231312, Kapla2004, KaragouniS, Karan9005, KarlDubost, Karthik Jagadeesh, Kate, Katerg, Katimawan2005, Katoh, Katydidit, Kbrose, Kea2, Keensdesign, Keeperofthesea1, Keepsleeping, Keilana, KeithD, Kencf0618, Kendrick7, Kenyon, Kernigh, Kernow, Kertof, Kevinmon, Kfeto, Khanbhaijaan, Kidlittle, King kilr, Kingboshcash, Kingboyk, KirbyMaster14, Kiwi Ranger, Kiy765630, Kkm010, Kkrouni, Klingon83, Kmsiever, Knowledge Seeker, Koavf, Komitsuki, Koolgiy, Kormin, Kozuch, Krylonblue83, Ktr101, Kudelv, Kukini, Kurt Shaped Box, Kuru, Kurykh, Kushboy, Kusma, Kwamikagami, Kycowboyntv, Kyle1278, Kyleoz, Kylevk, KyuuA4, LAX, LGagnon, LIVERPOOLFCCFLOOPREVIL, LOL, La Pianista, Laguna72, Lala887, Lambiam, Lambyuk, Lamperta, Larry laptop, Lasdlt, Laserusjm, LastLived, Latics, Latish redone, Law, Laxg0alie, Lazerhawk, Lbh1402, Lcarscad, Leafyplant, LeeHunter, Leftydan6, LegitimateAndEvenCompelling, Leki, Lemjok, Lesley.wheeler, Leuqarte, Level plus, Levineps, Liface, Lightmouse, Lights, Ligulem, Lihaas, Likeitsmyjob, Likelife, LilHelpa, Lilac Soul, Lincolnite, LindsayH, Lineface, Ling.Nut, Lither, Little Professor, Ljkitson, Lkprinceton, Llywrch, Lmdxx, Lmessenger, LmfaoManX2, Localbatman, Locos epraix, Logan, Loganberry, Longshot.222, LookingGlass, Lord Hawk, Lord Pistachio, Loren.wilton, Lost4eva, Lost98789, LostLeviathan, Lostart, Lotje, Louisstar, Lowellian, LoyolaDude, Lradrama, Luboogers25, Luisztdt, Luk, Lukeconnell, Luna Santin, Lutzee, Lvivske, M.O.X, M412k, MASTERuser, MBK004, MC32, MER-C, MMSwa02, MOF, MUFC47JJ, MacTire02, Mackatacka123, Macman16a, Madchester, Madras fp, Magacid, Magentabanana, Maggiecuda, Magister Mathematicae, MainBody, Majorly, Makgraf, Malakai777, Malickfan86, Malinaccier, Manderson198, Manop, MarXidad, Marcoboy, Marcus Qwertyus, Margetheintern, Mariomedici707, Mark, Mark0528, MarkHab, MarkS, Markeilz, Markharding93, Markiyan, Markmayhew, Marlova, MarmadukePercy, Marozols, MarritzN, MarsRover, Martarius, Martianlostinspace, Martin Hinks, Martinovic, MaryseHelene, Master of Puppets, Mathewd48, Mathprog777, Matt Gies, Matt107bghs, Mattdaley1, Matteh, Matterson52, Matthew Komorowski, MatthewBurton, MatthewTStone, Maurice Carbonaro, Maury Markowitz, Mav12321, Max rspct, MaxVeers, Maxim, Maximilian Caldwell, Maxí, Mazphd, Mcemce123, Mcmillin24, MdReisman, Mdavidson98, Mdawg728, Mdb20, Mdlawmba, Mdriver1981, Mdwh, Meandyou22, MearsMan, Mecanismo, Meco, Meeples, Megandiamond, MegastarLV, Meishern, Melb113, Meme918, Mememe909, MementoVivere, Memoirofdarkness, Memorized, Mencey, Meno25, MercolaOverMerck, Merrickb, Metallurgist, Mharb12, Mhiji, Michael Hardy, Michael J Swassing, Michael Leap, Michael lambert84, Michaelkourlas, MichaelsProgramming, Michaelvkim, MickMacNee, Mickleib, Micro101, Mido, Midway, Mieciu K, Mierdaan, Mike 7, Mike Halterman, Mike Schwartz, MikeAllen, MikeMorley, Mikeistheman, Mikieminnow, Mild Bill Hiccup, Minimac, Mintchocicecream, Mipadi, Miranda, MississippiBeau, Mitch1981, Mjayers, Mjb1981, Mjbugeja, Mjm46530690, Mkdw, Mm40, Modster, Mohammed2696, Mohnkern, Moncrief, Mongol, MoodyGroove, Moooon25, Mooseking0, Morgensternen, MorrisS, Morshem, Mostlyharmless, Moveoverlol660, Mr Beale, Mr Chuckles, Mr. 57, Mr. Absurd, Mr.Slinks, Mr.whiskers, MrBoo, MrJaywod1, MrOllie, MrZeebo, Mreditguy, Mrestko, Mrmuk, Mrprasad, Mrrightguy10, Mryozocripz, Mswer, Mtd074, Mukkakukaku, Mullahmatt, Mumble45, Murph146, Mustycrusty, Mutchy126, Muzzamo, Mx3, Mypantsarefun, Mysdaao, Mysekurity, N Shar, N-edits, N.B.Kitsune, N96, NAHID, NBS525, NCSS, NHRHS2010, Nadyes, Nakon, Namdlefhtes, NameThatWorks, Nareshov, Nasht, Nastajus, Natalie Erin, Nathan Williams, Naturada137, Nauticashades, Navigation12, NawlinWiki, Ndboy, Ndickson, Nealmcb, NederlandsNederlands, Neelix, Neo-Jay, NeoVampTrunks, NeonMerlin, Neorge, Netwhizkid, Neverquick, Neward Rylet, Newkai, Ngb, Nhprman, Nic Waller, Niceley, Nickb32, Nicolas1981, Nightdevil40, Nightstallion, Nihiltres, Niljay, Nima1024, Nippoo, Nishantman, Nishkid64, Nitelighter, Niteowlneils, Nitya Dharma, Nivix, Nixdorf, Nixeagle, Nlsanand, Noeticsage, Nol888, Nomader, Nomore, Nopetro, Northern, NorthernThunder, Not a dog, Noteremote, Nothlit, Nowa, Nslimak, NuclearWarfare, Numbo3, Nurg, NurseryRhyme, Nutanthakurlko, Nvm, Nyroska, Nyttend, O, OCNative, ONEder Boy, OSUKid7, Octahedron80, Octane, Oddtoddnm, OhanaUnited, Ohconfucius, Ohnoitsjamie, Oli Filth, Ombudswiki, Omicronpersei8, Omphaloscope, Oneupthextraman, Onorem, Ont, Oore, Ophois, Opokoko22, Ordinaterr, OregonD00d, Oreo Priest, Orfannkyl, OsFan, OsamaK, Oscarthecat, Osiriscorleone, Oskar Mayer Nguyener, Ott2, Ottawahitech, Overandover, OwenX, Owu07, Oxwil, Oxymoron83, Oyg, Ozzmosis, PGPirate, PRRfan, Pablothegreat85, Paddonm, Pais, Palashrijan, Palmiped, Pancakelizard, PandaSorn, Paridox, Parralax, Passingtramp, PassionoftheDamon, Patriarch, Patstuart, Paul Magnussen, Pauswa, Paxse, Peanut4, Peatymasta, PedroPerez, Penarc, Pengo, Pentasyllabic, Pepsidrinka, Per Abrahamsen, Perfecto, Perlman10s, Perseus, Son of Zeus, Perspicacite, Peschomd, Peter Napkin Dance Party, PeterSymonds, Peterwhy, Petey05, Phansen, Phgao, Philip Trueman, PhilipO, Philippe, Philwelch, Phoenix2, Piano non troppo, Pigsonthewing, Pilcrow, Pinas Central, Pinecar, Pinkadelica, Piotrus, Pip2andahalf, Pipep, Piper108, Pitoutom, Pixgarden, Pizza1512, Pkninja, Plasticbadge, Plasticup, Plazmatyk, Plm209, Plop, Poddarrishabh, Polarix, Pollo9087, Pomte, Pontillo, Pontus Lindengren, Poolboy8, Possum, Pradeepmallika, Pressforaction, PrezCRG, Proger, ProhibitOnions, Protiek, Prowikipedians, Pruneau, Ps2avery, PsY.cHo, Psantora, Pscheimann, Psellis, Pswiney, Ptothej, Purple Paint, Purpledigital, Pwnage8, Pwu2005, Pxma, Pyroponce, Pyrospirit, Quadratic, Quantumor, Quarl, Quatloo, Quibik, Quiname, Quinsareth, Quintin3265, Qviri, R'n'B, R27182818, RG2, Racso, RadioActive, Radon210, RainbowOfLight, Raineybt, Rajington, Ral725, Rami83, RandomHumanoid, Raprules7942005, Rapterrorist, RaseaC, Rat144, Rathfelder, Ravanacker, Raysonho, Razvanus, Rbarpar, Rdc525, Rdsmith4, Rebroad, Red marquis, RedHouse18, RedRose333, Redeyed Treefrog, Redgecko20, Redgwan, Redsully, Redthoreau, Refsworldlee, Reh303, ReidarM, Relly Komaruzaman, Remy B, Renosecond, Requestion, Ret.Prof, Retired username, RexNL, Reywas92, Rgb1110, Rgsupplies16, Rhetoricity, Riana, Ricebowl81, Rich Farmbrough, Richard001, Richard0612, RidinHood25, Rigid ember, Rikki agarwal, Rimush, RjCan, Rjd0060, Rjwilmsi, Rlarue1, Rm999, Robbor, Rober1236jua, Robert9673, Roberta F., Robertson-Glasgow, RobinsonWM, Roboguyspacedude, Robor09, Robstothard, RockMFR, Rockapoc, RocketJohnson, Romit3, Romney yw, Ronline, Ronz, Ronzie, Rorschach, Rory096, RossPatterson, RoyBoy, Royalguard11, Rprpr, Rrjanbiah, Rrlynch, Rsciaccio, Rspahnn, Ru-G Corp., Ruckruck, Rusted AutoParts, Rusty8, Rwwww, Rwxrwxrwx, Ryalesw, RyanH135, RyanHassall, Ryn2me, Ryulong, S.dedalus, S.Örvarr.S, SE7, SF007, SFGiants, SQGibbon, ST47, STM86, SWAdair, Saeed Jahed, Sahasrahla, Salacio, Sallysafety, Salspsyche, SaltyBoatr, Sam77g77, SamTheOptomist, Samuel Buca, Samueljeisen, Samvscat, Sanajcs, SandManMattSH, Sander123, SandyDancer, Sannse, Santaduck, Sanxiyn, Sasha Callahan, SatansAngel231, Saulcruz, Saulesha, Savidan, Savirr, Sbamkmfdmdfmk, Sbressler, Scartol, Scepia, Sceptre, Schmancy47, Schmloof, Schultz5, SchuminWeb, Schutz, Sclarfie, Scm83x, Scootnasty, Scottandrewhutchins, Scwlong, Scythe33, Scythre, Sean c griffin, Seaneld86, Seazzy, Sebcastle, SecretIdentityNumber26, Sepreece, Sepulveda, Seraphimblade, Sesshomaru, Shadow1, Shagmaestro, Shah.akshay15, ShambhalaFestival, Shannonwulff, Shantavira, Shawnc, Shenme, Sheppa28, Shii, Shimgray, Shirik, Shoecream, Shoeofdeath, ShootFrank, Shovonma17, Shuipzv3, Sicronet, Sidhekin, SilkTork, SilkySword, Silver mask cube, Simetrical, Simon Shek, Simon lock, SimonP, SimplySweet, Simulation90, Sincityaustyn, Singularity, Sinn, Sir.xerces, SirJibby, SixxiA, Sizzlemctwizzle, Skatolopunksax, Sketchmoose, Skier Dude, Skinnypez, Skitedude, Sko1221, Skomorokh, Skysmith, Slavakion, Slavatrudu, SlimVirgin, Slowking Man, Slysplace, SmartGuy, Smartse, Smelendez, SmokeyTheCat, Smyth, Snail Doom, Solomonmaimen, Solphusion, Somertime, Something9162, Somody, Souljamike, Soulmerge, Soundcomm, Sp35k3r, Spangineer, Sparkyingva, SparqMan, SparrowsWing, Spartacusprime, Spartanfox86, Spartas, Spectorza, Spell4yr, Spiffy sperry, SpikeZoft, SportsBrain2009, Spud Gun, SpuriousQ, SqueakBox, SquidSK, Sreejith M S, Ssj5perfect cell, St ttb, St.daniel, Staka, Stakelum, Starbuzz3d, Starrynite81, Startstop123, Startswithj, Steamroller Assault, Stephen MUFC, Stephenb, Stepheng3, Stepho22224, StepsTogether, Stevage, Steve Winter, Steven Walling, Stevenmansour, Stickee, Stoboe, Strawberryfire, Straxus, Student4, Stunetii, Subdolous, Subsume, Sue Gardner, Suhel1992, Suhmeister, Sujeet787, SujinYH, Sulinda11, SummerWithMorons, SuperHamster, Superbeecat, Superbowlbound, Superfascist, Supersaiyan474, Superstan999, Supersuzanne, Susan118, SusanLesch, Susanwell, Swarm, Swechsle, Swerty, SwisterTwister, TAGosselin, TEApollonius, TGilmour, TJRC, TKD, TPIRFanSteve, Tackyjulio, Tagus, Tajalam2, Tanvir Ahmmed, Taopman, Taras, Tarheelcoxn, Tavix, Taylorhope, Tbhotch, Tcalight, Tcwilliams, Tdl1060, Tea and crumpets, TeaDrinker, Teanywini123, Teapotgeorge, TeddyCarey, TedlyW, TehBrandon, Telstar2, Templetongore, Tenebrae, Tennisuser123, Terrett101, Tetobigbro, Tetzcatlipoca, Tewfik, Tezero, Thadius856, ThatWikiGuy, Thatperson, Thbsp, The Evil Spartan, The Founders Intent, The GOAT, The Giant Puffin, The Horned Water, The Jacobin, The Nut, The Obento Musubi, The Person Who Is Strange, The Realms of Gold, The Rock And Roll Pirate, The Wednesday Island, The lorax, The undertow, The wub, TheAznSensation, TheBilly, TheCustomOfLife, TheGerm, TheNewPhobia, ThePedanticPrick, TheQuaker, TheThomas, TheTrueAPlus, Theanphibian, Thebrandonshow, Thecurran91, Theda, Thelegendofvix, Themaludude101, Thepulse2007, Thesquire, Thessaysno, Thingg, Thirdeyeopen33, Thisbites, Thomassnee, Threeafterthree, Thumperward, Tide rolls, Tigerghost, Timothyarnold85, Timsdad, Timstown, Tinton5, Titoxd, Tj21, Tkessler, Tkgd2007, Tktktk, Tm1000, Tobor0, TobyDZ, Toddfast, Tolbert5, Tom, TomServo, Tomfisherman, Tommy2010, Tomroes, Tony1, Tony4346, Tony7444, Tooto, Topher8, Topperray, Tosenton, Tourettes1993, Tpbradbury, Tranix, TrbleClef, TreasuryTag, Tree Biting Conspiracy, Tremolo, TrendyLegs, Trevor MacInnis, Treyp, Treyt021, Tri400, TriciaAustin, Trivialist, Troysteinbauer, Truth2008Exists, Trvsdrlng, Tundern, TwilligToves, Twrdave, Tygar, Typhoonchaser, Typogr, TyrS, U21980, UCLARodent, URORIN, Ubiq, Ugen64, Uiteoi, UkPaolo, Ukulele, Ulflarsen, Ulkomaalainen, Ultiam, Ultimus, Ultra-Loser, Umawera, Umer88, Uncfan2000, Uncle G, Uncompetence, Undertaker2134, Unitalk, Unitanode, UnitedStatesian, Universal Hero, Uogl, Userpd, Utcursch, UtherSRG, Utubegangsters, VKokielov, Vagary, Valley2city, Vanis314, Varco, Veetrag, Vegaswikian, Ventusa, Verdlanco, Veritycowper, Versageek, Vgmddg, Vic93, Vicarvictor, Vikipediisto, Vilefile, Violacadenza, Violiszt, Viriditas, Virtual Particle, VirtualSteve, Vlad, Vlad788, Vn4m, Vsmith, Vvuser, WAS, WILLY ON WHEELZzzz, WODUP, WTGDMan1986, Wabed, Wackywace, Wahabijaz, Waleed, Walloon, Walor, Wapondaponda, WarpstarRider, Waterjuice, Wavelength, Wayne Slam, WebHamster, Webfan29, Weedar, Weesnaw117, Weierstrass, WestJet, WhatisFeelings?, Wherewithal, WhisperToMe, White eskimo, Whitecap, Wickethewok, Wiki alf, WikiAnthony, WikiDan61, WikiLaurent, Wikichange, Wikidemon, Wikidrone, Wikifox, Wikiklrsc, Wikiloop, Wikimalta, Wikipedian06, WikipedianMarlith, Wikipedical, Wikipidyst, Wikitonic, WikkiBurr, William Graham, Wimt, WinusB, Wirewad, Witz87, Wizardman, Wj32, Wknight94, Woober, Woody, Woohookitty,

Wumas214, Wwallacee, XGA geek, Xaosflux, Xavier andrade, Xeno, Xijjix, Xkfusionxk, Xlittlewhitelieo, Xmnemonic, Xnatedawgx, Xnuala, Xobxela, Xp54321, Xqt, Xxxfy123xxx, Y2kcrazyjoker4, Yabaa, Yaifuz26, Yamamoto Ichiro, Yaoming7511, Yboord028, Yelsent, Yeshyesh93, Ygfperson, Yizmo, Yjo, Yk Yk Yk, Yuccara, Yug, Yuggihol, Yvesnimmo, ZacBowling, ZacharyM001, Zambaccian, Zamkudi, Zanimum, Zaphraud, Zararo, Zaskie, Zchris87v, Zebov, Zeke72791, Zellin, ZimZalaBim, Zime2005, Ziva David, Zohaib ather, Zonath, ZoomDude, Zubair71, Zummis, Zzomtceo, Zzuuzz, ^demon, Александр Мотин, Петър Петров, 达伟, 2714 anonymous edits

Twitter *Source*: http://en.wikipedia.org/w/index.php?oldid=439241856 *Contributors*: (npcserver), *Αλέξανδρος, 10metreh, 16@r, 1973mfb, 1wolfblake, 22dahit, 242Selby, 2z, 336, 45ossington, 4urge, 68DANNY2, 7OA, A Macedonian, A.Ward, A3camero, AMK1211, APassionCane, Abunet, Acalamari, AdamG-PhotoShare, AdamJGSea, Adamwilcox, Adremja, Adrian232, Adwiii, Aeon17x, Aerodude96, Ageekgal, Agentbla, Aglyad, Ahirreddy, Airplaneman, Akamad, Al3xpayne, Alansohn, Alarics, Albertlg, Alboran, Aldaron, Aldnonymous, Alegoo92, Aleksandrit, Alex Neman, AlexBriggs13, Alexhch, AlexiusHoratius, Alhutch, AlisonW, Aliwa156, Alix.simon, Alyssa711, Amalthea, AnOddName, Anaxial, And3k, Andrew Filipe, Andrewlp1991, Andy, Andy Dingley, Andy Marchbanks, Anirvan, Anna, Anomie, Anonymous Dissident, Anonymoususer666, Anthony Appleyard, Antilived, Antonio Lopez, Antrikshy, Anwar saadat, Apoorv020, Arctic Night, Areeb cool, Aremisasling, Arsonal, Art LaPella, Arthena, Aschmidt, Ashanda, Ashton Rainwater, Ashwin.sri, Asruge, Atavi, Attilios, Auréola, AussieSamiLOL, Autarch, Avaarga, AvicAWB, Avicennasis, Avoided, Awb49, AxelBoldt, Aye Carumba Fajita Pizza, Ayrton Prost, Azure, BLOLMOM, BWP1234, BabbaQ, Backtable, Banaticus, Bansipatel, Barefootmeg, Barek, Barkman, Barnabypage, BarretBonden, Bart133, Baseball Watcher, Bblboy54, Bejinhan, Beland, Bellagio99, Bellewroy, Bender235, Bennylin, Bento00, Bevo, Beyoncé Superfanatic, Bhood4550, BigSexyJoe76, BigToe7000, Bigturtle, Biguana, Billbowery, Billinghurst, Billwhittaker, BillyPreset, Black Condor, Blainster, Blanchardb, Bnordlund, Boaf, Bob bobato, Boba-Fett64, Bocskey5, Boerewors, Bogey97, Boing! said Zebedee, Boleyn, Boots908, BorisVeldhuijzenvanZanten, Borkert, BostonRed, Boud, Boul22435, Bowmanjj, BradHD, Bradleytee, BrainyBabe, BrekekekexKoaxKoax, Brettstaylor, BritishWatcher, Britonkolber, BrotherSulayman, BrownHairedGirl, Browndog72, Brownsteve, Brucelee, Bryan.burgers, Bsadowski1, Bubba73, BullRangifer, BurtAlert, C.Fred, C6541, CAH-x-, Cacuija, Cae1990, Cagedether, Calliopejen1, Cameron Scott, Camoz87, Can't sleep, clown will eat me, CanadianLinuxUser, Canaima, Candoent, CapitalR, Capitalistroadster, CardinalDan, Carmichael95, Carolinesedda, Carre, Carruthk, Casassussan, Catgut, Catheorz, Cbreitel, Ccacsmss, CcolbyS, CecilWard, CenterofGravity, CerberuS, Cgmusselman, Chadfmartin, Chainsawriot, Charithjayanada, Charlette Proto, Chatfecter, Ched Davis, Cheermusic, Cheong Kok Chun, Chexov29, Chicago2011, Chickenlittle 850, Chitetskoy, Chost2016, ChrisThomson24, Chzz, Cic, Cindamuse, Cjvandyk, Ckatz, Ckdaro, Ckedwell, Clamshell Deathtrap, Cleany12, Cleared as filed, Clerkwheel11, CliffC, Cluetrainee, Cmadler, Cntras, CobiJa, Colbpa, Comccoy, Compasshc, Computerjoe, ConcernedVancouverite, Confession0791, Conti, Corbett3000, Courcelles, Crarysocom, Crash Underride, Crimsonnail, Crisco 1492, Cswpride, Cultureoftrust, Cursif, Cuteybubble, Cutfromtheteam, CyberSkull, Cybercobra, Cymru.lass, Cyvh, D-Notice, DAG JM, DARTH SIDIOUS 2, DMacks, DMahalko, Da Joe, DaRaeMan, Dabomb87, Daedalus969, Dagko, Dagmon, Daj12192, Dancraggs, Daniel Hen, Danlev, Danzigland, Darcyj, DasallmächtigeJ, Daven200520, Davewho2, David Rush, David Shankbone, Dcljr, Deanybabeh, Deathgleaner, Debresser, Decora, Dejaphoenix, DelPlaya, Delish90, Denelson83, Dennis Brown, Dennistoninc, Dentren, Deoma12, Derek.munneke, Deshabhakta, DeusExa, Diannaa, Dicesitalianice, Diobaithyn, Dionyziz, Discospinster, Dissolve, Diving2010, Diza, Dizikaygisiz, Djc wi, Dmarquard, Docu, Dodiedodie, Dodomonkey221, Dogfacebob, Doh5678, Donebythesecondlaw, DonnaTC, Doomsdayer520, Dottydotdot, Doug, Download, Dr. Blofeld, Dr.K., Draxtreme, Dreadstar, Dream out loud, Dreamyshade, Drewclick77, Drmies, Drone007, Drpickem, Drummerblvd, Duagloth, Dumshizz, Dwell88, Dy2007, Dycedarg, EEMIV, EHartwell, ERcheck, Eagle744, Eastlaw, Ebe123, Ed g2s, EdJogg, Edgarde, EditorOf2011, Edkollin, EdoDodo, Eduardoferreira, Edward, Eenu, Efcmagnew, Egil, Eiland, Einstein runner, El Pocho, Elassint, Elb2000, Electricalaskan, EliasG21, Elipongo, Elizium23, Elsheimy, Emerson7, Emiltsch, Emma23 K, EmuhGurrl.08, Eneteng Kabisote, Engl102amm, Enviroboy, Epbr123, Epeefleche, Epgui, Eric, Ericlee, Erifneerg, ErrantX, Es330td, Escape Orbit, EscapedGorilla, Esprit15d, Ethel the aardvark, EurekaLott, Everard Proudfoot, Everyonee-anything, Everything counts, Evgenimakarov, Evildeathmath, Evyn, EwokiWiki, Explicit, ExplicitImplicity, F00P, FHen, Fabian5003, Faithlessthewonderboy, FaktneviM, Falcon9x5, Fanatix, Fancy-cats-are-happy-cats, Fastily, FatalError, Father Goose, Fayenatic london, Feduciary, Fetchcomms, Ff1959, Fifthnail, Finetooth, Finin, Fischer.sebastian, FlamingSilmaril, Flowanda, Fluppy, Fly by Night, FlyingToaster, Foodimentary, Foofighter20x, Fordmadoxfraud, Fram, FrameWave20, FrankCarper, FrankTobia, Frankarr, Fraxtil, Freakedout, Frecklefoot, Frehley, Fresheneesz, Fruitbat101, Fruitking98, Funandtrvl, Funguy06, Funtaff, Furrykef, Fusho, Fvw, Fw5150, G.W., GDallimore, GFellows, GSK, Gabrielseed, Gaga111, GageSkidmore, Gaius Octavius Princeps, Galahaut, Gallery J, Gameplaya888, Gareth E Kegg, Gargaj, Gary King, Gavint0, Gavreh, Gccheer, GearedBull, Geni, Geobpenguin, Geoffman13, Georger55, Gerardw, Gfoley4, Gforce20, Gfp1968, Gil mo, Giveitlegs, Glasscity09, Gleask, Glennwells, Glst2, Goalloverhere, Gogo Dodo, GoingBatty, GoodbyeRosie, Googy, Gpia7r, Gpwhld, Grafen, Graham87, Grampion76, GreenGourd, Greenrd, Greg Tyler, GregC, GregManninLB, Ground Zero, Grunge6910, Gsarwa, Gsthst, Gunmetal Angel, Guy Harris, GyroMagician, H3llkn0wz, Haha169, Halemane, HalfShadow, HandThatFeeds, Happyflappy1, Harry Lake, Haza-w, HeadlightMorning, HelloImStorm, Heroeswithmetaphors, Hervegirod, Historypundit, Hjones567, Hmwith, Honeytech, HordeFTL, Horkana, Hrothgar15, Htanna, Hughtcool, Hullaballoo Wolfowitz, Hum0hallelujah, Human.v2.0, Humanisticmystic, Husky, Hydrargyrum, Hydrogen Iodide, HyperCapitalist, Hzshen, IGAT, ISD, Iamdeadnow, Iamhappy :), Iamzim93, Ianmacm, Ida Shaw, Ike-bana, Ilsjwnmcgbob, Iluvwiki1, Ilyakub, Imorthodox23, Indon, Indonesiahits, IngerAlHaosului, Inknoise, Insanatic, Insommia, Intelati, Ioeth, Ipsofacto123, Iridescent, Isaac Rabinovitch, Isaiah(creator), Ithizar, IvanLanin, IveFoundit, J o, J.delanoy, JBsupreme, JCDenton2052, JForget, JGXenite, JHunterJ, JMS Old Al, JTroisi89, JV Smithy, JacksonProductions, Jacob Poon, Jacobownsnoobs1, Jahsonic, Jakobalewis, Jalabi99, JamesMLane, JamesMcGuiggan, Jamessssss147258369, Jamiedixon, JanCK, Jansegers, Jarhed, Jasondburkert, Jasperrees, Jatkins, JavaTenor, Jay2009m, JayJasper, Jayglenn204, Jcarroll, JeevesWilliams, Jeff G., Jenkinsp, Jenks24, Jenmitch, Jeppesn, Jeremy Bolwell, Jerzy, Jessaharp, Jgera5, Jhenderson777, Jhw57, Jibbist, JimParsons, Jivecat, Jjd24, Jjron, Jmatthew3, Jodi.a.schneider, Jodrell, Joelrex, JohnCD, Johndburger, Johnjohn142, Johnred32, Jolly Janner, JonGarfunkel, JonSmet, Jonathanmjefferies, Jonathannip, Jopo sf, Josephgrossberg, JoshMarino420, Jouva, Joycloete, Jpbowen, Jpgovekar, Jrobin08, Juancnuno, Jujubean55, Julesd, Juliancolton, Julle, JustinArmstrong, Jwihbey, Jwmsfoben, K ideas, Kaarlows, Kai Tatsu, Kamath.nakul, Kapanka, KarenViceroy, Kayvee, Kbh3rd, Kehrbykid, Kennedymmkay, Kenyon, Keristrasza, Kessler, Kevang, Kevin, Kevphenry, Khalfani khaldun, Kichwa, Kigabo, Kimmylimmited, Kingpin13, Kkm010, Klelith, Klondike, Kmote, Koavf, Kolocha, Koman90, Komitsuki, Kriskras, Kross, Kshieh, Kuralyov, KuroiShiroi, Kyle1278, Kyng, L Kensington, Labboy, Lamename3000, Langhorner, Languagehat, Lansey, Lars Washington, Lars005, Laurence891, Lawl95, Lboulton, Leachyboy77, Leftmostcat, Legion fi, Lentower, Leroy573, Lester, Leszek Jańczuk, Levineps, Lewis TCM, Lexington96, Lightmouse, LilHelpa, Lilac Soul, Limideen, LinguistAtLarge, Linguisticgeek, Livecrunch, Livrachelle, Llusiduonbach, Locos epraix, Lollbirdsey, Loranp, Lordb, Lotje, Louiemantia, Lucyatchalk, Lukep913, Lwc, Lynbarn, Lyverbe, M7, MER-C, MJ94, Ma sassan, Macman44, MacsBug, Madberry, Magentabanana, Mandarax, Manonfire94, Manop, Manormadman, Marasmusine, Marcus Qwertyus, Margetheintern, Marianastrenchfreak, Mariomedici707, MarkGGN, Markdandrea, MarmadukePercy, Martarius, Martin451, MartinPackerIBM, Martindiano, Martnym, MassvMaster, Mattarata, Matthew Fennell, Matthewrlee, Mattisse, Matttwd, Mattybusiness1, Mauler90, Maxamegalon2000, Mc8755, Mcdy, Mcld, Mcmahonc28, Mczapp, Mdaniels, Mdl53711, Meaghannf, Melikbilge, Melissabrah, Melvalevis, Meno25, Mentifisto, Meowmix4jo, Mercury McKinnon, MetaManFromTomorrow, Michael Hardy, MichaelJohnNielsen, Michaelh2001, Michaelpraetorius, Midnight Love, Midway, Micciu K, MikeLynch, Mikecraig, Mikewax, Mimzy1990, Mipadi, Mjquinn id, Mmcneish, Mmmmm1000, Mmolaire, Mohamed mashaly, Mojei, MonkeyHouseOfPain, Mono, Montrealais, Moodymoon2598, Moozipan Cheese, Morgankevinj, Moritherapy, Mortense, Motormat, Movieguruman, Mpalermo14, MrHighway, MrOllie, Mrflip, Msnicki, Msr69er, Munchman, MylesCallum, Myomancer, Mzajac, NCSS, Naftprod, Nagy, Nakon, NameThatWorks, Nasa-verve, Nate1481, Nathan7la, Naumov, NawlinWiki, NecroBlze, Neon white, NerdyScienceDude, Netweb, Neustradamus, Nicholaidrevin, NicholasSThompson, NickD, Nickyus, Nicolas1981, Nicster09, Niekfct, Nightscream, Nihil, Nips, Noleander, Norquist9, Northumbrian, NortyNort, Not a dog, Notyourbroom, Notyourhoom, Nsaa, NuclearWarfare, Nyenyec, Nz101, O.neill.kid, ONEder Boy, Ocaasi, Occono, Offenbach, OhSqueezy, Ohnoitsjamie, Old Guard, Oliphaunt, OliviaPhelps, Onebravemonkey, Onesius, Optimist on the run, Orange Suede Sofa, Orbixhost, Orfen, OsamaK, Osborne, OsvaldoGago, Ottawahitech, Ottre, Outsidethewall, Ouvyt, OwenBlacker, Ozzdawg, PBP, PKT, Pafferguy, PahaOlo, Palfrey, Palmiped, Pankkake, PatrickMcGaha, Pauglester, Pauliewaulie64, Pauljtaylor, Pb30, Peascourt117, Pedro96, Pennstatephil, Pepper, Percy Snoodle, PercyLogan!, Petelead, Petey Parrot, Petriedn, Pgan002, Phattcityusa, Philg88, Philip Trueman, Phinicky, Phocks, Photographerguy, Phraine, Pigsonthewing, Pilotguy, Pinethicket, Piotrus, Pizza1512, Pjhsv, Pjoef, Pmlineditor, Pmsyyz, Poeloq, Pol098, Poshi, Ppival, Prettyblossom, Proxy User, PsY.cHo, Ptemples, Ptomblin, Qawswaq, Qrsdogg, Quantamm, Quantumobserver, Quillaja, Quiname, QuiteUnusual, Qwyrxian, R'n'B, RJW Times, Radagast3, Radiant chains, Rafelio, Rafiqphillips, Ragib, RainbowOfLight, RandyWine, Rapachella, Ravendarque, Ravensburg13, Rbaal, Rchandra, Rcnaranja, Rcsprinter123, Rculatta, Reach Out to the Truth, Realm of Shadows, Redthoreau, ReinforcedReinforcements, Rejectwater, Remember the dot, Renaissancee, RenniePet, Rich 99123, Rich Farmbrough, Richiekim, Richmond96, Riker666, Ripalda, Risker, Rjanag, Rjwilmsi, Rlancefield, Rnb, Rnc000, Robert Skyhawk, Robert1947, Robofish, RockMFR, Rockfang, Rockysmile11, Rodhullandemu, Rodrifranc, Ron Ritzman, Ronestar, Rookmdc, Rsrikanth05, Rufus12, Russavia, Rwiggum, RyanCross, S-Ranger, S0aasdf2sf, S4xton, SAVE US.L2P, SJP, Salamurai, SamJohnston, Samati, SandyGeorgia, Sarz, Sashreek2011, Saxsux, Scarce, ScarletPepper, Scarletdivision, SchuminWeb, Scientus, Scifiintel, Scole01, Scoops, Scootey, ScottMHoward, Scottcampbell195, SeanMooney, Seansinc, Seaphoto, Seav, Secretlondon, SensuiShinobu1234, Sentryspotter2121, Sepahvand, Sepreece, Sevela.p, Sgt. R.K. Blue, Shabock193, Shacksmonkey, Shadowjams, Shafqatislam, Shameonyoko, Sheilakinsella, Sherenk, Showmenights, Showtime2009, Sibeco, SigKauffman, Simon.painter, Simonxag, Sin-man, SirZidan, Sjc2128, Sjö, Skarebo, Skew-t, SkyeWaye, SlapTheTurtle, Slon02, Sluzzelin, SmartGuy, Smartse, Smdali, Snifyoner, Snori, Snowmanradio, SoWhy, Softytop, Solphusion, Spanglej, Sparkyomega, SparsityProblem, Species8473, Speer320, Spice3d, Spike the Dingo, SquierTheAspie, Sscheper, St ttb, StAnselm, Staka, Stennyg, StepmaniaGod, Sternenmeer, Steve2k2k3, Steven Walling, Steveradford, Stgreat, Stickee, Stifle, Storm Rider, Stormofthought, Stringanomaly, Studerby, Studio17, Stybn, Sublime98, SudoGhost, Suffusion of Yellow, SummerWithMorons, SunCountryGuy01, Super5h33p, SuperChencho, SusanLesch, Svandy624, Svick, SyncopatorSyncopator, SynergyBlades, TJDay, TJRC, Tabledhote, Tarotcards, TastyCakes, TastyPoutine, Tbhotch, Tbone2001, Tchalvak, Techman224, Technobuzz, TerraHikaru, Terryheath, Tetzcatlipoca, TexMurphy, The C of E, The Founders Intent, The Gnome, The Simpsons Fan100!, The Utahraptor, The lorax, TheChrisD, TheHills14, TheListUpdater, TheRedPenOfDoom, Theda, Themfromspace, Themichaeljones, Thumperward, Thw416, Tide rolls, Timberframe, Timdorr, TimonyCrickets, Timrollpickering, Tinton5, TippTopp, Tkasmai, Tlogmer, Tobeprecise, Tofutwitch11, Tommy2010, Toncek, Tony Sidaway, Topgear8, Topgun530, Tophee1, Topynate, Totnesmartin, Toxicityj, Tpbradbury, Trackdoodle, Tranquileye, Treasuretrooper55, TreasuryTag, Trendfreaks, Treybien, Tris2000, Trödel, Turtelmonk, Tuxlie, Tvoz, Tweetcash, Tweeteo, Twinsday, Twp, Tyler Watson, Uch, Uhai, UkePete, Unfree, UnicornTapestry, Unionhawk, Unreal ed, UpperPuppy, Usmme h8er, UtahSurfer, Utc in DC, VanTaylor12, Vanhoosear, Vencel, Verdecchia, Versageek, Versus22, Verticalanswer, Vertott, Vicenarian, Victor falk, Vitund, Vj0su3, Wackywace, Wafulz, Waldir, WaldoJ, Walterk29, Wanderingstan, Waterjuice, Wavelength, Wayfarer, Web20junkie, Webulite, Weedwhacker128, Wellbelove, Werd678, Wgreaves, Whalemobi, WhatisFeelings?, Whats new?, Whir, WhisperToMe, White 720, Whoisalejandro, Wickb55, Wickethewok, Wiki pv, Wiki1010101, Wiki845, WikiAC, WikiDan61, WikiaAlexC, Wikidemon, Wikiimam, Wikipedian06, Wikipedian2, Wikipedian64, Wikiuserj11, William Avery, Within a dream, Wizardist, Wolfrock, WombatSamWilson, Woodbed71, Woohookitty, Worm That Turned, Woz2, X!, Xposurepro, Y2kcrazyjoker4, Yeshejampa, Yomama123987, Yousou, Yoyolise, Yulia Romero, ZacharyM001, Zak110695, Zeejay92, Zeldex, Zenohockey, ZeroOne, Zhou Yu, Zollerriia, Бегемот, דוד ש", 达伟, 1300 anonymous edits

Social media *Source*: http://en.wikipedia.org/w/index.php?oldid=439478162 *Contributors*: *drew, -sd-, 1ForTheMoney, 3000records, 4twenty42o, A.DesAutels, A.Ward, Aarkangel, AaronEndre, Abdull, Abuain543, Accounting4Taste, AceofSpades9, Acroterion, Addept, Adrian 1001, Adwalker1019, Afonvill, AgadaUrbanit, Ageekgal, Ahallaz, Alansohn, Alex de carvalho, AlexTheHorrible, AlexanderShelton, Alphabettyjen, Amanverma121, Amberine, Amzimti, Anastrophe, Andy Dingley, Andy120, Angela, Angrysusan, Ankitwizard, Anne LB, Anthere, Apeelsolutions, ArcAngel, Arnastya, Arnoutf, Arthur Rubin, Asdfgbnmkiuytfv, AspectusPR, Atravisscorry, Audiovocal, Axelschultze, Azapatatx, Bagworm, Bakheer, BamukaDelish, Barek, Battoo, Bbb23, BeTheVillain, Beckshow, Benjaminvermersch, Bermudadr, BigDunc, BiggersBetter, Bigted1, Binaemanvel, Bonadea, Boomshakaknacker, Boones6433, BradyHarquin,

Image Sources, Licenses and Contributors

License

CPSIA information can be obtained at www.ICGtesting.com
Printed in the USA
LVOW061905050313

322834LV00013B/368/P